Public History and Heritage Today

Also by Paul Ashton

THE ACCIDENTAL CITY: Planning Sydney Since 1788

CENTENNIAL PARK: A History (*with Kate Blackmore*)

ON THE LAND: A Photographic History of Farming in Australia (*with Kate Blackmore*)

SUTHERLAND SHIRE: A History (*with Jennifer Cornwall and Annette Salt*)

SYDNEY TAKES SHAPE: A History in Maps (*with Duncan Waterson*)

Also by Hilda Kean

ANIMAL RIGHTS: Political and Social Change in Britain Since 1800

CHALLENGING THE STATE: The Socialist and Feminist Educational Experience

DEEDS NOT WORDS: The Lives of Suffragette Teachers

LONDON STORIES: Personal Lives, Public Histories

RUSKIN COLLEGE: Contesting Knowledge, Dissenting Politics (*co-edited with Geoff Andrews and Jane Thompson*)

SEEING HISTORY: Public History in Britain Now (*co-edited with Paul Martin, Sally J. Morgan*)

Public History and Heritage Today

People and their Pasts

Edited by

Paul Ashton
Professor of Public History, University of Technology, Sydney, Australia

and

Hilda Kean
Former Dean and Director of Public History, Ruskin College, Oxford

First published 2008
First published in paperback 2012 by
PALGRAVE MACMILLAN

Palgrave Macmillan in the UK is an imprint of Macmillan Publishers Limited, registered in England, company number 785998, of Houndmills, Basingstoke, Hampshire RG21 6XS.

Palgrave Macmillan in the US is a division of St Martin's Press LLC, 175 Fifth Avenue, New York, NY 10010.

Palgrave Macmillan is the global academic imprint of the above companies and has companies and representatives throughout the world.

Palgrave® and Macmillan® are registered trademarks in the United States, the United Kingdom, Europe and other countries.

ISBN: 978-0-230-54669-1   hardback
ISBN: 978-1-137-28590-4   paperback

This book is printed on paper suitable for recycling and made from fully managed and sustained forest sources. Logging, pulping and manufacturing processes are expected to conform to the environmental regulations of the country of origin.

A catalogue record for this book is available from the British Library.

A catalog record for this book is available from the Library of Congress.

10   9   8   7   6   5   4   3   2   1
22 21 20 19 18 17 16 15 14 13

Printed and bound in Great Britain by
CPI Antony Rowe, Chippenham and Eastbourne

Contents

v

List of Figures

Acknowledgements

A number of individuals and institutions have contributed to the evolution of this book. First, we would like to acknowledge the support of Ruskin College, Oxford, where the conference 'People and their Pasts' – on which this book is based – was held as part of its ongoing series of conferences and public seminars devoted to public history. The Faculty of Arts and Social Sciences at the University of Technology, Sydney, supported Paul Ashton to bring this volume to completion. We also wish to acknowledge a British Academy grant, which assisted in developing the conference as an international event.

Many people have also contributed in various ways to this publication. We would like to thank Phil Coward, David Chandler, Paula Hamilton, Ken Jones, Jorma Kalela, Brenda Kirsch, Paul Martin, Steve Mills, Ron Noon, Melanie Reynolds, Martin Spafford, Melanie Tebbutt and all those who participated in the 'People and their Pasts' conference. We would like to also thank Margaret Malone for her excellent editorial work.

We are grateful to: the Tokomairiro History Society, Milton, New Zealand, for permission to reproduce Figure 13.5 on page 250; Simon Russell at Boing Graphics for Figure 12.1 on page 228; Steve Whiting at loopimages.com for Figure 12.2 on page 230; Lambeth Archives for permission to reproduce Figures 14.2, 14.3 and 14.4 on pages 257, 272 and 274; and Lowell National Historical Park for Figures 3.3 and 3.4 on pages 66 and 69. Thanks to Jon Newman of Lambeth Archives for permission to use the cover image for the paperback edition.

Notes on Contributors

Paul Ashton is Professor of Public History at the University of Technology, Sydney. Co-editor of the journal *Public History Review* and Co-Director of the Australian Centre for Public History. His latest book is (with Paula Hamilton and Rose Searby) *Places of the Heart: Memorials in Australia.*

Meghan O'Brien Backhouse is a Doctoral Candidate at the University of Oxford, in the Material Anthropology and Museum Ethnography programme at the Institute of Social and Cultural Anthropology. Her fieldwork has focused on understanding the use of history and historical re-enactment within Britain, and this forms the basis of her prospective doctoral thesis. Her research interests include material culture, museum interpretation and documentation and the construction of history and identity.

Martin Bashforth is Assistant Archivist at the National Railway Museum in York and an independent researcher. He graduated from the University of Sheffield (1967, BA Modern History and Politics) and the University of York (2003, MA Local History). He is currently researching the Barnsley Cordwainers Society from 1747. His latest book is *The 11ᵗʰ Durham Light Infantry: In Their Own Names.*

Toby Butler is Programme Leader MA Heritage Studies at the Raphael Samuel History Centre at the University of East London. After working on oral history projects in India, USA and Wales Toby undertook an MA in public history at Ruskin College, Oxford, and then a PhD at Royal Holloway, University of London and the Museum of London where he developed the oral history trail concept (www.memoryscape.org.uk). He is currently developing oral history trails with community groups in Silvertown, East London.

Bronwyn Dalley has been a public historian for over a decade. She is Chief Historian at New Zealand's Ministry for Culture and Heritage where she manages the work of the History Group. She has authored or edited several books about New Zealand history, as well as a large number of articles, chapters in books and website features. In 2005, she co-edited *Frontier of Dreams: The Story of New Zealand*, published by Hodder Moa Beckett.

Paul Gough is Pro Vice Chancellor, Executive Dean and Professor of Fine Arts at the University of the West of England, Bristol, UK. A painter, broadcaster and author, his recent published research has examined the contested memorial spaces of cities in England after the First World War, the articulation of national memory through landscape design, and the relationship between business and corporate memory. His monograph on Stanley Spencer as a First World War artist was published in 2006. Homepage: http://www.vortex.uwe.ac.uk/

Paula Hamilton is Professor of History at the University of Technology, Sydney, where she is co-Director of the Australian Centre for Public History. Her publications include *History and Memory in Twentieth-Century Australia* (which she co-edited) and the community history *Cracking Awaba: Stories of Mosman and Northern Beaches Communities During the Depression*. She has recently, with Linda Shopes, edited *Oral History and Public Memory*, which was published by Temple University Press.

Bernard Eric Jensen is Associate Professor of History and History Didactics at the School of Education at Aarhus University, Denmark. He has been the head of an inter-disciplinary research project about the ways in which history is represented and used in present-day Danish society. The results of this project are summarised in *At formidle historie – vilkår, kendetegn, formål* (1999). Among his most recent publications are *Gads Historieleksikon* (2001/2006) and *Historie – livsverden og fag* (2003/2006).

Hilda Kean is former Dean and Director of Public History at Ruskin College, Oxford. Her books include *Seeing History: Public History in Britain Now* (with Paul Martin and Sally J. Morgan); *London Stories: Personal Lives, Public Histories* and *Animal Rights: Social and Political Change in Britain since 1800*.

Brenda Kirsch is a freelance writer and editor. She has been co-editor of *UC*, the magazine of the University and College Union, editor of reports for Her Majesty's Chief Inspector of Prisons, and contributor to the publications of the Trades Union Congress, PCS, UNICEF-UK,

Foreign and Commonwealth Office, Commission for Racial Equality and other public sector organisations.

Darryl McIntyre was Group Director, Public Programmes at the Museum of London where his responsibilities included the design and content for the major gallery redevelopment project. Formerly General Manager Public Programmes and Content Services at the National Museum of Australia, Darryl has worked in the Australian cultural heritage sector for over 30 years, including a decade at the Federal Ministry for the Arts. In November 2008 he became Chief Executive Officer, National Film and Sound Archive in Canberra, Australia.

Jon Newman is the Archive Manager, job-share, for Lambeth Archives, a local authority record office in South London. He also works as a freelance researcher and consultant and is currently working on 'Revisiting Archive Collections' for MLA London, a project which is investigating ways to incorporate user generated content into archive descriptions.

John Siblon teaches at City and Islington College in London. He is involved in the Black and Asian Studies Association, on whose behalf he has lobbied the government for a more inclusive history curriculum. He has written many articles and devised web trails on the Black and Asian Presence in Britain. He teaches courses on Black British history at Ruskin College, Oxford.

Cathy Stanton is a cultural anthropologist with an interest in heritage, museums, tourism, re-enactment and culture-led redevelopment. She currently advises in the area of historical and cultural studies in the B.A. program of Union Institute & University. Her book *The Lowell Experiment: Public History in a Postindustrial City* (2006) won the National Council on Public History's 2007 book award. A native of Canada, she has lived in central Massachusetts for many years.

Mary Stewart studied at St Peter's College, Oxford, gaining a BA (Hons) in Modern History in 2002. She then travelled to New Zealand to undertake postgraduate study at the University of Otago, completing her MA thesis on William McCaw in 2004. At present, Mary is Assistant Curator for Oral History at the British Library Sound Archive and is editing a collection of McCaw's writings.

Vasiliki Tzibazi is a Senior Lecturer in Primary Education at Winchester University, England. Her research interests and teaching are focused on museum education, communication and interpretative strategies.

Preface to the Paperback Edition

Hilda Kean

The first edition of this book, as reviewer Adam Gutteridge acknowledged, was not about rigid definitions of public history but rather, he argued, 'what does public history look like?'.[1] As such the collection was concerned with interrelationships between 'between national, state or élitist versions of the past, and the ways in which individuals and smaller social groupings remember and imagine the past, often privileging the personal over and above abstract notions such as nation and patriotism' as Lucy Noakes has put it.[2] The essays were – and remain – part of a debate on the way in which people were connecting with the past. While the editors of the book have situated such debates within a framework of public history others have discussed these ideas in the context of heritage. In a new collection, *Heritage from Below*, Iain Robertson, for example, has contended that heritage is 'about more than visitors, audience and consumption'. He suggests that it is also about people's sense of inheritance from the past and uses to which it is put and the way in which people make their own histories.[3] Similarly Laurajane Smith et al in *Heritage Labour and the Working Classes* draws on her own key work that challenged an authorised heritage discourse to create an international collection with a focus on people making their own histories usually through trade unions or labour movement organisations.[4]

This emphasis on the process of history-making and the choices taken in the creation of history that these essays represent has been developed in different ways in a recent book by Jorma Kalela, *Making History: The Historian and Uses of the Past*. His starting point is that 'History is an everyday matter'[5] but his focus is upon the role of historians urging us to think analytically about the reasons for the questions they are seeking to answer. His response to the creation of a participatory culture, which we too have emphasised, was for professional historians to work with others to 'tackle their own concerns and thinking over how to make a better future for themselves'. Thus participants in history-making would both come to grips with the conditions of their living 'but also learn that the implied strings attached to the social and political engagement offered "from above" are not inevitable'.[6]

Working within different cultural concerns in Australia Ashton and Hamilton have also revisited the role of 'professional' historians and, like Kalela, have certainly seen a role for such historians while being conscious of the particularities of working in a 'post-colonial era where history has been democratised' and where people 'will produce their own histories and engage with historical representation in an increasing range of forms'.[7] Their vision is more cautious than that of Kalela. They conclude that whether history-making activities will in the future be carried out in partnership with professional historians of all kinds, or largely independent of them, remains to be seen.[8]

Debate on the processes of public engagement with the past and the creation of different historical meaning has not, of course, been left to those employed as historians to explore. Within the archival field both in their own practice and conceptual exploration archivists have taken forward some of the issues raised in Jon Newman's essay. In community archives, for example, archivist Andrew Flinn sees possibilities for 'radical public history' where the archive 'can represent not only the establishment of a place where the past is documented and passively collected but, crucially, also a space in which the archive can become a significant tool for discovery, education and empowerment'.[9] As Richard Cox has suggested with the advance of technology in the future 'Archivists will be ... more archival activists than passive reference gatekeepers'.[10]

In museums exhibitions crossing over between different 'disciplines' have opened up these institutions to new audiences. Such innovation has included, for example, Turner prize winning artist Grayson Perry's work at the British Museum, engagement with the fictional material of 'war horse' at the National Army Museum and reflective work on the depiction of slavery in museums.[11] The Pew Centre for Arts and Heritage in Philadelphia has published a substantial volume entitled *Letting Go? Sharing Historical Authority in a User-Generated World*. In the Introduction, the editors argue that: 'The traditional expertise of the history museum seems to be challenged at every turn. Web 2.0 invites ordinary people to become their own archivists, curators, historians, and designers as they organize images on Snapfish, identify artifacts through Flickr, post text on wikis, and create websites with WordPress and Weebly. Bricks-and-mortar museums, meanwhile, in pursuit of "civic engagement," give community members more say in what stories the museum showcases and how they get told. Exhibitions frequently shun the authoritative voice.'[12]

Within academic circles discussion of public history has also continued to develop. *The Public Historian* has attempted to move out from its concentration on practice in the USA to acknowledge developments in other parts of the English-speaking world with special issues devoted, for instance, to practice in Canada and Britain.[13] In Germany the magazine *Hard Times*, dedicated to British Studies, has both explored public history in Britain but also started discussion of such practice in Germany with explorations of the influence of re-enactment in school museums.[14] Journals such as *Public History Review* and the *International Journal of Heritage Studies* continue to explore conceptual debates as well as including a range of international case studies on creative practice. Recent essays have included an exploration of the social construction of historical knowledge in online communities, and special issues on the role of bio-cultural diversity and transforming narratives in historic house museums.[15] The *History Workshop Journal* has revisited its participatory past and recently set up an associated website it has defined as 'a forum, laboratory, and virtual coffeehouse devoted to the practice of radical history'.[16] Debate has also continued in specific conferences such as an international colloquium at the Australian Centre for Public History in Sydney at UTS resulting in special editions of *Public History Review*; a conference on education and public history; and one on unofficial histories bringing together artists, activists, archivists and academics.[17]

The subsequent activity of contributors to this volume has also reflected the breadth and imagination of the scope of public history they embrace in this collection. Many have developed websites taking forward ideas in their essays. Martin Bashforth, for example, is using this form to develop ideas on radical family history[18] while others have taken forward such ideas in print or at conferences with works, for example, on museums, education and oral history.[19]

The collection emphasises that history is never settled but changes and is contested. Here Paul Gough, for example, discusses the changing role of the National Memorial Arboretum. His essay concludes with the laying of the foundation stone of the Armed Forces Memorial: this now physically dominates the site and has become a focus of national memorialisation as exemplified by the staging of a memorial service on the thirtieth anniversary of the Falklands war.[20] Yet it continues as a site of memorialisation also initiated by individuals who visit and plant their own trees to remember dead relatives. The site is a national memorial, acknowledged as such through royal visits and steady attendance figures: it is also a place in which those working inside and outside universities as historians, artists, museum curators, archivists, or religious ministers have come together to analyse the way the past is remembered in the present.[21]

Public history and heritage today reflects multiple strands of interest but as this second edition continues to recognise at the heart of both concepts of history are *people* who continue to grapple with the past.[22]

Notes

1 A. Gutteridge, Review of *People and their Pasts*, http://www.york.ac.uk/ipup/projects/packaging/history/discussion/ashton.html (accessed 7 June 2012).

2 L. Noakes, Review of *People and their Pasts*, *English Historical Review*, Volume CXXVI, Issue 518, 2011, pp. 248–9.

3 I. Robertson ed. Introduction, *Heritage from Below* (Aldershot: Ashgate, 2012), pp. 1, 7.

4 L. Smith, P. Shackel and G. Campbell, *Heritage, Labour and the Working Classes* (Abingdon: Routledge, 2011).

5 J. Kalela, *Making History: The Historian and Uses of the Past* (Basingstoke: Palgrave, 2012), p. 1.

6 Kalela, *Making History*, p. 164.

7 P. Ashton and P. Hamilton, *History at the Crossroads: Australians and the Past* (Ultimo, New South Wales: Halstead Press, 2010), p. 132.

8 Ashton and Hamilton, *History at the Crossroads*, p. 137.

9 A. Flinn, 'Archival Activism: Independent and Community-led Archives. Radical Public History and the Heritage Professions', *InterActions UCAL Journal of Education and Information Studies*, 7(2) (2011), http://www.escholarship.org/uc/item/9pt2490x, p. 9.

10 R. J. Cox, 'Appraisal and the Future of Archives in the Digital Era', in J. Hill (ed.) *The Future of Archives and Recordkeeping: A Reader* (London: facet publishing, 2011), p. 231.

11 G. Perry, 'The Tomb of the Unknown Craftsman', British Museum 2011–2 http://www.britishmuseum.org/whats_on/exhibitions/grayson_perry/introduction.aspx accessed 8 May 2012; D. Pakeman, Review of War Horse exhibition at the National Army Museum, *Society and Animals*, 23(3) (2012) (forthcoming); A. Rice, *Creating Memorials, Building Identities: The Politics of Memory in the Black Atlantic* (Liverpool: Liverpool University Press, 2012).

12 B. Adair, B. Filene and L. Koloski (eds) *Letting Go?: Sharing Historical Authority in a User-Generated World* (Philadelphia: The Pew Centre for Arts & Heritage, 2011), p. 11.

13 L. Dick, 'Public History in Canada: An Introduction', *The Public Historian*, 31(1) (2009), pp. 7–14; H. Hoock, 'Professional Practices of Public History in Britain: Introduction', *The Public Historian*, 32(3) (2010), pp. 7–24.

14 R. Wandel, 'Victorian Lessons – Unterricht wie zu Kaisiers Zeiten Ein Beispiel fur nachlerlebte Geschichte', *Hard Times*, 88 (2010), pp. 25–31. See also M. Stevens, 'Public Policy and the Public Historian: The Changing Place of Historians in Public Life in France and the UK', *The Public Historian*, 32(3) (2010), pp. 120–38.

15 P. Martin, 'A "Social Form of Knowledge" in Practice: Unofficial Compiling of 1960s Pop Music on CD-R', *Public History Review*, 18 (2011), pp. 129–50; *International Journal of Heritage Studies*, 17(2) (2011) Special Issue: Dwelling: Transforming Narratives at Historic House Museums and 17(6) (2011) Special Issue: Conserving Biocultural Diversity on a Landscape Scale: The Roles of Local, National and International Designations.

16 http://www.historyworkshop.org.uk/about-us/ (site accessed 7 June 2012).

17 ed. P. Ashton and L. Di Bartolomeo, *Public History Review*, 17 (2010); ed. H. Kean and P. Ashton, *Public History Review*, 18 (2011); Legacies and Futures, public history conference, Ruskin College, September 2009; http://unofficial-histories.wordpress.com/.

18 http://radfamhist.wordpress.com/ (Martin Bashforth) see also: www.cathy-stanton.net/; www.vortex.uwe.ac.uk/ (Paul Gough); http://hildakean.com/; Toby Butler is co-editor of http://www.historyworkshop.org.uk/ (all accessed 7 June 2012).

19 http://www.winchester.ac.uk/academicdepartments/poststudiesed/People-profiles/Academicprofiles/Pages/DrVasilikiTzibazi.aspx; http://pure.au.dk/portal/da/persons/id%281ea28fd9-ea06-4028-8428-5a2e3c4a558c%29.html (Bernard Eric Jensen) http://www.raphael-samuel.org.uk/events/history-nation-and-schools-0 (John Siblon, Toby Butler) http://www.bl.uk/researchregister/1.10/?app_cd=RR&page_cd=PUBLICATION&l_researcher_id=178 (Mary Stewart) http://datasearch2.uts.edu.au/fass/staff/listing/details.cfm?StaffId=1640 (Paula Hamilton).

20 Falklands conflict memorial service April 2012 http://www.youtube.com/watch?v=byrnjCV59DY&feature=player_embedded.

21 Publications have followed including M. Andrews with C. Bagot Jewitt and N. Hunt (eds) *Lest We Forget. Remembrance and Commemoration* (Stroud: History Press, 2011) (It includes essays by Paul Gough and Hilda Kean).

22 Thanks to Paul Ashton for his helpful comments on this introduction and to Jon Newman for suggesting the cover image.

Introduction: People and their Pasts and Public History Today

Hilda Kean and Paul Ashton

> ... history is not the prerogative of the historian ... It is, rather, a social form of knowledge; the work in a given instance, of a thousand different hands ...[1]

The first international public history conference was held in Britain at Ruskin College, Oxford, in September 2005, with the title 'People and their Pasts'.[2] In earlier years Ruskin public history conferences had covered a range of topics including official and unofficial histories, personal and public histories, placing history and seeing history. All emphasised the processes by which histories are created. At the same time, some recent university conferences in Britain had been held with the titles of 'Historians and their Publics' or 'History and the Public' in which the stress had been on communicating history as a given body of knowledge by academically trained historians to 'the public'.[3] Such frameworks concentrate on the form and nature of transmission, rather than explore the idea of how the past becomes history. However, the 'People and the Pasts' conference had a different emphasis. It sought to explore the range of historiographical processes that could lead to the possible creation of shared meaning and different understandings of the past between people with a keen interest in the role of the past in the present. This lively sharing of ideas and projects at the conference was the starting point for putting this collection of essays together.

The ideas explored in this collection are based on the premise that people are active agents in creating histories. Rather than a rigid demarcation between 'historians' and 'their publics', we include within this concept of the active agent professional historians, as well as those involved in community, local and family history projects.[4] Participants at the conference – and contributors to this collection –

include academic or professional historians, community historians, archivists, museum curators and educators, re-enactors, teachers, artists and family and local historians, all of whom are passionately concerned about the interpretation of the past. Underpinning this understanding is the notion that 'public historians do not own history' but are merely collaborators, particularly in community-based histories.[5] This book seeks to explore the possibilities of a participatory historical culture, as David Thelen has phrased it, where the 'past should be treated as a shared human experience and opportunity for understanding, rather than a ground for division and suspicion'.[6] This emphasis on collaboration has the capacity to lead to 'a broadly distributed authority for making new sense of the past in the present.'[7]

We recognise that there may be a gap in historical understandings between those trained as historians and the audiences for their work but this gap will not be bridged by 'historians' merely reaching out to 'the public'. Rather, as David Glassberg has argued, new ways of thinking about the past may be achieved by 'reaching in to discover the humanity they share'. The recognition of the historian's – as much as the public's – personal need for the past is key to different understandings of the past.[8]

The essays chosen for this collection cover a wide range of projects and contributors. Thus it is hoped that this book will appeal to a diverse audience and facilitate open-ended discussion of the role and interpretation of history in a multitude of contexts.

The intellectual influence of Raphael Samuel

> If history is an arena for the projection of ideal selves, it can also be a means of undoing and questioning them, offering more disturbing accounts of who *we* are, and where *we* come from than simple identification would suggest.[9]

This acknowledgement of the value of historical study in relation to our very identity as human beings was made by the late Raphael Samuel, former tutor at Ruskin College and promoter of the History Workshop movement in the 1970s, as a way of thrashing out contemporary historical issues. This emphasis on a past usable in the present has also been a concern of recent public history thinking, including events at Ruskin College.[10] As Bernard Jensen argues in his chapter in this collection, Samuel asserted that the overarching purpose of studying history was 'to historicise [our] understanding of the present' and to make us 'more aware of [our] own historicity'. Across the range of his research, Samuel returned:

> [A]gain and again to the idea of history as an organic form of knowledge, and one whose sources are promiscuous, drawing not only on real-life experience but also on memory and myth, fantasy and desire; not only on the chronological past of the documentary record but also the timeless one of 'tradition'.[11]

History was thus 'a social form of knowledge; the work in any given instance, of a thousand different hands.'[12] As Samuel elaborated in *Theatres of Memory*, there is a long legacy of historical practice by self-educated 'amateurs', such as John Aubrey, the seventeenth-century notator of places including the world heritage site of Avebury.[13] An exploration of the past was not – nor could be – neatly divided into 'professionals' and 'public'. Rather, if 'history was thought of as an activity rather than a profession, then the number of practitioners would be legion'.[14]

In both *Theatres of Memory* and in his earlier work Samuel developed historiographical insights into the nature of material suitable for writing history and the validity of personal experience and memory in this process. In their recent collections on memory and history Katharine Hodgkin and Susannah Radstone situate their work as a development of Samuel's ideas contained in *Theatres of Memory*, stating that work on social and cultural memory 'has come to be known as "public history"'.[15] Certainly Samuel recognised the value of autobiography, stories, legends or songs that a child might learn at a grandparent's knee, noting that a 'different order of evidence' would lead to a 'different kind of inquiry'.[16] As early as 1976 in an important article on the diverse, non-traditional range of materials used by local and oral historians he had shown the possibility of constructing different histories by using different materials.[17] This position was later exemplified by his historically imaginative book on the miners' strike of 1984–85, *The Enemy Within*. Here letters, diaries and speeches made during the strike allowed for a focus on individual experience, rather than on the nature of collective acts. It was 'about moments rather than movements'.[18] Using such material created and collected by activists, the book attempted to show 'the ways in which history is made behind our backs, in spite of our best intentions rather than because of them.'[19]

Such thinking is one of the areas of exploration in this collection. Non archival experience has led to different forms of historical inquiry. Thus, from floating down the river Thames an object made out of driftwood found trapped behind his houseboat and interviewing people where the object stopped, Toby Butler has created new ways of reading this national site. Hilda Kean and Brenda Kirsch, also in Britain, have used a mark book of their former primary school teacher to revisit their experiences of taking the 11+ exam in primary school and as a way of exploring wider, national debates on grammar school education. Other contributors have also used different starting points: an iconic photograph and family archive to develop fresh understandings of the impact of international migration, in the case of Mary Stewart's contribution; or John Siblon's image of a child photographed outside Buckingham Palace as an impetus for an exploration of the monuments at the heart of empire; or Meghan Backhouse's engagement with Wars of the Roses re-enactors to explore aspects of national identity. While broad questions of identity and nationality are explored, this is done largely by using materials from personal, local and familial domains, which have been mined to develop new perspectives on the past. The use of such non-archival materials also gives a greater appreciation of the many ways in which the past is validated in people's daily lives. This approach to the study of the past has been defined by some as public history. Like many definitions, however, this term is contested. However, we see the work of particular scholars in this field as providing useful contexts for this collection.

Pasts in the present

Roy Rosenzweig and David Thelen's *The Presence of the Past: Popular Uses of History in American Life*[20] has been influential in thinking about the past in the present for a number of reasons. In an extensive national survey of North Americans they investigated historical activities and the social needs and historical sensibilities underlying them. In particular they demonstrated the complex ways in which people used the past in making sense of themselves and their lives, as well as to negotiate the present and navigate the future. The past and the present were brought together in an analysis of the ways in which people made the past part of their everyday routines and turned to the past 'as a way of grappling with profound questions about how to live'. People used their pasts, their findings suggested, to address questions about 'relationships, identity, immortality, and agency'.[21] The past was not a distant or abstract, insignificant entity but a key feature of their present lives.

The Presence of the Past was written against a politically conservative climate in the US in which debates about the nature and presentation of history were fiercely and publicly disputed. Just one example, that of the arguments surrounding the display by the National Air and Space Museum in Washington DC of the Enola Gay, the plane that dropped the atom bomb on Hiroshima, showed, if nothing else, that the authority of official history-makers can be, and is, up for fierce discussion.[22] Rosenzweig and Thelen's book was seen as controversial since it discredited both conservative and elitist claims that there was indeed a collective 'national' history, essential to civic co-operation and advancement in difficult times, and that the general public did not understand such frameworks and needed to be schooled in them. Such sentiments had been in part expressed in 1996 when Professor Sheldon Hackney, former Chair of the National Endowment for the Humanities, announced that 'there is an inclusive historical narrative in which we all recognise not only the stories of our kith and kin but in which we acknowledge that we are playing roles in a common story'.[23] At stake were social cohesion, the 'national character' and the authority of the professional historian.[24] But Rosenzweig and Thelen, among others, were challenging the concept of a common story and national character needing to be asserted against a tide of ignorance. Of particular concern was their suggestion that people's understanding and use of the past was 'intimate and personal'.[25]

For some historians working in the presentation of history, for example in museums, this contention was seen as potentially threatening. As James Gardner, Associate Director of Curatorial Affairs at the National Museum of American History, Smithsonian Institution, acknowledged in his presidential address to the National Council on Public History, the 'public's understanding and use of the past', as noted in the Rosenzweig and Thelen study, provided a 'fundamentally different sense of the past than what we as public historians are committed to exploring and sharing.'[26] Particularly worrying was the concept of valuing individuals' experience of the past, unmediated by the professional input of historians, and thus in one stroke undermining the raison d'etre of those seeking to present 'history' to 'the public' outside academic institutions.[27] As Thelen observed in his afterthoughts on the project, their book provided 'evidence that academic history differs from everyday history'.[28] Thelen has been critical of professionals who dismiss experience as inconsequential, private or self-deceptive[29] or fail to respect 'differences in grandmothers' stories, museum exhibitions, and manuscript collections as trusted sources for approaching the past.'[30]

In his own afterthoughts entitled 'Everyone a Historian', Roy Rosenzweig argued that he had attempted to bring the spheres of the professional and popular history-maker together. While recognising 'the terrain of the past that is so present for all of us' he did not dismiss the role of professional historians but rather sought to explore how such scholars can talk to, 'and especially *with*, those audiences'. This involved working harder at listening to and respecting the work of popular history-makers to see the common experience that bound them.[31] For his part, Thelen maintained that in practice there was a blurring between the personal/private and public. Such categories, he declared, were artificial: 'The dichotomy between "intimate" and "national", public and private, dissolves into dynamic and reciprocal interaction'. Respondents to their survey, he pointed out, 'more often mentioned public experiences than private ones as the most formative of their lives, but they mentioned those public events most often as intimate experiences'. This was not a rejection of national pasts, for example as treated in museums, or important political events. Instead, it was an acknowledgement that these occurrences are often remembered and perceived as personal events. Such a participatory historical model 'would take seriously how... [people] live lives and meet needs in relationships driven by forces different from those that power institutions and cultures'.[32]

The validity of this approach can be illustrated by the number of projects established in the US in the aftermath of the bombings of September 11, 2001. Oral history interviews, thousands of photographs, digital images, emails, instant messages and material from 30,000 websites were archived. By 2005, the September 11 digital archive, overseen by Rosenzweig, had collected more than 150,000 items from thousands of individual contributors.[33] Using such material Michael Kazin discovered that 'fewer Americans than one might imagine saw 9/11 in terms of nationalism or another abstract framework. Instead, most saw the events in personal and local terms, the loss of a friend, the effect on a town or community, the impact on their family or job'.[34] In New York a very popular exhibition of the work undertaken by rescue workers at the twin towers has not been staged in a museum or university but in St Paul's Chapel, the oldest building in continuous use in Manhattan, and where fire fighters and police came to rest between shifts. Here spontaneous sites of memory have been created with police and fire fighters' badges from many states and countries, while the church pews themselves have been re-configured to reflect this recent New York past.[35]

Challenges: historians and materials for history

For Rosenzweig and Thelen, academic history was but one of many historical practices. Such an understanding does not deny the work of professionally trained historians but equally does not reserve for them an exclusive role. Of course, not all historians have seen their role in this way. As Paul Ashton and Paula Hamilton discuss in their chapter, for some Australian academic historians, cultural authority about the past rests solely with them. Thus a popular and well-written book might be dismissed as the work of a talented interloper largely because the author was writing for a wider audience. Similar debates have take place in Canadian public history networks.[36]

As this book itself demonstrates, however, many view 'non-academic' engagements with the past more positively. As Hilda Kean, Paul Martin and Sally J. Morgan suggested in the introduction to the collection *Seeing History: Public History in Britain Now*, 'Public History relies on a collective and collaborative effort of people often working in different fields.' Moreover, they contend that what united the contributors in their book was an understanding that:

> what is seen and what is experienced in our everyday lives is as likely to be as significant in our understanding and creation of history as the reading of books or archives.[37]

This approach emphasised the value of different material in the writing of history, freeing a writer from the apparent constraints of the archive, and simultaneously acknowledging that materials found in the course of everyday life were important in understanding the past. Valuing local and personal experience and material is not necessarily counterposed to broader understandings of the past but rather can challenge and alter our perception of them, as Alessandro Portelli has shown in his studies of Italian post-war politics. He has combined his professorship at La Sapienza University in Rome with a position as the mayor of Rome's representative for historical memory. His emphasis is usually upon using individual experiences of the past to investigate and re-assess grand narratives of history. In analysing his approach to oral history, Portelli has challenged the conventional notions of an historian recording and analysing the material of the interviewee. Rather than privileging the role of the professional he suggests that *both* participants in this form of history-making are subjects. There is no oral history before the encounter of these two different subjects, 'one with a story to tell and the other with a history to reconstruct'.[38]

The impetus for his recent work, *The Order Has Been Carried Out: History, Memory, and Meaning of a Nazi Massacre in Rome*, was the election in 1994 of Silvio Berlusconi at the head of a right wing coalition which, Portelli argued, 'challenged the meaning of the Resistance as the foundation of the Italian state'.[39] In 2002 the government wished to purge history textbooks of anti-Fascist 'bias',[40] leading Portelli to examine the way in which the memory of Italy's partisan history was being re-worked. Major historical events, such as the Nazi massacre at the Ardeatine caves in Rome, were re-appraised by Portelli in the light of the oral testimony and collective memory of hundreds of Roman citizens that he gathered together. Here the personal and the public were elided, rather than counterposed.

The role of the state in constructing pasts

In Australia, Paul Ashton and Paula Hamilton have also explored the complex relationship between state-initiated events and individual experience. Their seminal study, 'Australians and the Past', analysed the importance of place, locality, material culture and family as factors contributing to the creation of a national understanding of the past. They note the large numbers of respondents who felt connected to the past through public anniversaries, particularly Anzac day, but that such events were significant for their local, rather than national, value.[41] Their chapter here further elaborates on these ideas as does, for example, Cathy Stanton's work on the Lowell National Historical Park in the US. Her chapter explores, in part, the 'rituals of reconnection' where middle-class Americans connect with their working-class heritage.

This relationship between state or official depictions of the past and popular expressions of it has also been explored by Jeremy Black.[42] In his book *Using History* he focuses on the way in which the past has been re-worked in different nation states. Rejecting the importance of academic historians as the 'drivers' of history, his central claim is that 'changes in the public usage of history are crucial to the general understanding of the past, and that these developments stem largely from current political shifts and pressures'.[43] While valuing the role of collective memory and oral history in the public usage of history he suggests that the role of the state and its political direction are often underrated.[44] Certainly in countries forging new identities the role of the state has been key. As Kate Flynn and Tony King have discussed in their work on post-apartheid South Africa, while the state has, in the main, left the old South African heritage sector relatively untouched, a series of high profile developments, known as the 'Legacy Project', have attempted to 'redress the balance in presentation and create new museums and monuments reflecting a post-apartheid civic identity and nationhood that transcends ethnic division'.[45] In a different vein, recent initiatives such as the CBC/Radio Canada millennium project to chronicle the history of Canada on film or the founding of the Historica project to promote Canadian history education have helped to foster debates in that country on the role of official national history in the twenty-first century.[46]

Ludmilla Jordanova has also suggested that public history can both be a 'tool of establishments' as well as a feature of radical history movements, which are 'critical of elitist, over-professionalised history' and instead 'seek to promote politically self-conscious, community-based histories, open to all'.[47] Significantly, her analysis covers discussion on the difference between 'the past' and 'history', thus opening up the debate on the nature of historical knowledge, ownership of the past and the nature of the materials used in creating meaning. The recognition that 'the past is essentially open-ended, and accounts of it are public property should help historians', she argues, 'to see their own activities in a wider perspective and to raise broad questions about the practice of history'.[48] As Paul Gough demonstrates in this collection, while the intention of the Millennium Commission in funding a National Memorial Arboretum in Staffordshire was to create a national site of memory, the result has been irretrievably altered by the contributions to the site by individuals and groups, who have privileged the personal and local above abstract ideas of nation.

The difficulties of the phrase 'public history'

The directions we hope this book explores – the breaking down of knowledge barriers, the promotion of the use of different materials, valuing engagement – might be seen as a form of public history in which people and their lives and experiences are central to the work in hand. As such it might be said to have long traditions. However, for some, the phrase public history relates to the place of employment of a professionally trained historian. In the US, where contemporary public history is most firmly established and widely practised, the term is commonly attributed to Robert Kelley, an environmental historian then at the University of California, Santa Barbara. Writing in the first issue of *The Public Historian* – the journal of the National Council on Public History (NCPH) – Kelley stated that 'public history' referred 'to the employment of historians and historical method outside of academia'.[49] Some 25 years later, while acknowledging the inter- and multi-disciplinary nature of public history, David Vanderstel, Executive Director of the NCPH, wrote that public historians were 'those [who were academically trained but] engaged in work outside the halls of the academy and those within the academy who prepare students for careers in government agencies, museums, libraries, historic preservation, and in private business enterprises'.[50] This definition was taken further by Jill Liddington.

In a broad ranging, exploratory article in the journal *Oral History*, Liddington suggested that '[s]ome public historians are surely just "private historians" in cunning disguise: may not writing a commissioned history for a private corporation be nearer "public relations" than "public history"'?[51] Most controversially, as she admits, Liddington questioned the public worth of genealogy, family and local history. Positing a binary, and we would contend artificial divide, she asks: 'who are public historians: publicly-funded, publicly-accountable academic historians or enthusiastic grassroots practitioners?'[52] The answer was academic historians. Public historians, she concludes, 'provide refreshing, inspiring and necessary *expert* mediation between the *past* and its *publics*.'[53] Professionally trained historians would 'maintain the highest standards of scholarship and critical rigour'.[54] This, Liddington suggests, distinguishes them from other 'Purveyors of the past to popular audiences'.[55]

Some, including contributors to this collection who have undertaken consultancies and drafted commissioned history, see the issue less starkly. In their collection on New Zealand public history, *Going Public*, Bronwyn Dalley and Jock Phillips define public history as 'historical work undertaken according to the research priorities, agendas or funding capacities of another party other than being self-directed by the Historian'.[56] They note in particular the progressive role played by New Zealand public historians employed directly by the state either in the history group of the Ministry for Culture and Heritage or as experts in the Waitangi Tribunal established in 1975 to determine Maori claims to land.[57] As Bronwyn Dalley argues in this collection, had it not been for state sponsorship, few studies of New Zealand's military history would have appeared before the 1980s when it began to gain popularity among other historians and writers.

Public history has a long history. Even in the self declared 'first book length reference work' on the subject, *The Craft of Public History*, published by the NCPH in 1983, the authors debunked the apparent newness of the term describing public history as an ancient approach to the study of past processes.[58] Professional status was not important. While official or government history was specifically excluded from their definition, genealogy and family history were acknowledged as being 'among the oldest fields of historical practice'.[59]

Although the term 'public history' was not adopted until the late 1980s in Australia, public historians could be traced back at least to Charles Bean, who played a major role in shaping the national Anzac legend from the First World War. He was also largely responsible for the establishment of the Australian War Memorial in Canberra – a major museum and one of the most popular in Australia today – as well as a national archives for war records that is frequently used by a range of history practitioners.[60] Significantly, however, Bean was not an academically trained historian but studied law at Oxford University before becoming a journalist and turning his hand to writing nationalist history. Although Graeme Davison has described Australian public history as the 'practice of history by academically trained historians working for public agencies or as freelancers outside the universities',[61] he has also hinted at tensions raised by the notion of 'public history'. In Australia this 'public' scrutiny of the work of academic historians has been termed the History Wars. Led largely by the press, radio and television, heated debate and vilification has resulted from challenges to historical depictions of nineteenth-century white Australians as invaders or colonists who deliberately, and physically, eradicated the indigenous population. Established historians have had their tenure threatened and museum curators, sympathetic to this stance, have been silenced or become self-censoring. Indeed, in one high profile case, a senior museum director was dismissed from her job in this climate of political backlash.[62]

Perhaps understandably then, some historians have felt threatened by such public discussion of the past, as Paul Ashton and Paula Hamilton explore in their chapter. Others, however, have chosen to recognise the potentially inclusive nature of the term 'public'. In his collection, which positively recognised the role of 'amateur' practitioners interacting with archaeologists, Nick Merriman helped unpack different ideas of 'the public'. He considers, for example, how the word 'public' can be understood as something that encompasses both the role of the state in the establishment of the British Museum in 1753 as a public institution and the potential for archaeologists to engage with alternative 'public' opinion to their mutual benefit.[63] Merriman notes that however hard archaeologists try, 'non-archaeologists will re-appropriate, re-interpret and re-negotiate meanings of archaeological resources to their own personal agendas.'[64] Certainly those who engaged in metal detecting used to be frequently derided by archaeologists, but have now been recognised by many for their work in mapping important English sites of battle, such as the civil war site at Naseby.[65]

Public history today: promoting practice and forwarding debate

As indicated in the pages of the North America journal *The Public Historian*, published by the NCPH, there remains a 'considerable diversity of approaches to the definition and practice of public history'.[66] Since its establishment in 1980 the NCPH has contributed greatly to enhancing history's place in both public and corporate culture in the US, an achievement reiterated in a special issue of *The Public Historian* in 2006 that addressed public history as reflective practice.[67] Noel Stowe defined reflective practice as the professional habit of 'thinking about and rethinking intellectual, practical and moral issues'.[68] But contributors to *The Public Historian* have not always agreed on their practice. While some have emphasised public history as 'using' history 'out there ... in the real world',[69] others have situated public historians' work within explorations of people's personal pasts and engagement with community practitioners.[70] Certainly New York historians such as Mike Wallace have promoted community practice in different ways. The Gotham Centre for New York City History, which Wallace founded at the City University of New York, Graduate Center, is a public centre drawing in scholars, librarians, teachers, film-makers, preservationists and history 'buffs' in a study of the city in which they all live.[71] In 1999, under the direction of Daniel Walkowitz, a professor at New York University who ran a graduate programme in public history, the American journal *Radical History Review*, a left-wing, scholarly journal established in the 1970s, launched, as a regular feature, a series in public history aimed at broadening understandings of the field. The first feature examined how 'racial' others and imperial pasts played out in national histories. Another looked at the extent to which national narratives constructed by previous political regimes were questioned by public representations of the national story commissioned or endorsed by succeeding regimes.[72] And this series has led to the publication of two edited collections.[73]

The Australian journal *Public History Review*, founded in 1992 by Paul Ashton, Christopher Keating, Paula Hamilton and Christa Ludlow, and now available online, established its direction from the first issue. As Ann Curthoys and Paula Hamilton argued:

[F]or us a commitment to the idea of public history is a commitment to a concern with audience and an awareness of the complex relationship between audience, historical practice and institutional context. It places academic historical work in a broader framework seeing it as only one kind of historical practice, constantly in a process of negotiation and dialogue with other forms of history.[74]

Subsequent articles have considered, for example, the nature of gender and heritage, the development of gay history or the role of historical re-enactors or monuments in the creation of the past.[75] And the current editors are keen to develop consideration of explicitly historiographical and political issues. Although debate establishing and contesting the nature of public history has thrived in the US and, to a lesser extent, in Australia, the historiography of public history is less well established in Europe. While public discussion has recently flourished – for example, in Germany over the ways in which the Nazi or Communist past might be acknowledged and commemorated in a reunified nation – looking backwards, as W. G. Sebald explored, has been problematic.[76] Similarly, Brian Ladd has observed that in the new German capital 'Each proposal ... for construction, demolition, preservation, or renovation ignites a battle over symbols of Berlin and of Germany'.[77]

In Britain some journals have seen public history as a new concern with which they seek to engage. Thus the *Labour History Review* has sought to explore heritage in relation to labour history while *Oral History* has established a vox pop section inviting public historians to define their understanding of the topic and has set up a section in the journal designed to separate discussion on public history from that on oral history and memory. New journals such as the *International Journal for Heritage Studies* have promoted discussion on aspects of public history while the *History Workshop Journal* has continued to discuss the role of film in the making of historical knowledge and to review exhibitions.[78]

But, unsurprisingly, for the most part it is outside journals that historical engagement is blooming. As Martin Bashforth explores in his chapter, the proliferation of family history fairs and family history societies and magazines devoted to the subject is an indication of how seriously the community of family historians see themselves. Moreover, this makes them, he suggests, probably the single biggest constituency of practising historical researchers within the wider public history community. While Patrick Wright has criticised the BBC television programme *Restoration* for seeing 'conservation as a wholly good cause: a secular version of churchgoing, which only a satanic monster would question,' he nevertheless acknowledges its popularity in attracting over three million people for most episodes.[79] And certainly, the

difficult questions of whether, and how, politically discredited buildings or structures should be preserved have resulted in a more problematic positioning – and critical engagement – for the programme than is
usually found in a ratings-driven television show.[80]

The BBC show highlights the popular engagement that is occurring
with questions of national historical significance, but it is just one
example. In England alone, there have been a number of recent campaigns to erect new memorials to forgotten – or discredited – pasts. The
memorial of the slave trade in Lancaster, for example, has drawn in a
range of local people including historians, teachers, artists and politicians, as has the currently unsuccessful campaign to erect a monument
to socialist Sylvia Pankhurst near Parliament.[81] In his chapter John Siblon
discusses the new group Memorial 2007, which is composed of individuals linked to the Black and Asian Studies Association and sponsored
by the Museum in the Docklands. The group is attempting to raise funds
to erect a permanent memorial in the Rose Garden of London's Hyde
Park to 'honour and acknowledge the millions of enslaved Africans and
their descendants'. Such initiatives suggest to us that critical engagement
with the past is flourishing.

Conclusion

At a conference in London's Conway Hall on the tenth anniversary of
Raphael Samuel's death, several of the invited speakers and contributors from the floor talked almost sentimentally of a past golden age
of 'people's history'. Allegedly, local projects involving working people's
autobiographies or oral history projects had been, some suggested,
entirely independent of state intervention and represented a now totally
defunct example of radical history-making. Such an elegiac tone seems
inappropriate and premature. While the parameters have changed, critical explorations of engagement with the past continue. Clearly, some
work is funded through state priorities. As Jon Newman discusses in his
chapter, there is a growing expectation, in part shaped by central government agendas, 'that archives, museums and other heritage institutions
should hold and proactively seek content that is "relevant" to current,
new and future audiences'. But, as Newman argues, this approach is also
driven by 'bottom-up demands and expectations of communities and
individuals as to the perceived shortcomings of public collections'. There
is an ongoing debate both about the meaning of relevance and the nature
of audience.[82] This challenge to national funding priorities is also
explored by Cathy Stanton in her analysis of the role of the US National

Park Service in relation to post-industrial towns. Paradoxically, as the number of such projects continues to increase in the US and as the role of vernacular memories and voices within them expands, the actual range of participation seems to be shrinking, sharply raising the question of who is able to access the benefits of this growing embrace of the past as a public good. Those, too, who write here about the experience of public history practice in museums, do not understand this solely in terms of access. For Darryl McIntyre the challenge for new museums is in creating a conversation with its audiences and realising the ways in which a museum can bring communities and groups together to examine and seek answers to *collective* questions. Even when museums are presenting history to children, as Vasiliki Tzibazi discusses, the performances are still negotiated and contested by the young museum visitors themselves.

History in the public arena has been defined as 'the ensemble of activities and practices in which ideas of history are embedded or a dialectic of past-present relations is rehearsed'. In this sense, public history is an engagement with such activities and practices.[83] These range from ceremonies and rituals of 'social integration'[84] to everyday material, public landscapes, monuments and memorials, museums and exhibitions, school texts and classrooms, historical films and novels, family stories, songs, memories and family and local history-making.[85] North American oral historian Charles Hardy III has recently reflected on community oral history projects he conducted in Philadelphia some 25 years previously. He acknowledged that the interviews were as much about the elderly people he interviewed and the community and city of their youth as they were about him and Philadelphia at that time. He concluded his article with a sentiment that we also find helpful in furthering ideas of historical understanding:

Interviewers and interviewees, insiders and outsiders, subjects and objects, we are all historians.[86]

Notes

1 R. Samuel, *Theatres of Memory: Past and Present in Contemporary Culture* (London: Verso, 1994), p. 8.
2 Thanks to Brenda Kirsch, Jorma Kalela, Stephen Mills and Melanie Tebbutt for their helpful comments on earlier drafts.
3 The 'Historians and their Publics' Conference held at York University in 2001, as discussed by S. Ditchfield, 'It Pays to Help the Public Meet the Ancestors', *The Times Higher Education*, 20 April 2001; 'History and the Public' was organised by the Institute of Historical Research, University of London, Spring 2006.

4 See for example, the discussion of 'the parallel roads taken by amateur and professional historians' in M. Conrad, 'How Historians Complicate Things: A brief survey of Canadian Historiography', see www.histori.ca/prodev/article.do?id=11635

5 R. Archibald, *A Place to Remember: Using History to Build Community* (Walnut Creek, CA: AltaMira Press, 1999), pp. 155–6 as quoted in A. S. Newell, '"Home is What You Can Take Away with You": K. J. Ross Toole and the Making of a Public Historian', *The Public Historian*, 23: 3 (2001) 70.

6 D. Thelen, 'Afterthoughts: A Participatory Historical Culture', http://chnm.gmu.edu/survey/afterdave.html, p. 2, accessed 4 January 2007.

7 As Michael Frisch suggests, 'projects which involve people in exploring what it means to remember and what to do with memories to make them active and alive, as opposed to mere objects of collection' can stand as 'an alternative to imposed orthodoxy and officially sanctioned versions of historical reality'. M. Frisch (ed.) *A Shared Authority: Essays on the Craft and Meaning of Oral and Public History* (Albany: State University of New York Press, 1990), pp. xiii, 27.

8 D. Glassberg, *Sense of History: The Place of the Past in American Life* (Amherst, MA: The University of Massachusetts Press, 2001), p. 210.

9 R. Samuel, *Island Stories: Unravelling Britain* (London: Verso, 1998), p. 223: our emphasis.

10 H. Kean, 'Public History and Raphael Samuel: A Forgotten Radical Pedagogy?', *Public History Review*, 11 (2004), 51.

11 Samuel, *Theatres of Memory*, p. x.

12 *ibid*, p. 8. See also J. Kalela, 'Politics of history and history politics: Some conceptual suggestions as to political aspects of history', *Ajankohta*, Finland (2004).

13 Samuel, *Theatres of Memory*, p.11; Brian Edwards, 'Avebury and Not-so-ancient-places: The Making of the English Heritage Landscape', in H. Kean, P. Martin and S. J. Morgan (eds) *Seeing History: Public History in Britain Now* (London: Francis Boutle, 2000), pp. 65–80.

14 Samuel, *Theatres of Memory*, p. 17.

15 K. Hodgkin and S. Radstone (eds) 'Introduction', *Contested Pasts: The Politics of Memory* (London: Routledge, 2003), p. 3. See also Kean, 'Public History and Raphael Samuel'.

16 Samuel, *Theatres of Memory*, p. 11.

17 R. Samuel, 'Local History and Oral History', *History Workshop Journal*, 1: 1 (1976) 191–208.

18 R. Samuel, B. Bloomfield and G. Boanas (eds) *The Enemy Within: Pit villages and the Miners' Strike of 1984–5* (London: Routledge and Kegan Paul, 1986), p. xvii.

19 *ibid*, p. xv.

20 R. Rosenzweig and D. Thelen, *The Presence of the Past: Popular Uses of History in American Life* (New York: Columbia University Press, 1998).

21 *ibid*, p. 18.

22 L. Jordanova, *History in Practice* (London: Hodder Arnold, 2000), p. 156; 'A Big Museum Opens, to Jeers as Well as Cheers', *New York Times*, 16 December 1993; www.lehigh.edu/~ineng/enola/ accessed 25 May 2007.

23 S. Hackney, 'The American Identity', *The Public Historian*, 19: 1 (1997) 22.

24 See, for example, E. Foner, *Who Owns History?: Rethinking the Past in a Changing World* (New York: Hill and Wang, 2002), pp. 149–66.
25 J. B. Gardner, 'Contested Terrain: History, Museums and the Public' (NCPH president's annual address), *The Public Historian*, 26: 4 (2004) 13.
26 *ibid.*
27 *ibid*, pp. 12, 13.
28 Thelen, 'Afterthoughts: A Participatory Historical Culture', p. 2.
29 *ibid*, p. 3.
30 *ibid*, p. 11.
31 R. Rosenzweig, 'Afterthoughts: Everyone a Historian' http://chnm.gmu.edu/survey/afterroy.html#32 accessed 7 February 2007.
32 Thelen, 'Afterthoughts', pp. 7–8.
33 See George Mason University's History News Network, 'In memory of Roy Rosenzweig 1950–2007' http://www.hnn.us/articles/43739.html accessed 2 March 2008.
34 D. J. Cohen, 'The Future of Preserving the Past', *CRM: The Journal of Heritage Stewardship*, 2: 2 (2005) 11.
35 Examples of the exhibition can be found at: http://www.saintpaulschapel.org/pyv/
36 See, for example, F. Pannekoek, 'Who matters? Public History and the Invention of the Canadian Past', *Acadiensis*, XXIX, 2 (2000) 205–17.
37 Kean, Martin and Morgan, 'Introduction', in Kean, Martin and Morgan, *Seeing History*, p. 15.
38 A. Portelli, *The Battle of Valle Giulia: Oral History and the Art of Dialogue* (Madison: University of Wisconsin Press, 1997), p. 9.
39 A. Portelli, *The Order Has Been Carried Out: History, Memory, and Meaning of a Nazi Massacre in Rome* (New York: Palgrave Macmillan, 2003), p. 12.
40 *ibid*, p. 12.
41 P. Ashton and P. Hamilton, 'At Home with the Past: Background and Initial Findings from the National Survey', *Australian Cultural History*, 22 (2003) 27, 23.
42 J. Black, *Using History* (London: Hodder Arnold, 2005).
43 *ibid*, p. 2.
44 *ibid*, p. 9.
45 M. K. Flynn and T. King, 'Museums and Symbolic Reparation in Post-Apartheid South Africa', paper presented to Ruskin public history group 13 May 2006, subsequently published as 'Renovating the Public Past: Nation-building, Symbolic Reparation and the Politics of Heritage in Post-Apartheid South Africa', in C. Norton (ed.) *Nationalism, Historiography and the (Re)construction of the Past* (Washington DC: New Academic Press, 2007). See also discussion over the future of the site of the Long Kesh internment camp/Maze prison in the north of Ireland as analysed in B. Graham and S. McDowell, 'Meaning in the Maze: The Heritage of Long Kesh', *Cultural Geographies*, 14 (2007) 343–68 and L. Purbrick, 'The Architecture of Containment', in D. Wylie (ed.) *The Maze* (London: Granta, 2004), pp. 91–110.
46 www.histori.ca; Conrad, 'How Historians Complicate Things'; J. L. Granatstein, *Who killed Canadian History?* (Toronto: HarperCollins, 1998).
47 Jordanova, *History in Practice* p. 141.

48 *ibid*, p. 155.
49 R. Kelley, 'Public History: Its Origins, Nature and Prospects', *The Public Historian*, 1: 1 (1978) 16.
50 D. G. Vanderstel, 'The National Council on Public History', *Public History Review*, 10 (2003) 131.
51 J. Liddington, 'What is Public History?: Publics and their Pasts, Meanings and Practices', *Oral History*, 30: 1 (2002) 90.
52 *ibid*.
53 *ibid*, p. 92 (our emphasis).
54 *ibid*, p. 91.
55 *ibid*, p. 92.
56 B. Dalley and J. Phillips (eds) *Going Public: The Changing Face of New Zealand History* (Auckland: Auckland University Press, 2001), p. 9.
57 M. Belgrave, 'Something Borrowed, Something New: History and the Waitangi Tribunal', in Dalley and Phillips, *Going Public*, pp. 92–109.
58 D. F. Trask and R.W. Pomeroy III (eds) *The Craft of Public History: An Annotated Select Bibliography* (Connecticut: Greenwood Press for NCPH, 1983), p. xi.
59 *ibid*, p. xii.
60 S. Macintyre and A. Clark, *The History Wars* (Melbourne: Melbourne University Press, 2003), pp. 201–61. See also Peter Stanley, 'Happy Birthday HRS: A decade of the Australian War Memorial's Historical Research Section', *Public History Review*, 2 (1993) 54–65.
61 G. Davison, 'Public History', in G. Davison, J. Hirst and S. Macintyre (eds) *The Oxford Companion to Australian History* (Melbourne: Oxford University Press, 1998), p. 532.
62 Macintyre and Clark, *History Wars*.
63 N. Merriman, 'Diversity and Dissonance in Public Archaeology' and T. Schadla-Hall, 'The Comforts of Unreason: The Importance and Relevance of Alternative Archaeology', in N. Merriman (ed.) *Public Archaeology* (London: Routledge, 2004), pp. 1–2, 255–71.
64 Merriman, 'Diversity', p. 7.
65 Glenn Foard, Field Offensive, *British Archaeology*, 79 (2004), accessed at www.britarch.ac.uk 27 May 2007.
66 See, for example, 'Editorial Policy', *The Public Historian*, 19: 2 (1997) 152.
67 See N. J. Stowe, 'Public History Curriculum: Illustrating Reflective Practice' and Shelly Bookspan, 'Something Ventured, Many Things Gained: Reflections on Being a Historian-Entrepreneur', *The Public Historian*, 28: 1 (2006) respectively 39–66, 67–74.
68 *ibid*, p. 40.
69 See for example, the editorial 'Public History/Public Activism: Looking Ahead in the Twenty-First Century', *The Public Historian*, 24: 3 (2002) 5–7.
70 See, for example, the presidential lecture of Alan Newell which drew on the work of K. Ross Toole and R. Archibald: A. S. Newell, '"Home is What You Can Take Away with You": K. Ross Toole and the Making of a Public Historian', *The Public Historian*, 23: 3 (2001), 62–71.
71 http://www.gothamcenter.org/about accessed 27 May 2007.

72 D. Walkowitz, 'Series in Public History: "Around the Globe"', *Radical History Review*, 75: 79 (1999).
73 D. Walkowitz and L. M. Knauer (eds) *Memory and the Impact of Political Transformation in Public Space* (Durham, NC: Duke University Press, 2004) and D. Walkowitz and L. M. Knauer (eds) *Narrating the Nation: Memory, Race and Empire* (Durham, NC: Duke University Press, forthcoming, 2008).
74 A. Curthoys and P. Hamilton, 'What Makes History Public?', *Public History Review*, 1 (1992) 13.
75 See for example, M. Anderson, 'In Search of Women's Public History: Heritage and Gender', *Public History Review*, 2 (1993) 1–17; Stephen Gapps, 'Out of Time, Out of Place: Re-enacting the Past of a Foreign Country', *Public History Review*, 9 (2001) 61–9; P. Ashton and P. Hamilton, 'On not Belonging: Memorials and Memory in Sydney', *Public History Review*, 9 (2001) 23–36; A. Gorman-Murray, 'Gay and Lesbian Public History in Australia', *Public History Review*, 11 (2004) 8–38.
76 W. G. Sebald, *On the Natural History of Destruction* (London: Penguin, 2003), p. 7.
77 B. Ladd, *The Ghosts of Berlin: Confronting German History in the Urban Landscape* (Chicago: University of Chicago Press, 1997), pp. 234–5. See also S. Macdonald, 'Undesirable Heritage: Fascist Material Culture and Historical Consciousness in Nuremberg', *International Journal of Heritage Studies*, 12: 1 (2006) 9–28; P. Carrier, *Holocaust Monuments and National Memory Cultures in France and Germany since 1989* (Oxford: Berghahn Books, 2006).
78 J. Kuehl, 'History on Film: T.V. History', *History Workshop Journal*, 1 (1976) 127–35; J. Champion, 'Seeing the Past: Simon Schama's "A History of Britain" and Public History', *History Workshop Journal*, 56 (2003) 153–80; K. Loach, 'In Mortal Combat with the Laura Ashley School of Film-making', unpublished paper, Radical and Popular Pasts Public History Conference, Ruskin College, Oxford, 17 March 2007.
79 P. Wright, 'Restoration Tragedy', *The Guardian*, Saturday 13 September 2003, viewed online.
80 See, for example, the removal by the Federal Office for Building and Regional Planning of one of the last remaining sections of the Berlin Wall which provoked controversy (De-World.De Deutsche Well, 11 April 2007); and Louise Purbrick, 'A Haunted Peace: Long Kesh/Maze Prison and the Past in "post"-conflict Northern Ireland', unpublished paper, Ruskin Public History discussion group, Saturday 21 October 2006 and L. Purbrick, 'The Architecture of Containment', in D. Wylie, *The Maze* (London: Granta, 2004).
81 H. Kean, 'Personal and Public Histories: Issues in the Presentation of the Past', in B. Graham and P. Howard (eds) *The Ashgate Research Companion to Heritage and Identity* (Aldershot: Ashgate, 2008); A. Rice, *Radical Narratives of the Black Atlantic*, (London: Continuum, 2003); Lancaster.gov.uk 'Stamp unveils memorial "Captured Africans" 23 September 2005' accessed 30 November 2006; The Sylvia Pankhurst Memorial Committee http://sylviapankhurst.gn.apc.org/.
82 Archives Task Force report, *Listening to the Past, Speaking to the Future* (London: MLA, 2004). See also the National Council on Archives Road to Relevance Conference, 2003 and MLA London, *Revisiting Collections* research, 2005–07 http://www.mlalondon.org.uk.

83 Samuel, *Theatres of Memory*, p. 8.
84 E. J. Hobsbawm and T. Ranger, *The Invention of Tradition* (Cambridge: Cambridge University Press, 1983), p. 263.
85 Also see J. Kalela, *The Historian in Society* (forthcoming Palgrave 2009).
86 C. Hardy III, 'A People's History of Industrial Philadelphia: Reflections on Community Oral History Projects and the Uses of the Past', *The Oral History Review*, 33: 1 (2006) 30.

Section 1   The Making of History

History does not reside in the archive or the filing cabinet, behind the glass case or in the lecture theatre or the classroom. Nor is it the preserve of academic historians or a fixed entity that is merely communicated to passive publics. History is an active and complex process that involves an ensemble of practices.[1] In various ways, using a range of materials, people make history; it is a construction that is inevitably both personal and contingent.[2]

The chapters in this section address some of the ways in which history is constructed. In discussing the controversy that emerged over Rosenzweig and Thelen's book *The Presence of the Past*,[3] Bernard Jensen notes that for most people the terms 'history' and 'the past' are not synonymous. While many academic historians use the terms interchangeably, thus indicating a desire for critical distance, others use the past to make history that is meaningful and useful in their present, while some found academic history to be 'estranged from everyday life'. Jensen examines this divide, exploring ways in which the nature of public history has been conceptualised.

One issue discussed by Jensen – the relative authority of history-makers – is also explored in Chapter 1 by Paul Ashton and Paula Hamilton. The burgeoning of historical activities and the diversification of history making has challenged the cultural authority of professional historians. Ashton and Hamilton observe that while many academic historians continue to assert their role as leaders in the field of history, there has been an eruption in the amount of interest shown towards history and its practices from all sections of the community. Most of this has been in popular forms and forums with which academics have had little involvement. Indeed, their national survey, 'Australians and the Past' – one of a number of studies of historical consciousness undertaken since the 1990s in response to the history boom – found that many people wanted to 'choose their own past' and make their own histories.

Cathy Stanton's chapter reinforces the dynamism and complexity of the history-making process through a discussion of the development of two historical national parks in the USA. She asks: 'Does "public history" simply mean the presentation of history by [professional] historians to the public, or does it connote a more radically inclusive vision of history-making activities in the public realm?' She argues for the latter, noting the interactions of local historians, professional historians, various levels of government, private enterprise and a diversity of vernacular and local materials in developing these resources for cultural tourism, which allow some North Americans to reconnect to their pasts. Bronwyn Dalley, in her discussion of the New Zealand government's facilitation of, for example, military and indigenous history, also demonstrates a more complex relationship between the state and producers of history, the latter involving a range of participants, not simply an 'author'.

Public history is 'part of a living present constantly being re-created, contested and challenged'.[4] This section explores the issues around how and by whom history is made and re-made.

Notes

1 R. Samuel, *Theatres of Memory: Past and Present in Contemporary Culture* (London: Verso, 1994), p. 8.
2 'Editorial', *Public History Review*, 2 (1993) vi.
3 Roy Rosenzweig and David Thelen, *The Presence of the Past: Popular Uses of History in American Life* (New York: Columbia University Press, 1998).
4 H. Kean, P. Martin and S. Morgan (eds) *Seeing History: Public History in Britain Now* (London: Francis Boutle, 2000), p. 15.

1
Connecting with History: Australians and their Pasts

Paul Ashton and Paula Hamilton

> Australian history is almost always picturesque; indeed, it is so
> curious and strange, that it is itself the chiefest novelty the
> country has to offer, and so it pushes the other novelties into
> second and third place. It does not read like history, but like
> the most beautiful lies. And all of a fresh new sort, no mouldy
> old stale ones. It is full of surprises, and adventures, and
> incongruities, and contradictions, and incredibilities; but they
> are all true, they all happened.[1]

Mark Twain (Samuel Langhorne Clemens), the famous American writer
and humourist, visited Australia in 1895 as part of a moneymaking
lecture tour around the equator. He was broke. Of the many things
about the continent with which he was taken, one was its 'picturesque
history – Australia's speciality', as he called it.[2] By this he meant in the
then relatively recently established colonies the propensity of individuals and institutions to make convenient pasts that were usable in
the present. History was everywhere to be found in public. Civic pro-
moters gave a 'capital of humble sheds' the trappings of 'the aristo-
cratic quarters of the metropolis of the world'. Didactic monuments
and memorials were scattered across the landscape. Tall tales but true
were built around self-made men.[3]

In piecing together his glimpses into Australia's past, Twain drew on
bits of oral histories which he took down from people as he travelled
around, historic landscapes, civic building and private homes over which
he mused, newspapers, books, official publications and the contents
of a number of Australian museums where, he told his readers,
'you will find acres of the most strange and fascinating things'.[4] Many
of these historical artefacts revealed to Twain contradictory and

incongruous stories, few of which could not be reconciled with the landscape.

Mark Twain's late nineteenth-century literary sensibility is a useful reminder of some of the key concerns confronting public historians in Australia and elsewhere over a hundred years later, particularly the challenges to the authority of the 'expert' to interpret the meaning of the past to their society. This chapter examines these shifts against a background of considerable change in the historical landscape over the last few decades. To do this we draw on some results from our national survey, 'Australians and the Past',[5] which was based on an American survey conducted during the mid-1990s in the United States by Roy Rosenzweig and David Thelen and subsequently published as *The Presence of the Past*.[6] We thought that material interpreted from our Australian study could help us connect the work of professional historians with public historical understandings, linking history as a professional study with history as a form of social knowledge and activity. Both contribute to 'public history', defined here as the practice of historical work in a wide range of forums and sites which involves negotiation of different understandings about the nature of the past and its meaning.[7]

Australians and the past

Our primary aim in conducting this three-year project was to interview people who had no formal interest in 'History'. The many issues involved in how people learn and understand history and their attitudes to and ideas about it is of continual concern to secondary school teachers who must make decisions not only about emphases and interpretation within syllabi but about teaching styles and methods. It is of similar concern to the producers of history in the public domain: museum curators, heritage practitioners, directors of historical films and writers of historical novels. All are acutely aware that they must interact with their audience.[8] We asked: 'How are professional historians, history-makers and educators to communicate the past to their publics if we do not understand the historical sensibilities of our own culture?'

Broadly then, our project set out to try and chart forms of historical consciousness, or history-mindedness in Australia. As authors and history-makers we did not stand outside these shifts in the historical climate. To some extent, even to consider such an unusual undertaking as this survey meant our understanding about the nature of historical work and its role in society had already been challenged.

As public historians each with over 20 years experience we were in a good position to observe the politicising of 'History' in public arenas and the many disjunctions between the rhetoric of politicians and commentators, who claimed that the public were generally uninterested in history or had an imperfect knowledge of the past, and what ordinary people were actually doing. On the one hand, a national discourse about historical 'amnesia' in contemporary Australia has been pervasive for the last few years.[9] On the other, remembering the past in a wide range of sites was everywhere becoming more popular along with a growing number of ceremonies and commemorations.[10] Fierce 'history wars' were breaking out on numerous fronts, the most controversial of which was the public debate about the dispossession and treatment of indigenous people, termed the 'stolen generations' due to the policy of removing 'half-caste' (mixed race) children from their families up to the 1960s and 1970s. As David Carter has observed, 'We are not used to thinking of *our* history as contentious, morally compromised or volatile, as dangerous as, say, Japanese or South African history, the American Civil War history, or recent Russian history.'[11]

In addition history teaching in classrooms was under fire from politicians, media commentators and a number of academics for seemingly failing to deliver students with a particular narrative of Australian History.[12] Progressive academic historians were being pilloried in the press and on television for being overly concerned with documenting indigenous dispossession and focusing on a negative and dark past, the 'black armband view' as it was called'.[13] From its opening in 2001, the National Museum of Australia (NMA), which averages about 800,000 visitors per year (against a population of 20 million), became an object of censure. Initially, it faced strong media criticism. One reporter insisted that the NMA represented a 'nation trivialised'. Traditionalists condemned it for its supposed 'sneering ridicule at white history'. Some visitors claimed that it was 'profoundly offensive', 'letting the country down, [with] too much "blackfella history"', though official surveys indicated that the vast majority of visitors had positive reactions to the museum.[14] Its director, Dawn Casey, was sacked in 2003. Attacks on the NMA were quietly encouraged by the conservative Federal Howard Government which pushed for an official appraisal of its content. A review panel reported in July 2003, recommending a more chronologically-based, coherent story of the progress to nationhood.[15] In this environment the survey led us to think differently about the traditionally understood purpose of historical practice, the raft of activities we associate with the term 'doing history' or 'history-making' and the contentious nature of History.

Our research has led us to ask questions about the traditional framework for the formal teaching of history in classrooms and lecture theatres as well as its presentation in a range of institutions such as museums and heritage agencies. For example, in response to the deceptively simple question – 'What is history for?' – both the USA and Australian surveys charted the increasing range and diversity of its use in contemporary society. What also became apparent was that the definition of 'History' itself has become more elastic. There is increasingly a politics of even defining the subject: traditionalists seek to defend its institutional basis as expert knowledge, insisting on the term 'History' or 'Public History'. Academic historians have traditionally relied on a discourse that in one sense is unassailable: history entails 'ruthless analysis', critique and rigorous interrogation. Their business, according to a recent address by an Australian historian, is demolishing myths.[16]

But such a definition to which all others should aspire and the long-standing normative hierarchy it invokes has come under threat in myriad ways. For one, historians, recognising History's western origins, are being forced to share the ground with others seeking epistemological answers to those indigenous people traditionally 'without a history'. An Australian history that truly takes into account Aboriginal perspectives would need to recognise indigenous custodianship of the land prior to British invasion, as well as the shameful treatment of indigenous people by Australian bureaucracy.[17] Many Aboriginal communities also insist on the ownership and control of their own histories. We have also seen the increasing authority of the eyewitness to experience as a powerful correlative to the absence of 'formal evidence.' Some progressive historians now prefer a more broad-ranging understanding of history/histories, while many outside educational institutions have turned to 'remembering' and interpreting the meaning of the past through a memorial framework.[18]

Perhaps the greatest threat to the authority of the traditional historian is the recognition that formal written history is only one mode of understanding the past. Museums in particular claim an increasingly larger share of this institutional high ground though at the same time museums have been challenged by the large numbers of popular collectors who are creating their own collections and archives. While the survey process itself can give us no real idea of how long some history-making activities have been in existence, we have tried to provide the historical context when possible and to indicate the shifts from one form to another. The internet has had considerable impact, for example, on the practice of family reunions and family research and has no doubt stimulated their growth. Other activities such as those undertaken by local historical societies have a longer history but particularly since the 1970s must take their place alongside re-enactment societies or genealogy as a choice of historical pursuit.[19]

The practice of history

Australian histories and historical activities have over time grown in various places and institutions. Academic history, which was a very small field for many years, initially developed partly as a response to the beginning of the nation state. (Australia's six colonies federated in 1901.) The first Professor of History in Australia, George Arnold Wood, who worked at the University of Sydney, said in 1921 that 'the study of history and the practice of patriotism are very closely connected'.[20] Prior to the First World War, Australia had only six small Universities with five professors of history and one associate professor.[21] (By the early 1970s, most professional historians – around 750 – were concentrated roughly equally in universities and colleges of advanced education.) Outside the academy, early trade union histories challenged those of commerce though they too adopted the 'great man' genre and generally reflected the dominant theme of wealth and progress.[22] Textbooks and picturesque atlases traced the development of the colonies and later the states and the nation.[23] Local histories emerged as communities matured, reinforcing local identity and a sense of belonging, though this usually involved erasing indigenous pasts.[24] Australia's first historical society – the Royal Australian Historical Society – was founded in 1900, a year before federation.[25] Some of it members spearheaded the historic preservation movement.[26] Historical societies, which often established museums, were highly influential in framing local pasts though the mean founding date for historical societies across Australia is 1973.[27]

There continues to be a booming public interest nationwide by many different groups (particularly Anglo-Australians and indigenous people) in local history and family history research and a lucrative industry in historical novels and biographies has mushroomed since the 1990s.[28] Some, such as novelist Penelope Fitzgerald, have claimed that the current preoccupations with the past 'arise out of the shortcomings of history'.[29] This is familiar rhetoric. Though many have berated professional historians for their absence from broader public arenas, this argument does not sufficiently explain the increasing interest in the past since the late twentieth century. This phenomenon has more to do with contemporary challenges to cultural identities, social authority and institutional shifts within a context of globalisation and rapid technological change. These endeavours by countless individuals and local groups were at least in part concerned with establishing continuity in time and place, resisting change and avoiding oblivion.

Despite only a sketchy knowledge of the factors that shape historical sensibilities, it is still possible to discern some trends over time. Across generations many will have different levels of knowledge and understanding about the past. Those over 60, for example, have had very little of their historical knowledge informed by school learning, since only 17 per cent of Australians before 1945 completed high school. For those born after the Second World War in an era of mass secondary schooling and increased tertiary education, a larger number will have been exposed to formal history classes at school, especially since in states such as New South Wales it is a compulsory area of study in the middle years of high school.[30] The rapid expansion of historical sites since the 1960s, alongside a proliferation of historical organisations, has also no doubt had considerable impact on inter-generational knowledge and attitudes. The number of people growing older and surviving longer and the growth of cultural diversity in Australia's population have created a very different context for the transmission of historical knowledge in Australian society. Certainly these changes have meant that more people become historical 'monuments' (or living treasures) in their own lifetime as the society increasingly values those who remain to tell the stories of their past experiences. When the last Anzac veteran from the disastrous Gallipoli campaign in the First World War died at the age of 103 in May 2002, he was given a state funeral.[31]

The tumultuous social change of the last four decades has seen up to four different generations shaped by quite divergent understandings about 'race' and 'empire'. Some still living remember a time when their sense of belonging rested with England, which they called 'home'. Others, now middle-aged, grew up identifying with the British Commonwealth, rather than with a strong sense of Australia as sacred territory and nation. What we may be currently experiencing in the traditional Anglophone population, then, is the final death of a consciousness justifying the national and colonial projects of European powers.

One of 'Australia and the Past's' principal findings was that history-making activities allow people to structure themselves in time and space and to make the past familiar: the purpose of their history work is to make connections with the past and to bring the past into the present. Tessa Morris-Suzuki has similarly observed that people constantly draw on a 'kaleidoscopic mass of fragments ... [to] make and remake patterns of understanding which explain the origins and nature of the world we live in'. Through this process, people also 'define and redefine the place that we occupy in that world'.[32] History, in this sense, is as much about identification – about empathetic understanding and intimate connection – as it is about interpretation.[33]

Alan Atkinson has argued that we need to consider 'ideas about the past which are embodied in action and habit and which involve a mostly unreflecting, or at least compulsive, participation, by communities and individuals, in the continuum of past-and-present'.[34] These embodiments of ideas can also be sources for history-making and we would argue that they are culturally constructed. But he ultimately concedes that the past is an artefact of the present which has vital political and social uses. In discussing regional and local heritage, he notes that:

> Important here are the ways in which the uses of the past are linked to the uses of power and to the means of resistance to power. As a source of legitimacy, the past is a fund of precedent. It can be a means of maintaining not only privilege and power but also the everyday decencies, comforts and pleasures – plus varieties of spiritual attachment – to which everyone can feel entitled by the passage of time.[35]

This past as a form of social knowledge and the professional skills of the historian as 'advocate' can legitimate geographical communities and social identities. Every social movement constructs its own past. These histories legitimate their place in the world, their perspectives and their visions of the future.[36] For the many Australians involved in the process of 'reconciliation', the national term chosen to mark a putative turning point in the relationship between Australia's indigenous peoples and the continuing legacy of European colonialism, the past is not the preserve of any one group. We concur with Marnie Hughes-Warrington's view that:

> [T]here is no 'history' apart from historical practices. Nor, in consequence, is there any logical, universal or unchanging reason to

talk of one practice as 'more historical' than another. If we value some historical practices over others, it is because of historical decisions. And because our views on what history is are themselves historical, they are subject to re-evaluation and change.[37]

These practices include history on film and television, as historical novels, in newspapers,[38] in universities, in museums, in schools and in the home, as well as the practice of academically trained professionals who work in 'the field'.

In their northern American study, Rosenzweig and Thelen found a gap between 'history' and 'the past'. For them, it reflected a seeming divide between the academic discipline of History – with a capital H – as opposed to histories which were personal, local or communal. In the Australian survey, this was apparent in responses about history in schools. One north Queensland respondent, for example, recalled that:

> We were taught a lot of dates ... we should have done more work on Australian history. I've had to read up myself most of what I know. Different things come up and I think – God I never learnt about that. We did war and 1788. Nothing on the Mount Morgan mine. We were never taught about our own backyard at school ...[39]

In this view, traditional approaches to history appear to be failing some people. Irrespective of age, for some who did connect with the local at school, this exposure often shaped a lifelong interest in history. For the majority, however, interests in the past had not been stimulated primarily by formal history teaching: many older respondents reported being alienated during didactic history teaching at school. Most participants said their high school history study, whether enjoyable or not, failed to deal with the most significant questions they had about the past generally and their own past in particular.[40]

While some respondents remembered teachers drawing on their local area as a source for historical research and meanings most respondents found classroom history dull and remote. In the late 1990s, in response to a startling decline in the number of high school students taking history, some academic historians accused history teachers of being the main cause of the unpopularity of the subject. During 1998, Alan Ryan – at the time an academic at the University of Notre Dame Australia – asserted that history teachers were a major factor in the nationwide crisis that history was facing. The 'simple fact', he claimed, 'is that children are being introduced to history by people who know nothing about it'.[41] Ryan's intervention sparked a heated debate again reflecting issues around authority and expertise. History educators and others accused him of presuming to understand how the discipline of history operated in classrooms. Carmel Young, who was lecturing in history curriculum at the University of Sydney, rightly noted Ryan's 'failure to comprehend the distinctiveness of school history'.[42] This was one highly public historical practice that had its own set of needs.

It was, however, the family, not the classroom, that was shown in the survey to be the principal site for exploration and teaching about the past across all cultures and religions. Most respondents reported changes in their view of the past as they reached life passages such as having children or losing parents. Interviewees typically said they were seeking answers to the personal questions: 'Who am I? How does the present come to be as it is?' Many interviewees, including those with no expressed leisure interest in history, were nevertheless actively involved in constructing an account of the past and present to be preserved within their family and passed on to their younger relations or friends. These may range from the taking and collecting of photos, to recording videos of major events, collecting memorable objects and recording older relatives' memories. The past that inspires genealogists, local and community historians and collectors is not random but connected to their personal identity, most often their genetic heritage. Genealogy locates people in time and place. Many of these people saw themselves as involved in the preservation of records or objects, as being 'archivists' for the community, locality or family. It was these people who were most likely to locate personal pasts in broader themes and stories.[43]

Museums and heritage sites were also highly valued by respondents in their learning about and connecting with the past. The reasons were partly that great authority was ascribed to material culture as a 'real' testimony from the past, but also partly that places such as museums and heritage sites allowed opportunities for family visits and questions to older relations. Museums were also useful as sites for the negotiation of the past between generations. James Gardner of the National Museum of American History, Smithsonian Institution, however, has argued that a simple trust in what is perceived to be unmediated objects indicates that most people do not understand the role of the contemporary museum.[44] People inscribed historical associations and meanings onto physical objects, special things, structures and places that act as triggers of memory.[45] These objects often connect personal pasts to historical processes such as colonialism, migration and suburbanisation, to community and family history and to national narratives. Sometimes they confirm official accounts of the past and at other times they show these to be contestable. They physically anchor the past in the present. They are perceived to be 'real'.

Contemporary historical culture, too, is not solely aimed at transmission of historical knowledge. Instead it has more complex understandings and uses. There is a very widely held and sophisticated awareness, for example, of the processes of constructing an interpretation of the past in film and television historical products. While programmes promoted as 'documentary' are more widely regarded as reliable on detail and interpretation, electronic media history is subject to sceptical critique among many ordinary Australians. Nevertheless, these products are also widely consumed, enjoyed and discussed. While received critically, most interviewees across all ethnic groups regarded film and television, whether fiction or documentary, as a major source of historical knowledge. This is part of a wider shift towards material objects and the visual, supporting the idea of direct access to the past, of immersing oneself in the 'experience' of the past.

These foregoing observations arise from the voluminous qualitative material collected in the course of the 'Australians and the Past' project.[46] Corroborative examples abound. One older man with grandchildren felt connected to the past through

> medals and old watches. Old jewellery that was my grandmother's ... An old vice that was my grandfather's when he was a blackie [blacksmith] and I use it still today and it'll be passed on. They give you a grounding in where you come from: if you don't know where you've come from you don't know where you're going. There's china too. There's a dinner set my grandfather bought piece by piece.[47]

This reflection had a number of meanings. It valued, for example, the careful and sustained nature of collection while indicating a desire to keep alive the memory of former work practices.

In response to being asked what she wrote in her diary, one woman, clearly conscious of herself as an historical subject, said:

> Everything. Everyday happenings, the weather. When I get letters I put them in too. I think it's important to own the past, not just throw it away. I emigrated in 1969 [to Australia] and I wish I had

started my diary then. My grandmother lived in the bush in Western Australia and there are no records of that at all.[48]

A male school teacher who strove to bring the past into the present liked

to look at historical sites as I go around Melbourne and outside Melbourne. I read plaques and look at architecture. Then I may look at books at home and think about their purpose and previous purpose. I look at old signs. It has become part of the fabric of my life.[49]

Another respondent was not so keen on books. These, he said, 'are just imaginary stories. But Museums have real things in them'.[50] Someone else indicated that through '[m]useums and historic sites – I feel as if I'm transported, as if I'm there, stirring deep memories which are not available to me day by day.'[51] Similarly, one man was taken with '[h]istoric sites. The atmosphere. When I was in England the old castles. When I was young', he remarked, 'I was affected by them. Like a vibration. I can tune into that.'[52]

Understandings of 'history' in these accounts are tied to objects and places. They are mnemonic whiteboards that flag meanings, connections and associations. 'I've got some old clocks', one middle-aged woman said, 'that me dad gave to me. I look at them because it's nice to feel something in my hand that has belonged to family to bring me closer to them; to remember when I touch that thing'.[53] Personal and public pasts, however, blur. A middle-aged man confided that although his family discussed the great depression's disastrous impact on his relatives, war 'wasn't talked about, but I said to dad when I was older: "You have to share it. I want to know what happened out there." He was a stoker and never wanted to talk about it'.[54] Many stories revealed, as Harry Harootunian has eloquently put it, the 'ceaseless interrelationship between public and private that register large and small events alike'.[55] At different stages of their life or at times of significant change or trauma many people became sharply aware of a sense of history, of living in time, of themselves as historical beings. This awareness involves a sense of shared experience, of being shaped by and participating in events larger than oneself.[56]

Historical authority

Questions of historical authority lay at the heart of many comments made by 'Australians and the Past' participants in relation to their feeling of historical connectedness. Many wanted to be reassured that the historical knowledge and insights gained from various sources was reliable. Debates over historical authority have been brewing in Australia for over two decades. When Robert Hughes' epic work on convict Australia, *The Fatal Shore*, became an international bestseller in the mid-1980s some eminent academic historians reacted defensively.[57] Stuart Macintyre portrayed Hughes as a talented interloper largely because he was 'writing for a wider audience'.[58] Marion Aveling argued that there was an almost natural 'antithesis between powerful popular writing and the hesitations and qualifications of academic history'.[59] Clearly there are differences between these forms of historical presentation. Hughes' book, over 700 pages in length, was largely a work of synthesis but it gained wide critical acclaim from literary critics and academics, including eminent historians.[60]

Inga Clendinnen, a senior academic and author of *Reading the Holocaust*, took an even harder position in a condescending foray into the history wars during 2006. In her essay, 'The History Question: Who Owns the Past?', Clendinnen provided the following answer to this question: academic historians were in possession. In one section, Clendinnen dismissed Orange prize-winning novelist Kate Grenville's historical novel, *The Secret River*, as an inadequate representation of the past. (Grenville was taken aback by this attack.) Placing traditional written academic history at the summit of a hierarchy of historical forms, Clendinnen wrote that Grenville 'sees her novel as a work of history sailing triumphantly beyond the constrictions of the formal discipline of history-writing'.[61] She is annoyed by would-be historians who claim their fiction as a 'serious work of history' while at the same time supposedly using their literary art as a shield against historical criticism.[62] Real history for Clendinnen is a moralistic, 'critical discipline'[63] and the stakes – cultural authority – are high. This history war was a turf war. For Clendinnen, it was the 'confusion between the primarily aesthetic purpose of fiction and the primarily moral purpose of history which makes the present jostling for territory matter.'[64]

Mark McKenna, an historian at the University of Sydney who has shown a commitment to accessible history in his writing, commented along similar lines to Clendinnen in a public lecture held the previous year. He lamented that in recent times historians had 'lost much of their earlier cultural authority'. 'A cultural space', he noted, 'has opened up into which writers of fiction are now more commonly seen as the most trustworthy purveyors of the past'. This had also allegedly contributed to the 'decline of critical history in the public domain'.

McKenna argued that this was in part a legacy of the history wars which left some wounded and other academic historians looking like 'cultural warriors peddling rival versions of the truth'.[65] Thus critical historians found themselves and their 'real pasts' out in the cold in a 'great age of historical mythology', as McKenna put it. Everywhere, individuals and groups seem to be making new pasts or remaking old ones; growing numbers of novelists turn to historical perspectives and sources for inspiration; and while history continues to act as a powerful force in the culture it is seemingly out of the control of academics and not of their making. Is it not, however, surprising that some people had drifted away from the work of history scholars who show disdain for wide audience appeal and 'powerful popular writing' while issuing permits for permissible pasts.

Who has authority in different historical practices and how is it gained? Professional associations can lend authority via accreditation. Legislation, such as heritage acts, can give practitioners authority through the force of law, tying them into the state. Academics gain authority by processes of peer review and academic promotion. Re-enactors gain authority through authenticity: they pride themselves on using genuine reproductions or, if at all possible, 'the real thing'.[66] Communities can also confer authority. This can take the form of 'trust bestowed' and access granted to archives or memories or of collaborations with communities. In terms of indigenous communities, an outstanding example is the film *Ten Canoes*. This powerful work won an award at the New South Wales' Premier's History Awards in 2006.

Rolf de Heer and co-director Peter Djigirr produced a visually stunning and historiographically noteworthy work. Inspired by a photographic collection made in the 1930s by anthropologist David Thomson, the film was shot in Central Arnhem Land in the Northern Territory, south of Darwin, in both black and white – for the pre-contact period – and colour – for Dreamtime (when ancestral creation heroes shaped the earth as it is today). It centres on two brothers and their eight companions who set out into the Arafura swamp in ten canoes to search for goose eggs and tells a cautionary tale involving kinship laws. The film entails these stories being re-enacted by the Yolngu of Ramingining in their own language and in line with kinship laws; in doing so they have reclaimed their past.[67] The judges for the award commented that as 'the community use the medium of film to do what they have done for millennia through the mediums of painting and dance and song, the result is one of the most significant histories told in this country, in any art form'.[68]

Questions of authority – or its recognition – in part underlie continuing tensions between academic and other historians. For public and community historians, however, issues of authority can be particularly fraught when working with communities. In a post-colonial era where history has been democratised, professional practitioners can find themselves in negotiation with a range of individuals, groups and organisations over the content and nature of history.

Kate Waters, a consultant historian who does a lot of work with indigenous communities' histories, says that the history she puts together 'is not *her* vision'. The whole process, she says, 'of collection, structuring and analysis of the material is always impacted upon by the perceptions, desires and demands of the community'. 'Overall, the main issue for me', she contends, 'is that it is a constant negotiation between the ethics of the analytical historian [truthful to the discipline] and the ethics of the practising historian engaging with people and their personal, political concerns.' There is frequently conflict between these two sets of ethics.[69] This is particularly acute when dealing with histories of massacres, the forced separation of children and violence, which have often been known for generations but hidden or unacknowledged.[70]

Conclusion

This chapter has touched on a number of historical practices and activities, some of which have been operating in our culture for many generations. Collectively, they shape the vast majority of people's understandings of 'history' in Australia. And they form part of what has been called 'history in public'[71] – collective, history-based activities or history practices which are undertaken for a broad audience. These activities have expanded exponentially in recent times as more history is being made for public consumption and as the diversity of popular historical pursuits have grown significantly.

Our national survey has investigated some of the ways in which people work with the past in their everyday lives, their attitudes to it and the uses they make of it. Most if not all of the people who took part in the survey would have wholeheartedly agreed with the assertion of one participant that 'history is not just ancient history or famous people... the everyday person has more interesting history.'[72] Many people also had a strong sense of ownership of, or desire for control over, the past. Reflecting on a question in the survey: 'Do you think people think differently about the past as they grow older?', one respondent said: 'Definitely. People realise more how much a part of the past they are, both psychologically and physically; in doing so they realise they can choose their own past.'[73]

Traditional history was widely respected in the survey. And academic historians were highly trusted. But they were only one of many sources of knowledge about the past and their practice was often perceived to be foreign to everyday lives. (Ironically, too, a number of people in the survey admitted to not knowing what academic historians did while simultaneously ranking them highly on the basis of trust. This might suggest that authority is in part conferred on academics by an institutional framework.) As a female respondent in her early sixties told one survey interviewer, 'to actually feel connected [to history] it needs to be part of my past'.[74] A man in his seventies likewise said that his feeling of connectedness to history depended on whether it had 'a bearing on me or my family's past'.[75] For those who made their own histories, there was a strong sense of what Michael Frisch called a 'shared authority'.[76] This term has since become very popular, particularly in fields of historical endeavour that involve working with people to make histories outside the institution – in the case of museums – or the academy. Attempts at democratising history, however, have had uneven effects and have not on the whole disturbed the balance of power except, in the Australian case, for historians working with some indigenous people. Shared authority is a term still in wide usage but more often than not it is a signal of worthy intentions rather than an actual description of how people negotiate knowledge about the past.

What has changed is that historians are being forced to recognise the legitimacy of people as makers of history who have been the subjects of history. 'Expert' historians – professional, public, academic – have variously claimed that there is a 'crisis' in history and some contend that they are losing their authority. But there is a certain irony in claiming expert status. In some countries the main arenas for negotiating the past are now located in popular culture, specifically media, which can satisfy a range of constituencies. New and culturally influential forms of historical knowledge have emerged relatively autonomously from the work of professional historians.

While professional historians in Australia continue to exercise significant authority, their influence today resides more in places such as courtrooms – over native title and other legal disputes – that demand 'expert witnesses'. For the historical profession, the question of 'expert authority' is not in any real doubt. But the arenas in which history is practiced and historical understandings are generated have widened as public appetites for accessible pasts have grown. This is clearly reflected in the rise of words that go with history – history-making, practising history, recreating and using history, witnessing, testimony, memorialising and remembering. As Greg Denning has observed,[77] to think that academic history is the only 'real history' is 'a mere claim to territoriality'.

Notes

1   M. Twain, *The Wayward Tourist: Mark Twain's Adventures in Australia* (Melbourne: Melbourne University Press, 2006), p. 65; extracts from Mark Twain, *Following the Equator*, first published 1897.
2   *ibid*, p. 75.
3   *ibid*, pp. 70, 71, 75.
4   *ibid*, p. 64.
5   See P. Hamilton and P. Ashton (eds) *Australians and the Past*, special issue of *Australian Cultural History*, 22 (2003). This project was carried out at University of Technology, Sydney by Paul Ashton, Jane Connors, Heather Goodall, Paula Hamilton and Louella McCarthy.
6   R. Rosenzweig and D. Thelen, *The Presence of the Past: Popular Uses of History in American Life* (New York: Columbia University Press, 1998).
7   See, for example, D. Thelen, 'But is it History?', *The Public Historian*, 22 (2000) 39–44.
8   M. Frisch, *A Shared Authority: Essays on the Craft and Meaning of Oral and Public History* (Albany: State University of New York Press, 1990); D. Thelen, 'History Making in America', *The Historian*, 53 (1991) 631–48; R. Samuel, *Theatres of Memory: Past and Present in Contemporary Culture* (London: Verso, 1994); D. Lowenthal, *Possessed by the Past: The Heritage Crusade and the Spoils of History* (London: Viking, 1996).
9   See, for example, J. Howard, Sir Robert Menzies Lecture, 'The Liberal Tradition: The Beliefs and Values which Guide the Federal Government', 18 November 1996.
10   See, for example, K. Inglis, *Sacred Places: War Memorials in the Australian Landscape* (Melbourne: The Miegunyah Press, 1998), ch. 8 'Australia Remembers', pp. 412–79.
11   D. Carter, 'Working with the Past, Working on the Future', in R. Nile and M. Peterson (eds) *Becoming Australia: The Woodford Forum* (St Lucia: University of Queensland Press, 1999), p. 10: emphasis added.
12   P. Ashton and P. Hamilton, 'Facing Facts?: History Wars in Australian High Schools', *Journal of Australian Studies*, 91 (2007), pp. 45–59.
13   See S. Macintyre and A. Clark, *The History Wars* (Melbourne: Melbourne University Press, 2003), pp. 164–5.
14   D. Casey, 'Culture Wars: museums, politics and controversy', *New Museum Developments and the Culture Wars*, special issue of *Open Museum Journal*, 6 (2003) 8–10.
15   For detailed accounts of the controversy see G. Hansen, 'White Hot History: the Review of the National Museum of Australia', *Public History Review*, 11 (2004) 39–50, which is an insider's response; and 'Review of the National Museum of Australia, its Exhibitions and Programs: A Report to the Council

of the NMA', July 2003. This can be downloaded from the NMA website www.nma.gov.au; a summary can be found at Georgina Sale, 'Museum told it's lost the plot', *The Australian*, 16 July 2003, p. 5.

16 See I. Clendinnen, 'The History Question: Who Owns the Past?', *Quarterly Essay*, 23 (2006) 32–68.

17 See B. Attwood, 'Introduction: The Past as Future: Aborigines, Australia and the (Dis)course of History', in B. Attwood (ed.) *In the Age of Mabo: History, Aborigines and Australia* (Sydney: Allen and Unwin, 1996), pp. vii–xxxviii.

18 P. Hamilton, 'Memory Studies and Cultural History', in H. Teo and R. White (eds) *Cultural History in Australia* (Sydney: University of NSW Press, 2003), pp. 81–97.

19 W. Tyler, *Survey 2000: A Report of the Survey of Member Societies of the Federation of Australian Historical Societies* (Canberra: Federation of Australian Historical Associations, 2000), p. 8.

20 *Sydney Morning Herald*, 20 June 1921, p. 3.

21 Macintyre and Clark, *The History Wars*, p. 25.

22 P. Ashton and C. Keating, 'Commissioned History', in G. Davison, J. Hirst and S. Macintyre (eds) *The Oxford Companion to Australian History* (Melbourne: Oxford University Press, 1998), p. 140.

23 See, for example, A. W. Jose, *History of Australasia from the Earliest Times to the Present Day with a Chapter on Australian Literature* (Sydney: Angus and Robertson, 1899) and Picturesque Atlas of Australia (Sydney: Picturesque Atlas Publishing, 1886).

24 B. Kingston, 'The Use and Function of Local History', in The Local History Co-ordination Project, *Locating Australia's Past* (Kensington: University of NSW Press, 1988), p. 7.

25 G. Griffith, 'The Historical View from the Royal Australian Historical society', in The Local History Co-ordination Project, *Locating Australia's Past*, p. 9.

26 S. McClean, '"Progress the Iconoclast": Campaigns, Ideologies and Dilemmas of Historic Building Preservation in New South Wales, 1900–1939', *Public History Review*, 7 (1998) 25–42.

27 Tyler, *Survey 2000*, p. 8.

28 J. Spurway, 'The Growth of Family History in Australia', in *The Push: A Journal of Early Australian Social History*, 27 (1989) 7–12.

29 Quoted in P. Ashton and P. Hamilton, 'At Home with the Past: Background and Initial Findings from the National Survey', in Hamilton and Ashton (eds) *Australians and the Past*, 6.

30 C. Young, 'Recasting School History: For Better or For Worse?', *Public History Review*, 7 (1998) 9–12. The middle years of high school refers to years 9 and 10 in which students are generally between 14 and 15 years old.

31 ABC Radio National, 'The World Today', 17 May 2002, www.abc.net.au/worldtoday/stories/s558041.htm accessed 6 March 2007.

32 T. Morris-Suzuki, *The Past Within Us: Media, Memory, History* (London: Verso, 2005), p. 2.

33 *ibid*, p. 22.

34 A. Atkinson, 'Heritage, Self, and Place', in Hamilton and Ashton, *Australians and the Past*, p. 162.

35 *ibid*, p. 165.

36   A. Curthoys and P. Hamilton, 'What makes history public?', *Public History Review*, 1 (1993) 8.

37   M. Hughes-Warrington, *History Goes to the Movies: Studying History on Film* (Abingdon: Routledge, 2007), p. 32.

38   For newspapers, see P. Hamilton, '"Stranger than Fiction": the *Daily Mirror* "Historical Feature"', in J. Rickard and P. Spearritt (eds) *Packaging the Past? Public Histories*, special issue of *Australian Historical Studies*, 24: 96 (1991) pp. 198–207.

39   Australian and the Past Survey (hereinafter Survey), interview GZ 11. Interviews held at the Australian Centre for Public History, University of Technology, Sydney. For this respondent, both the local event was important as well as its connection to broader Labour history.

40   Ashton and Hamilton, 'Facing facts?'.

41   A. Ryan, 'Developing a Strategy to "Save" History', *Australian Historical Association Bulletin*, 87 (1998) 42.

42   C. Young, 'Historical Revivalism', *Australian Historical Association Bulletin*, 88 (1999) 24.

43   Ashton and Hamilton, in Hamilton and Ashton, *Australians and the Past*, 21.

44   J. B. Gardner, 'Contested Terrain: History, Museums, and the Public', *The Public Historian*, 26 (2004) 12.

45   P. Read, '"Before Rockets and Aeroplanes": Family History', in Hamilton and Ashton, *Australians and the Past*, 135–6.

46   For quantitative material see Ashton and Hamilton, 'At Home with the Past', in Hamilton and Ashton, *Australians and the Past*, 14–17.

47   Interview, FW/08, Survey, text units 176–7.

48   Interview AP/01.vic, Survey, text units 42–3.

49   Interview AP/05.vic, Survey, text units 105–8.

50   Interview AP/01.vic, Survey, text units 42–3.

51   Interview MH/20, Survey, text units 142–5.

52   Interview PA/02, Survey, text units 140–2.

53   Interview ME/18, Survey, text units 34–5.

54   Interview KC/33, Survey, text units 85–90.

55   H. Harootunian, *History's Disquiet: Modernity, Cultural Practice and the Question of Everyday Life* (New York: Columbia University Press, 2000), p. 19.

56   P. Ricoeur, *Time and Narrative*, vol 1 (Chicago: University of Chicago Press, 1984), p. 274.

57   R. Hughes, *The Fatal Shore: A History of the Transportation of Convicts to Australia, 1787–1868* (London: Collins, 1987).

58   S. Macintyre, 'Hughes and Historians', *Meanjin*, 46: 2 (1987) 245.

59   M. Aveling, review of *The Fatal Shore*, *Australian Historical Studies*, 23: 90 (1988) 127.

60   A. Forst, 'Fatal ambivalence towards our past', *The Weekend Australian*, 21–22 February 1987, p. 14.

61   Clendinnen, 'The History Question: Who Owns the Past?', p. 17.

62   *ibid*, p. 31.

63   *ibid*, p. 64.

64   *ibid*, p. 34.

65   M. McKenna, 'Writing the Past', 2005, www.humanitieswritingproject.net.au/mckenna.htm accessed 1 November 2006.

66 S. Gapps, 'Authenticity Matters: Historical Re-enactment and Australian Attitudes to the Past', in Hamilton and Ashton, *Australians and the Past*, pp. 105–16.

67 *Ten Canoes* (Adelaide: Vertigo Productions/Adelaide Festival of Arts, 2005).

68 Arts NSW, *NSW Premier's History Awards 2006* (Sydney: Arts NSW, 2006), p. 12.

69 K. Waters, personal communication, 29 September 2006: emphasis added.

70 G. Blomfield, 'Hidden History: Conflict and Community History', in Community History Program, *History and Communities: A Preliminary Survey* (Kensington: University of New South Wales, 1990), p. 59.

71 C. Stanton, *The Lowell Experiment: Public History in a Postindustrial City* (Amherst and Boston: University of Massachusetts Press, 2006), p. 8.

72 Interview AP/06.vic, Survey, text units 149–50.

73 Interview KC/07, Survey, text units 152–3.

74 Interview FW/22, Survey, response to question 3.2.

75 Interview RD/38, Survey, response to question 3.7.

76 Frisch, *A Shared Authority*.

77 G. Denning, 'Some Beaches are Never Closed: Foundation and Future Reflections on the History Institute, Victoria', *Rostrum*, 19 (2001) 29.

2
Usable Pasts: Comparing Approaches to Popular and Public History

Bernard Eric Jensen

The publication of Roy Rosenzweig and David Thelen's *The Presence of the Past: Popular Uses of History in American Life* in 1998 signalled a landmark in the empirical study of popular and public history.[1] It outlined a way of conceptualising the character of popular and public forms of history, and was the first major attempt to generate sociological insight into the ways in which ordinary people understand and use history in their everyday lives.

The publication of this survey also generated an eye-opening controversy about what is at stake when one starts to compare the approaches of popular and public history on the one hand and academic history on the other. This became apparent in the responses to Rosenzweig and Thelen's book generated in the course of a roundtable discussion published in *The Public Historian: A Journal of Public History* during the winter of 2000.

Michael Zuckerman, an American university-based historian, was the most adamant critic of Rosenzweig and Thelen's results. As he saw it, they had overlooked a central fact revealed by their own survey for the reason that they had looked 'at their data through rose-colored glasses.' What their survey had disclosed, Zuckerman asserted, was the existence of 'a pathological, nonparticipatory, and ahistorical culture' among white adult Americans.[2] Rosenzweig responded to this by countering that he and his co-author could not 'recognize our respondents ... in this indictment'.[3]

These incompatible interpretations of the findings of *The Presence of the Past* cannot be explained by a difference in professional ideals, since Zuckerman professed to share 'Rosenzweig and Thelen's desire for a healthy, participatory, historical culture'.[4] How then is it to be explained? It is due – I suggest – to a difference in their underlying conceptions of history.

Zuckerman entitled his contribution *The Presence of the Present, The End of History*, pointing out that Rosenzweig and Thelen's respondents had 'defined the past in terms of their own experience.' To this he added: 'But history addresses exactly what is beyond immediate experience.'[5] Thelen admitted that a key issue raised by their survey concerned the question: 'What do the book's findings about individual uses of the past have to do with "history", the domain of our competence as professionals?'[6] He therefore entitled his reply: *But Is It History?*

When Zuckerman had stressed the pastness of history he was advocating a view prevalent among academic historians. It is an approach that treats 'history' and 'the past' as synonymous terms and therefore views the past as a bygone, foreign country. What *The Presence of the Past* had revealed is that adult Americans do not think along these lines. What counts for them is the uses of the past in the present: that is, the availability of usable pasts rather than the pastness of history.

Different ways of understanding how the present relates to the past is the factor that underlies and can explain many of the clashes between public and academic historians in recent years.[7] I will only dwell upon one aspect of this conflict here – the conceptual frameworks employed to account for the character of popular and public history.

American and British approaches

There is no consensus about definitions of the terms 'popular' and 'public' history at the present time.[8] Not all popular history can be meaningfully called public history insofar as the former category includes more intimate uses of history that are not made publicly available in any form. Moreover, there are also some forms of public history that seem to be virtually indistinguishable from academic history. Yet, in many settings it is quite justified to treat popular and public history as a set of largely overlapping if not wholly synonymous terms. People working in these fields share the conviction that there are other forms of history besides the academic variant. In their view, history should not be treated as if it were a prerogative of academic historians. However, this in turn raises a pertinent question: which conceptual frameworks should be employed when treating popular or public forms of history?

A strongly argued case for the existence of various forms of history was offered in the presidential address delivered by Carl L. Becker to the American Historical Association in 1931. It was entitled *Everyman*

His Own Historian, and it outlined some of the basic premises of popular and public history. When this address has subsequently been taken up for discussion, it has usually been in the context of an epistemological debate focusing on the type of historical scepticism that Becker espoused. However, his address can also be interpreted within the context of an anthropology or sociology of knowledge, and then his ideas appear to be a remarkable anticipation of key findings of *The Presence of the Past.*

Becker made it clear at the outset of his address that the past should not be regarded as an integral feature of a definition of history. He argued that this view of the matter would be 'misleading, because the past, used in connection with history, seems to imply the distant past, as if history ceased before we were born.' Instead, he defined history as 'the memory of things said and done' and claimed that such a definition included 'everything that is essential to understanding what [history] really is.'[9] Becker in effect identified history with memory. He thereby took a stance that clearly diverged from the viewpoint, still prevailing, among academic historians who tended to stress the difference rather than the similarity between history and memory.[10]

Becker did not use the terms 'academic' and 'popular' or 'public' history. He spoke instead about professional and informal historians. With regard to the latter, he pointed out that 'Mr. Everyman, being but an informal historian, is under no bond to remember what is irrelevant to his personal affairs.'[11] This was the key issue as far as Becker was concerned. The only history, he argued, that is truly worthwhile is the pragmatic kind. The proper function of history, he claimed, 'is not to repeat the past but to make use of it.'[12] He therefore sought to clarify what this would mean in an everyday setting:

> Mr. Everyman ... remembers things said and done, and must do so at every waking moment. Suppose Mr. Everyman to have awakened this morning unable to remember anything said or done. He would be a lost soul indeed ... Normally the memory of Mr. Everyman, when he awakens in the morning, reaches out into the country of the past and of distant places and instantaneously recreates his little world of endeavour, pulls together as it were things said and done in his yesterdays, and coordinates them with his present perceptions and with things to be said and done in his tomorrows. Without this historical knowledge, this memory of things said and done, his today would be aimless and his tomorrow without significance.[13]

In *Everyman His Own Historian,* Becker put forward two important points about the use of history. The first is that people use memories of the past in their everyday lives; the second, that people must inter-relate their understanding of the past, present and future in order to be able to participate in the ongoing making of history. Thus, as Becker saw it, the primary use of the past lies in the actual making of history.

The Presence of the Past by Rosenzweig and Thelen bears the marks of being influenced by Becker's way of thinking – a fact made apparent by Rosenzweig entitling his postscript *Everyone a Historian*.[14] At the same time, it should be noted that Rosenzweig and Thelen did not make any attempt to use Becker's concept of history as concerning 'the memory of things said and done.' As a matter of fact, the concept of memory plays no significant role in their analysis of the popular uses of history. Thus, on this point they appear to have adapted their thinking to the prevailing norm among academic historians; that is, to keep the study of history and memory clearly apart.

When Rosenzweig and Thelen began listening to the interviews with a cross-section of Americans, they became excited but also worried because as they point out 'nothing in our professional training had prepared us to interpret what we were hearing.'[15] They were therefore under pressure to develop a new conceptual framework for their analysis of the ways in which ordinary Americans relate to the past.

In *The Presence of the Past* they made use of well-known terms such as 'public history', 'people's history' and 'heritage'. They also mention that they had considered using the concepts 'historical consciousness' and 'historical memory', but had decided to bypass these concepts because they 'told more about how the past had been popularly presented [rather] than about how it been popularly understood.'[16]

Their intent to design a new conceptual framework becomes apparent with their introduction of new terms such as 'popular historymaking' and 'popular historical methodology'. By introducing these terms, they wanted to highlight the fact that just as there is an academic history-making, there also is a popular history-making. Rosenzweig and Thelen wanted to bring across one of the key findings of their survey in this way, emphasising that adult 'Americans take active part in using and understanding the past – that they're not just passive consumers of histories constructed by others.'[17] However, it should be noted how the term 'historymaking' was being used in this context. It did not refer, as in the case of Becker, to the ongoing making of history in the present. Rather, it referred to the construction of stories about the past that are produced by both popular and professional historians.

While the term 'popular historymaking' drew attention to points of similarity between public and academic history, another set of terms introduced by Rosenzweig and Thelen made apparent a point of difference. The terms 'a user of the past', 'a usable past' and 'an intimate use of the past' were introduced in order to convey that Americans treat 'the past as a reservoir of experience', to which they can turn and which they may use in their everyday lives.[18]

The idea of usable pasts is similar to Becker's conception of history as 'the memory of things said and done'. It appears to be a way of holding on to the classical idea of history as a teacher of life *(magistra vitae)* at a time when that notion no longer plays any significant role within academic history. However, it is not the only point on which *The Presence of the Past* reveals important differences between academic and popular historians. Whereas the former treat 'history' and 'the past' as synonyms, these terms have rather different connotations in the minds of popular historians. Adult Americans, the survey shows, view 'the past' as something 'omnipresent' and 'pervasive, a natural part of everyday life, central to any effort to live in the present', but feel fairly alienated from 'history' because they see it as something 'formal, analytical, official or distant'.[19]

The approach adopted by the British historian Raphael Samuel converges on important points with that of Becker, Rosenzweig and Thelen. This convergence partly stems from a shared desire to lessen the authority of academic history and thereby further a democratisation of the study and use of history. It is also due to similar ways of understanding the relationship between past and present. In 1980, when Samuel singled out the defining features of the History Workshop movement, he made the following point:

> The Workshop ... has implicitly challenged the Chinese wall between past and present which is one of the chief legacies of the Rankean revolution in historical scholarship, and which has been powerfully reinforced in more recent times... The division ... impoverishes the study of the past as well as limiting the critical understanding of the present ... It also effectively insulates historians from the wider questions of social and ideological formation ... It deprives them, in brief, of the precious advantage of hindsight.[20]

In much the same way as Americans use the past as a reservoir of experience in their ongoing lives, the History Workshop movement wanted to promote an approach that would make it possible to draw lessons from the study of the past. However, Samuel went on to assert that the overarching purpose of studying history is 'to historicise [our] understanding of the present' and to make us 'more aware of [our] own historicity'.[21] The idea of bringing the past to bear on the present was further developed in 1990 when Samuel and Paul Thompson published the proceedings of the Oral History Conference on *The Myths We Live By*:

> In identifying mythical elements in our own cultural or professional assumptions, we threaten our ethnocentric self-confidence. We discover a psychic dimension which recognizes the power of myth and unconscious desire as forces, not only in history, but in shaping our own lives. We open up a history which refuses to be safely boxed away in card indexes or computer programs: which instead pivots on the *active* relationship between past and present, subjective and objective, poetic and political.[22]

Samuel refined this viewpoint when he began writing his study entitled *Theatres of Memory*, of which only the first volume subtitled *Past and Present in Contemporary Culture* (1994) was published during his lifetime. He entitled its preface *Memory Work* and used a phrase from William Faulkner's *Requiem for a Nun* (1951) – 'The past is not dead. It is not even past yet' – as his point of departure, thereby making it clear that the focus would be on how the past lives on in memory and thereby can exert a continuing influence upon the present.[23]

When Becker pinpointed his understanding of history, he had defined it as 'the memory of things said and done'. Samuel, it should be noted, reached a similar conclusion, seemingly without having been influenced by Becker. By employing a concept of memory Samuel wanted to sketch a framework that would permit one to understand popular and academic history as related – yet distinct – ways of constructing knowledge. Academic history, he pointed out, tended to become 'an esoteric form of knowledge'.[24] By examining the interrelationship between history and memory, Samuel sought to outline an alternative way of understanding history:

> The starting point of *Theatres of Memory* ... is that history is not a prerogative of the historian ... It is, rather, a social form of knowledge; the work ... of a thousand different hands. If this is true, the point of address in any discussion of historiography should [be] the ensemble of activities and practices in which ideas of history are embedded or a dialectic of past-present relations is rehearsed.[25]

In this light it becomes clear that Zuckerman's guiding assumption that 'history addresses exactly what is beyond immediate experience' is precisely the point that has been disputed by both American and British historians in their studies of popular and public approaches to the past.

A Central European approach

The historians considered thus far – Zuckerman excepted – shared a common commitment. Their interest in popular and public history formed an integral part of their political commitment to a history from below. The field of interest for German historians to be considered now is rather different. They have been mainly concerned with history education, and therefore tend to approach popular and public history from a perspective within the educational system.

In the course of the 1970s, it became apparent that a new conceptual framework was needed in order to respond to the fact that history is not merely learned and used in schools and academic institutions, but it is also learned and used in many other cultural and social settings. The concept of 'historical consciousness' (*Geschichtsbewusstsein*) was developed in this setting, resting upon the assumption that this type of consciousness is developed and used in all walks of life. The first attempt to develop an actual theory of historical consciousness emerged in West Germany – a theory that has shaped Central and Northern European approaches to the study of popular and public history during recent decades.

For instance, I have sought to develop this approach in *Historie – livsverden og fag (History – Life-world and Academic Discipline)*[26] – a study that examines the ways in which history is conceived and used in everyday and academic settings. Its starting point is the idea that history and history-making as they occur in our 'life-world' should be considered the more basic form of history. It is from this perspective that the book goes on to explore similarities as well as differences between the concepts of history employed in everyday life, in the educational system and in the academic world.

The diffusion of the theory of historical consciousness was initially furthered by the publication of *Handbuch der Geschichtsdidaktik,* a work looking at many aspects of history education as well as its broader context. Originally published in 1979, a third revised edition appeared in 1985 and a fifth revised edition in 1997. It is worth noting how the broader context of history education has been conceptualised in successive editions of this handbook. The term 'history as life-world' (*Geschichte als Lebenswelt*) was employed in the 1979 edition. An extra section was added to the 1985 edition entitled 'History in an extra-curricular setting' (*Geschichte in der ausserschulischen Öffentlichkeit*). That section was then re-titled in the 1997 edition, 'Aspects of historical culture' (*Aspekte der Geschichtskultur*).

The task of introducing the idea of history as life-world had been given to Rolf Schörken, and his presentation in the first edition was mainly inspired by the work of Edmund Husserl, Alfred Schütz, Peter L. Berger and Thomas Luckmann. Schörken focused especially on their attempts to develop a theory regarding the foundational importance of life-world experiences and common-sense modes of thinking in everyday life. It was against this background that he undertook the task of outlining the ways in which ordinary people relate to the past, present and future:

> The life-world is 'obviously there' and its presence requires no further corroboration... The self experiences the life-world in varying degrees of spatial and temporal nearness and distance ... The interest of the self is preoccupied with its own present-day world, which constitutes its sphere of action. But also past and future times belong to the life-world. Yet, the interest therein is usually less pronounced than the interest in what is immediately present.[27]

This is a point of departure that accords well with the ideas of Becker, Rosenzweig and Thelen concerning usable pasts. In the 1985 edition Schörken argued that, insofar as one's theoretical point of departure is history as life-world, this also entails a rejection of the viewpoint that scientific reasoning is the only true form of rationality (*Allmachtansprüche wissenschaftlicher Rationalität*).[28] It was necessary to challenge the latter viewpoint since a phenomenological approach understands scientific thinking as a mode of reasoning that represents a specialised development of common-sense thinking. Schörken then made the further point that when one employs a theory of the life-world, history is primarily understood as a basic feature of human life:

> The historicity of man is considered a constitutive feature. Man, according to Husserl, is always standing 'in history' – he has a past when glancing backwards, a future when looking forward towards the *eschaton* (i.e. last things), and a present in which he plainly stands. Historicity constitutes the structure of human life.[29]

On this point Schörken's position converges with some of the basic tenets of Samuel's thought. Importantly, it is not an approach that seeks to stress the pastness of history; that is, the mode of thinking favoured by Zuckerman. On the contrary, history is defined as a constitutive feature of the ongoing lives of ordinary people. In the process of living, people must constantly inter-relate their perceptions of past, present and future in their attempts to work out and realise their various projects.

It was in the context of spelling out the implications of the life-world approach that the concept of historical consciousness was introduced, together with a series of other concepts such as 'everyday consciousness', 'time', 'tradition', 'socialisation' and 'identity'. For the 1979 edition, Karl-Ernst Jeismann was charged with the task of presenting the theory of historical consciousness. His initial definition was in line with a phenomenological approach to history, and it reads as follows:

> Historical consciousness encompasses the inter-connection between an interpretation of the past (*Vergagenheitsdeutung*), an understanding of the present (*Gegenwartsverständnis*) and a prospect for the future (*Zukunftsperspektive*).[30]

It is this definition of historical consciousness that in the course of time has become the classical one in Central and Northern Europe. It was employed for instance by Schörken when exploring the different dimensions of popular and public history. In 1981 he edited a collection of essays entitled *Der Gegenwartsbezug der Geschichte* that explored how interest in history is shaped by present-day concerns. It also described how a re-actualisation of the idea of history as *magistra vitae* was taking place at that time. 'There can be no history', it was asserted, 'which does not at the same time offer advice about the present and future'.[31] Schörken went on to publish an extensive study, *Geschichte in der Alltagswelt* (1981), that explored how history is used in everyday life. Moreover, this was undertaken with the following perspective as to how academic and popular historians tend to see each other:

> Viewed from the position of academic history the life-world approach to history appears naïve ... Seen from the pragmatic viewpoint of ordinary people academic history appears estranged from everyday life (*lebensfremd*).[32]

Yet, the main objective of publishing *Handbuch der Geschichtsdidaktik* had not been to explore how history is used in everyday life. The main concern had been with questions of how to teach history within an educational system. The following question was an urgent one in that context: to what extent should the teaching of history be obliged to employ the methods and results of academic history?

When first reading the handbook on history teaching, one may get the impression that it represents a thoroughgoing attempt to ground the teaching and study of history in a phenomenological approach – that is, following Husserl's idea that people are always living their lives 'in history'. Yet, upon scrutiny, it becomes clear that the commitment to a phenomenological approach is somewhat half-hearted. A careful analysis shows that many of the contributors to the handbook appear to be deeply ambivalent about committing themselves to such an understanding of history.

Why this ambivalence? Close examination shows that many contributors seem keenly aware that a phenomenological understanding of history is in conflict with the view prevalent among academic historians – that 'history' should be conceived of as synonymous with 'the past'. A way of handling such ambivalence has at times taken the form of attempting to find a theoretical halfway house or compromise between a phenomenological and a traditional academic approach by trying to blend the concepts of history as life-world and history as the more distant past.

This theoretical ambivalence appears to be operative in Jeismann's outline of the theory of historical consciousness. He first presents a definition of historical consciousness in line with a phenomenological approach but, on closer inspection, he in fact puts forward several definitions. One of his other definitions reads: 'Historical consciousness [is] the manner in which the past is present in ideas and knowledge'.[33] Here the idea that historical consciousness concerns how the past, present and future are inter-related is being modified in order to give preference to the notion that history concerns the past.

Even Schörken, who made a serious attempt to outline a phenomenological approach to history, shows traces of theoretical ambivalence. In the 1985 edition of the handbook he concludes by arguing that to learn history in a life-world setting is the outcome of non-intentional and non-organised processes of learning, while learning history within an educational system and at university will be the outcome of intentional and organised processes of learning.[34] Jochen Huhn pursues this line of thought when introducing the idea of history in extra-curricular settings. One of the tasks of history teaching, Huhn asserts, is to discipline the form of popular history that pupils bring with them from their lives outside the educational system, in order to ensure that their approach to history will come to respect the norms of academic history.[35]

The 1997 edition differs from earlier editions by making the concept of historical culture (*Geschichtskultur*) an integral part of *Handbuch der Geschichtsdidaktik*. But even at its introduction, in a contribution by Jörn Rüsen, that same theoretical ambivalence is present:

> Historical culture names all the activities within the field of historical consciousness. ... Historical memory (*Historische Erinnerung*) is the anthropological base of any activity related to historical consciousness. Moreover, a memory is historical whenever it time-wise and in a fundamental way goes beyond the limits of the lifetime of the remembering self – i.e. goes further into the past and from there projects long-range prospects for the future (*Zukunftsperspektive*).[36]

Although Rüsen's definition of historical culture at first sight appears to be an attempt to apply Jeismann's classical definition of historical consciousness – the inter-connectedness of past, present and future – it actually represents a significant modification of that definition. Moreover, this way of defining historical memory implies that it should be possible to distinguish between non-historical and historical memory in a meaningful way. Thus, what a person remembers about interacting with their parents during childhood would be classified as non-historical memory, whereas what the same person comes to know about their parents' life before they were born would be credited as constituting historical memory.

This way of understanding history and memory is incompatible with a phenomenological approach to history. A phenomenological approach is based upon an exploration of the various kinds of time consciousness operating in human life. It therefore inquires into how inner, subjective and lived time contributes to the shaping of people's lives. This is the point at which a phenomenological understanding of history converges with the work being done in contemporary studies of memory. Academic historians, by contrast, focus their attention on how objective or chronological time works and normally show little or no interest in clarifying how interior (subjective) and exterior (physical and biological) modes of temporality are related to each other.[37]

Moreover, Rüsens's definition of historical memory seeks to uphold the very idea that Becker had warned against – that of understanding history as 'the distant past, as if history ceased before we were born'. Therefore, his wish to introduce a distinction between non-historical and historical memory can be seen as an attempt to revise the theory of historical consciousness in such a way that it would appear to be more compatible with the conception of history prevalent among academic historians which emphasises the pastness of history.

Points of convergence

When one surveys the available attempts to characterise popular and public history, it becomes apparent that different conceptual frameworks are being employed. The work of Carl L. Becker and Raphael Samuel is centred upon the concept of memory. Roy Rosenzweig and David Thelen make the idea of a user of the past their focal point. Finally, the historians associated with *Handbuch der Geschichtsdidaktik* have set out to develop a theory of historical consciousness.

These may appear to be three very different conceptual frameworks. However, close analysis indicates that there are important points of convergence between these approaches. Becker's concept of history, as 'the memory of things said and done', accords fully with Rosenzweig, Thelen and Samuel's findings about the character of popular and public history. Becker's description of the ways in which people inter-relate past, present and future when they use history in their everyday lives can be seen as an early formulation of what later has come to be known as a theory of historical consciousness.

How can these points of convergence be explained? When one begins to enquire into how ordinary people – Becker's Mr. Everyman – approach and relate to the past, it becomes clear that what is being focused upon is not the question of how to study and write about the past, but rather how people make use of available and relevant pasts in their everyday living. Rosenzweig formulates this point as follows:

> In our interviews, the most powerful meanings of the past come out of the dialogue between the past and the present, out of the ways the past can be used to answer pressing current questions about relationships, identity, morality, and agency ... For our respondents, the past is not only present; it is part of the present. That powerful sense of connectedness to the past (and between the past and the present) ... we find in everyday life.[38]

One of the pressing questions would appear to be whether the concept of history as memory is compatible with a theory of historical consciousness that emphasises the ways in which people inter-relate their perceptions of past, present and future in their ongoing lives? This is by no means an insurmountable task once one begins to look into how memory work is being understood in contemporary memory research.

Humans do not have one kind of memory. They make use of different inter-related kinds of memory. They have a 'procedural' memory (remembering how to perform certain activities), as well as a 'semantic' memory (remembering the meaning of words). They have an 'emotional' memory (remembering the feelings different experiences evoked), as well as an 'episodic' memory (remembering specific or types of events). However, the kind of memory that appears to be most relevant when examining points of convergence with the theory of historical consciousness is termed 'autobiographical' memory.

Autobiographical memory appears to be specific to human beings. It is the decisive one when seeking to understand human action; that is, the ongoing making of history. Moreover, exploration of this kind of memory has demonstrated that the memory work undertaken by human beings is not merely retrospective in character. It also has a prognostic or prophetic function, focused upon the future. In the context of surveying what presently is known about autobiographical memory, two German memory researchers, Harald Welzer and Hans J. Markowitsch, draw attention to the following features:

> The stage of fully developed autobiographical memory is attained when the individual can classify information according to the temporal dimensions, when he or she has a concept of the past and the future and performs 'mental time travels' backwards in time and prospectively.[39]

This description might well have been an account of the key features of what has been termed 'historical consciousness' (*Geschichtsbewusstsein*). The central points are the same. What is important from a theoretical point of view is that this way of understanding memory takes as its starting point the matter of how people make history in and through their everyday lives. When it comes to understanding what history is, the approaches adopted by popular and public historians appear therefore to be on the right track. It is crucial that we continue to examine the different ways in which people's pasts shape their ongoing lives – ways that vary from one culture to another and from one epoch to another.

When it comes to the question of how best to further the appreciation of popular and public history, the preceding analysis indicates that attempts to incorporate insights from memory research into the study of popular and public history could prove to be very fruitful indeed. People working in these fields share an interest in seeking to understand how the subjective experiences of time operate in human life, a decisive element in regard to the ways people relate to their pasts.

Notes

1 R. Rosenzweig and D. Thelen, *The Presence of the Past: Popular Uses of History in American Life* (New York: Columbia University Press, 1998).
2 M. Zuckerman, 'The Presence of the Present, The End of History', *The Public Historian*, 22: 1 (2000) 19.
3 R. Rosenzweig, 'Not A Simple Task: Professional Historians Meet Popular Historymakers', *The Public Historian*, 22: 1 (2000) 37.
4 Zuckerman, 'The Presence of the Present', p. 19.
5 *ibid*, p. 20.
6 D. Thelen, 'But Is It History?', *The Public Historian*, 22: 1 (2000) 40.
7 However, there are also those historians who seek to bridge the gap between popular and academic history. *Cf* H. Kean, P. Martin and S. J. Morgan (eds) *Seeing History: Public History in Britain Now* (London: Francis Boutle, 2000).
8 L. Jordanova, *History in Practice* (London: Arnold Publishers, 2000) chapter 6 and J. Liddington, 'What Is Public History?', *Oral History*, 30: 1 (2002) 83–93.
9 C. L. Becker, *Everyman His Own Historian: Essays on History and Politics* (New York: Crofts & Co., 1935) p. 235.
10 Similarly, Susannah Radstone and Katharine Hodgkin felt the need to include a section entitled 'What history forgets: memory and time' in their book S. Radstone and K. Hodgkin (eds) *Regimes of Memory* (London: Routledge, 2003).
11 Becker, *Everyman His Own Historian*, *ibid*, p. 247.
12 *ibid*, p. 253.
13 *ibid*, p. 236.
14 Rosenzweig and Thelen, *The Presence of the Past*, pp. 177–89.
15 *ibid*, p. 8.
16 *ibid*, pp. 3–4.
17 *ibid*, pp. 3, 114.
18 *ibid*, pp. 11–13, 37–9, 65–6.
19 *ibid*, pp. 6, 9.
20 R. Samuel, 'History Workshop Methods', *History Workshop Journal*, 9 (1980) 168.
21 *ibid*, p. 169.
22 R. Samuel and P. Thompson (eds), *The Myths We Live By* (London: Routledge, 1990), p. 5.
23 The quote from Faulkner is not wholly accurate. The phrase in *Requiem for a Nun* reads: 'The past is never dead. It's not even past'. W. Faulkner, *Requiem for a Nun* (Harmondsworth: Penguin, 1960), p. 81.
24 R. Samuel, *Theatres of Memory: Past and Present in Contemporary Culture* (London: Verso, 1994), p. 3.

25 *ibid*, p. 8.
26 B. E. Jensen, *Historie – livsverden og fag* (Copenhagen: Gyldendal, 2003).
27 R. Schörken, 'Geschichte als Lebenswelt', in K. Bergmann *et al* (eds) *Handbuch der Geschichtsdidaktik*, 1st edn (Düsseldorf: Schwann, 1979), pp. 3–4.
28 R. Schörken, 'Geschichte als Lebenswelt', in Bergmann *et al* (eds) *Handbuch der Geschichtsdidaktik*, 3rd edn (Düsseldorf: Schwann, 1985), p. 5.
29 *ibid*, p. 6.
30 K. E. Jeismann, 'Geschichtsbewusstsein', in Bergmann *et al* (1979), p. 42.
31 E. Kessler, 'Historia magistra vitae. Zur Rehabilitation eines überwundenen Topos', in R. Schörken (ed.) *Der Gegenwartsbezug der Geschichte* (Stuttgart: Klett, 1981), p. 28.
32 R. Schörken, *Geschichte in der Alltagswelt. Wie uns Geschichte begegnet und was wir mit ihr machen* (Stuttgart: Klett-Cotta, 1981), p. 18.
33 Jeismann, 'Geschichtsbewusstsein', in Bergmann *et al* (1979), p. 42.
34 Schörken, 'Geschichte als Lebenswelt', in Bergmann *et al* (1985), p. 8.
35 J. Huhn, 'Geschichte in der ausserschulischen Öffentlichkeit', in Bergmann *et al* (1985), pp. 717–22.
36 J. Rüsen, 'Geschichtskultur', in Bergmann *et al* (1997), p. 38.
37 In '"Already in the Past": Memory and Historical Time', in Radstone and Hodgkin, *Regimes of Memory*, Bill Schwarz tries to persuade academic historians to re-consider their traditional thinking about the relationship between history and memory.
38 Roy Rosenzweig, 'How Americans Use and Think about the Past', in P. N. Stearns *et al* (eds) *Knowing, Teaching, and Learning History: National and International Perspectives* (New York: New York University Press, 2000), p. 280.
39 H. Welzer and H. J. Markowitsch, 'Towards a Bio-psycho-social Model of Autobiographical Memory', *Memory*, 13:1 (2005) 73. *Cf* also K. Nelson and R. Fivush, 'The Emergence of Autobiographical Memory: A Social Cultural Developmental Theory', *Psychological Review*, 111: 2 (2004) 486–511.

3
The Past as a Public Good: The US National Park Service and 'Cultural Repair' in Post-Industrial Places

Cathy Stanton

The practice of public history in the US, as elsewhere, has always had a paradoxical quality. Although it draws primarily on vernacular and local materials, it has often depended on the support of government at many levels. Indeed, as Ludmilla Jordanova has suggested, the state is at the very heart of public history.[1] Inflected by a generally left-leaning political sensibility, the work of American public historians has nonetheless frequently contributed – in ways that this chapter will discuss – to projects that preserve rather than challenge *status quo* relationships of power and inequality. And the field's expansion and professionalisation over the past three decades has in many ways worked against practitioners' own goals of fostering broad public participation in historical inquiry and expression.

These tensions between vernacular and official,[2] critical and hegemonic, professional and populist, have been present within American public history from its beginnings in the 1970s. The field began to try to define itself in that decade in response to three developments: an academic job shortage, substantial state support for history-related projects, and social and civil rights movements that prompted many scholars to shift their intellectual emphasis to what was then called the 'new social history', as well as seeking new ways of supporting critical public activism with their work. Although American public historians continue the work of self-definition and promotion through the development of professional organisations, academic credentialing programmes, publications and other efforts,[3] they are not necessarily any more certain now how to articulate a core identity for the field. Are American public historians defined by the kinds of jobs they do – archivists, curators, museum educators – or is there some set of core principles that unites their practices? How should those practices position themselves in relation to tourism, economic development efforts, nationalist projects and personal or 'popular' historical expression? Does 'public history' simply mean the presentation of history by historians to the public or does it connote a more radically inclusive vision of history-making activities in the public realm? Within these debates, the inherent tensions present at the genesis of the field continue to make themselves felt.

Nowhere are these paradoxical pairings clearer than in public historical work located within what James Abrams has called 'cultural repair' efforts[4] – state-sponsored regeneration projects in economically depressed or obsolete places. As knowledge- and service-based post-industrial economies continue to develop worldwide, a growing proportion of public history projects take place within such settings. Because these strategies are so linked with change and new cultural and economic patterns, it is easy to overlook the considerably longer history that exists in the US of state-sponsored history-related projects. This chapter will explore that longer history – and its relationship with the American public history field – by comparing a national historical park created in a deindustrialised area in the 1930s with one created in the 1970s. In the first example, a long-inactive Pennsylvanian iron-making site called Hopewell Furnace was transformed into a national park as part of the federal government's efforts to alleviate the worst effects of the Great Depression during the 1930s. In the second case, the New England textile city of Lowell, Massachusetts, was used as the site for an experiment in creating a new kind of urban national park that would help to reinvent a deindustrialised community for a post-industrial economy. The two projects offer a particularly useful pair of case studies for thinking about public history in relation to the state – in this case represented by the US National Park Service (NPS). Studying the intersections of the state, those who identify themselves explicitly or implicitly as public historians, and the various 'publics' involved in cultural repair projects over time can illuminate some key aspects of public historical practice in the US.

Early post-industrialism: Hopewell Furnace National Historic Site

A little-known site within the American national park system, Hopewell Furnace is a small park in southeastern Pennsylvania that preserves an eighteenth- and nineteenth-century iron-making site.[5] This part of the mid-Atlantic area was an important centre of pre-Civil War US iron production, but the small 'cold-blast' furnaces that dotted the region began to close after the advent of new technologies in the mid-nineteenth century. By the 1930s, iron- and steel-making had long since been concentrated in urban centres, leaving older sites like Hopewell as little more than crumbling ruins in the midst of the forests that had once supplied the wood to make the charcoal that fuelled their operations (see Figure 3.1).[6] The population around Hopewell Furnace in this period included a high proportion of long-settled families, many of Pennsylvania German ancestry,[7] and a considerable number of farmers as well as metalworkers and other skilled tradespeople who worked in nearby towns and cities.

While Hopewell's immediate vicinity had, in a sense, already been deindustrialised by the late nineteenth century, the industrial economy of Pennsylvania and the American northeast remained generally strong until the Great Depression of the 1930s. The shock of economic collapse in that decade was met by the Roosevelt administration's massive effort at recovery. This included projects designed to create new employment and undo some of the environmental damage caused by a century of rapid industrial growth. Just as in later twentieth-century state responses to deindustrialisation, culture, history and recreation were often integrated into these efforts – for example, through Works Progress Administration (WPA) art projects and publications that employed histor-

Figure 3.1   Remains of the Hopewell Furnace stack in 1939
(US Library of Congress)

ians, artists, writers, folklorists and others in documenting local pasts, and through the creation of NPS-administered 'Recreational Demonstration Areas' (RDAs) in areas of depleted land. An RDA was established around Hopewell Furnace in 1935, with federal relief workers constructing outdoor recreational facilities that were intended to provide an experience of healthy rural life for people from nearby industrial cities.

But the Hopewell site offered another intriguing possibility. Although project supervisors regarded the furnace ruins merely as useful raw materials to be used in constructing dams, roads and new park structures, architects and historians working for the US National Park Service quickly raised questions about their possible heritage value.[8] The NPS had only recently begun to turn its attention to historic preservation and interpretation. Founded in 1916 to preserve and administer sites deemed to be of national significance, the agency had at first been responsible largely for areas of natural splendour such as Yellowstone, Yosemite and other iconic western natural parks.[9] Many of these had contained 'antiquities' – primarily prehistoric Indian sites. But history was not a direct concern of the NPS until the 1930s when Director Horace Albright began to push for the inclusion of historical areas within the growing system.

In 1933, the transfer of stewardship of all the historic forts and battlefields from the War Department and the creation of the Historic American Buildings Survey (HABS) gave a tremendous boost to the Park Service's fledgling historical programme as did the passage of the Historic Sites Act in 1935.[10] This legislation reinforced the emerging sense that the federal government had an important role to play in preserving the nation's historic places. At the same time, the NPS embrace of historical interpretation intersected with widespread public desire for a sense of reconnection to values and practices – for example, small-scale communities, meaningful hand-work, a sense of common purpose – that seemed to offer an alternative to the problematic present of industrial capitalism. Hopewell Furnace, which combined early industry, village life and a rural setting, offered a symbolically-rich location for this kind of communion. From being a half-remembered footnote to the area's more modern iron and steel industry, Hopewell's history became a kind of public good that could be used within the larger redevelopment and relief effort.

Cultural workers at Hopewell Furnace

As part of this exploration of how vernacular histories, public historians and the state have intersected over time, it is worth inquiring into the types of people involved in transforming this derelict iron-making site into a national park. Initially an effort that made use of but did not deeply engage with local memory, the development of Hopewell Furnace NHS has come to include more local participation over time – but only of quite a limited segment of the local population.

The process of making Hopewell Furnace into a national park took place in three general stages. During the first stage, non-local Park Service professionals gathered and created data about the site from primary sources, excavations and oral history interviewing. In an important sense, these professionals were proto-public-historians, academically-trained, in search of employment at a time of limited opportunity and interested in using their skills to support the presentation of history in the public arena.[11] Some local people worked as skilled and unskilled labourers on the building of recreational infrastructure and on the restoration of the iron-making village, which began around 1937 and continued into the 1960s.[12] But only one local man, Jackson Kemper, took part in collecting oral histories and helping to document the furnace site.

Kemper's case is revealing: he was hired at the park because he was eligible for federal relief work, happened to have a college degree and possessed useful connections in the local community. But his own goal was to work in the metal industry, an aim he eventually achieved. The creation of Hopewell Furnace NHS, then, was not a locally-inspired effort to commemorate a particular past but a project that emerged from the historical sensibilities of a particular new class of professional worker in the National Park Service within the context of a broader, state-supported effort at cultural and environmental repair. Local people – except for a single short-term worker who served as a liaison between local and outside knowledge – were not a part of the process of conceptualising the park or shaping its interpretation. This was a case of professional historians presenting history to the public rather than a collaborative effort between historians and their publics.

Much of the work of restoring and rebuilding structures at Hopewell Furnace was done between the mid-1950s and the mid-1970s. In this period, the NPS's 'Mission 66' programme of park improvement and modernisation and the celebration of the US Bicentennial provided funding and impetus for countless public historical projects throughout the country. This second stage of Hopewell's development was something of a 'golden era' for the park, with high visitation and a well-staffed and popular summer living history programme. An examination of the staffing and interpretation patterns in this period reveals that the park, the people associated with it, the iron industry, and the changing economy of the region all overlapped in intriguing ways.

The park's full-time interpretive staff continued to be drawn mostly from the national pool of career NPS workers rather than from the local community. But its seasonal interpreters – those who most often interacted with visitors – included many long-time local residents, some of whom were descended from former furnace employees. Unlike Jackson Kemper, for whom work at the park had been a temporary expedient during an industrial downturn, these seasonal workers were often people who were making a transition out of the industrial economy and into service or knowledge work – a common trajectory in this period of macroeconomic shifts in the US and other developed nations. This was precisely the period when public history was beginning to emerge as a distinct professional field, and some of the tensions and paradoxes of that field made themselves felt among Hopewell's interpretive workers in this period. Did their interpretive authority derive from education, the legitimising force of the National Park Service, local memory or all three? Were these 'real' jobs, or something more akin to a hobby or a vocation? Where was the balance between celebrating and commemorating local culture and performing a serious educational service for the public?

The seasonal rangers included many teachers, typically a 'gateway' profession into the middle or professional classes. One seasonal interpreter, a Hopewell descendant and second-generation newspaper editor who had himself become a high school print shop teacher, joked that he 'very quickly realized that there was no such thing as a real national park employee—they're all schoolteachers!'[13] Skilled craftsmen – for example, iron moulders and charcoal-makers – were still brought in for occasional demonstrations at the park but this became less frequent as these workers aged and industrial production in the region continued to dwindle after the Second World War. By the bicentennial years, local historical knowledge had been fully absorbed into the park's professional structures via the hiring of seasonal interpreters and living history demonstrators. The vernacular pasts represented by iron-making, open-hearth cooking and other skills were, in part, a resource mobilised by a particular type of local worker to produce supplemental income and further their experience as educators. One woman who was descended from families long associated with Hopewell Furnace and with the area's farming economy noted of her work as a seasonal costumed interpreter: 'Sometimes the children would ask me, how did I know to do this, and

I'd say, well, I was raised on this big farm with my Grandmother, and Grandmother was doing all these things, so of course I tagged along and I learned how to make soap and how to make butter and how to make apple butter and whatever... I'm never sorry that I learned what Grandmother taught me, because it came in very handy when I wanted to go down there and work.' In addition to whatever personal satisfactions accrued from practicing hand skills and crafts and displaying them for others, these aspects of the past became personal resources that could be used to obtain new kinds of employment – a process that Barbara Kirshenblatt-Gimblett has referred to as giving aspects of the past a 'second life as exhibitions of themselves.'[14]

Over the past 25 years, Hopewell Furnace NHS has entered a quieter phase, more oriented to maintenance than development. Two aspects of the park's work in this period reveal the continuing evolution of its intricate relationship with locality and vernacular histories. First, in an era of steeply declining funding at US national parks, Hopewell has become much more dependent on volunteers for its public presentations, particularly for its living history programmes. These volunteers strikingly resemble the seasonal workers of the earlier period. Most have ethnic, occupational, family or other ties to the history of the local area and they occupy transitional niches between rural and urban, working class and middle class. They also straddle the line between popular history, undertaken for personal reasons, and public history, which seeks in some way to engage with the idea of a 'public' for whom historical knowledge is or should be important.

There is a recreational aspect to many of the volunteers' activities, but it is blended with a desire to educate others or to pay homage to a shared local past. The hybrid quality of volunteers' participation at Hopewell occasionally causes some tensions with the NPS staff, for example when the volunteers wish to emphasise 'generic' historic crafts – spinning, weaving, blacksmithing, cooking and so on – through which they experience their own sense of connection to the past while the park argues for a more concentrated focus on iron-making and its closely-associated trades such as charcoal-making. A charcoal-making programme instituted in the 1990s has proved to be a boon for the park in this sense, as it allows for professional and vernacular visions of the past to coexist within the same activity. The experience of holding a charcoal 'burn' two or three times a year has created a community of quite close-knit volunteers who feel a sense of stewardship for a body of local historical knowledge that has come down to them in large part through the preservationist work of public historians at the national park.

Figure 3.2   National Park Service workers and living history volunteers at a charcoal 'burn', May 2005
(Photograph: Cathy Stanton)

A second factor shaping the current phase of Hopewell Furnace's existence is that this small and rather isolated national park is becoming more fully absorbed into the regional cultural economy of Pennsylvania and the northeastern US. Where the cultural and environmental repair efforts of the Depression Era tended to produce clearly-bounded historical and recreational parks, recent approaches to revitalising deindustrialised areas and creating a 'sense of place' have been much broader in both a geographical and a conceptual sense. These approaches rely on multi-layered partnerships among different levels of government, businesses, non-profit groups, educational institutions, private landowners and others. They also draw on the expertise of an ever more specialised cadre of planners, designers, educators, researchers and other kinds of cultural workers. These people supply much of the professional infrastructure for projects like large-scale land trusts and conservancies, local and regional 'branding' and 'smart growth' campaigns, heritage areas or heritage corridors and so on – forms that have become almost ubiquitous in the US and that are also being adopted worldwide. Hopewell Furnace NHS has become a partner in the Schuylkill River

Heritage Area, a three-county, 185-mile corridor; the park is also part of several regional conservation projects, including a three-million-acre 'Highlands' green belt that borders the northeastern seaboard megalopolis. Within such structures, the kinds of vernacular and professional knowledges of the past found at Hopewell Furnace NHS must now be understood as part of a multi-layered regional, national and global network of historic and heritage sites that allow us to envision what Kirshenblatt-Gimblett has called a 'global cultural commons'[15] – a type of cultural production that draws local, personal and professional histories into a more globalised frame.

The new post-industrial model: Lowell National Historical Park

The former textile city of Lowell, Massachusetts, about 25 miles outside Boston, served as an important laboratory for the development of this new kind of network.[16] Built in the 1820s as one of the first planned industrial communities in the US, Lowell was a dominant US textile producer until the late nineteenth century. It was among the first American places to experience the now-familiar shock of large-scale deindustrialisation when many of its major textile corporations moved or closed during the 1920s. In the late twentieth century, it found a position on the leading edge of another economic trend – the increased attention to culture and knowledge as products within the new economies of formerly industrialised places.

An important difference between Hopewell and Lowell is that Lowell's turn toward preservation, recreation and performance as a way of re-inventing itself in a changing economy was much more locally-initiated and locally-driven. After several failed attempts at attracting new industry and remaking the urban landscape through draconian 'urban renewal' strategies, a broad coalition began forming within the city's educational and social service communities in the 1960s and 70s to advocate for the idea of creating a national historical park to commemorate Lowell's industrial past. As the idea gathered momentum, political and business leaders signed on to it, prompted in large part by then-US Senator and Presidential aspirant Paul Tsongas, a Lowell native who was instrumental in convincing Lowell's power brokers that supporting historic preservation and interpretation could be a viable strategy for revitalising the city's economic base.[17]

Lowell National Historical Park was created by federal legislation in 1978 after a well-orchestrated lobbying effort. It differed from Hopewell

Figure 3.3   US Senator Paul Tsongas, a Lowell native, presides over the opening of the Lowell National Historical Park Visitor Center in September 1978 (Photograph: Lowell National Historical Park)

Furnace NHS and other traditional national parks in that only a few parcels of property in Lowell were bought outright by the federal government. Instead, the park was one of the first to follow a new pattern of NPS involvement in cultural and economic repair projects. The role of the NPS in these newer efforts is to help establish an interpretive agenda, foster alliances among different stakeholders and serve as a conduit for federal funding. Thus Lowell NHP incorporates a number of NPS-created exhibit sites in the downtown area, but it also interprets properties it does not own – for example, the 5.6 mile long canal system that once powered the textile mills. It is also a partner in many of the city's major cultural and educational ventures. This partnership model – what one early consultant called a 'new educational/cultural/economic animal'[18] – was explicitly designed to encourage 'public/private' redevelopment ventures, in which public investment was to serve as seed money for local projects that would eventually become self-sustaining. This has happened to a relatively high degree in Lowell where heavy initial public support for the city's regeneration efforts (along with a spillover effect from the flourishing post-industrial economy around Greater Boston) has paid off in the form of greatly increased property values, many new residents and businesses, continued public and private reinvestment in the city's downtown and an improved reputation in the region and beyond.

The local efforts that produced these changes coincided and over-lapped with state, regional and federal anti-poverty and economic redevelopment initiatives in the 1960s and 1970s. This was also a period of expansion in the National Park Service, which sought to establish new parks and recreation areas geographically closer to the urban populations of the eastern part of the nation. At the same time, the reframing of histories like Lowell's took place in parallel with the emergence of the nascent public history movement and a 'new social history' that focused on the 'subaltern' histories of working-class people, immigrants, women and others who had been neglected by traditional 'great man' histories. Some within these fields – and within many related scholarly disciplines – questioned the close linkages between business interests and historic preservation and interpretation in the city.[19] Others, however, saw partnerships with business as an opportunity for truly active participation in the civic culture of the places where their work was being used. One public historian at Lowell NHP noted to me: 'We felt that the purpose of public interpretation is to give people a sense that you make your own history, and if making your own history means using your history to make money, then that's a good thing.' Just as early Lowell was widely studied as an exemplary industrial city, its post-industrial redevelopment has been viewed by many in the fields of public history and urban planning as an important test case for the viability of public/private partnerships and culture-led regeneration strategies.

Like those who collected and generated the historical and archeo-logical data that was used to reframe Hopewell Furnace as a national historic site, the majority of Lowell NHP's knowledge workers – the public and academic historians, planners, folklorists, artists, archeo-logists, architects, National Park Service staff and others whose work helped create the national park – have not been local people. However, strong and politically savvy local voices in Lowell have always insisted that these outsiders be accountable to local agendas and interests. During the earliest discussions about the park, NPS planners expressed skepticism about whether enough remained of Lowell's original indus-trial landscape to be worth preserving. They were also initially resistant to the assertions of local leaders that any park commemorating the city's past should include attention to its immigrant history and present-day ethnic communities.[20] Many in the Park Service contended, as one early manager recalled in an interview with me, that 'after 1860, it's just another mill town' among countless ethnically-diverse industrial places in the region and the nation. However, this was a 'deal-breaker' for those who had bought into the local coalition in large part because it promised to represent their own family and ethnic community histories within the national park's interpretive scheme and who were suspicious of giving too much representational control to 'blow-ins' without deep roots in the community.[21]

Due to the strength of the political network that had aligned itself with the park proposal, the locally-important element of ethnicity remained in the plans and the park's enabling legislation asserts that Lowell was 'historically *and culturally* the most significant planned industrial city in the United States.'[22] Ethnicity, immigration and working-class history continue to be an important component of the national park's interpretation. Although the best-known labourers represented at the park are the early workforce of 'Yankee mill girls', considerable attention is also paid to the Irish, French-Canadians, Greeks and others who came to Lowell in the late nineteenth and early twentieth centuries. Supported by the work of the new social historians of the 1970s and by the political will of civic and cultural leaders who have retained a strong interest in the park, the work of non-local public historians in Lowell has always been shaped by vernacular memories and agendas, much more so than in earlier projects such as Hopewell Furnace.

Limits to local participation in the 'New Lowell'

This greater accountability to local voices and agendas, however, does raise some troubling questions about the practice of public history in post-industrial settings. Over the lifetime of Lowell's culture-led re-development project, the range of people speaking on behalf of 'the community' has in fact been quite limited, and it has grown narrower over the decades. For a variety of reasons, including the tendency of cultural and educational power structures to reproduce themselves[23] and the desire of local people in Lowell to safeguard their hard-won gains, those who act as gatekeepers into the city's tight-knit network of cultural production have been cautious about allowing newcomers into their inner circles. These gatekeepers have typically been educated professionals with family connections to the city's longest-established ethnic communities and to its educational, arts and social service sectors.

Most of the newcomers recruited into the cultural network fit the same occupational and class profile, which also closely matches that of the public historians working in the city and the majority of those who visit the park. As with those who have worked, volunteered and visited Hopewell Furnace NHS, these people exist in a somewhat tenuous or ambivalent relationship to post-industrial capitalism. They appear to make use of historic sites and historical or cultural work as a way of finding a their own niche within volatile post-industrial economies or as a way to reconnect with pasts from which generational and socio-economic change has left them feeling disconnected. Thus these sites are used less to explore the political and social effects of particular histories – ostensibly a primary goal for many self-identified public historians – than to facilitate individual reconciliations with the past, to negotiate the rough waters of the advanced capitalist economy or to provide fulfilling employment in increasingly market-dominated settings.

And while local voices and experiences are to be found throughout Lowell's cultural realm, including in the interpretation of the national park, the actual participation of local people is uneven and sharply unequal. People from Lowell's many new and ethnic immigrant communities – including Cambodians, Latinos, Brazilians and others – have been welcomed into the city's cultural production realm. But they are

Figure 3.4   A Lowell National Historical Park ranger leads a group of visitors on a walking tour of one of the city's poorest neighbourhoods in 2003 (Photograph: Cathy Stanton)

much more often found in the role of colourful performers than as high-level decision-makers, while their public representations have sometimes been re-scripted to fit existing Euro-American templates.[24] And the cultural performances of the newer groups have been influenced by a celebratory multiculturalism that tends to exert a depoliticising, aestheticising effect. Lowell's public historians, who were initially able to create sharply critical and questioning exhibits about industrial capitalism and labour, have always been much more limited by entrenched local opinion in interpreting the topics of immigration, ethnicity and the city's contemporary economy.

From Hopewell to Lowell: progressions and questions

The seven-decade history of Hopewell Furnace NHP and Lowell NHP offers an opportunity to assess some of the implications of doing public history in the emerging settings of post-industrial societies. This allows the drawing of some preliminary conclusions about the ways in which the state, the professional field of public history and expressions of local vernacular culture and memory have intersected over time in the US.

First, these two case studies suggest that within the trend toward partnerships with market-oriented ventures and the overall shift of the US economy toward neoliberal market-driven philosophies, the state retains a central role in helping local places leverage their histories as part of economic redevelopment efforts.[25] While direct public funding for the development of historic sites and interpretation has decreased sharply in the US over the past 25 years, government at all levels remains actively involved in collaborative relationships driven by economic redevelopment plans, many of which include adapting local pasts and places to new purposes.

Second, the proliferation of larger-scale projects suggests that the past is more and more commonly viewed as a public good by those seeking to draw interest and investment into former industrial places and to assert the importance of local memory and experience within a globalising cultural economy. During the Depression-era transformation of the area around Hopewell Furnace, history was something of an afterthought, and it was still a tough sell when the idea of history-based revitalisation was first broached in Lowell. But the specific histories of local places are now very widely seen as a resource that can readily be mobilised in aid of strengthening local reputations and economies. From the ongoing development of heritage areas to now-commonplace local 'branding' and 're-localisation' campaigns, it is clear that local and vernacular pasts – the raw material with which public historians often ply their trade – are assumed by many people to be integral to successful place-making and place-marketing.

Local histories remain a resource for the work of professional cultural workers just as they were at Hopewell Furnace in the 1930s. But the cultural workers themselves have increasingly become resources for communities seeking to reposition themselves within global capitalism. The history of Hopewell Furnace NHS shows us these roles in their infancy, with the progenitors of professional public historians arguing for the value of preserving the material evidence of America's industrial past in an era of widespread anxiety about the effects of industrial development. By the time Lowell NHP was created in 1978, new professional identities and affiliations – public history among them – were emerging from the assortment of disciplines and roles that had always clustered around cultural repair projects. Over time, these fields have become much more rationalised, professionalised and interconnected and people within them have come to constitute a mobile sector of professional workers who are increasingly sought by local places to facilitate the development of Lowell-like projects elsewhere.[26]

Finally, this sector resembles and overlaps in significant ways with the local publics and communities of memory with whom public historians interact. The two examples of Hopewell and Lowell challenge a too-simple distinction between public historians and their various publics and suggest that while the borders between producers and audiences are permeable, travel across that border is being done primarily by people who are very similar to one another. In some important ways, these postindustrial public history projects appear to be resistant to greater inclusivity, just as they tend to sidestep the most urgent and critical questions relating to the contemporary arc of industrial capitalism and its aftermath. Paradoxically, as the number of such projects continues to increase in the US and as the role of vernacular memories and voices within them expands, the actual range of participation seems to be shrinking, raising the question of who is able to access the benefits of this growing embrace of the past as a public good.

Notes

1 L. Jordanova, *History in Practice* (London: Arnold, 2000), p. 155.
2 The terminology is John Bodnar's. See J. Bodnar, *Remaking America: Public Memory, Commemoration, and Patriotism in the Twentieth Century* (Princeton, NJ: Princeton University Press, 1992), p. 14.

3 For an overview of the American public history movement and its ante-cedents, see R. Conard, *Benjamin Shambaugh and the Intellectual Foundations of Public History* (Iowa City: University of Iowa Press, 2002) and C. Stanton, *The Lowell Experiment: Public History in a Postindustrial City* (Amherst and Boston: University of Massachusetts Press, 2006), pp. 8–16.

4 The term 'cultural repair' is drawn from J. F. Abrams, 'Lost Frames of Refer-ence: Sightings of History and Memory in Pennsylvania's Documentary Landscape', in M. Hufford (ed.) *Conserving Culture: A New Discourse on Heritage* (Urbana and Chicago: University of Illinois Press, 1994), pp. 24–38.

5 My research on Hopewell Furnace National Historic Site was carried out under the auspices of the Northeast Ethnography Program of the NPS. The final report, *Cultures in Flux: New Approaches to 'Traditional Association' at Hopewell Furnace National Historic Site*, will be available in 2008. I am indebted to Chuck Smythe of the Northeast Ethnography Program and to the staff, volunteers and others at Hopewell Furnace NHS for their assistance on this project.

6 On the history of Hopewell Furnace, see J. Walker, *Hopewell Village: The Dynamics of a Nineteenth-century Iron-Making Community* (Philadelphia: University of Pennsylvania Press, 1966).

7 'Pennsylvania German' and 'Pennsylvania Dutch' are terms used to describe the descendants of German-speaking immigrants to Pennsylvania starting in the late seventeenth century.

8 L. Glaser, *Hopewell Furnace National Historic Site: Administrative History* (Philadelphia and Boston: National Park Service, Northeast Regional Office, 2005), pp. 25–6.

9 For an overview of the development of the US National Park Service, see *The National Parks: Shaping the System* produced by the Harpers Ferry Center of the NPS (Washington, DC: US Department of the Interior, 2005).

10 See B. Mackintosh, *Interpretation in the National Park Service: A Historical Perspective* (Washington, DC: National Park Service. Electronic document, http://www.cr.nps.gov/history/online_books/mackintosh2/).

11 For an in-depth analysis of another such proto-public-historian, see Conard, *Benjamin Shambaugh and the Intellectual Foundations of Public History.*

12 Glaser, *Hopewell Furnace National Historic Site: Administrative History*, p. 334.

13 Direct interview quotations throughout this paper are drawn from my ethnographic fieldwork. In keeping with the conventions of ethnographic interviewing and writing, I do not quote interviewees by name or cite archived transcriptions of interviews. Rather, these quotes are intended to illustrate patterns of thought or behaviour that are shared by the people or groups whose experiences I am discussing.

14 B. Kirshenblatt-Gimblett, *Destination Culture: Tourism, Museums, and Heritage* (Berkeley: University of California Press, 1998), p. 7.

15 B. Kirshenblatt-Gimblett, 'World Heritage and Cultural Economics', in I. Karp *et al* (eds) *Museum Frictions: Public Cultures/Global Transformations* (Durham, North Carolina: Duke University Press, 2006), pp. 160–202.

16 The ethnographic research on which this section of the chapter is based was conducted at Lowell NHP between 2000 and 2002 as part of my doc-toral dissertation work at Tufts University in Medford, Massachusetts.

17 For an exploration of the creation of Lowell NHP, see L. Ryan, 'Lowell in Transition: The Uses of History in Urban Change', (unpublished PhD dissertation: Columbia University, 1987).

18 Ryan, 'Lowell in Transition', p. 301.

19 For example, historian Mike Wallace insisted that the historic preservation movement had deeply weakened itself by forging allegiances with its 'traditional enemies' in the economic development sphere. See M. Wallace, *Mickey Mouse History and Other Essays on American Memory* (Philadelphia: Temple University Press, 1996), p. 179. Like Wallace, sociologist Sharon Zukin pointed to the ways in which culture and history have been co-opted by profit-driven development within neoliberal economies. See S. Zukin, *Loft Living: Culture and Capital in Urban Change* (Baltimore and London: Johns Hopkins University Press, 1982).

20 Ryan, 'Lowell in Transition', p. 187.

21 'Blow-in' appears to originate as an Irish term for British colonial administrators and other professional outsiders. It is often used in Lowell to describe outsiders in the city's planning and heritage realms.

22 United States Congress, Public Law 95-290 (HR 11662), *An Act to Provide for the Establishment of Lowell National Historical Park*, 1978, p. 1: emphasis added.

23 The classic analysis of this process can be found in P. Bourdieu, *Outline of a Theory of Practice* (Cambridge: Cambridge University Press, 1977).

24 For an analysis of this relationship, see Stanton, *The Lowell Experiment*, pp. 185–228 and C. Stanton, 'Serving Up Culture: Heritage and its Discontents at an Industrial History Site', *International Journal of Heritage Studies*, 11: 5 (2005), 415–31.

25 In particular, national heritage areas continue to be designated across the US, with ten new projects being added in 2006 to the existing 27 areas. See http://www.cr.nps.gov/heritageareas/ for more on US national heritage areas.

26 For a fuller exploration of this aspect of post-industrial cultural production, see M. M. Breitbart and C. Stanton, 'Touring Templates: Cultural Workers and Regeneration in Small New England Cities', in M. K. Smith (ed.) *Tourism, Culture and Regeneration* (Wallingford, UK: CABI, 2006), pp. 111–22. See also B. Dicks, *Culture on Display: The Production of Contemporary Visibility* (UK: Open University Press, 2004), pp. 138–9 for a discussion of cultural workers within heritage projects.

4
Shades of Grey: Public History and Government in New Zealand

Bronwyn Dalley

As an undergraduate over 20 years ago I was once asked what I was studying at university. 'New Zealand history', I replied, as over half the papers in my history major were in this area. The question, 'So, what do you do after lunch?', was shot back at me. All the Important People, Significant Places and Big Events, it seemed, were found elsewhere – Britain, Europe, North America. New Zealand's indigenous inhabitants, Maori, may have lived in this country for half a millennia, and Europeans for about 150 years, but New Zealand was, quite simply, too young to have a past.

This mid-1980s exchange spoke volumes both about what constituted history, but more importantly, about a popular conception of New Zealand history: there wasn't any. In fact, a sizeable body of New Zealand history writing existed at a popular and 'amateur' level. More academic and scholarly treatments came out of universities and the ranks of professional historians and government or self-employed commentators. Local television screened *Landmarks*, a series about New Zealand history, and the country's built heritage and material culture were there for the viewing, even if people had to know where to look (and what to see).[1]

New Zealand history, however, was still too easy to dismiss as not worthy of consideration. That situation began to change from the mid-1980s as the volume and type of history made available grew in response to many stimuli: an ageing and educated population, more New Zealand history graduates, the rise of the heritage industry and a cultivation of cultural nationalism, among other things.[2]

Since then, New Zealand history (and culture more generally) has enjoyed an unprecedented public appreciation and engagement. History, I have argued elsewhere, is 'the new black'; everyone seems interested in it.[3] In just the last decade, at least a half-dozen national histories have appeared in print and more are in the pipeline.[4] New Zealand's stories are explored or brought to the fore in many places: museums, heritage sites, books, websites, history tours, novels, memorials, film, genealogies, courtrooms, in song, dance, art and design.

Academic treatments of the past continue. But in New Zealand, history has gone public. Within public history, government-sponsored work is a significant part, either directly employing historians or creating the conditions under which public history work is done. New Zealand's experience differs markedly from that of other societies where the state may not play such a direct and varied role in producing history. Here I consider why this is the case and explore the particular characteristics of this form of public history in New Zealand.

Black, white and shades of grey

I want to start with an acknowledgement: the New Zealand government pays my salary. For some readers, this position will fundamentally compromise my ability to discuss the evolution of the government's role in public history in New Zealand or to speak 'impartially' about the connections between government and the production of history. My hope is that my experience of this sector can offer a more nuanced and complex understanding of this area of public history; to suggest some shades of grey in what can be seen as a black and white issue.

I work as a public historian in the Ministry for Culture and Heritage that includes a section – the History Group – entirely devoted to the production of scholarly historical works aimed at a broad public audience.[5] The Group's organisational antecedents stretch back to 1937 when planning began for a series of historical works to mark the centenary, in 1940, of the signing of New Zealand's 'founding document', the Treaty of Waitangi. A 'Centennial Branch' in the government's Department of Internal Affairs was established to undertake the series. It morphed into the War History Branch in 1945. Several name changes and one organisational 'home' later, the History Group of the Ministry for Culture and Heritage (from 2000) continues the 70-year tradition of history within government. The nature of the work has undergone considerable change, sometimes in parallel with shifts in historical research. Since the late 1980s, the focus of work has been on histories of New Zealanders at war, the relationships between government and society and the workings of government – all through a broad social history approach. Increasingly the History Group's work examines New Zealand history in a general sense; its history website, for example, includes material designed specifically for schoolteachers of New Zealand history.[6] Since the late 1980s other government agencies or external groups have periodically commissioned and paid for a history.

The Group gives advice to government on historical matters – regarding, for example, the commemorations marking the landing in 1915 of New Zealand and Australian troops on the Gallipoli peninsula, seen by some as a key moment in New Zealand's national story. It administers grants for community-based historical research and writing, and assists publishers produce works of New Zealand history. It also gives professional historical advice to groups and individuals outside government and is broadly engaged in public history. This may include work with local communities and groups running history projects or with museums on exhibition programmes. In recent years the Group has had considerable involvement in the production of history on television or radio. Between 2000 and 2005, for example, it was the historical consultant for *Frontier of Dreams*, a 13-part television series about New Zealand history.

When public history was just history

New Zealand has, in Chris Hilliard's phrase, a 'prehistory of public history' – a body of work that we now identify as public history but which was simply called 'history' at the time of its creation. Much of this came from within government. Significantly, it was not necessarily different from other types of historical practice. Works from within or outside government could be propagandist, or sanitised or highly academic and critical in tone and content. Government origins, Hilliard suggests, do not adequately explain differences.[7]

New Zealand governments took on the direct sponsorship of history writing from the early twentieth century. War history was the initial focus. Before the 1930s, accounts of the nineteenth-century New Zealand Wars, the South African War and the First World War all appeared with state support. Works came from within various parts of government, including the Defence Department and the Department of Internal Affairs. Some writers had backgrounds in journalism. Others were in the military. But most had no formal historical training.

A number of the pieces were called 'official' histories although the meaning of the term is moot in this context. It sometimes meant a record compiled from government documents rather than a broad range of historical sources. It could mean explicitly nationalist projects, but it could also include more popular or accessible accounts. James Cowan's two-volume history of the New Zealand Wars, published in 1922–23, is a case in point. Produced from within what he rather grandly called the 'Maori Wars Section' of the Department of Internal Affairs – of which he was the only staff member – this was 'the Official History of the Wars in New Zealand'. Cabinet approved the proposal for such a history in part because of the rapidly declining number of veterans from both sides of this 1860s conflict. Cowan himself, fluent in Maori, had spent many years collecting the testimony of combatants from both sides. This hardly constituted 'official' given the predominance of these types of records used although it certainly was a monument to those who had been involved.

A much more considerable record of New Zealand's involvement in war occurred from within government after 1945. The War History Branch of the Department of Internal Affairs became home to the massive official history series of New Zealand's involvement in the Second World War. The series eventually saw 48 volumes and 24 short booklets produced by the mid-1980s when it came to a close. Authors of the volumes included journalists, university history lecturers, military officers and history graduates.[8] Through its long life, the series was variously overseen by a professional writer, a former high-ranking soldier who was interested in military history and trained professional historians. 'Official' meant government sponsored and carried out within central government rather than presenting the government's 'view'. Editorial discretion of the head of the War History Branch was accepted and seemed to have remained unchallenged.[9]

Government-sponsored war histories were, Hilliard suggests, 'historiographical monuments' intended to be a tribute to those who served. Jock Phillips likens them to 'a form of literary medal', a bookish equivalent to a physical war memorial.[10] More prosaically, Ian McGibbon contends that government-sponsored histories of war were also to provide a record that might be of use in future conflicts. In a narrow military definition, official war history was to be of use to the military student by being an 'exact statistical and chronological record of all events'.[11]

Other forms of government-sponsored history appeared particularly from the 1930s.[12] New Zealand's first Labour government, enthusiastic about history and state assistance, initiated several major projects as part of the country's centennial in 1940. Like other aspects of this government's view of citizenship, history was a form of public good and could be used as a clear story of and for national development. A range of projects was instigated and several completed, including a Dictionary of New Zealand Biography, a series of 30 pictorial surveys of New Zealand history and life and 13 books. A historical atlas was planned and although some work was done, it was never finished. A major encyclopedia of New Zealand, approved in principle under another Labour government in the late 1950s, appeared in 1966.[13]

Some of the works took New Zealand history to a popular and broad public audience, such as the highly illustrated and topically diverse *Making New Zealand* series. Others explained significant if select and highly skewed features of the past: the role of (white) pioneers or the various steps to European colonisation of the country. Large projects such as the 1940 *Dictionary of Biography* or the 1966 *Encyclopaedia* attempted to create a permanent and explanatory record of people or events (past and present), although the results could be idiosyncratic or, at worst, self-serving and uncritical.[14]

The emergence of a public history identity

The flurry of state-sponsored historical activity engendered by New Zealand's centennial in 1940 and then the official series of the Second World War did not last. Comparatively few works appeared out of government from the mid-1960s and for a brief period the Historical Publications Branch (as the War History Branch had become in 1963) was disbanded. That situation changed markedly in the mid-1980s as government investment and interest in history increased as part of a broader declaration of New Zealand's 'national' identity and culture. Growing globalisation played a role in this: a local identity rooted in the Pacific seemed to be more important as the rest of the world loomed large. Specific events also contributed, such as the 150th anniversary (in 1990) of the signing of the Treaty of Waitangi, and a new 'application' of history through the investigation of relations between the Crown and Maori.

Historians have expended considerable quantities of ink in describing public history. Differing definitions mirror national practice but they are also rooted in time and intricately embedded in professional issues and politics. Robert Kelley's notion of public history as the employment of historians and historical method outside academia suitably described and gave meaning to a 'new' community of scholars in North America in the late 1970s. At about the same time, but on the other side of the Atlantic, connections with radical or people's history gave public history in the United Kingdom a particular identity and purpose.[15]

The articulation of public history practice and the formation of a public history community appeared later in New Zealand. PHANZA, the Professional Historians' Association of New Zealand/Aotearoa, emerged in 1994 to represent the interests of historians working beyond or in academic institutions. Such historians had, it was argued, a set of interests and issues that were distinct from matters relating to the teaching of history or the production of work for academic audiences. The choice of name was deliberate. The term 'professional' suggested an approach to history that was rooted in the discipline and paid heed to historical method. It was, in effect, a credential for historians working in the marketplace to distinguish them from enthusiastic amateurs. Ludmilla Jordanova has commented on the proliferation of organisational and professional groupings as history becomes more specialised. PHANZA is one of these 'instruments of legitimation', influential in defining disciplines and creating communities.[16]

The notion of 'public history' was largely absent from the discussions of PHANZA's initiators, of which I was one.[17] We considered – correctly as it turned out – that the term was too new in New Zealand and liable to be misunderstood. If pushed, we would probably have had difficulty defining its meaning ourselves as the label had gained little currency among New Zealand historians, public or otherwise.

In PHANZA, historians from several areas – museums, libraries, archives, the heritage sector, government, a few university academics, freelancers or 'feral historians' unaffiliated to any institution – came together for the first time, united by similarities in employment or purpose rather than through subject matter.[18] Common ground was found and within a few years of PHANZA's appearance, the term 'public history' was used to describe these historians' work. The first university course on public history appeared in 1996 and an inaugural public history conference was held in 2000.[19]

In 2000 and 2001, published collections of essays appeared in which practitioners attempted to map out the field. Defining what public history could mean in New Zealand was a core part of this. Alex Trapeznik and Gavin McLean appreciated the difficulties in defining public history, but suggested that two main elements mattered. Audience – the first – was important and it would always be broader than for academic history. The second – the utilitarian – indicated that applied aspects were to the fore, such as commissioning a history for an anniversary or undertaking a heritage inventory for a local council.[20] I suggested that public history covered many things, but the glue that bound public historians was working to the broad requirements of another agency or individual – answering questions that someone else had asked. Public history was done for a particular purpose, regardless of the size of its audience, which could, in fact, be very narrow or specialised.[21] Giselle Byrnes merged these views and saw public history as history applied to a particular outcome, done in such a way as to make it accessible to a variety of audiences.[22]

Importantly, each of these working definitions attempted to present public history positively. In the Australian context, Ann Curthoys and Paula Hamilton had noted the looming presence of 'academic history's Other': a public history that gained its meaning by being something that academic history was not.[23] From the outset, New Zealand public historians attempted to avoid this by considering what public history was, rather than what it was not.[24]

The state steps in, again

The burgeoning market for public historians made such a process easier. The state was a key player in the development of that market from the mid-1980s, so when, a decade later, a professional group began articulating its identity, there was a sizeable body of work that pointed to common elements. I am not suggesting that state-sponsored historical work 'invented' public history in New Zealand, but that government policies and programmes influenced some of its trajectory.

Two areas in particular stand out. The first is the growth in the volume of historical work undertaken by the Waitangi Tribunal and the subsequent employment of historians in Treaty claims work. The Tribunal was established in 1975 as a permanent commission of inquiry to receive and report on claims regarding the Crown's alleged breaches of the Treaty of Waitangi.[25] The British Crown and Maori signed the Treaty in 1840, both agreeing to rights and responsibilities. Many of the Crown's subsequent actions regarding Maori land in particular broke its agreement.

Initially claims could only be about Crown actions after 1975. In 1985 the Tribunal's jurisdiction was extended back to 1840 and the situation changed markedly as historical claims were lodged. One politician predicted this would be 'the greatest heyday for lawyers in the history of the country'.[26] That may have been the case but it has certainly proved a boon to historians. The Treaty sector is the single largest employer of New Zealand historians in the country.[27] Professional historians work not only with the Tribunal as researchers or writers but they work with other parts of government (directly negotiating with claimants or investigating the Crown's position) and with claimants. Over 1,200 research reports have been commissioned by the Tribunal and the majority of its time since 1985 has been devoted to inquiring into historical land grievances.[28]

There is now a substantial body of literature in this area of New Zealand history. Within two decades, historical Treaty claims have generated a unique historiography and have had an impact on historical research, writing and direction.[29] The nature of the work and its 'product' are very specific types of public history. It occurs within a government-sponsored context and can have significant outcomes for the claimants themselves; this is 'applied' history. The Tribunal has the power to make recommendations only but some settlements reached with claimants after the Tribunal process have been considerable. The Waitangi Tribunal also has some of the social functions of a truth commission, Richard Boast suggests.[30] Here, the issuing of a formal apology as part of a settlement process can be significant for claimants who have lived with the consequences of Crown actions for generations.

History in Treaty claims work is part of a judicial and legalistic process and this fundamentally affects its nature. Historians not only have to follow the 'normal' methods of historical research but their work may also be tested within a legalistic framework where cross-examination and matters of burden and standard of proof are vital. The work is produced for a distinct purpose, reports and research answer particular questions and the audience can be specific: the 'rules of the game', Michael Belgrave notes, are different from academic history, and so is the product.[31] It is, Giselle Byrnes argues, a form of 'public ethnohistory' – a response to particular needs of government for specific types of data from which conclusions can be drawn.[32]

Such an area of public history is fundamentally political for all concerned but in a different way from the second main area of government-sponsored work. From the mid-1980s there was an explosion in historical work from within the Department of Internal Affairs, home to government history since the mid-1930s. Importantly, the nature of government history within this agency was set upon a clear footing. The work of the current Ministry for Culture and Heritage builds on this process set in train in the 1980s.

Substantial new projects were initiated which, it was assumed, only the government was in a position to fund (through a lotteries grant or direct government funding). The first and longest running of these was the Dictionary of New Zealand Biography project. It received government approval in 1982 and, at the time of writing, is still operational although in much reduced form and with no new volumes in train.[33] The project was managed and produced within government under a team of professional historians, editors and translators but its liaison with the wider community was close. Community-based regional and subject working parties suggested names of likely people for inclusion and the biographies were predominantly written by historians and other specialists outside government.

The *New Zealand Historical Atlas*, published in 1997, was also in this mould. It used 'external' writers and had external advisory groups, with government management and production under an academic historian especially recruited for the task. The tradition of the government producing large-scale reference works in this vein has continued more recently with *Te Ara: the Encyclopedia of New Zealand*.[34] Funded directly by government, it is produced and managed from within the Ministry for Culture and Heritage, with entries prepared by project staff and external writers and advisory groups offering specialist input. This web-based project is a general encyclopedia rather than an historical work but historical topics play an important part.

The areas of history produced from within government were also clarified from the mid-1980s as the work of the Department of Internal Affairs was reviewed in a process that also examined the wider sphere of New Zealand history. Studies of New Zealand's involvement in war would continue alongside histories of government and government policy. Since then, government historians from the Department of Internal Affairs and now the Ministry for Culture and Heritage have concentrated their work in these areas. In recent years, Ministry historians have also begun to develop more general treatments of New Zealand history, particularly in web-based publications.

The focus on government and war was a deliberate decision to undertake research on topics that showed no other signs of being examined by the historical community. As a consequence of this, government-sponsored history has been the only major work in some areas of New Zealand history. Topics in diplomatic history, somewhat unfashionable in university academic circles, have been covered, as have broadly constitutional areas such as the history of the office of the governor-general. Had it not been for state sponsorship, few studies of New Zealand's military history would have appeared before the 1980s when it began to gain popularity among other historians and writers. Even as broader interest in this area has grown, the government has continued to play a role, completing studies of New Zealand's involvement in conflicts since the Second World War and collecting the oral histories of war veterans. Now, however, the aim is not so much to 'rescue' topics from historical oblivion but to produce works of history that are accessible to a wide audience.

Major anniversaries also boosted the work of government historians. The centenary of women's suffrage in 1993, for example, generated historical research about women within government as well as in the broader community and academic environments. A number of government agencies marked their centenary, or other significant anniversaries, with an organisational history or study of their policies. Government restructuring from 1984 spawned a flurry of historical works as agencies rushed to 'capture' institutional memory before the institutions themselves disappeared.

Government agencies commissioned many of these works. From 1989, such agencies had no choice but to use professional historians. In that year, a Cabinet minute stipulated that any history of a government department or policy should be written within or under the supervision of the Historical Branch of the Department of Internal Affairs (the forerunner of the present History Group); its field of operation had already been identified as government history. This was, in effect, to avoid the production of 'PR with footnotes' – a public relations or propaganda exercise glossed with a veneer of scholarship. Historians commissioned for such projects had to be monitored by historians in the Historical Branch and work to the standards of accepted academic scholarship.

A recently completed review of the Historical Branch had already assigned its head, the Chief Historian, authority over the final content of any work before it proceeded to publication. The decision about whether or not something was good history rested with historians, not commissioning agents or politicians. In this way, it was believed, professional history would be produced and the credibility and independence of historians protected. To attempt to safeguard academic standards even further, academic and general publishers were (and still are) requested to submit proposals for the publication of any work produced. Publishers followed their regular procedures regarding the quality of the work, such as sending the work out for further peer review.

The system, still in effect, has worked reasonably well in practice. It has largely gone unchallenged by those commissioning work. This is not to suggest that issues have not arisen. Once the past catches up with the present those commissioning history can display a more lively interest in the depiction of events and personalities. Historians employed by government are, of course, public servants, bound by public service codes of ethics concerning public comments on current government policy, positive or negative. Regardless of whether a work is commissioned, the government's public historians, like everyone else, have to contend with the litigious living. Like other historians, they may display a degree of self-censorship or feel a reluctance to speculate on the significance of recent events without the benefit of time to place things in perspective; they have a professional duty to present a balanced and fair account.[35]

Government historians may have to be careful in presenting potentially difficult material that covers current events. In such cases, intensive use of quotations from external commentators can be a key way of including highly critical assessments of policies or actions. Historians may not necessarily use their 'own' words to critique an issue or piece of policy, but alternative assessments to an agency's or politician's own can be included in this way.[36]

Reviewers sometimes point to the government origins of work to explain its content or tone. The fact that the work has been commissioned by government, or completed within government, can be sufficient to question its basis. Rarely, however, has its academic credentials been challenged or instances of institutional bias or censorship been identified. Individual historians bring their own views and interpretations to bear on a topic and 'positions' identified by readers or reviewers may have little to do with the commissioned nature of the work or its government origins. The practice of government history is, I suggest, more complex than it may at first seem.

Government history and the history of government

Government involvement in history is inextricably part of New Zealand's history of government. It sits within the long tradition of state support for literature and other cultural activities in New Zealand. Successive New Zealand governments, including those of the twenty-first century, have considered state support of the arts – directly as well as indirectly – an important activity. A belief that cultural activities form part of modern civil society and an acknowledgement that without state support some of those activities may never occur play a significant role here.

So too do issues of nation-building and the fostering of national identity. Rob Rabel classes official war histories as a collective example of nation-building and the creation of national stories. Such works are, he suggests, as nationalist as the wars they recorded: 'lest there be any doubt that the interest of successive governments in sponsoring war history was conceptually bounded in nationalistic terms', he argues, 'one need only recall that all the official histories have strictly focused on New Zealand's national effort and the state has shown little interest in promoting historical writing about war in general or the war experiences of other nations.'[37] Here they differ little from any other war history produced within New Zealand, whether from university academics, public historians or 'enthusiastic amateurs'. Yet some government-sponsored war histories, particularly collections of interviews with former servicemen and women, also tell that 'national' story through a personal lens. Such oral histories are more concerned with injecting the individual into history and uncovering personal experience than offering a narrative of events.

These works are part of, and display, a cultural nationalism – New Zealanders finding a 'home in thought within their own country rather than simple pining for the traditions of older worlds', as Jock Phillips expresses it – that has particularly influenced New Zealand history as well as government public history.[38] Within government, the historical activities marking the centenary in 1940 exemplify an early example of this cultural nationalism. National progress was the key here, with New Zealand moving steadily forwards and the state playing an important role in this modernising enterprise. Maori and other 'alternative' views were marginalised.

It is also a mark of government involvement in large-scale history production in more recent times. The constituent parts of 'New Zealand', however, are conceived more broadly than earlier, as they are in New Zealand history more generally. An awareness that New Zealand had stories to tell lay behind the commissioning of many anniversary projects from the mid-1980s; an acknowledgement that the stories of individuals 'on the ground' mattered as much as the view 'from the top' lay behind the collection of oral histories from former servicemen and women.

Large-scale projects founded within a national framework have sought to complicate matters of identity and nation. The *Dictionary of New Zealand Biography* was designed to mark the 1990 celebrations of the sesquicentenary of the signing of the Treaty of Waitangi, rather as its counterpart from 50 years before had marked the centenary. Its conception was certainly linked with notions of national identity and celebration, but its first editor, W. H. Oliver, was determined to oversee a project that was much more than this, and which would push the boundaries of what and who should be included in national biographies. For him, selecting individuals was more than satisfying criteria such as 'national significance', regional or local importance; he wanted a cross-section of society that included the notorious, the eccentric, the inarticulate and the silenced.[39]

The conception of the Historical Atlas project also sat within a context of national celebration and identity building. A Labour government, eager to complete a task that its 1930s' predecessor had initiated but never finished, approved the project in 1988–89, just in time for the 1990 sesquicentennial events. Editor Malcolm McKinnon was determined that the work would break new ground for a reference work. Its purpose was not, in his view, to settle arguments, but to suggest further questions and voyages of discovery. A story of nation-building may have lain behind the project's conception. But 'the nation' as 'a central reality around which historical explanation should revolve' was untenable in this work, McKinnon argued.[40]

A similar attempt to broaden New Zealand's stories informs *Te Ara*, the contemporary encyclopedia of New Zealand. This is most evident in the first 'theme' of the encyclopedia, online in 2005, that outlined the different cultural, ethnic, national and iwi (Maori tribal) groups that comprise New Zealand. Maori tribal histories from a tribal perspective may contain interpretations that differ markedly from those provided by other tribes or commentators.

Such examples show the important place that public history can have in what Jill Liddington refers to as 'newer nation states and newer democracies'.[41] Public history can be a powerful tool in offering national stories, and there is risk about what types of national stories are constructed in the process. Debates in Australia over the national history taught (or not) in the classroom have raised concerns that the state may want to impose an 'authorised' version: 'the government seems to be looking for its War of Independence, its Battle of Hastings, a series of historical and momentous events and struggles to define and bind the Australian people', Bill Kyriakopoulos suggests.[42] Those stories can and do take many different forms.

It is not just in 'newer' societies where this occurs. Government intervenes in the historical landscape of many societies, in subtle and not so subtle ways. Decisions about whether to fund national museums or heritage organisations, whether or not to conserve particular Crown-owned heritage landscapes and built environments or whether to make formal apologies – or to refuse to do so – regarding actions and policies of former political regimes are all part of this continuum. As Liddington notes, 'Public Historians will probably need to be aware of the state, nationally, regionally and … locally.'[43]

Conclusion

Government involvement in history often attracts a degree of suspicion. Ludmilla Jordanova claims that 'departments of government ... frequently buy in the services of historians, who become dependants, losing a measure of intellectual freedom. Such relationships are never unproblematic ... are commissioned historians able to pass whatever judgements they think fit, or is the account to be written in order to show the company or organisation in a good light?'[44] Musing on Otis Graham's definition of public history as 'someone else who asks the questions', Rob McLachlan noted that it was not so simple when the 'someone' was a bureaucrat; that was hardly 'public' history but more like 'professional history', he suggested.[45] 'State propaganda or balanced professional histories?', Tom Brooking asked of the New Zealand government histories; 'jackals of the Crown?', Giselle Byrnes wondered of the position of historians working in the government end of Treaty claims.[46]

It is important to question the basis of government involvement in public history, just as it is to consider the basis of any work of history. I agree with Jordanova's advice to 'be aware of the possible pitfalls – he who pays the piper'. But as she notes, practice can be less clear-cut than this.[47] It is equally important, however, to try to understand this practice and consider how historians may work in government. It is not just an issue for countries such as New Zealand where there has been a long – accepted and expected – state role in history. Or perhaps it is not such an issue at all: there is, as others have said, only good history and bad history – and the struggle to tell the difference.[48]

Notes

1 Better-known examples of general works of New Zealand history include W. P. Reeves, *State Experiments in Australia and New Zealand*, 2 vols (London: Grant Richards, 1902), J. B. Condliffe, *New Zealand in the Making: A Survey of Economic and Social Development* (London: George Allen & Unwin, 1930), K. Sinclair, *A History of New Zealand* (Harmondsworth: Pelican Books, 1959), W. H. Oliver, *The Story of New Zealand* (London: Faber and Faber, 1960), W. B. Sutch, *The Quest for Security in New Zealand 1840 to 1966* (Wellington: Oxford University Press, 1966), P. Munz (ed.) *The Feel of Truth: Essays in New Zealand and Pacific History* (Wellington: A.H. and A. W. Reed, 1969). Publisher A. W. Reed produced an enormous volume of historical works aimed at a general and younger audience; over 200 of his publications are histories.
2 J. Phillips, 'Introduction', in B. Dalley and J. Phillips (eds) *Going Public: The Changing Face of New Zealand History* (Auckland: Auckland University Press, 2001), pp. 7–13 explores this in more detail.

3   'Introduction', in B. Dalley and G. McLean (eds) *Frontier of Dreams: The Story of New Zealand* (Auckland: Hodder Moa Beckett, 2005), p. 11.

4   J. Belich, *Making Peoples: A History of the New Zealanders from Polynesian Settlement to the End of the Nineteenth Century* (Auckland: Allen Lane/Penguin Press, 1996) and *Paradise Reforged: A History of the New Zealanders from the 1880s to the Year 2000* (Auckland: Allen Lane/Penguin Press, 2001), Dalley and McLean, *Frontier of Dreams*, M. King, *The Penguin History of New Zealand* (Auckland: Penguin, 2003), P. Mein Smith, *A Concise History of New Zealand* (Cambridge: Cambridge University Press, 2005), M. Wright, *Reed Illustrated History of New Zealand* (Auckland: Reed Books, 2004). Giselle Byrnes is editing essays for a new Oxford history of New Zealand, due for publication in 2009/2010.

5   See www.mch.govt.nz for further information about the organisation.

6   See www.nzhistory.net.nz for this.

7   C. Hilliard, 'A Prehistory of Public History: Monuments, Explanations and Promotions, 1900–1970', in Dalley and Phillips, *Going Public*, pp. 30–52; see also his 'Textual Museums: Collection and Writing in History and Ethnology, 1900–1950', in B. Dalley and B. Labrum (eds) *Fragments: New Zealand Social and Cultural History* (Auckland: Auckland University Press, 2000), pp. 118–39. These two articles inform this and the following paragraphs.

8   See I. McGibbon, '"Something of Them is Here Recorded": Official History in New Zealand', in J. Grey (ed.) *The Last Word? Essays on Official History in the United States and the British Commonwealth* (Westport CT: Praeger Publishers, 2003), sourced in this instance from www.nzetc.org. For discussion about the type of historians and writers employed and the writing of official war history more generally, see R. Rabel, 'War History as Public History', in Dalley and Phillips, *Going Public*, pp. 58ff.

9   McGibbon, 'Something of Them', p. 10.

10 Quoted in Rabel, 'War History', p. 61.

11 Quoted in McGibbon, 'Something of Them', pp. 2–3.

12 These projects are discussed in Hilliard, 'A Prehistory', pp. 30–54; see also R. Barrowman, unpublished paper delivered at Historical Branch seminar, 'Government History: Past, Present, Future', November 1995; and M. Bassett, *The Mother of All Departments: The History of the Department of Internal Affairs* (Auckland: Auckland University Press, 1997).

13 Discussion of the Dictionary, the abandoned atlas, and the encyclopedia is in P. Gibbons and J. Graham, 'Adventures in Scholarship: State-sponsored Reference Works, 1940–2000', in Dalley and Phillips, *Going Public*, pp. 74–8.

14 See C. Hilliard, 'Stories of Becoming: the Centennial Surveys and the Colonization of New Zealand', *New Zealand Journal of History*, 33: 1 (1999) 3–19 and 'A Prehistory', pp. 43–5; also www.nzhistory.net.nz/culture/centennial for a discussion of the role of history in the centennial. The variety of centennial activities is discussed in W. Renwick (ed.) *Creating a National Spirit: Celebrating New Zealand's Centennial* (Wellington: Victoria University Press, 2005).

15 R. Kelley, 'Public History: Its Origins, Nature and Prospects', *The Public Historian*, 1: 1 (1978) 16.

16 L. Jordanova, *History in Practice*, 1st edn (London: Hodder Arnold, 2000), pp. 14–15.

17   Tony Nightingale, Helen Walter, Buddy Mikaere and I formed a small work-
     ing group in 1994 to consider ways to further the professionalism of histor-
     ians working outside the academy. Tony, Helen and I went on to develop
     proposals for an association for such historians. A larger interim group of
     historians came together to design the association, and PHANZA emerged
     in 1994.
18   For a discussion of the term 'feral historian' see S. Butterworth, 'Thoughts of
     a Feral Historian', in Dalley and Phillips, *Going Public*, pp. 204–16.
19   This was taught by Associate Professor Geoff Rice in the History Depart-
     ment at the University of Canterbury from 1996.
20   A. Trapeznik and G. McLean, 'Public History, Heritage, and Place', in
     A. Trapeznik (ed.) *Common Ground? Heritage and Public Places in New Zealand*
     (Dunedin: University of Otago Press, 2000), pp. 13–23.
21   B. Dalley, 'Finding the Common Ground: New Zealand's Public History', in
     Dalley and Phillips, *Going Public*, pp. 16–29.
22   G. Byrnes, *The Waitangi Tribunal and New Zealand History* (Melbourne:
     Oxford University Press, 2004), pp. 3–4.
23   A. Curthoys and P. Hamilton, 'What Makes History Public?', *Public History
     Review*, 1 (1993) 10.
24   See D. Hamer, 'Book Review', *People's History*, 24 (1997), 6–8.
25   Useful discussions of the Tribunal's emergence and historical work are
     found in J. Hayward and N. Wheen (eds) *The Waitangi Tribunal: Te Roopu
     Whakamana i te Tiriti o Waitangi* (Wellington: Bridget Williams Books,
     2005), especially P. Hamer, 'A Quarter-century of the Waitangi Tribunal:
     Responding to the Challenge', G. Phillipson, 'Talking and Writing History:
     Evidence to the Waitangi Tribunal' and R. Boast, 'Waitangi Tribunal Pro-
     cedure'. See also G. Byrnes, 'Jackals of the Crown? Historians and the Treaty
     Claims Process' in Dalley and Phillips, *Going Public*, pp. 110–22 and *The
     Waitangi Tribunal*; also M. Belgrave, 'Something Borrowed, Something New:
     History and the Waitangi Tribunal', in Dalley and Phillips, *Going Public*,
     pp. 92–109 and *Historical Frictions: Maori Claims and Reinvented Histories*
     (Auckland: Auckland University Press, 2005).
26   R. Austin, *New Zealand Parliamentary Debates*, 6 August 1985, vol. 465,
     p. 6071, quoted in Hamer, 'A quarter-century of the Waitangi Tribunal', p. 6.
27   Belgrave notes that this role should not just be assumed and a similarly
     important role has not been evident in other jurisdictions such as Canada
     or Australia, see 'Something Borrowed', p. 96.
28   D. Edmunds, 'The Commercial Reports', in Hayward and Wheen, *The
     Waitangi Tribunal*, p. 113; see also www.waitangi-tribunal.govt.nz/publica-
     tions for a list of the publications and reports, many of which are available
     online; and www.ots.govt.nz for the work of the Office of Treaty Settlements.
29   Byrnes discusses this in detail in *The Waitangi Tribunal*.
30   Boast, 'Waitangi Tribunal Procedure', p. 63.
31   Belgrave, 'Something Borrowed', pp. 97–8.
32   Byrnes, *The Waitangi Tribunal*, pp. 3–5.
33   See www.dnzb.govt.nz/dnzb.
34   www.teara.govt.nz.
35   For more on this, see M. Tennant, 'History and Social Policy: Perspectives
     from the Past', in B. Dalley and M. Tennant (eds) *Past Judgement: Social*

Policy in New Zealand History (Dunedin: University of Otago Press, 2004), pp. 19–21.

36 For a recent example, see B. Dalley and G. McLean, 'Breaking Free, 1984–2005', in Dalley and McLean, *Frontier of Dreams*, p. 381 for comments about the economic policies of the government in power at the time of writing.

37 Rabel 'War History', pp. 61ff, discusses this aspect of official war histories in some detail.

38 Phillips, 'Introduction', in Dalley and Phillips, *Going Public*, p. 11.

39 See Gibbons and Graham, 'Adventures in Scholarship', pp. 79–80; see also *The Dictionary of New Zealand Biography*, 1 (1769–1869) (Wellington: Allen and Unwin/Department of Internal Affairs, 1990).

40 'Preface' in M. McKinnon (ed.) *Bateman New Zealand Historical Atlas* (Auckland: David Bateman Ltd/Department of Internal Affairs, 1997), pp. 12–14.

41 J. Liddington, 'Public History in Britain', *NCPH Public History News*, 23: 3 (2003) 1–2. This piece follows her fuller discussion on public history published in *Oral Historian* in 2000 where she compares the public history landscape in Britain, North America and Australia. She does not refer to New Zealand in these pieces, but the argument applies by extension.

42 B. Kyriakopoulos, 'Can There be an Official History?', *BBC History Magazine*, 8: 3 (2007) 90.

43 J. Liddington, 'What is Public History? Publics and their Pasts, Meanings and Practices', *Oral History*, 30: 1 (2002) 91.

44 Jordanova, *History in Practice*, pp. 159–60.

45 R. McLachlan on www.h-public.msu.edu, 12 August 1996.

46 T. Brooking, 'State Propaganda or Balanced Professional Histories? The Historical Branch and the Production of History', and Byrnes, 'Jackals of the Crown?', both in Dalley and Phillips, *Going Public*.

47 Jordanova, *History in Practice*, p. 159. For some thoughts on this in a New Zealand context see Butterworth, 'Thoughts of a Feral Historian', pp. 204–16.

48 C. Moore, on www.h-public.msu.edu, 14 August 1996. A similar argument has been mounted for the Australian experience. See P. Ashton and C. Keating, 'Commissioned History', in G. Davison, J. Hirst and S. Macintyre (eds) *The Oxford Companion to Australian History* (Melbourne: Oxford University Press, 1998), pp. 139–41.

Section 2   Presenting the Past in Place and Space

In explorations of unofficial understandings of the past attention has been drawn to the role of the visual in creating different public histories. Landscape, statuary and the built environment have all been deemed important in allowing for a sense of the past that is separate from that of the 'heavyweights' of the history profession with their 'autarchic tendencies'.[1] This crucial role played by visual representations of the past in the public landscape is the focus of this section. These forms of representation – which here include fifteenth-century battlefields, an officially designated memorial site, museums and public squares – are indicative of a varied and dynamic engagement by people with the past.

Dolores Hayden has noted how places, such as ordinary urban landscapes, are powerful in nurturing public memory.[2] Certainly the histories being presented in public places through monuments and memorials have been sharply contested in countries witnessing significant political change.[3] David Glassberg has discussed the way in which value is attached to a place because of the memories and historical association we have with it but, as controversy over statues of discredited politicians reveals, places potentially contain many stories and pasts; it is too simple to see statues or places as representing just one narrative.[4]

As John Siblon discusses in this section, there can be a mismatch between minority communities' memories of the past and state-initiated historical representations. To look at a place critically is to also consider the often-competing histories that are told of them.[5] While Siblon considers the imperial histories promoted at the heart of London, Paul Gough examines the way in which people have created and re-created their own sites of memory in the National Memorial Arboretum specifically designated to be an 'inclusive, non-aligned memory space' in the 'unmarked backwaters of central Staffordshire'. Here, the space itself, unconnected with any specific past events related to popular memory, has been created with the intention of providing a comprehensive account of a half-century of war and peace. But grand narratives of warfare have been subject to different readings by those who have planted the memorialising trees. Their labels often denote locally significant or personally known people rather than conforming to an abstracted memory summarised on many war memorials. Individual stories and experiences have become counterposed to the grand designs of the original owner's intentions. The creators of such forms of public history include those who create their own memorials but also commissioned artists, rather than historians. Andy de Comyn's ten-foot sculpture, for example, modelled on 17-year-old Private Herbert Burden, executed for desertion, is at the centre of the Shot at Dawn memorial in the National Memorial Arboretum. And John Carew's mid-nineteenth-century sculpted reliefs at the base of Nelson's Column present a particular and persistent narrative of empire in Trafalgar Square.

A popular public location of history-making is found in museums and galleries. Conventionally, museums may be seen as employers of professional historians committed to presenting engaging exhibitions, but how visitors themselves negotiate, interpret and interact with such displays is also a key aspect of public history practice.[6] For example, while the architectural form and internal organisation of nineteenth-century museums was significant in creating particular ideas of the nation, contemporary curators, as Darryl McIntyre explores in his chapter, are faced with the problem of creating spaces in which local communities may feel a sense of ownership.[7] And though museums may be facilitators and mediators of cultural exchange their collections are also open to challenge by visitors. The problems inherent in presenting a multi-layered and dynamic past were evident, for example, at the National Museum of Australia when the initial displays presenting particular histories of indigenous peoples were contested by some visitors, funders and key commentators. Approaching the past as shifting and open to appropriation by different generations has also been tackled by interpreters employed in museums who adopt the role of an historically-documented or a fictional character, in an improvisational and interactive way to encourage visitors' participation. As Vasiliki Tzibazi discusses here children who engaged with museum theatre brought their own agendas, expectations and pre-understandings to the event. Their own understanding of the relationship between the past and the present and their own subjectivity was key in analysing the events of 'Roman daily life' to which they were exposed.

The rationale for engagement with the past is explored by Meghan O'Brien Backhouse in her analysis of the enthusiastic activities of plumbers, builders or IT workers who engage in historical re-enactments in their leisure hours. Here narratives of the past are being produced and presented as a way of creating a particular contemporary identity of Englishness as an historic birthright: as she puts it in her chapter, it is 'an idealized representation of the vivacity of the non-noble people of an island country based on a long and thriving past'. Their particular way of turning to the past narratives they create suggests a dislocation from the present. This theme is also present in John Siblon's chapter in which he suggests that the experience of black and ethnic minority communities has failed to be represented adequately in the public monuments of Britain's imperial past.[8]

Notes

1 R. Samuel, *Theatres of Memory: Past and Present in Contemporary Culture* (London: Verso, 1994), pp. 4, 11, 23, 39.

2 D. Hayden, *The Power of Place: Urban Landscapes as Public History* (Cambridge, Massachusetts: MIT Press, 1995), p. 9.

3 For example, K. Lunn, 'War, Memorialisation and Public Heritage in South-east Asia: Some Case Studies and Comparative Reflections', *International Journal of Heritage Studies*, 13: 1 (2007) 81–95; M. K. Flynn and T. King, 'Symbolic Reparation, Heritage and Political Transition in South Africa's Eastern Cape', *International Journal of Heritage Studies*, 13:6 (2007) 462–77; C. Norton (ed.) *Nationalism, Historiography and the (Re)construction of the Past* (Washington: New Academic Publishing, 2007); L. Purbrick, J. Aulich and G. Dawson (eds) *Contested Spaces: Sites, Representations and Histories of Conflict* (Basingstoke: Palgrave Macmillan, 2007); R. Bevan, *The Destruction of Memory: Architecture at War* (London: Reaktion Books, 2006); catalogue of the touring exhibition against the Duke of Sutherland monument in Golspie, Scotland: B. Wilson, D. Thomson, I. Stephen, P. Seddon, R. Gibson and R. Murray, *MacTotem: Reviewing the Duke of Sutherland Monument* (Stornoway: An Lanntair, 1998).

4 D. Glassberg, *Sense of History: The Place of the Past in American Life* (Amherst: University of Massachusetts Press, 2001), p. 112.

5 D. Massey, 'Places and Their Pasts', *History Workshop Journal*, 39 (1995) 186–7.

6 R. J. Grele, 'Clio on the Road to Damascus: A National Survey of History as Activity and Experience', *The Public Historian*, 22: 1 (2000) 31–4.

7 See, for example, C. Duncan, *Civilizing Rituals: Inside Public Art Museums* (London: Routledge, 1995); T. Bennett, *The Birth of the Museum: History, Theory, Politics* (London: Routledge, 1995); C. Whitehead, *The Public Art Museum in Nineteenth Century Britain: The Development of the National Gallery* (Aldershot: Ashgate, 2005).

8 See also B. Batten, 'Monuments, Memorials and the Presentation of Australia's Indigenous Past', *Public History Review*, 11 (2004) 100–21.

5

'Garden of Gratitude': The National Memorial Arboretum and Strategic Remembering

Paul Gough

A vignette of commemoration in Middle England

My first visit to the National Memorial Arboretum (NMA) in 2003 was memorable for two things: first, the inordinate difficulty of locating it amidst the unmarked backwaters of central Staffordshire; and secondly, for the incongruent (but no less moving) sight of a group of New York firefighters in uniform unveiling a memorial plaque to their colleagues who died following the collapse of the Twin Towers at the World Trade Center in 2001. On a more recent visit, in September 2006, the site was more accessible and the compulsory entry charge had been reduced to a voluntary contribution. With a slightly more permanent ambience, it was also a busier place, made more noisy by construction traffic engaged in the early stages of building a huge circular earthwork at the heart of the arboretum, planned to be surmounted by a vast stonework intended to become the 'nation's principal alternative site to the Cenotaph'.[1] Just over a year later, in October 2007, the monument was unveiled by H.M. the Queen.[2]

In this chapter I want to explore the NMA as a self-proclaimed and now officially recognised centre for national memory. By adopting Lacquer's notion of 'anxieties of erasure', I will examine the tensions between public and private memories as represented through the design of the NMA, a design that has grown largely out of corporate and official sponsorship, but where 'private voices' can occasionally (perhaps increasingly) be heard. As a vaunted site of national memory, the NMA must be understood in the context of the 'Millennium Period', a time of systematic audit, enumeration and data gathering often carried out by volunteers, remembrance societies and local history groups. With the unveiling of the new Armed Forces memorial the NMA is now considered 'full' and its complement of national memory 'achieved'. I finish by asking whose voices have been heard and whose not; who has been remembered and who forgotten? And are these acts of forgetting in effect acts of exclusion?

Many of the arguments in this chapter also have to be understood in the context of public history. Like many commemorative sites, the NMA is a significant example of the past being fashioned and presented, perhaps even reasserted, into a public arena that may look back but is very much of the 'here and now'. To an extent, the NMA is presented as a condensed site of multiple memory, just as former battle sites have been preserved as hallowed places of national memory. Lowenthal argued that the identification and preservation of a battlefield as a physical and inviolable entity can help maintain a consciousness of the past which is 'essential to maintenance of purpose in life, since without memory we would lack all sense of continuity, all apprehension of causality, all knowledge of our identity'.[3] Roland Barthes argued, similarly, of the past being brought into the present if it is not to disappear.[4] However, as is evident from the contested terrain of many former battlegrounds and sites of remembrance, memory, identity and purpose are seldom shared values. Nevertheless if, as has been argued, landscape is 'memory's most serviceable reminder' then preserved sites or 'memory parks' can help to make concrete significant public and private experiences and evoke profound reflections. Despite the need for occasional artifice, such memorial landscapes can assume significance because they 'challenge us to recall basic realities of historical experience, especially those of death, suffering and sacrifice.'[5]

Monuments to the millennium: moments of dissent

As the year 2000 approached and the 'Millennium period' beckoned, a burgeoning fascination for systematised private and public reflection was discernible. In the UK a predilection for gathering together traces of the past into the present was nourished by greater internet access, the release online of the 1901 Census and by a plethora of mass participation schemes that included the campaign to understand the apparent demise of the common sparrow in British cities, to counting and recording species of hedgerow flowers. Such programmes were encouraged by the availability of some financial support through competitive schemes such as the Heritage Lottery Fund (HLF).[6]

Perhaps nowhere was this fascination more evident than in the campaigns that were co-ordinated across the UK to compile comprehensive

lists of public artworks. During the late 1990s exhaustive recording
schemes were undertaken by, amongst others, the Public Monuments
and Sculpture Association (PMSA), the United Kingdom National
Inventory of War Memorials (NIWM) and the Local Heritage Initiative
(LHI). Aiming to be inclusive and authoritative, these schemes were
extraordinarily ambitious in their scope. The PMSA's National Recording Project, for example, was established to catalogue 'every piece of
public sculpture and every public monument in the British Isles'. The
catalogue was expected eventually to contain descriptions and illustra-
tions of many thousands of pieces of art. Relying on a network of
volunteer and amateur historians, underpinned by association with
regional universities, the recording project also aimed to establish and
maintain a catalogue of images and texts in digital form for public
access.[7]

Equally ambitious, the NIWM estimated its task was to record over
54,000 war memorials throughout the UK in such diverse forms as
lychgates and church organs, as well as the more common chapels,
windows and reverential monuments. The template for recording the
details of each memorial runs to four pages and the project has since
expanded from its millennium ambitions to a 12-year long campaign
involving three full-time and five voluntary staff and over 500 volunteer fieldworkers.[8]

Running in parallel with this mass recording project, a number of ex-
servicemen's and 'remembrance' organisations have been purposefully
adding to the network of war monuments and memorial schemes.
Voluntary and subscription bodies such as the Western Front Association (WFA), the Royal British Legion (RBL), the Friends of War Memorials (FWM) and a distributed network of affiliates have become
dedicated not merely to the preservation of memory but the creation of
new sites of 'strategic memory'. The WFA, for example, has purchased
the Butte De Warlencourt, an isolated hillock on the former Somme
battlefield that was of strategic value during the battles of 1916. The
WFA has fenced off the hillock and erected explanatory texts and stone
markers. These organisations boast impressive organisational structures.
With its simple motto '1914–1918 Remembering', the WFA, for example, has over 6,000 members in 46 branches across the UK and 15 overseas branches including five regional 'chapters' in the US. Among its
trustees are an 'Historical Information Officer' and a 'Memorials Officer.'
Its executive committee has also an official cartographer. Like The Friends
of War Memorials, the WFA is committed to educating the public about
the First World War, largely through an infinite appraisal of the most

visual residue of that war – its numerous memorials and sites of battle. A programme of maintenance and refurbishment of the original head-stones, obelisks and crosses has been complemented by an active cam-paign to build further monuments and, where that is not possible, planting trees and preferencing natural forms and shapes on sites of actual or assumed import. Their enthusiasm for such acts of memory retrieval is a manifestation of a need to fill the 'absent space of memory'.[9] It also meets the need to capture personal and family his-tories that – with the vanishing of the last veterans of the First World War – are now slipping out of first-hand experience.

Arguably, such remembrance organisations have started to assume – perhaps even supplant – the 'memory work' once managed by the state. Indeed, we have seen a significant (perhaps an irreversible) shift to a memorial framework as the preferred way of interpreting and pre-senting the past. As Paul Ricoeur has argued, the beginning of the twenty-first century has seen a heightened sense of historicity in a global, rapidly changing environment, where people are increasingly coming to understand 'the fundamental and radical fact that we make history, that we are immersed in history, that we are historical beings'.[10] On occasion this erupts into internal disputes as to who controls 'proper' memory and how this ought best be marked. In 2001, for example, a fierce wrangle was conducted in the letters column of the WFA magazine about the appropriateness of raising the flag of the European Union during a service to mark the erection of a new memorial tree. Many cor-respondents felt that this was a distinctly British ceremonial moment lodged in a specific past which pre-dated European union. More recently there has been a prolonged dispute between who has the rights to access certain memorial battlegrounds in northern France.[11] In fact, there is little new in such tensions between 'top-down' ideologies and private mani-festations of memory. As Raphael Samuel recognised, in parallel with the shared appreciation and recognition of local memories, there has been a democratisation in the actual forms of memorial expression. Whereas most nineteenth-century monuments had tended towards the allegorical or metaphoric or had stood as effigies of the good, the great and the wealthy, the most common monumental forms of the early twentieth century – cenotaphs, obelisks, and empty tombs to the 'Unknown Soldier' – stand as a singular abstraction of mass death. These monuments do not celebrate individual heroics or leadership. Rather, they mourn the common man, for in the project of national memorialisation after the mass death of the First World War, the foot soldier was considered the equal to the field marshal.[12]

Despite the democratisation of memory and history, dissenting voices existed. In the 1920s, Armistice Day services were disrupted by unemployed veterans and successive peace marches.[13] On occasion, one finds bitter words amongst the inscriptions at the foot of military gravestones in the otherwise pristine cemeteries so scrupulously managed by the Commonwealth War Graves Committee (CWGC). Indeed, it is within the confines of these 'silent cities' that we can detect surviving evidence of private dissent – unofficial memorials, rogue planting, unplanned interventions – and these tell us a great deal about the hidden tensions in the process of remembering. It is, perhaps, brilliantly encapsulated in Julian Barnes' short story *Evermore,* which tells the story of the redoubtable 'Miss Moss' who, in the decades after the First World War, undertakes an annual pilgrimage to visit her brother's gravestone in Cabaret Rouge Military Cemetery in northern France. Her attempts to personalise the graveside environment of her brother's stone are frustrated by the strict procedures of official protocol:

> There had been problems with the planting. The grass at the cemetery was French grass, and it seemed to her of the coarser type, inappropriate for British soldiers to lie beneath. Her campaign over this with the commission led nowhere. So one spring she took out a small spade and a square yard of English turf kept damp in a plastic bag.
> After dark she dug out the offending French grass and relaid the softer English turf, patting it into place, then stamping it in. She was pleased with her work, and the next year, as she approached the grave, saw no indication of her mending. But when she knelt, she realised that her work had been undone: the French grass was back again.[14]

Such dissent has contemporary origins. In May and June 1919 Mrs Sara Smith from Stourton, Leeds, organised a petition, eventually signed by 1,400 families mainly from the Leeds district, arguing that the Imperial War Graves Commission (IWGC) was morally unjustified in denying families the right to repatriate the bodies of those servicemen who had died and been buried overseas. Mrs Smith's campaign was formalised in February 1920 when she founded the Yorkshire Association of Claiming the Fallen. Two months later, she announced that the British War Graves Association had been formed 'with the object of banding together the relations and friends of all those who fell in the Great War and to protect their rights and interests'.[15] Mass meetings were held in

Leeds and Wakefield throughout 1920 and 1921, causing embarrassment to the government and the IWGC who were busily involved in
exhumation, burial and the building of thousands of military cemeteries along the old battle lines. Her relentless campaigning floundered
when, in answer to another petition, the Prime Minister of the day
pointed out on 28 February 1924 that one only had to look at the
beautifully maintained cemeteries to recognise that the commission
had been right. As Dominiek Dendooven has written, 'The Prime Minister's stance convinced Mrs Smith that she was fighting a battle she
could not win'. Disappointed she wrote:

> We are being treated with great harshness and with far more cruelty
> than the bereaved of other countries. We are only asking for our just
> rights and it is high time we should be helped and not put off again
> and again ... The finished cemeteries certainly look peaceful but the
> cramped space of the graves and their being buried without coffins
> is a horrible thought.[16]

While both Miss Moss and Mrs Smith had eventually to resign themselves to alien turf and 'dusty geraniums', Barnes' story brings out
some of the key issues in the tensions between a public and private
agenda of grief. How, in the face of a complex administration, heavy
monuments and distant cemeteries, could an individual mourner hope
to personalise the symbols of commemoration? What role might
plants, shrubs and trees play in opening up and making fluid the
processes of remembrance? And could the natural form of things –
as distinct from hewn stone, shaped bronze and formal arrangement –
act as metaphors for collaboration and interaction in the future design
of new commemorative landscapes? Would this allow the private voice
to be heard with equal status alongside the high diction of official
slogans?

The National Memorial Arboretum, Alrewas, Staffordshire

Conceived by a retired British Royal Navy Commander, David Childs
in the late 1980s, the National Memorial Arboretum (NMA) was initiated by Second World War veteran Group Captain Leonard Cheshire,
founder of the eponymous ex-servicemen's homes and charitable services. Cheshire was anxious lest his and others' military and civilian
contributions to the Second World War be forgotten, perhaps indeed
even overshadowed by the resurgence of interest in the First World

War. Childs' visit to Washington in 1988, where he witnessed the multi-layered memorial schemes of Arlington National Cemetery, stimulated a wish to create a single focal point for national commemoration in Britain, one that might usefully encapsulate the country's military involvement during, and since, the Second World War.[17]

Specific places of memory – 'lieux de memoire' as Pierre Nora has coined the term – do not, however, simply rise out of the ground, nor can they be easily imposed upon any given landscape.[18] They have to be created. To this end, the NMA was intended to be an account of the British experience during and since the Second World War. Here, it was hoped that a wide range of voices would be heard, and many sentiments expressed – from deeds of heroism to daily acts of common work. As an index to twentieth-century British uniformed conflict, the NMA was intended to be an inclusive, non-aligned space that combined a comprehensive account of a half-century of war and peace ('this happened and is here recorded') with an iconic marking of the terrain ('this matters and is here enshrined').[19] As a 'permanent' floral tribute to 'human endeavour', the NMA is an ideal leitmotif for a population popularly characterised as a 'nation of gardeners'. As Paul Fussell so brilliantly observed of the 'English' passion for the rural and the bucolic, 'if the opposite of war is peace, the opposite of experiencing moments of war is proposing moments of pastoral'.[20]

However, when the appeal to create an arboretum was launched by the then Prime Minister John Major in November 1994, the project lacked a site and any long-term endowment. Soon after, however, an 82-acre tract of reclaimed gravel workings was donated by Redland (now Lafarge) Aggregates in Staffordshire, central England. A further 70 acres – including a lake – were gifted to the project. Start-up funding came from several sources – a grant from the National Forest in 1997, ongoing support from the armed services and veterans' and ex-servicemen's organisations and in 2001 a commitment for £2.25 million from the Millennium Commission (provided the sum could be funded with equal amounts from other sources). Having achieved match-funding the NMA commissioned and erected a Visitor's Centre and a Chapel which carries the distinction of being the only place of worship built in this country to specifically mark the Millennium, and the only place to mark a two-minutes silence every day. Since 1997 over 50,000 trees have been planted and over 100 dedicated plots created. The site does include non-military monuments and memorials – there is a plot maintained by the British Royal National Lifeboat Institution, another to those who died as a result of accidents on Britain's roads. Of the 56 identified monuments

Figure 5.1 Plaques to Police forces, 'The Beat', National Memorial Arboretum, Alrewas, Staffordshire, UK
(Photograph: Paul Gough)

counted in a visit in 2006, 12 refer to non-military activities but most have been established to represent interest groups associated with uniformed civilian services – the Police Force, Fire Service or the General Post Office.

In plan, the arboretum forms a simple right-angled triangle; its hypotenuse is formed by the north to south flow of the River Tame (and beyond that the main rail line to London); its lower edge follows the line of the minor road that leads from the main access road (the A513); while the left-hand side is currently bounded by a gravel works. Arranged geometrically within the arboretum are two principle sight lines: 'Millennium Avenue' runs in a north-easterly direction from the rear of the Visitor Centre; while another slightly shorter avenue, 'The Beat' – an avenue of horse chestnuts, each dedicated to a regional constabulary – runs in a straight line to the south-east, ending in a circular planting described as the 'Golden Grove' where trees can be dedicated by those celebrating fiftieth wedding anniversaries. Balanced originally between these two axes was a low circular earthwork known as the 'UN Spiral'. This has now been built up into a vast circular earthwork, which (now that the necessary funding has been achieved) is surmounted by a substantial architectural feature – the Armed Forces Memorial – that commemorates members of the UK armed forces killed on duty since 1945. The parkland around the Visitor Centre and Chapel is laid out as a succession of formal geometric plots either side of a shorter avenue. One of the arboretum's best known sculptures – the 'Shot at Dawn' monument – is concealed in the least formal, and perhaps the most remote, area of the park towards the north-east.[21] Around the Visitor Centre the arboretum is arranged with relics brought from distant battlefields. There are, for example, two lengths of railway from the notorious Burma-Siam railway that were delivered amidst great public ceremony in early 2002.[22]

The majority of the trees are part of a regimented design comprising some 50 dedicated plots. Trees tend to be planted in straight lines, though an air of informality has been allowed in some of the outlying tracts of the park. Each major planting has been inaugurated with a ceremony – invariably military or uniformed – and is usually co-ordinated by a recognised group or charitable concern. The dedication

Figure 5.2   Plaque to the Rugeley Phoenix Activities Club, National Memorial Arboretum, Alrewas, Staffordshire, UK
(Photograph: Paul Gough)

of the Ulster Ash Grove in September 2003, for example, was attended by the Secretary and Minister of State, a Chief Constable and Director-General of the Prison Service in Northern Ireland, and a clutch of officiating clergy led by the Lord Bishop of Armagh. By mid 2003 the site was considered full; its capacity to absorb any further planting schemes exhausted. Management rejected all further organisation and corporate overtures[23] though there is still some infilling as the plots around the chapel are decked out with statuary and smaller gardens. Instead of larger official initiatives it is intended that individual veterans, families and relatives will adopt individual trees or pay for new ones to be planted in their name. In this process, it is expected that their names and stories will populate the arboretum, slotting into the meta-narrative and adhering to the grand design.

Grand design: private statements

The NMA was inspired by memorial gardens in the USA. Reflecting on such spaces, Michel Foucault might have regarded them as 'utopian' projects. For him, utopias were the antithesis of homogenised and unified places, instead they were 'arrangements which have no real space: arrangements which have a general relationship of direct or inverse analogy with the real space of society. They represent society itself brought to perfection, or its reverse.' And, in any case, he added 'utopias are spaces that are by their very essence fundamentally unreal.' In trying to capture the disparate nature of these places, Foucault developed the term 'heterotopia', using it to describe places that have the power to create unusual or discordant juxtapositions, divergent memory systems and collapsed temporal dimensions in a 'single real place'.[24]

Can the NMA be understood as a heterotopia? Given that most of the tree growth is still modest, even minimal, the mnemonic role of the arboretum is currently played out by the numerous monuments, trophies and inscribed stones that furnish the park. These objects take multifarious forms, from simple brick pedestals to wrought-iron gateways and carved statuary, many of which are three-dimensional renditions of badges or insignia. There has been some effort to harmonise the design of the Arboretum so as to unify the extraordinary matrix of monumentalia, badges, texts and plants. However, in places there are some unfortunate aesthetic and symbolic clashes. (Although Foucault might not have worried unduly, it being the nature of heterotopia to be spontaneously dissonant). But the following excerpt, drawn from

Figure 5.3   The 'Shot at Dawn' memorial, National Memorial Arboretum, Alrewas, Staffordshire, UK
(Photograph: Paul Gough)

the original NMA Visitor's Guide, give both a flavour of the strident variety of the NMA and the underlying rigidity of the design:

> As the river turns North there is the option of turning into the vast spiral of Plane trees that will form the United Nations Circle or moving into the Royal Air Force Wings where trees have been planted for RAF Squadrons, Wings, Commands and Stations. Beside the river are Maritime Pine, planted for Coastal Command and those who served in Flying Boats, while the main feature is a collection of Silver Birches in the shape of eagle's wings wheeling in flight ... In between a walnut, a tree from which the first propellers were made, has been planted for the Aircrew Association while the WAAF have a selection of trees with 'Star' in their name shaped in the form of the constellation Cassiopeia, herself an Ethiopian Queen.
>
> Leaving the RAF plot by the southern entrance one crosses between the Adjutant General's Corps Plot and the Staffordshire Regiment Plot. The former is fronted by pleached Limes laid out to

resemble the West Front of Winchester Cathedral, the Corps' home city. The central Beech Tree reflects the species common to the Corp's Headquarters, while the varied collection of trees separating this plot from the Staffordshires symbolise the constituent elements of the Corps, such as *Cupressus sempervirens* 'Green pencil' for the Clerks and *Malus* 'red Sentinel' for the Royal Military Police (the 'Red Caps').[25]

Alongside the official military stories stand the corporate contributions of banks, savings societies and multinationals. Other than their role as sponsors, their relationship to the NMA is difficult to fathom. The arcade alongside the Millennium Chapel holds dozens of memorial plaques contributed by P & O Ferries, Sun Life Assurance and other financial bodies. One of the benches facing the wooden poles at the 'Shot at Dawn' memorial is sponsored by a tabloid Fleet Street newspaper. Another bench is dedicated by the Black Police Association from Northamptonshire, a county that is some distance from the Arboretum. Nearby, but looking out over the river, is a single bench marked with a

Figure 5.4 General view of the aboretum's western aspect, National Memorial Arboretum, Alrewas, Staffordshire, UK
(Photograph: Paul Gough)

brass plaque commemorating 'Workers Memorial Day' and sponsored by one of the largest trade unions in the UK. Even those trees planted to celebrate local civilian organisations – Rugeley Phoenix Social Club, for example – are arranged in symmetrical lines, bound by the didactic planting regime and its rigid format. Like the Northamptonshire memorial bench, Rugeley is a town that is some distance from the NMA.

What place then have private or individual voices in such a didactic environment? How authoritative is its assertion to be a national memorial, located at the very 'heart of the country'? And who is being remembered, and who not? As Samuel observed, it is what civic memory contrives to forget that may be as important as what it includes and remembers.[26]

The answer may lie in the function of the texts attached to many of the trees. In similar memorial environments in the US – notably Forest Lawn in Glendale, California – the arboreal and memorial iconography is reinforced by text and narrative. Occasionally prolix, these words and labels dispel any ambiguity. At every step a strict typology of meaning is

Figure 5.5   Grove of trees, National Memorial Arboretum, Alrewas, Staffordshire, UK
(Photograph: Paul Gough)

evoked: explicit captioning, weatherproof labels and guidebooks rule out any grounds for misinterpretation or ignorance. This widespread inscribing effectively glosses the memorial space with indelible readings, which act as unambiguous captions to the landscape.[27]

Similarly, at the NMA the labeling is intended to operate as a sub-text (but not a counter-text) to the grander design. As sub-text, however, it is somewhat indiscriminate. Almost everything is labeled, even the hedgerows are described in an 'accompanying description' as being of a particular design and material. Brass plates have been attached to five large boulders in the 'Normandy Garden'. One plate is inscribed with the word 'Gold', which might seem surreal in any other context, but here at the NMA it is immediately understood as a historical metonym.[28] Nearby, the 'Police Memorial Garden' also sprouts labels and inscriptions but with little apparent consistency: one sapling commemorates a police constable who died ('lost his life') aged 27, while an adjacent tree marks the longest serving police officer (1851–1903). Another tree close by marks the 175th anniversary of the Special Constabulary. To the right, one of the 'Groves' dedicated to a military unit – in this case, The Royal Logistics Corps – is a somewhat sparse space where trees are variously dedicated to constituent regiments, individuals who served in peacetime and others who were taken prisoner. Even the 'City of Coventry' is marked on one label.

At first glance there is no obvious rationale for the choice of tree or of its accompanying texts: nothing to indicate why a city is remembered by one plant, a Prisoner of War by another. Some of the smaller trees have large labels; some of the larger trees have tiny tags. What is clear is that in the military plots most of the people who are remembered are defined almost exclusively by their military service. Their civilian lives are left unrecorded or are deliberately forgotten. A good example is tree number 78/5 with its accompanying plaque to Captain John B. N. Armstrong. Born in 1928, he died in 2002; his service history is clearly laid out so that we can follow that he was with the Royal Inniskilling Fusiliers in 1944, had two years in No. 5 Commando until 1947, then a year back with the Fusiliers. From 1949 until 1971 he served with the Royal Army Pay Corps and from 1980, he saw out a further 11 years with the Royal Ulster Constabulary. Of the period 1971–80 there is a conspicuous gap, which is now impossible to fill, his life having been thus inscribed, framed and remembered entirely by his service in khaki.

What we are seeing at the NMA is a gradual reclaiming of the grand design. The labels quietly contest the meta-narrative: they favour the local and the known rather than the abstracted memory summarised on many war memorials. As poly-vocal mutterings, they act as a running sub-text to the larger ambitions of the site, a quiet, unassuming graffiti that is slowly reasserting the private voice within the high diction of the garden's larger plan. Family members play a major part in contesting the terrain. Once embarked on the project of remembering their dead, relatives become engaged in the particular rather than the general. In such circumstances, and within these remembrance organisations, there are few unknown soldiers or unremembered campaigns. The dead come from suburbs, neighbourhoods, chapels and churches, families and schools. They are not British: they are Mancunian; Bristolian; Brummies. More than that, they are Accrington Pals, Bedminster Boys, Ladywood Chums. They are bound by regional and local identities, not national ones. As Paul Gough and Sally Morgan have argued, they are 'identified by local boundaries and affiliations. They are "our" dead in a localised and exclusive sense. They are known, they are particular, and, even when dead, they are part of networks of power and identity.'[29] Over time, their voices may hold sway over the imposed design and high diction of the NMA.

Conclusion

Does the National Memorial Arboretum meet an invocation expressed after the Second World War for a grand national shrine, a garden that would provide a place where 'people can rest, meet and talk'?[30] In time, possibly. But the NMA develops arboreal themes that were far beyond anything envisaged by Arnold Whittick in the 1940s. In its current arboreal layout, the NMA is a highly complex site: inconsistent, selectively politicised and partial in its representation of national remembrance. Although it purports to be inclusive and broadly consensual it is subject to the vagaries of public interest and the volatility of commemoration. Only time will tell whether the 'nation' adopts and embraces the huge architectural monolith of the Armed Forces Memorial. Despite its massive presence, the Arboretum is quintessentially a place of floral and arboreal display. It is regarded as a garden that contains a monument, rather than a monument surrounded by a garden. In time the tree growth will harmonise the awkward visual clashes between some of the sites and soften the more crude *objets de memoire* that litter the green spaces. Whether or not the Memorial supplants the Whitehall Cenotaph as the alternative site for national commemoration is impossible to guess: it is, after all, situated in a rather remote location, its transport infrastructure is underdeveloped and its identity as a place of national remembering is only slowly emerging from a period of uncertainty and delay. The success in raising millions of pounds for the Armed Forces Memorial (which was so close to floundering) was revived because of grass-roots pressure and low-level interventions, generated by remembrance leagues, ex-service organisations and interest groups. Although the stone has now been laid and the monument unveiled, their contribution is far from complete: through a gradual programme of public inscription and the laying down of personal histories, what we will continue to see is an ongoing process of remembering, a slow encroachment of individual voices, achieved through private plantings, small words, handwritten tags and modest captions, which over time will complement the didactic grandiosity of the official design.

Notes

1 For the Armed Forces Memorial see: www.forcesmemorial.org.uk/the-memorial-project.asp/
2 See *The Lichfield Mercury*, 18 October 2007, and the official web site: http://www.friendsofnma.org.uk/
3 D. Lowenthal, *The Past is a Foreign Country* (Cambridge: Cambridge University Press, 1985), p. 103.
4 R. Barthes, *Mythologies* (Paris: Seuil, 1970).
5 R. M. Rainey, 'The Memory of War: Reflections on Battlefield Preservation', in R. L. Austin (ed.) *Yearbook of Landscape Architecture* (New York: Van Nostrand Reinhold, 1983), p. 76.
6 Between 1994 and 2001, the HLF has awarded £3.3 billion to more than 18,000 projects across the UK, primarily on buildings, museums, natural heritage and the heritage of cultural traditions and language.
7 By early 2004, the National Recording Project was able to claim that much of England and all of Wales, plus Glasgow and Edinburgh, had been surveyed, amounting to 70 per cent of Britain. The exercise is managed from a network of Regional Archive Centres mostly run from academic institutions. The information is conveyed to the National Archive Centre for collation, storage and dissemination in digital form.
8 N. Hewitt, 'The National Inventory of War Memorials: Profile of a National Recording Project', in J. M. Teutonico and J. Fidler (eds) *Monuments and the Millennium* (London: James and James, 2001), pp. 13–23.
9 The notion of the 'absent space of memory' is a phenomenon identified by de Certeau who captured the notion of 'alterity', the propensity of individuals and groups to implant and re-implant memories in 'forever new places'. M. de Certeau, *The Practice of Everyday Life* (Berkeley: University of California Press, 1984), pp. 88–9.
10 P. Ricoeur, *Time and Narrative*, vol 1 (Chicago: University of Chicago Press 1984), p. 274.

11 P. Gough, 'Sites in the Imagination: the Beaumont Hamel Newfoundland Memorial on the Somme', *Cultural Geographies*, 11: 3 (2004) 235–58.
12 See P. Gough and S. J. Morgan, 'Manipulating the Metonymic: The Politics of Civil Identity and the Bristol Cenotaph 1919–1932', *Journal of Historical Geographies*, 30 (2004) 665–84.
13 A. King, *Memorials of the Great War in Britain: Symbolism and Politics of Remembrance*, (Oxford: Berg, 1998), p. 235.
14 J. Barnes, *Cross Channel*, (London: Jonathan Cape, 1996), p. 108.
15 *Yorkshire Evening Post*, 24 April 1920.
16 D. Dendooven, unpublished paper given at 'Bodies in conflict: Corporeality, Materiality, Transformation in Twentieth-century War, Materialities and Cultural Memory of Twentieth-century Conflict', 3rd University College London/Imperial War Museum Conference on Materialities and Cultural Memory of Twentieth-century Conflict (16 September 2006).
17 Having been established as a registered charity in 2003, the administration of the NMA was assumed by the Royal British Legion.
18 P. Nora, and L. D. Kritzman (eds) *Realms of Memory: Rethinking the French Past, vol. 1 – Conflicts and Divisions* (New York: Columbia University Press, 1996), p. 160.
19 J. Forster, 'Creating a Temenos, Positing "South Africanism": Material Memory, Landscape Practice, and the Circulation of Identity at Delville Wood', *Cultural Geographies*, 11: 3 (2004), 259–90.
20 P. Fussell, *The Great War and Modern Memory* (Oxford: Oxford University Press, 1975), p. 231.
21 The memorial remembers the names of the 306 British and Commonwealth servicemen who were executed for cowardice and desertion during and just after WWI. The memorial was created by the artist Andy De Comyn and unveiled by the Duchess of Kent in 2001.
22 The 30 metre piece of rail track from the former Thai-Burma railway line was collected by a Royal Navy frigate, HMS Northumberland, and transported back to UK after several years of negotiations between the NMA and the Kwai Railway Memorial Group. Recent research has shown that the track had, in fact, been manufactured by Bolckow, Vaughan & Co Ltd of Middlesborough before the Second World War, later to be transported to Asia. See Friends of the NMA, *Newsletter* (autumn 2003).
23 P. Gough, 'Corporations and Commemoration: First World War Remembrance, Lloyds TSB and the National Memorial Arboretum', *International Journal of Heritage Studies*, 10: 5 (2004) 435–55.
24 M. Foucault, 'Other spaces: The Principles of Heterotopias', paper presented in March 1967, first published in English in *Lotus International*, 48/49 (1986) 9–17, reprinted in J. Ockman (comp.), *Architecture Culture, 1943–1968: A Documentary Anthology* (New York: Columbia Books of Architecture/Rizzoli, 1993), p. 422.
25 National Memorial Arboretum (NMA), *Guidebook* (2003), pp. 6–9.
26 R. Samuel, *Theatres of Memory: Past and Present in Contemporary Culture*, (London: Verso, 1996), pp. ix–x.
27 See M. Treib, 'The Landscape of Loved Ones', in J. Wolschke-Bulmahn (ed.) *Places of Commemoration: Search for Identity and Landscape Design* (Washington, DC: Dumbarton Oaks, 2001), p. 82.

28 'Gold' was the codename for one of the five Normandy beaches that were invaded by Allied forces in 1944.
29 Gough and Morgan, 'Manipulating the Metonymic, p. 672.
30 A. Whittick, *War Memorials* (London: Country Life, 1946), pp. 6–11.

6
Re-enacting the Wars of the Roses: History and Identity

Meghan O'Brien Backhouse

Historical re-enactment is a popular activity for thousands of people in the UK, and nearly every era and its associated activities from the distant past through to the near present day are represented. Here, the terms 're-enactment' refers to a hobby enjoyed by participants and 're-enactors' to unpaid, non-professional history enthusiasts who spend time, energy and money to investigate a particular period of history and then join a group of other enthusiasts in dressing in period-appropriate clothes, living in period-appropriate accommodation and demonstrating period-appropriate activities, from war to domestic life. It is important to categorise them as such to separate them from paid interpreters who are employed and usually trained by a site, such as a museum or heritage organisation, to embody a person, real or composite, based on historic records. These paid 'professionals' may be actors or storytellers or musicians or enthusiasts, but they work according to a script, either literally or improvisationally, which provides the guidelines for accuracy and the institutionally determined narrative. Re-enactment groups also determine what activities will occur during each event, and they regulate what objects may be used and what must be worn, but they do so for their own purposes and without an external editorial voice directing a specific narrative. While they visit libraries to view texts, visit museums to look at objects, buy collection catalogues and books about the period, generally and specifically, what they are most interested in is the *experience* of history – going beyond the books and lessons to discover what it would have been like had they lived 'back then'.

Roy Rosenzweig and Dave Thelen have found that by eschewing the history lessons taught in the classroom in favour of actively pursuing a first-hand understanding of the past, people are looking to 'strip away layers of mediation' and thereby 'engage in historical texts (and all

113

cultural forms) in ways molded by their own personalities, experiences, and traditions'.[1] This not only defines my understanding of public history – members of the non-academic public engaging with the past in ways that make it relevant to them – but it finds wider resonance in how people define themselves today: what 'back then' influences how we understand ourselves today? What can we learn? What should we remember and what should we, can we, or do we ignore? What do the people of the past represent that we would like to see in ourselves today and tomorrow?

The events and people portrayed in the British re-enactment world span the continents with Romans, Germans, Americans, even Native Americans being represented.[2] The eras can be just as diverse: Roman, 'Dark Age' or Viking era, the medieval period, the English Civil War, the Napoleonic Wars, the American Civil War and the First and Second World Wars.[3] The re-enactors themselves are a dedicated and enthusiastic cross-section of the upper-working and middle-class[4] British population who, for the most part, participate in these groups for personal enjoyment and edification, even though it can be quite costly both in regard to finances and time.

Figure 6.1   English Civil War Re-enactors: English Civil War re-enactors at a multi-period event at Warwick Castle, Warwick, UK, in 2000, displaying their military capabilities
(Photograph: Meghan O'Brien Backhouse)

Figure 6.2   Twelfth Light Dragoons: Re-enactors of the Napoleonic era British Army's Twelfth Light Dragoons at a multi-period event at Warwick Castle, Warwick, UK, in 2000
(Photograph: Meghan O'Brien Backhouse)

The re-enactment group on whom this chapter is based situated their primary activities within the years of the Wars of the Roses (1455–87), a period of civil unrest brought on by the desire of two English Households, Lancaster (symbolised by the Red Rose) and York (the White Rose), to control the throne and royal succession and thereby secure influence and wealth for the household from which the king was descended or allied. The Re-enactors are specific in their focus, and so have chosen to represent a Yorkist camp. Specifically, they represent the billmen, or foot soldiers comprised of freemen and yeomen who carried in battle long poles (bills) topped with hooks or blades, and the accompanying retinue of wives and children, of a household aligned with the Yorkist cause.

The group itself began as a military drill company comprised of primarily single young men who displayed military manoeuvres, techniques and equipment. They took great pride in their military prowess, especially in recreated battles with other groups. As the group has grown and wives and partners have joined, and some of the men have grown older, the activities now include more informal demonstrations of cooking, sewing, wood and leather work, herbal medicinal preparations, as

Figure 6.3 War of the Roses Battle display. Here members are demonstrating how a battle between bill-lines would take place. Members of one group are representing both Yorkist and Lancastrian sides for this small display at Warwick Castle, Warwick, UK, 2000
(Photograph: Meghan O'Brien Backhouse)

well as singing, storytelling, dancing and games. In the same way, the events at which they perform have diversified as well. They continue to include the major battle site re-enactments of the Wars of the Roses, including those at Tewkesbury, Blore Heath and Bosworth, as well as multi-group events like the now defunct History In Action Days,[5] but now many events also occur on the sites of castles or recreated living history villages like Cosmeston in Wales. While all of the non-battlefield sites include military drill demonstrations, the emphasis there is more firmly on camp life and material culture.

At this point, it should be mentioned that I am an American woman who joined this group while doing post-graduate work in anthropology in the UK. At first, due to my student-status, domestic status (I joined as a single woman) and my accent I was greeted with some concern: female students often wanted to fight, which was not allowed in this group, and with a large number of single men there was scepticism about my intentions towards them. However, I made an effort to participate in every aspect of camp and group life that was open to me, given my financial and transportation restraints (which precluded owning much 'authentic' kit or helping to transport group-owned

Figure 6.4 War of the Roses Camp: Quiet time in camp after the midday meal. Notice the cleaned plates and bowls drying on the table, and while most of the men are demonstrating or drilling, the women pass the time by sewing or catching up on chores such as mending torn clothes. Warwick Castle, Warwick, UK, 2000 (Photograph: Meghan O'Brien Backhouse)

materials). I also found that once it was known I had a partner (who is British and was also welcomed despite the fact that he had no interest in fighting), I was treated with less suspicion on that account. It would not be fair to say that all members were fully open with or to me but that was related to the view that it was a newcomer's job to make every effort to integrate and commit themselves over years of membership. (I was told at my first event that it was perfectly normal for people to try out several groups and periods before committing, and it was almost expected.) This probational participant status and my viewpoint as an American with a background in anthropology and history positioned me as the 'Other' on the inside and gave me analytical distance from the interactions which played out within the group as well as their general activities.

It was from this position, as participant observer, that the conclusion drawn earlier was formed: re-enactment is about the experience of history. Re-enactors are interested in taking an active role in a documented narrative of past events, and from the understanding they gain from their participation they not only create their own narratives of what happened in the past, which is endowed with their own personalities and experiences, but they create a narrative of their own personal history, or identity. So, while re-enactment has a nominal and superficial purpose of providing entertainment and education for the public, it is more for the re-enactors themselves. Their personal enjoyment of an event derives from what insights the experience provides. In this light, historic re-enactment is equally about the 'now' as it is about the 'then'. It is about what defines the group and the individuals today based on the exploration of English 'everyday' history (including possible embellishment and elision).

Involvement in re-enactment, like involvement in most groups, is as much about the participating as it is about the actual activity. Identification with something larger than the self is always one motivation in re-enactment. Yet, what is interesting about the Yorkist re-enactors is the overt integration of history and identity – the literal use of a commonly understood but very remote past to subtly separate oneself from today's commonly understood and assigned identity. It is more than simply wanting to live in the past: given the foreignness of life in the fourteenth century and its hardships, there must be additional motivations. The narrative being produced and presented in the guise of history creates a contemporary experience from which members can derive their own identity.

'We few, we happy few ...'[6]

Identity is 'the ways and circumstances in which people define themselves and are defined by others ... in specific historical contexts'.[7] But groups, which can be as complex as communities or as simple as a group of people with shared hobbies, have their own complex identities which are absorbed and redefined by the members because 'every and each collective identity construction highlights assumed similarities while obscuring presumed differences that at times may become more or less significant'.[8] This collective identity is reiterated by means of cultural performances such as traditions, objectified in material goods and by imbuing the natural and built landscapes with commemorative meanings. These symbols not only come to represent a moment or event of particular importance, but they serve as mnemonic devices for personal, group, and even national characteristics (whether true or assumed).[9] These representations, however, are only *lieux de mémoire*,[10] memories and culturally-informed ideals objectified into repeated actions or events, which have become important symbols of identity, or at the very least, of group association, but have lost the original imperative and spontaneity of the originating people.[11] The vibrancy is no longer the same. So while it appears that the symbols have remained the same as the years pass, the original meanings have changed. Each generation imposes its own experiences onto the object or tradition adding layer upon layer of understanding and perspective to the artefacts of culture. And as such these representations of identity become more heavily burdened with expectation and contested meanings as each year passes. Identity is not only layered, it is also reflexive, malleable, ambiguous and sometimes tenuous.

One way to begin to approach the issue of identity is to view it as a narrative: 'how I, as a finite, concrete embodied individual, shape and fashion the circumstances of my birth and family, [and] linguistic, cultural and gender identity into a coherent narrative that stands as my life story'.[12] This can be expanded to refer to groups attempting to reinforce a chosen identity felt to be at risk because 'identities are based on a *version* of the past rather than any conception of absolute truth about the past'.[13] But identity is not the only narrative that considers the past and its influence on the present. History, viewed from the standpoint of anthropology, is also a narrative. History is a cultural performance, a means of interacting with the past, a means of understanding how people have come to understand themselves in relation to others through past events and experiences. It is a human construct, a form of consciousness and therefore an interpretation, not just a written or ordered narrative of past events. By accepting this view of history and by understanding how people *create* histories, a more expansive view of historical narratives opens up, and parallels and interactions with identity can be drawn. History goes beyond the recording of facts from the past to include how, over time, people, both as individuals and groups, integrate past experiences into their consciousness of self in such a way that they can be used as references for responding to similar situations in the present and in the future.[14]

Richard Handler in *The New History in an Old Museum: Creating the Past at Colonial Williamsburg*[15] suggests that the goal of history is to connect structural conditions and cultural patterns of the past to those of the present. In a museum or heritage setting this can be best achieved through transparent interpretation, which allows for fully participatory history. This fully participatory history is gained when visitors feel that they can connect and hold a dialogue with the narrative to which they are being exposed. The outcome is the connection of those involved in the dialogue (visitors and interpreters) with the larger 'community of memory' in which 'people agree that they do, indeed, share some kind of cultural heritage and they talk about that heritage in ways that celebrate what is good or beautiful in it but criticise what is not'.[16] But, as Bernard Jensen pointed out in his presentation to the People and their Pasts International Public History Conference at Ruskin College in 2005, a problem emerges for both historical educators and a society as a whole, when groups within a society cannot connect to a larger, national community of memory. What happens, then, if there is a group who want to connect to an identity, or larger community of memory, but cannot because their sense of identity has been subsumed into another?

For these re-enactors who are looking to regain a sense of Englishness, which has become subsumed into Britishness, the answer is found in the past, such as in the Wars of the Roses. In a mostly non-reflexive manner these medieval re-enactors take on the material culture and actions of the past, controlled with strict standards of 'authenticity', and infuse it with a contemporary interpretation which yields more to a view of how they understand 'Englishness' than to strict medieval English history. In viewing this contemporary performance of the past, it becomes clear that history as narrative reveals more about the identity of the performers than it does about their subject, and for this reason, it is an important exercise in understanding identity in twenty-first-century England.

Us and them: identity, history and memory

The use of 'narrative' as a metaphor for identity is very useful for discussing identities similar to the 'Englishness' under discussion here: identities that are trying to represent a historically rooted culture within a larger, more heterogeneous society. The term narrative evokes a story, like a history, and all of the literary tools employed in its creation: metaphor, exaggeration, the nuances of semantics and semiotics, point of view and the expansion and elision of time. What are also implied is the vernacular language and the ability to understand the story through first-hand experience of it or through translation. In the context of group identity, these tricks of language are crucial, if, as Handler argues, 'groups do not have essential identities':

> For any imaginable social group – defined in terms of nationality, class, locality and gender – there is no definitive way to specify 'who we are', for 'who we are' is a communicative process that includes

many voices and varying degrees of understanding and, importantly, misunderstanding.[17]

It can be suggested that the narrative the re-enactors are presenting is being told in at least two languages, that of history and that of English. Neither language is uncomplicated and both often lose something in the translation.

Historians, social scientists and anthropologists have debated extensively whether or not the past is a foreign country, and whether or not the past can ever be truly known, understood or expressed in such a way as to illuminate its dynamism and nuances.[18] By extension, this debate questions the ability of Western people today to assess themselves in relation to a past populated by people to whom they may not be able to relate. This goes to the heart of the debate over what place memory, communal and personal, has in identity. These debates are occurring now because of the past's alienation from contemporary, first-hand experience due to intense movements in technology and philosophy over the past two centuries.

When people today begin to search and encounter artefacts of the past, both physical (objects) and cultural (traditions and histories), there is no deep, individually-rooted explanation. And so these meeting grounds between the past and present are devoid of original meaning. This void leaves them open to constant re-interpretation by whoever views them. This is what makes histories so popular, pervasive – some might suggest subversive – and ultimately, useful in identity construction. As Beth Goodacre and Gavin Baldwin have observed, '... [p]ersonal, group and national identities are founded on "memories" often aided by artefacts of images that substantiate the information recalled'.[19] These *lieux de mémoire* provide the framework on which contemporary identities could be constructed by allowing comparisons with similar features found in the past. And yet, because of a discontinuity between the past and the present caused by constant change, too much emphasis has been placed on memorialising the events of the past and organising them or translating them into histories, while ignoring the historical associations of the events which effect identity, what Pierre Nora refers to as 'memory grasped by history':[20]

[W]e should be aware of the difference between true memory, which today subsists only in gestures and habits, unspoken craft traditions, intimate physical knowledge, ingrained reminiscences, and spontaneous reflexes, and memory transformed by its passage through history, which is the opposite: wilful and deliberate, experienced as a duty rather than as spontaneous; psychological, individual and subjective, rather than social, collective, and all-embracing.[21]

John Gillis is more explicit: 'Modern memory was born not just from the sense of a break with the past, but from an intense awareness of the conflicting representations of the past and the effort of each group to make its version the basis of national identity'.[22]

These views support a concern that memorialisations, which can be considered to include identities, are carrying the weight of expectations placed upon them by groups too removed from their creation to grasp their original intentions, and perhaps, without the desire to accept everything implied by the act of remembering. In the same way that one ethnographic object dating from a hundred years ago in a museum cannot be expected to represent an entire cultural group from either a hundred years ago or today, nor should its position in the museum mask how it arrived there. Similarly, nostalgic identities, physical recreations and memorialisations – three terms that can refer clearly to historic re-enactments – must be investigated. As Gillis has noted, identities and memories 'are not things we think *about*, but things we think *with*. As such they have no existence beyond our politics, our social relations and our histories'.[23]

Commemorative activity, itself a political and social statement, must be fully dissected to reveal the 'coordination of individual and group memories whose results may appear consensual when they are, in fact, the product of processes of intense contest, struggle and, in some instances, annihilation.'[24] This is a provoking proposition to consider in relation to the re-enactors. It may appear that they are rejecting the modern habit of making everything into history by trying to interact directly with the past: they are removing the separation of time and space and modern boundaries and so reconnecting the 'us' of today with their precursors. But these appearances are deceiving: the re-enactors are instead separating themselves from what they view as a 'British' identity by working with and through a *lieux de mémoire* of Englishness and thereby creating a new reflexive identity through experience. In the 'British' identity to which they are ascribed by society they see the annihilation or at least the covering up of elements of their English identity perhaps in the name of political correctness or multiculturalism. This is not to suggest they are right-wing nationalist extremists seeking an England for the English but rather a group proud of a past that is going unnoticed or under-appreciated.

Them and us: Britishness or Englishness

In the United Kingdom, two centuries of human movement, both physically and socially, has created a situation in which many of the symbols of nationhood are seen as hollow relics of a time of domination by the top down and of the English over the non-English. No longer do the crowns of the monarchy represent its position as the head of an empire. Most seats in the House of Lords are no longer hereditary and the House of Commons is elected by all men and women regardless of income or station in life. Yet as the old system of British nationhood gives way to a vocal multi-cultural, or at least multi-ethnic, and devolved Britain without an empire, the concept of 'the nation' is being reconsidered:

> [T]he integrative capacity of the nation comes soon enough to pose another question, this one concerned not with falsity or illusion but with actuality of the nation – with its practical truth as a cultural formation of enormous historical influence and power. What is the actual basis for the nation in contemporary experience and how can the forms of self-understanding which it promotes come to be shared by people of strikingly different situations and circumstances?[25]

For the re-enactors, England the country is the collective entity at the centre of their sense of self, not Britain or the United Kingdom, the nation.

In his investigation of Scottishness after devolution, Anthony Cohen suggests that nationalism is the mediation of the state through the self, and in a stateless (non-sovereign) nation it can be understood as an expression of peripherality with respect to the larger state, in this case Britain or the United Kingdom.[26] The latter half of this argument works well for Scotland, but less so for the re-enactors being discussed here, as England is the ruling country in the United Kingdom since its Parliament ultimately controls key issues such as taxation or war. And yet by and large, the re-enactors in this chapter do not see Parliament, or the government regardless of party affiliation, as representing them or their concerns. Rather being English for them suggests something less tangible or visible than the politics of Westminster or a powerful, wealthy head of an empire. It is in people's own minds that a sense of difference may be found, and in symbolism, rather than structure, that the boundaries of their worlds of identity and diversity are sought.[27] To be English, then, is something more akin to an ethnicity or historic birthright; it is an idealised representation of the vivacity of the non-noble people of an island country based on a long and thriving past.

Re-enactors are utilising one of the qualities shared by many modern Western European history narratives: a glaring lack of specificity about how the majority of the people in these places lived their lives. And, if the existence of 'ordinary' people were ever recognised, their stories would have been amalgamated into generalisations in order to provide a fuller and more uniform picture of the national character. But these generalised references and carefully chosen portraits of a 'representative' few made by the privileged authors, provided only empty outlines which could be coloured in by anyone, through supposition, interpretation, manipulation and redefinition, and more often than not, they were used to represent both the best and the worst of the 'national' values, morals and attributes.[28]

These blank pages of history are what make the past easily exploited by re-enactors who see themselves as providing a *service* which they sometimes referred to as 'doing Living History', by re-animating the unknown men and women of the past to prove any of a variety of points about the bravery, industriousness and the creativity of the forgotten people, including and sometimes especially women. They begin to echo the very narratives they are trying to overcome, however, by showing that they themselves are the embodiment of whatever quality they feel today's people are lacking. Through the very deliberateness of their actions and their intentions they are repeating the generalisations they say they are attempting to overcome while erecting boundaries around themselves. For example, the camps alone are organised in circles with guy lines overlapping and tent openings facing inward, making the entire area private and difficult to access. During meal times and other periods of rest throughout the day, re-enactors will sit at a large central table, facing inwards and showing their backs to the public, thereby using body language to keep members of the public from intruding. Re-enactors also carefully decorate their tents with authentic furnishings and open their tent flaps so that these may be seen, but one should not look too carefully without being invited by the owner. They will often remain in costume to go to a supermarket or to the pub after hours, thereby denoting themselves as a distinct group from the other patrons and carrying the experience of the 'past' into the 'present' by keeping at bay the roles, statuses and stereotypes assigned to them by their everyday clothes.

This is an example of what Eviatar Zerubavel might call a 'rite of separation', an act of historical discontinuity.[29] Zerubavel discusses the concept of historical discontinuity and the separation of identities as it is applied to 'contiguous yet conventionally separate historical "periods"',[30] not, as in this case, to groups who use the material of history to physically dissociate themselves from their contemporaries. Yet the application of his concept works. It thus makes sense, in light of this, that the Re-enactors should be interested in developing proof of ancestral connection with the fifteenth century, what is often referred to as common descent, since '[h]aving a common past also entails some general sense of sharing a common present'.[31] Yet membership is not reliant on English, or necessarily British birth or citizenship. In addition, to my knowledge, none, if any, of the re-enactors had done any thorough investigation into their genealogy, or if they had they made no explicit association between their interest in medieval history and their ancestral associations. So, instead of relying on common descent, they are trying to develop an identity that is basically contrary to the twenty-first-century British one to which they are commonly ascribed. As Zerubavel summarised it, '*rites of separation* are specifically designed to dramatize the symbolic *transformations of identity* involved in establishing new beginnings, essentially implying that it is indeed quite possible to turn over a new leaf and

Figure 6.5 English Civil War Tent: 'Authentic' English Civil War period tent, including period furnishings, clothing and firearm
(Photograph: Meghan O'Brien Backhouse)

Figure 6.6   Twelfth Light Dragoons Camp: An officer of the Twelfth Light Dragoons and his wife, also dressed in army-style dress, outside their tent in an 'authentic' camp at Warwick Castle, Warwick, UK, in 2000
(Photograph: Meghan O'Brien Backhouse)

somehow be "reborn"'.[32] Re-enactors are 'starting over' by choosing a period which is sufficiently different both physically and socially from the present that they can create situations which provide them with experiences they would be unable to attain through the normal circumstances of contemporary life.

Conclusion: twenty-first century billmen

For a group of working middle-class English people to explore these ideas of identity in a way that is most meaningful to them, they choose to ground these experiences in the 'everyday life' of 'everyday people' of the past. Patrick Wright argues that 'everyday life' 'define[s] the main characteristics of a vernacular and informal sense of history which is certainly not exhausted by the stately display of tradition and national identity in which [British identity] finds such forceful and loaded public expression'.[33] And as such, this approach complements the twenty-first-century experiences of the re-enactors and allows them to negotiate between the rigours of medieval life and those of contemporary existence. It is also the public aspect of the 'everyday past' and the resulting histories which allows for the many subtle manipulations and subversions of meaning that are accorded to assimilated group symbols and it is in these manipulations that new narratives are created.

As David McCrone has argued, '[i]dentities should be seen as a concern with "routes" rather than "roots", as maps for the future rather than trails from the past'.[34] The 'English' identity of the re-enactors should be seen as such a route. While superficially their activities are rooted in the past, their goals are a sense of belonging to a narrative, which with reference to the past will help them situate themselves with regard to the present and the future. What is more important than just getting onto the battle-field and swinging bills at each other in a choreographed manner with a pre-ordained outcome is one more opportunity to experience 'what it was like'.

Many re-enactors have stories about a moment of epiphany during a battle sequence at a particularly evocative location: when the blood and adrenalin was pumping, the smoke was billowing, making vision and orientation difficult, the noise of raised voices and bills colliding was ringing in their ears and they felt like they were 'really there'; they felt like they knew what it had been like 500 years previously. These revelations do not happen every time, but the actual experience and the hope of its repetition is what keeps many of them coming back. While the words they use to describe the modified *deja-vu* refer to the past, the experience is now, the present. The most enjoyable events are the ones in which the experiences were 'good' – when the surroundings, the camp itself, the activities and the level of authenticity all work together and the feeling of the past is evoked – and therefore memorable – and the politics of the group structure did not interfere. When this happens, and they can really experience their chosen history, it becomes more than another presentation of traditional activities, it is in fact a new narrative of Englishness being explored.

Notes

1   R. Rosenzweig and D. Thelen, *The Presence of the Past: Popular Uses of History in American Life* (New York: Columbia University Press, 1998), pp. 5, 6, 12.

2   The case is the same in Australia though re-enactors in that country tend to avoid re-enacting Australian history. See S. Gapps, 'Authenticity Matters: Historical Re-enactment and Australian Attitudes to the Past', in P. Hamilton and P. Ashton (eds) *Australians and the Past*, special issue of *Australian Cultural History*, 22 (2003) 105–16.

3   Historic eras re-enacted are not limited to those that occurred during wars, however, these are the most popular. Non-military re-enactment groups tend to break off from these groups and focus on other aspects of life from a larger period. Most re-enactment groups are affiliated with larger umbrella organisations, which provide standards of authenticity and insurance, and organise large, multi-group events. These organisations also provide forums for discussions on topics ranging from historic research and how to do it to evaluations of events and how to make period clothing. They also provide lists of affiliated groups. What follows is an *extremely* short list of UK-based umbrella organisations and websites for some of the periods mentioned, and where such a site could not be identified, websites for individual groups from particular eras:

Roman era: Brittania – www.durolitum.co.uk, Comitatus – www.comitatus.net, Legio VIII Augusta – www.roman.org.uk

Dark Age and Viking eras: The Vikings! Saxon, Norman, Celtic and Viking Re-enactment – www.vikingsonline.org.uk, Regia Anglorum – www.regia.org

Medieval eras: Livery and Maintenance – www.et-tu.com/livery/cgi-bin/index.cgi, Wars of the Roses Federation – www.et-tu.com/wotrf1/cgi-bin/index.cgi, Mediaeval Trust – www.mediaevaltrust.freeuk.com, Rent a Peasant www.rentapeasant.co.uk

English Civil War: Sealed Knot – www.sealedknot.org, The English Civil War Society – www.english-civil-war-society.org.uk/www/cms/index.php

Napoleonic Wars: Napoleonic Association – www.napoleonicassociation.org

American Civil War: American Civil War Association – www.acws.co.uk

World War I: The Great War Society – www.thegreatwarsociety.com

World War II: All Forces (formerly Axis Forces) Reenactment Association – www.afra.org.uk, World War Two Living History Association – www.ww2lha.com

General Living History site where re-enactment groups from all periods may be found: www.historic-uk.com/historyUK/livinghistory/LivingHistorySocieties.htm

4   For example, the members of the group with whom I participated, and who appeared typical, were employed in a variety of occupations including some of the following: plumbing, building, (including owning plumbing and building businesses), security, haulage, administration, information technology, the law (solicitor), publican, and the military. Some members had university degrees, but not a majority.

5   History in Action Days was an event organised by English Heritage which occurred over a long weekend in the summer, and for most of its history, it took place on the grounds of Kirby Hall in Northamptonshire. During this weekend, re-enactment groups from across the UK and Europe, and representing every time period previously mentioned, would camp side by side and put on displays of living history, storytelling, and military hardware throughout the day. The highlights would include multi-group displays of large, historic battles on a hillside overlooking the encampments. Aerial displays were also organised, including a World War I dogfight, and fly-overs of World War II planes including a Lancaster bomber. The last time this large event was held was in 2001.

6　While this quote from Shakespeare's *Henry V* is about the Battle of Agincourt and was written long after the Wars of the Roses, it was a favourite speech recited by the Castle Bowman (an archer dressed in period dress and employed by Warwick Castle) at the end of longbow demonstrations. During this demonstration periods of English history were elided and as such the Battle of Agincourt was not clearly placed outside of the Wars of the Roses, nor vice versa. As a result, this speech has come to symbolise for me the embodiment of what the Wars of the Roses re-enactors were seeking to identify with.

7　S. Macdonald, *Inside European Identities: Ethnography in Western Europe* (Oxford: Berg, 1993) as summarised by B. Goodacre and G. Baldwin, *Living the Past: Reconstruction, Recreation, Re-enactment and Education at Museums and Historical Sites* (London: Middlesex University Press, 2002), p.169.

8　D. Mato, 'On the Making of Transnational Identities in the Age of Globalization: The US Latina/o – "Latin" American Case', *Cultural Studies*, 12: 4 (1998) 598, as quoted in Goodacre and Baldwin, *Living the Past*, p. 169.

9　C. Palmer, 'An Ethnography of Englishness: Experiencing Identity Through Tourism', *Annals of Tourism Research*, 32 (2005) 7–27. There are also many references in the work of R. Samuel, *Island Stories: Unravelling Britain* (London: Verso, 1998), such as pp. 12, 14–17, 41–69.

10　P. Nora and L. D. Kritzman (eds) *Realms of Memory: Rethinking the French Past*, vol.1 – *Conflicts and Divisions* (New York: Columbia University Press, 1996), pp. xvii–xviii.

11　Rosenzweig and Thelen, *The Presence of the Past*; Nora, *Realms of Memory*; E. Hobsbawm and T. Ranger (eds) *The Invention of Tradition* (Cambridge: Cambridge University Press, 1983).

12　S. Benhabib and D. Cornell (eds) *Feminism as Critique: On the Politics of Gender* (Cambridge: Polity Press, 1987), p. 166 as quoted in Goodacre and Baldwin, *Living the Past*, p.170.

13　Goodacre and Baldwin, *Living the Past*, p. 172: emphasis added.

14　Rosenzweig and Thelen, *The Presence of the Past*.

15　R. Handler and E. Gable, *The New History in an Old Museum: Creating the Past at Colonial Williamsburg* (Durham and London: Duke University Press, 1997).

16　*ibid*, pp. 224–6, 235.

17　R. Handler, 'Is 'Identity' a Useful Cross-Cultural Concept?', in J. R. Gillis (ed.) *Commemorations: The Politics of National Identity* (Princeton: Princeton University Press, 1994), p. 30.

18　There are many references that could be cited from many subject areas, but the most relevant in my mind must include: E. H. Carr, *What Is History?* (Harmondsworth: Penguin, 1990); Nora, *Realms of Memory*; D. Lowenthal, *The Past is a Foreign Country* (Cambridge: Cambridge University Press, 1985); D. Lowenthal, G. Feeley-Harnik, P. Harvey and S. Küchler, '1992 Debate: The Past is a Foreign Country', in T. Ingold (ed.) *Key Debates in Anthropology*, (London: Routledge, 1996); G. Dening, *Performances* (Chicago: University of Chicago Press, 1996).

19　Goodacre and Baldwin, *Living the Past*, p. 170.

20　Nora, *Realms of Memory*, p. 8.

21　*ibid*, p. 8.

22　Gillis, *Commemorations*, p. 12.

23 *ibid*, p. 12.
24 *ibid*.
25 P. Wright, *On Living in an Old Country: the National Past in Contemporary Britain* (London: Verso, 1985), p. 5.
26 A. P. Cohen, 'Peripheral Vision: Nationalism, National Identity and the Objective Correlative in Scotland', in A. P. Cohen (ed.) *Signifying Identities: Anthropological Perspectives on Boundaries and Contested Values* (London: Routledge, 2000), pp. 146–69.
27 See especially the essays in A. P. Cohen (ed.) *Symbolising Boundaries: Identity and Diversity in British Cultures* (Manchester: Manchester University Press, 1986).
28 Samuel, *Island Stories*, pp. 14–17, 44.
29 E. Zerubavel, *Time Maps: Collective Memory and the Social Shape of the Past* (Chicago and London: The University of Chicago Press, 2003), p. 89.
30 *ibid*, p. 89.
31 *ibid*, p. 63.
32 A. van Gennep, *Rites of Passage* (Chicago: University of Chicago Press, 1960), p. 11; E. Zerubavel, *The Fine Line: Making Distinctions in Everyday Life* (New York: The Free Press, 1991), pp. 23–4; see also V. Turner, 'Betwixt and Between: The Liminal Period in Rites de Passage,' in Turner, *The Forest of Symbols: Aspects of Ndembu Ritual* (Ithaca, NY: Cornell University Press, 1970), pp. 93–111, all quoted in Zerubavel, *Time Maps*, p. 89: emphasis in original.
33 Wright, *On Living in an Old Country*, p. 5.
34 D. McCrone, *The Sociology of Nationalism: Tomorrow's Ancestors* (London: Routledge, 1998), p. 34 as quoted in Cohen, *Signifying Identities*, p. 167.

7
Creating New Pasts in Museums: Planning the Museum of London's Modern London Galleries

Darryl McIntyre

The past two decades have witnessed the establishment of many new museums with innovative approaches to interpreting both national and urban histories and with accompanying public programmes that include temporary exhibitions, learning programmes and public events. In addition, existing museums have also embarked on different means of communicating new stories and interpretations of their national, regional or urban histories. As an example, the Museum of London, in addition to its core permanent displays, has mounted a series of major temporary exhibitions that explored London in the 1920s, the creative contribution of London fashion designers, and the personal experiences of recent refugees and their interaction with local communities in London, as well as presenting a series of small 'platform' displays dealing with the urban environment, social housing and gay and lesbian London. The Museum has also supported a range of social inclusion programmes such as working with homeless teenagers and long-term prisoners in interpreting objects or creating guided tours for visitors. All of these activities are aimed at both providing new insights into London and Londoner's 'hidden' histories and reaching new audiences who traditionally do not visit museums. The lessons that the museum learns from undertaking these programmes also inform the future planning and direction of the museum. These activities are mirrored in a number of other museums – national and urban – in Britain, Europe, North America and Australasia. Museums, especially those in the process of reinvention and redevelopment, need to learn from and draw on these experiences, both of good practice and the occasional mistake.

During the past four years the Museum of London has been planning and working on the redevelopment of its exhibition galleries that interpret and depict the history of London since the Great Fire of 1666. To date the museum's exhibitions have been arranged chronologically, like chapters in the biography of a great city, and ended with the story of London in 1914. There was an expectation that another floor of the museum would deal with London from 1914. However, financial, architectural and design considerations and other realities have dictated that the existing floor dealing with London since the Great Fire will now tell the story of the past 350 or so years. This has provided the Museum with an opportunity to move away from a traditional, chronological, encyclopedic-driven approach as well as an exhibition design that was in many ways out of date and out of touch with visitor needs. Previously the gallery exhibits assumed that the visitor was well educated with knowledge of the city's history and made no allowances for families or children, the city's cultural diversity and rapidly changing demographic profile or the use of new media as a means of conveying the rich information resources now available to us. Moreover many of the Museum's visitors are from overseas and there is also now scope for London's rich histories to be compared with other great cities. The opening of the Medieval London gallery in November 2005, adopting a new design and interpretive philosophy, is the first of the new galleries that is taking the Museum in a new direction.

The Museum of London is perhaps unusual in comparison with most other major museums in terms of its dual status. It is seen as a national museum by the British government which provides half of its funding and trustees, and a local government in that the balance of its funding and trustees come under the aegis of the City of London Corporation. However, the Museum's status will become essentially local government when the Greater London Authority replaces the British government as funder from April 2008. While the collections will retain their national status, the Museum's focus will remain the greater London area and its people with perhaps an increasing interest in contemporary London but explored in the context of changes to place and inhabitants of the city over the past 2,000 or more years.

Planning the development of a new suite of exhibitions and public programming is a mixture of excitement, considerable debate and discussion (internal and external), shaping and responding to new expectations, and creating opportunities for new ways of telling the stories of London and Londoners. Learning is now at centre stage of a museum's purpose and the Museum has taken the opportunity to create a multidisciplinary approach from the outset by bringing together curatorial, learning, design, visitor services, information technologies, collection management and other subject specialists to collectively plan and develop the new exhibition galleries and associated public programming. The Museum has moved away from chronology as the sole driver and will use a thematic approach – although still using chronology as anchor points in telling the narrative as audience research firmly tells us that the public still want chronology in some form. Learning opportunities will be integrated much more strongly in the gallery and visitor experience – whether formal learning programmes for schools or informal learning through performances, debates, use of object trolleys and explainers – as well as through the layering of information from exhibition text to the use of information technologies that allow visitors to interrogate online resources about the collections, thus interacting with the Museum beyond its walls.

Recent developments in national and metropolitan museums

The planning of new exhibitions is not undertaken in institutional isolation. Museum staff needs to be aware of the latest and best examples of new approaches and interpretations, as well as to see where mistakes have been made. It is inevitable that we too will make some mistakes, but hopefully at the edges. The past five or more years have seen a global expansion in new and exciting museum developments such as the Deutsches Historisches Museum and the Jewish Museum in Berlin, the National Museum of World Cultures in Gothenburg, Sweden, the National Museum of the American Indian and the proposed African-American National Museum in Washington DC, the Capital Museum in Beijing, the National Museum of Australia in Canberra, the Melbourne Museum and Te Papa Tongarewa (Museum of New Zealand) in Wellington. At the same time the Museum should not be blind to another significant museum development – the creation of museums of conscience that reveal the failures of human society. They include the House of Terror in Budapest, Hungary, New York's Lower East Side Tenement Museum, the slave quarters of Gorée Island off the coast of Senegal and a group of human rights organisations called *Memoria Abierta* in Buenos Aires is working to build a museum that will recall the kidnap, torture and execution of thousands of Argentinian citizens by that nation's military dictatorship between 1976–83. There are many more such examples that explore connections with the past that are too often ignored or forgotten by the major museums.[1]

Importantly, the Museum is drawing on the experiences of major new and not so new institutions that have undergone major reviews since 2000, such as the review of Te Papa Tongarewa (Museum of New Zealand) in 2000; the review of the Canada Hall at the Canadian Museum of Civilization, although both these reports are not publicly available; the Blue Ribbon Commission on the National Museum of American History of 2001–02; and the review of the National Museum of Australia in 2003, both of which are publicly available.[2] A recent article by David Dean and Peter Rider in the University of Leicester's electronic journal *Museum and Society* compares the reviews at the Canadian Museum of Civilization and the National Museum of Australia and it provides a number of very valuable insights into the review process and their outcomes.[3]

It is not the aim of this chapter to undertake a detailed analysis of each review. A great deal has already been written about the reviews of the National Museum of American History and especially the National Museum of Australia. More important is the question of the application of outcomes both from these reviews and the growing corpus of books and articles that have been published in the past few years that explore the changing roles of museums in society, from issues such as identity and nation building to learning and the visitor experience.[4] The new museology that has evolved during the past 20 years has increasingly placed learning and engagement with audiences at the centre of a museum's role and responsibilities although the development, preservation and enhanced interpretation of collections are beginning to gain a much stronger place in the core business of museums. Museums are under pressure to broaden the scope of their collections and programmes in order to better reflect and be more relevant to the societies that they serve. How might these outcomes be applied to the planning processes at the Museum of London?

The National Museum of Australia might be a starting point and many of the following observations might also apply to Te Papa, which together with the Melbourne Museum and the National Museum of the American Indian, were influential in the planning of the National Museum of Australia.[5]

The National Museum of Australia

A cornerstone of the National Museum of Australia's mission is to explore and portray an Australian heritage that includes recognition of the achievements of a culturally diverse society. As is the case with other national museums, the initial choice involved how it would position these different cultures and values within the museum and depict the life of a nation: how was the nation to be defined?; what should be told about its past?; who was to be included in the story, and how?; who is excluded, and why?; how would local experience fit into the national narrative?; and what happens when the community that we call nation does not fully mesh with the territorial entity that we call country?

Faced with the enormous task of interpreting and communicating the stories of Australia for new generations of visitors, who arrive with varied backgrounds and understandings, the museum chose the intellectual framework of land, people and nation as opposed to a chronological interpretation of Australia's history. It explored those meta-themes by building exhibitions around personal stories that illustrated the themes. It was clear that a theme couldn't simply be about 'things' or 'events' and 'ideas': it must be about people. To present the past and the present, museums must portray the past on a human, even intimate scale that is about real people dealing with real life, and making choices. For each story objects with strong provenance depicting personal accounts from the collections were combined with explanatory text and images, and throughout the museum multi-media components are employed to unlock further layers of each story, or to link them with broader national issues. The museum also has a radio and television broadcast studio that allows it to be an active forum in presenting debates and discussion about contemporary national issues, to deliver programmes for schools and to reach audiences who are unable for reasons of distance to visit the museum in person.

The aim was to achieve a multi-disciplinary approach by combining subject areas such as science and technology, the creative arts and the social and historical sciences. The integration of the three meta-themes was always a fundamental planning concept. All the exhibitions and programmes interpret the meta-themes of land, nation and people in one way or another. The real story of any nation does not divide itself neatly into academic disciplines. Project teams comprised staff drawn from different disciplines. In addition, from the outset, the museum held a number of workshops involving historians, geographers, anthropologists and a range of other disciplines as well as members of the museum community, teachers, writers, dramatists and film makers to explore how best the museum might interpret and, importantly, communicate the vast canvas of Australia's history. The museum received criticism that it does not deal with particular subjects or, where it does, the treatment is superficial. Museums always receive such criticism and no doubt the Museum of London will also with its new exhibitions.

However, museums are not 'books on walls'. They have limited 'real estate' in which to convey so many stories, and increasingly museums need to take account of visitor and non-visitor consultations in shaping their exhibitions.

The National Museum of Australia has no single master narrative – the truth is complex and emerges not from a simple chronology, or a content's list of hard facts, but from the interplay of numerous individual stories and points of view. These can range from the profoundly tragic, through the ironic or quirky, to the absurd or the joyful. For example, the museum's innovative *Eternity* gallery explored ten emotions, such as passion, fear and hope, by taking one object that reflected an emotion and providing a range of personal narratives to explain the individual's emotional connection with the object. The stories ranged from Captain Arthur Phillip's hope for the creation of a new colony at the foundation of the first European settlement in 1788 (at Sydney) to a person's passionate belief in the football code Australian Rules. The 50 stories in this gallery are by and large the sum of us. However, some people, and this was very apparent during the review of the National Museum of Australia's exhibitions and public programmes, really wanted a 'master narrative' with a strong, authoritative voice presenting a simplistic chronology of civilisation and progress and a 'comfortable' view of history that does not confront the museum visitor. But the National Museum of Australia doesn't do that – why?

Two reasons were stated in the Museum's initial planning stages during the 1970s:

> A new national museum will illuminate new fields of knowledge and also link traditional fields in revealing ways. ...[It will] chart a course quite different to that followed by ... those earlier Australian museums which were founded during a different educational and scientific climate.

> The museum, where appropriate, should display controversial issues. In our view, too many museums concentrate on certainty and dogma, thereby forsaking the function of stimulating legitimate doubt and thoughtful discussion.[6]

The Museum was planned on the basis that it would be a forum, a place for dialogue and discussion, for the benefit of Australian citizens who visit the museum facility in Canberra and/or encounter its programmes in some other form. One of the museum's aims was 'to speak with many voices', to listen and respond to all and to promote debate about questions of diversity and identity. These values are also implicit in the Museum of New Zealand and in other major Australian museums, such as the Melbourne Museum and the Australian Museum in Sydney. Can the act of visiting a museum be part of such a consciously nation-building exercise?

To a large extent the answer is 'yes', posited on the notion that 'museums, collections and exhibitions are products and agents of social and political change'.[7] The National Museum of Australia embraced its role as an interpreter of societal change. The museum has much to explain about the complex origins of the continent and the nation now called Australia and it explains these concepts by presenting well-researched exhibitions, such as its environmental gallery (*Tangled Destinies*) and the *First Australians* gallery, and by inviting discussion and debate through its public programmes, which covers topics such as the impact of bush fires on urban and rural environments and the current drought engulfing much of Australia. As well, it has a monthly programme, *Talkback Classroom*, in which senior secondary school students interview leading politicians and other opinion makers on current issues. This programme is broadcast on the national radio network and reaches an audience in excess of one million listeners. .

Challenges to reinterpretation

It has been said that cultural institutions and their visitors need each other. As David Carr has noted, 'People go to museums for profound reasons of hope, identity, and self-construction.' Indeed, he continued, every 'cultural institution is challenged to live up to the trust placed in it by the mere presence of the user, a trust or contract or alliance devoted to creating a situation that offers the optimal experience.'[8] Carr was writing in 1999, prior to the Blue Ribbon Commission at the National Museum of American History. That review grew out of concerns about the modernisation agenda of the then Secretary of the Smithsonian, Lawrence Small, who believed the Smithsonian's exhibitions were run down, of little interest to young people, reflected a 'national cemetery of bric-a-brac' and were coupled with the influence of major donors who would advise on two new exhibitions on subjects of their choosing which turned out to be a celebration of American achievers and celebrities. Secretary Small also initiated some actions and a commercialisation agenda to improve the Smithsonian's financial 'bottom line' and attendance that appeared to attack the whole research function of the Smithsonian while draining its institutional lifeblood.

Following a campaign by scholars, one of the major donors withdrew her financial support and the Blue Ribbon Commission was established to advise on 'the most timely and relevant themes and methods of presentation for the National Museum of American History in the 21st century'. Issued in March 2002, the report's recommendations for the future development of exhibition themes and content are prefaced by the statement that the National Museum of American History 'must assure that the process of developing themes and topics is perceived as having legitimacy' and that the exhibits should 'meet the highest standards of scholarship'.[9] This has not stopped continuing criticism by some tourists and cultural commentators that the museum's exhibitions have 'washed out' the nation's European ancestry in favour of 'diversity' history which portrays America's repression of minorities ranging from the treatment of the Pueblo minorities in New Mexico to the forced Japanese-American internment camps of the Second World War and the discrimination against Hispanics and African-Americans. The museum quite rightly defends these exhibits as reflecting the complexity of American history, which involves people other than Caucasians and the need to address past omissions.

The challenges facing new museums and those in the process of re-invention include asking fresh questions about a nation or a city's histories and identities, and setting up conversations with its audiences. In its positive aspects a museum can bring communities and groups together to examine and seek answers to collective questions. Museums can generate pride and comfort in cultural identities that are a mosaic and provide a compelling picture made of different parts and diverse stories that collectively make up a great anthology. In 2006 the Museum of London was chosen by the families of those killed in the 7 July 2005 bombings to be the venue for a small display that commemorates those deaths through a book of tributes. It provides a quiet space for reflection in response to this tragic event. The proposed new exhibitions will incorporate this display as well as other spaces of reflection in recognition of other tragic events in London's history. In addition, the Museum will continue its tradition of hosting small 'capital concerns' displays that explore topical issues confronting London such as gun and knife crime, drugs and climate change.

An important key to how the Museum of London represents the city's voices lies in its determination to include them in the story from the start. Through the process of consultation and involvement the museum should aim to reflect the communities' inheritance and stories, which may not always have been part of the 'majority history'. Of course, dialogue between the museum and communities does not guarantee that things will run smoothly. Within each community there may be factions with differing views arising from religion, political outlook, socio-economic background, geographic location and the like. And the museum cannot consult with every community or group within London and be everything to everyone. But it does give people a feeling of owner-ship if they are involved in museum planning from the start and the museum's work can only be strengthened if it seeks partnerships with those communities whose cultures and identities it intends to represent.[10] The eminent American museologist Robert Archibald has observed that authoritarian voices sound hollow at this time in history.[11] But museums themselves do have authority in that visitors turn to museums for an authoritative version of national events and issues. Many American museums responded to the events of 11 September 2001 through a series of moving exhibitions that attracted large audiences. This bestows an enormous responsibility on museums.

Returning to the National Museum of Australia, it recognised that it had a conspicuous role to play in illuminating the full range of stories from the past and it would be failing in its duty if it shied away from controversy and disagreement in pursuing this role. Active social and political debate about its past and future is vital to any healthy society, and the museum has become a forum for such debate.

The National Museum of Australia accepted from the outset that there would be disagreements about the way it examines historic processes or about the choice of themes, stories and issues. It is never easy for a publicly funded cultural institution to become involved in controversy but that is probably inevitable if the museum is to do its job honestly. Differing value systems *will* meet and sometimes collide in what needs to be said about Australia's histories. But the museum must be able to show that careful balance has been given to different points of view and that the best academic advice about the accuracy of the statements and statistics involved are employed in its preparation. Controversial exhibitions mark the sometimes painful steps towards proper public discussion of issues and can make museum programming relevant and interesting to a broader range of audiences. While contro-versial exhibitions may be perceived to have failed on one level – and nobody ever enjoys being unpopular with the government, the press or a community lobby group – they can also be instrumental in focusing attention upon matters of public importance.[12] The Museum's *First*

Australians gallery sensitively explores issues such as the stolen generation (the forced removal of Aboriginal children to live with European families) and Aboriginal land rights, which provide Aboriginal
perspectives to these events in their history which traditionally have
only been seen from the viewpoint of white Australians.

Overall the National Museum's opening suite of exhibitions and
programmes were well received by the public. However, some neo-
conservative historians and commentators dismissed the National
Museum of Australia as 'politically correct' and concluded that post-
modernism had undermined not only the museum's ability to tell the
national story, but in fact the appeal of history in general. One critic
concluded that 'women and ethnic groups' deserve their own specialist
museums of minority interest, and do not deserve space in a *national*
museum. Why not? In his view, they have not contributed to 'real'
history. National history deals, he says, with 'the major structures of
the society and its culture, and the key decision-makers who brought
them into being or changed their direction.'[13] It was these types of
criticism that led to the review of the museum's exhibitions and public
programmes in 2002–03. While the review found in summary that the
museum was innocent of the charge of political bias, it recommended
that the museum should not focus on the untold and disparate stories
of the nation but rather on the important and traditional stories of the
nation, that is, the more traditional themes of European discovery,
exploration, convicts, settlement, agricultural and pastoral industries
and the like that held secure places in the school curriculum of the
1950s and 1960s. The museum is now embarking on implementing
these recommendations.[14] It is likely that the *Nation* and *Horizons*
(a history of immigration) galleries will be the first to be redeveloped.

The National Museum of Australia was not alone in attracting
criticism because it included alternative perspectives of history. The
Smithsonian National Air and Space Museum's *Enola Gay* exhibition in
1995 generated heated debate. There was a similar controversy in
Germany in 1995 when an exhibition displayed new evidence about
the role of the German army in wartime and questioned whether the
Wehrmacht was 'innocent' or had played an active role in the extermination of many civilians, especially from Jewish and other communities, in Poland, Russia and other countries in eastern Europe occupied
by the Nazis. It was bitterly attacked by some former soldiers, while
others agreed that it was factual and were pleased to see the story told.
A revised and toned down version of the exhibition later toured
Germany in 2001.[15] A 1991 exhibition at the Smithsonian Institution's

American Art Museum (formerly National Museum of American Art) showed romantic landscapes of the Wild West but challenged the Manifest Destiny viewpoint by suggesting that America's frontier had actually been characterised by racism and greed. It was deplored as 'perverse, historically inaccurate and destructive' – but also praised for its move away from traditional heroism to a more fluid, social history approach,[16] providing different perspectives of an episode of national history.

For many years Australian museums have been addressing major societal issues and not just the display of objects. Visitors will find startling – and very timely – insights into refugees, tolerance and multiculturalism in the Migration Museums of both Adelaide and Melbourne.[17] The Australian Museum in Sydney is a long-time exponent – even activist – on issues of indigenous histories and cultures, world population, environmental change, or the comparative value and richness of different cultures.[18] The new Melbourne Museum highlights significant present-day issues within historic, present and future contexts.[19] Museums provide a useful forum for debate and offer reflective spaces in which to consider current debates and controversial issues against their historic or conceptual background. They offer comfortable spaces and stimulus for thought – 'a safe place for unsafe ideas'[20] – and they present the evidence from many perspectives, some of them new or unusual, but they leave people to make up their own minds.

Most people are open to legitimate doubt, or have the gift of imagination that helps them to understand things from someone else's point of view. Museum educators recognise this moment of change and call it 'landmark learning'.[21] The visitor receives a brief but indelible sense of the subject, against which any subsequent exposures will be referenced. Not every visitor will discover every element, because exhibitions are not classrooms but rather immersive environments, offering a number of choices. Something that fascinates one person will be disregarded by another. What museums do is assemble the evidence, design it to be attractive and accessible and then guide the visitor in its interpretation.

What does all this mean in the case of the Museum of London? A major redevelopment programme is not restricted simply to the creation of new exhibitions and refurbished facilities. The Museum aims during the next four to five years to transform itself. The presentation of London's stories will be changed to make these stories more relevant and engaging to present and future audiences. New spaces and resources will be created that will actively encourage more people to use the

Museum's collections and knowledge base for their own learning and enjoyment. The Museum's reach will be extended by using this redevelopment project to engage new users and stakeholders locally, nationally and internationally. Energies will also be devoted to attracting families, children, diverse communities and particular socio-economic groups as our primary audiences following extensive user and non-user consultations and evaluation studies. The Museum wants also to convey a stronger sense of London's contemporary identity as a vibrant and dynamic city with diversity at its heart by exploring and portraying a London that recognises the achievements and contributions of a culturally diverse society.

The Museum is now well advanced in the detailed content development and design of the new galleries that will primarily explore London as both a global city and a people's city in the context of a meta-narrative of city, people and change. This will involve creating a new history of London by having the confidence to interpret new patterns for London's past within which all these stories can sit 'comfortably'. The museum has about 2,500 square metres in which to interpret societal change and the available physical space will fundamentally affect what the Museum will say. The challenge is what to include and headline and what to leave out – all the while bearing in mind the overarching authoritative voice.

By combining subject areas such as archaeology, history, geography and the visual arts and by ensuring that the exhibitions and programmes interpret the meta-narratives, the Museum will take a multi-disciplinary approach to tell stories of London and Londoners in ways that ask fresh questions about histories and identities. It will set up conversations with its audiences through exhibits, staff interaction and events in which they are reassured by the familiar and challenged by the new. In effect the Museum will show visitors those identities with which they are familiar and then stretch the boundaries. But it will also present themes, stories and issues about which there might be disagreement. In doing so, the Museum will show that careful balance has been given to different points of view and factual accuracy. What makes museums different from a newspaper when it comes to discussion of current and controversial issues is the museums' contribution to *informed* debate. Museums can make possible a crucial interplay between intellectual and emotional knowledge. Museums want visitors to say: 'I knew this happened, but I didn't realise what it was actually like.' Emotional connection, founded on scholarship, is what museums can do best.

It is perhaps also timely for the Museum to review the value, role and use of its collections and to develop new collection development strategies that more strongly reflect the city's rich cultural diversity, in the broadest sense, as well as future major transformational events such as the Olympic Games in 2012. Change will present a number of challenges. Should the Museum, for example, decide on the themes and stories primarily by using historical accounts and then select objects to illustrate that schema or should it interrogate the objects and see what themes can be deduced? To what extent can old collections embodying previous curators' views of what was 'important' or symbolic be re-purposed to address contemporary issues and new lines of historical enquiry? Or are they largely irrelevant and be deemed closed collections or even in some cases de-accessioned? What types of collections should the Museum be building now to represent current concerns, interests and the diversity of London? How far can such collecting be objective or is it reflective of our own subjective views as was the case with collections created in the past? This poses a question about the interface between 'historical' and 'contemporary' and how soon after an event has taken place – such as the recent terrorist attacks in London – does the historian take over from a journalist or commentator? The Museum's response here was to actively collect both journalists' accounts as well as individual stories placed on Internet sites. Finally, should the museum continue to de-contextualise objects or should it be recording contemporary 'supra-objects' – such as a room or a building in its entirety (as is the case in Sweden) – to give significant meaning to the individual meanings of that collage?

The Museum of London aims to challenge its visitors with a number of significant questions about the histories and identities of London and Londoners, and the issues of representing different cultures within society. The new galleries, which will open to the public in late 2009, must communicate to and provide visitors with a clear, coherent and engaging story that runs seamlessly over time, rather than a fragmented story broken into stand-alone periods. The core story is complex and multi-layered and will inevitably make demands of visitors, intellectually and emotionally. The design process will be a critical part of the planning of the new galleries and create an urban mood and a sense of the complexity, creativity, dynamism and diversity of the city itself. In drawing out these common patterns the galleries must strive to generate a sense of ownership of the past and the present, in particular breaking down the idea that the past is 'not about me'. This is just one of the many challenges facing the Museum in planning and creating its new galleries.

Conclusion

The role of museums is changing from one of focusing just on collecting, preserving and presenting static displays to being facilitators and mediators of cultural exchange. They can be places of both entertainment and discovery, with the potential to consider the great questions of our world and our time in ways that are matched to the interests and capacities of their audience. Museums are one of the new cultural frontiers and part of the cultural landscape of experiential consumption. They can show people the limits of their own experience, and help them to cross the imagination boundary to gain the insights we all need to enter into the viewpoints of other peoples, cultures and times.

Notes

1 S. Ashley, 'State Authority and the Public Sphere: Ideas on the Changing Role of the Museum as a Canadian Social Institution', *Museum and Society*, 3: 1 (2005) 5–17; H. Goodall, 'Museum Reviews: The Historical Museums of Ottawa; Canadian Museum of Civilization', *The Public Historian*, 24: 1 (2002) 55–64; J. M. Gore, 'Representations of History and Nation in Museums in Australia and Aotearoa New Zealand: The National Museum of Australia and the Museum of New Zealand Te Papa Tongarewa', (unpublished PhD dissertation: University of Melbourne, 2002); K. Windschuttle, 'How Not to Run a Museum: People's History at the Postmodern Museum', *Quadrant*, 45: 9 (2001); G. Davison, 'Museums and the Burden of National Identity', *Public History Review*, 10 (2003) 8–20; J. Philips, 'Our History, Our Selves: The Historian and National Identity', *New Zealand Journal of History*, 30: 2 (1996); S. Lubar and K. M. Kendrick, *Legacies: Collecting America's History at the Smithsonian* (Washington, DC: Smithsonian Institution Press, 2001); L. Young, 'Federation Flagship', *Meanjin*, 60: 4 (2001) 149–59.

2 Commonwealth of Australia, *Review of the National Museum of Australia, its Exhibitions and Public Programs. A Report to the Council of the National Museum of Australia* (Canberra: Commonwealth of Australia, 2003). See also G. Hansen, 'White Hot History: The Review of the National Museum of Australia', *Public History Review*, 11 (2004) 39–50 and two reviews of the National Museum of Australia: I. McShane, 'The Acton Funhouse?' and P. Ashton, 'A Trojan Horse?', both in *Public History Review*, 9 (2001) 122–5, 126–8.

3 D. Dean and P. E. Rider, 'Museums, Nation and Political History in the Australian National Museum and the Canadian Museum of Civilization', *Museum and Society*, 3: 1 (2005) 35–50.

4 For example, see J. B. Gardner, 'Contested Terrain: History, Museums and the Public', *The Public Historian*, 26: 4 (2004) 11–21; T. W. Luke, *Museum*

Politics: Power Plays at the Exhibition (Minneapolis: Minnesota University Press, 2002); S. S. Weil, 'The Proper Business of the Museum: Ideas or Things?', *Muse*, 7: 1 (1989) 28–38; D. J. McIntyre and K. Werner, *National Museums Negotiating Histories: Conference Proceedings* (Canberra: National Museum of Australia, 2001); S. Macintyre and A. Clark, *The History Wars* (Melbourne: Melbourne University Press, 2003); A. Witcomb, 'Editor's Introduction: New Museum Developments and the Culture Wars', *Open Museum Journal*, 6 (2003) http://archive.amol. org.au/omj/volume6/volume6_ index.asp (accessed 5 March 2005); A. Witcomb, 'Beyond the Politics of Representation: Towards a New Approach for Engaging with the Past in Museums' and G. Davison, 'Interpreting the Nation: Which Stories, Whose Voice?', Museums Australia National Conference, Sydney (2005) http:// www.museumsaustralia.org.au/site/page413.php (accessed 5 March 2005).

5 I was significantly involved with its conceptual development and subsequently the physical expression of the National Museum of Australia between 1985 and March 2001, when the museum opened to the public.

6 *Museums in Australia 1975: Report of the Committee of Inquiry on Museums and National Collections* (Canberra: Australian Government Publishing Service, 1975), sections 12.2, 12.16.

7 F. Kaplan (ed.), *Museums and the Making of 'Ourselves': The Role of Objects in National Identity* (London: Leicester University Press, 1994), p. 5.

8 D. Carr, 'The Need For the Museum', *Museum News*, March/April (1999) 11–21.

9 Smithsonian Institution, Blue Ribbon Commission report, http://american-history.si.edu/reports/brc/1a.htm

10 M. Simpson, *Making Representations: Museums in the Post-Colonial Era* (London and New York: Routledge, 1996), pp. 48–9.

11 R. Archibald, 'Narrative for a New Century', *Museum News*, November–December (1998).

12 Simpson, *Making Representations*, p. 261.

13 K. Windschuttle, 'How Not to Run a Museum', 16.

14 For a critique of this process, see G. Davison, 'A Historian in the Museum: The Ethics of Public History', in S. Macintyre (ed.) *The Historian's Conscience: Australian Historians on the Ethics of History*, (Melbourne: Melbourne University Press, 2004), pp. 49–63.

15 'War of Extermination: Crimes of the Wehrmacht 1941–1944', mounted by the Hamburg Institute for Social Research, 1995.

16 'The West as America: Reinterpreting Images of the Frontier, 1820–1920' National Museum of American Art, 1991.

17 For a discussion on the Migration Museum in Adelaide, see V. Szekeres, 'A Place for All of Us', *Public History Review*, 4 (1995) 59–64.

18 See Museum of Sydney, *Sites: Nailing the Debate: Archaeology and Interpretation in Museums* (Sydney: Historic Houses Trust of New South Wales, 1996).

19 See http://www.museum.vic.gov.au/about/.

20 A phrase first used by US museum consultant Elaine Heumann Gurian.

21 G. Durbin (ed.), *Developing Museum Exhibitions for Lifelong Learning* (London: Stationery Office Books, 1996), p. 4.

8

'Monument Mania'? Public Space and the Black and Asian Presence in the London Landscape

John Siblon

> What cheek! Mandella [sic] statue in Trafalgar Square. Who next? Hitler![1]

Monument mania?

Statues and monuments are not just a ghostly presence from the past in our public spaces. They have different meanings and significance in the present for different people. The prospect of the addition of a full-size bronze statue of Nelson Mandela to London's statuary landscape[2] and the temporary installation on the vacant fourth plinth of 'Alison Lapper pregnant' in Trafalgar Square proved too much for the graffiti writer or journalists working on the evening paper who contended that London was passing through a phase of politically correct 'Monument Mania'.[3] The primary intention of this chapter is to investigate the role today of London's statuary and monuments through the critical gaze of a public historian. In the heart of London, official imperial histories underwritten by the state have increasingly come to compete with the remembered pasts of minority communities. I argue that complex monuments and memorials that are focal sites of remembrance can become spaces in which entangled personal and national histories are contested. Such activity indicates a desire for a participatory historical culture.

The heart of London

If you are visiting London even for just a few hours but wish to take a whistle stop tour of the capital's establishment past and present you could do no worse than begin your tour in Trafalgar Square, both a

political and cultural centre of London and its symbolic heart.[4] From
there you might choose to walk down either the Mall to Buckingham
Palace or stroll along Whitehall to Parliament Square and the Houses
of Parliament. You could instead turn eastwards down the Strand along
Fleet Street and end your walk at St Paul's Cathedral. Along the route,
the abundance of public monuments might offer the viewer a kind of
history lesson. The monuments and statuary appear like bookmarks
in the development of Britain's national heritage and the ubiquitous
blue plaques add to the notion of visiting a space once inhabited by
the 'great and the good'. They are intended to be sites of memory, the
memorial heritage of a particular community.[5] They also serve as public
art and are free to be imagined and interpreted by tourist and resident
alike.

It is precisely at this junction between art, memory and landscape
that the tourist in me departs and the critical public historian takes
over. The personal question I invariably ask myself is: 'Where are the
monuments and statues to non-white people like me'? It is a response
that I have found hard to shake over the years. On the one hand, I feel
myself organically connected to a space and place called 'London', the
place of my birth, by familiarity, nationality and identity. On the other
hand, the symbols and icons of national identity on display in the symbolic centre of the capital appear remote and exclusive to me. I find it
hard to imagine that I have anything in common with the assortment
of royalty, aristocrats, military, imperialists and slave traders ever present
in London's landscape. However, I haven't always viewed its statuary in
this way.

The pilgrimage

I am the London-born son of immigrant parents who were enticed
away from Britain's former colony of British Guiana to London in 1961
with the prospect of work and a better life in the United Kingdom. As a
child, I always enjoyed our family trips to the centre of London.
Looking back through our family photo album, the most prominent
pictures are the ones of our family in the symbolic centre of London
posing outside of some of the capital's most famous historical landmarks. For many years I read these photos solely as our family as 'internal tourists' to the capital but recently I have come to look upon these
photos also as 'story containers'.[6] They acted as mnemonic devices to
retell a story to our family. But they also sent a message back to the
now independent Guyana to let relatives and friends know that my

Figure 8.1 The Siblon family (mother taking photo) outside Buckingham Palace, 1968. I am the young boy on the right
(Siblon collection)

mother and father had 'made it', not only materially but also in terms of arrival and settlement in Britain.

There are two photos in the album that stand out: one of our family posing in front of the Houses of Parliament, and another with my father parking his car as close as possible to Buckingham Palace in the Mall with the Queen Victoria Memorial behind us. Felix Driver and David Gilbert refer to memorials such as this as being part of 'pilgrimages of empire'.[7] My parents had indeed come a long way from the poverty of Georgetown, capital of Guyana, to make a pilgrimage to the imperial centre and its memorials. In the photos, at least, my parents are no longer outsiders looking in but insiders with a direct line, as British citizens, to the heritage on display; their British identity confirmed. The photos were to ensure that the moment itself was commemorated for posterity.

Time, though, has changed my perception of, amongst other things, the symbols of identity we posed before that day with such optimism. The years that followed were ones where my everyday experience was of exclusion because of my dark skin. The message being constantly reinforced was that Britishness equalled whiteness. A casual survey of London's statues and monuments of people, which revealed them to be exclusively white, confirmed this message. The result was that I often felt 'foreign' in the place that was supposed to be 'home'.[8] For a few years, the 'London' I had mentally constructed[9] in my earlier years was replaced by another 'London' of racial exclusion. Time, again, has made me reflect once more on the place I inhabit.

Such personal but social moments and memories have mostly gone unrecorded throughout history. There is also a sense that the pasts of public spaces and the events commemorated in them are more important than the people who visit them and try to find meaning in them. The stories and experiences of ordinary people have been displaced by the stories of stone or marble figures of 'great men'. In *Theatres of Memory* Raphael Samuel argued that a reason for this process was the 'unspoken assumption that knowledge filters downwards.'[10] History, put in this way, is something that we learn from other people (or statues) but not for ourselves; our thoughts and memories are not registered. Public history practice disputes this; in fact it encourages 'unofficial learning'[11] and emphasises that personal histories can intertwine with other histories, landscapes and memories. 'History', as Hilda Kean, Paul Martin and Sally Morgan have observed, 'becomes then not part of a past which has gone but part of a living present constantly being recreated, contested and challenged.[12] Approaching the past in this way black and Asian Britons may draw contradictory feelings and meaning from public spaces such as Trafalgar Square. These spaces were designed specifically to display imperial grandeur, military and racial superiority and exclude representations of, amongst others, the black and Asian presence in British history. They are, however, also important sites in which to investigate the past in the present.

The black and Asian presence[13]

There has been a black and Asian presence in Britain for 2,000 years and a settled presence for at least 500 years. London's population at the end of the eighteenth century was estimated at 700,000 and it is estimated that around 15,000 of these were 'black'.[14] The black population of this period inhabited a space described by Paul Gilroy as the 'black Atlantic'.[15] The period of settlement in the 'black Atlantic' corresponds with the rise of Britain as a maritime power, the development of the East India Company, conquest and settlement in North America and the Caribbean and the development of the transatlantic slave trade. In the nineteenth century with the onset of informal and formal imperialism around the globe, the black and Asian population of Britain's empire would rise to 400 million, many of whom travelled to, worked for and lived in the administrative and symbolic centre of the empire: London. However, this presence remained largely unacknowledged in history until the late 1960s.[16] Before then, the history of Britain taught in schools and printed in history books was a very white one indeed. Yet, in the capital city today, there is not a single public statue or monument to this enduring black and Asian presence in British history.

An African in Trafalgar Square

However, for those who are prepared to look for this presence in the landscape, there are traces. In the centre of Trafalgar Square, the 'national Valhalla'[17] of empire and militarism, stands the symbol of British maritime and imperial superiority: Nelson's column erected in 1843. At the foot of the column there are four bronze bas-reliefs that were added between 1849 and 1854. One of them, the 'Death of Nelson', was created by the sculptor, John Edward Carew. The relief was sculpted figuratively to represent death and conquest in the name of empire.[18] On the left of the scene is a black sailor holding a musket. He is looking towards the sharpshooter who has shot Nelson and signifies his rank as a marine in the navy. At the end of the eighteenth century, it is estimated that 25 per cent of the crew of British ships in the Atlantic were black.[19]

The image of the black sailor is replicated in another important centre of power: the Houses of Parliament. Inside the Royal Gallery of the House, there are two large frescoes painted by the artist Daniel Maclise between 1859 and 1865. One of the frescoes is *The Death of Nelson* at the Battle of Trafalgar and contains two images of black sailors. One is tending to the wounded and the other is pointing out a target to a sharpshooter.[20] Were they included as part of a naturalistic rendering of the battle scene? Was the image meant to convey a message about the important role of African crew in the battle? Or was it following eighteenth-century conventions of using the figure of a black servant as emblematic of loyalty and servitude or what is part of the nineteenth-century fashion for using Africans in sculpture?[21] Neither Carew's frieze or Maclise's fresco was primarily constructed to depict a black presence but a visual representation of the black and Asian presence in British history has nevertheless been registered in the symbolic heart of London. Its very existence allows space for a different interpretation of the nation's history to surface; one that has Africans, possibly enslaved, possibly free, almost certainly impressed, fighting to defend Britain and its empire from a foreign threat in a British ship in Mediterranean waters. This is at odds with the national story that omits those with a darker skin.[22]

Figure 8.2   A black sailor at the Battle of Trafalgar. (The black sailor is on the far left of the frieze).
(Photograph: John Siblon)

A monument like the Nelson Monument was designed to celebrate virtues such as 'British national greatness'.[23] Nelson's achievement in 'saving' the British Empire from the French challenge is commonly known and still celebrated but the lives of the multinational crew such as that of the African sailor and the context of the battle are less so. As John Oldfield writes, 'who or what a community chooses to commemorate is highly revealing ... monuments ... help to create national "histories", as well as national myths.'[24] This selective commemoration of a nation's high points and its memorable achievements serve to produce a 'national story'[25] crucial in constructing a nation's identity. The monuments and statuary of London's public spaces 'remember' a very white story whilst a more inclusive one is 'forgotten'. At the very least, the black sailor allows some contestation of this story.

White slave traders – white abolitionists

One reason for this selective amnesia and convenient colour blindness could be that the horror of the transatlantic slave trade and Britain's inglorious involvement in the acquisition of a vast global overseas empire has made any link to issues of 'race' in British history taboo and an embarrassment in our apparently post-colonial times.[26] Hence there is the reluctance to revisit Britain's massive involvement in enslavement and imperial expansion, the profits of which underpinned Britain's economy and society,[27] or to openly discuss the legacy of the slave trade, such as crude racism and notions of white superiority, that pervade not just Britain and Europe but their colonies and former colonies. Despite such elision, it is not too difficult to find visual traces of London's crucial involvement in the slave-trading past in the city's landscape and public spaces.[28]

Indeed, there are monuments in the capital to 'great men' directly connected to the slave trade and slavery. A statue of one of the most notable individuals involved in the slave trade, William Beckford (1709–70), Britain's first millionaire and twice Lord Mayor of London, stands in the Guildhall, the former centre of power in the city of London. With over 1,000 enslaved Africans on his Jamaican plantations, his ownership and management of slave plantations was widely acknowledged. In 1769 *The Public Advertiser* noted: 'To see a slave he could not bear, unless it were his own'.[29] Such was the integration of the slave trade into everyday British public life that when Beckford died a statue of him was quickly raised by public subscription. The monument commemorates, 'a typically impetuous and bellicose

Beckfordian incident' when 'he reduced the young King George to silence by one of his ferocious frowns'[30] whilst he delivered a remonstrance on the restriction of freedom. His defence of political freedom and commerce at home is revealed on the monument but the denial of

Figure 8.3 Statue of William Beckford in the Guildhall
(Photograph John Siblon)

freedom for enslaved Africans on his plantations is not. Madge Dresser argues that the legacies of men like Beckford are presented in ways which render the connection between their philanthropy and their slavery interests invisible and so the monument remains today silent over how Beckford was able to achieve his wealth and prominence in the first instance and an example of how memory can be an active, shaping force in 'contriving to forget'[31] as much as it remembers.

There has been a suggestion that Britain's involvement in the slave trade and its effect on the transatlantic economy and society has been obscured by a historical focus on the abolition movement. Marcus Wood argues that after 'its formal and legal abolition in 1807 the slave trade fairly rapidly developed into a site for national celebration'.[32] Involvement in the abolition movement had as much to do with purifying Britain from the taint of slavery as any great humanitarian concern for the slaves themselves,[33] to the extent that by the middle of the 1820s the memory of the slave trade had become the memory of abolition.[34]

This celebration of the abolition of the slave trade, as well as London's crucial involvement in the abolition movement, is evident in the London landscape. An example of this is the Buxton Memorial Drinking Fountain erected in 1865 with the support of the Metropolitan Drinking Fountain Association and originally located in Great George Street on the corner of Parliament Square. It was designed to commemorate both the activity of Sir Thomas Foxwell Buxton MP, the leader of the Anti-Slavery Society, and also the abolition of American slavery.[35] When the square was being redeveloped in 1949 there was a fear that the monument might be discarded. In the House of Lords, Viscount Simon protested that this was exactly the sort of memorial that should be found at the 'hub of the empire'.[36] An agreement was reached to site it in Victoria Tower Gardens, a small green next to the Houses of Parliament, where it remains today. A memorial plaque commemorating the 150th anniversary of the Anti-Slavery Society was added in 1989 and it has recently been spruced up to coincide with the 200th anniversary of the abolition of the slave trade.

This focus on equating the moral achievements of the abolitionists with the British nation and therefore, our 'national story', has been termed 'the culture of abolitionism'.[37] This culture is evident in another site of memory, Westminster Abbey, where there is an abundance of memorials to leading figures involved in the abolition of the slave trade and slavery itself. Thomas Clarkson is the most recent addition; Granville Sharp and William Wilberforce are all commemorated in the abbey. There are also memorials to the abolitionists Zachary

Figure 8.4 The spruced up Buxton Memorial Fountain in Victoria Tower Gardens
(Photograph: John Siblon)

Macaulay, Sir Thomas Foxwell Buxton and Charles James Fox.[38] There are also many blue plaques across London, as well as memorials to Wilberforce and the abolitionist group of evangelical Anglicans, the

Clapham Sect. Missing from these spaces are the black abolitionists who were central to the campaign – and residents of London – at the birth of the anti-slave trade movement.

Where are the black abolitionists?

The visual public memory of a settled black presence in British history before the twentieth century is virtually non-existent. Sam Walker argues that black people in Britain and Europe are invisible in the historic landscape, 'not because of their absence, but because of a myth that required their absence'.[39] However, visual representations of Africans can be seen in national sites of memory such as Westminster Abbey but only to show them giving thanks to the white abolitionists. The monument to Charles James Fox unveiled in the abbey in 1822 has a life-size figure of an enslaved African kneeling in gratitude to Fox. Near to Fox's monument is a bust of Zachary Macaulay, erected in 1842. Below the bust is a medallion with a kneeling figure of an enslaved African with the motif of the emancipation movement inscribed: 'Am I not a man and a brother'. This token representation serves only to perpetuate another myth – that black people played no part in their own emancipation.

Like other aspects of the black and Asian presence in the life of the city, African involvement in the anti-slavery movement is excluded by the warped culture of abolition, which favours white campaigners. Indeed, when the British and Foreign Anti-Slavery Society commissioned the painter, Benjamin Haydon, to commemorate the World Anti-Slavery Convention in 1840 with a painting, he originally inserted the names of William Wilberforce, Granville Sharp and Toussaint L'Ouverture on the curtain in the background. He was reprimanded by the society and told to delete the names as they had nothing to do with the convention.[40] L'Ouverture's deletion in particular was partly dictated by the reluctance to concede any agency to slaves who played a part in their own emancipation. The inclusion in the painting of Henry Beckford, a Jamaican ex-slave, was meant to signify the success of the abolitionists rather than represent the resistance of the slaves themselves.[41]

The African abolitionists in Britain included Ignatius Sancho, Ottobah Cugoano, Olaudah Equiano, Robert Wedderburn and Mary Prince.[42] Of these only Olaudah Equiano and Ignatius Sancho have any recognition in London's landscape and then only recently, Cugoano, Sancho and Equiano were the first Africans to have books published in Britain. The books of the latter two were bestsellers. Importantly the books informed society of the experiences of Africans, enslaved and free. They provided a moral imperative for abolition and were used extensively by abolitionists.[43]

Yet, even as their work was being utilised, these Africans were being written out of the memory of the campaign.[44] More recently, they have been incorporated into the public memory of abolition and the history of the black and Asian presence in Britain through contemporary publications and exhibitions.[45] There is some information on Sancho on a small council noticeboard placed in Broadway, a stone's throw from Westminster Abbey. In Greenwich, where Sancho spent most of his life in service at the now demolished Montague House, an alliance of The Greenwich Historical Society, The Friends of Greenwich Park and members of the public used the 200th anniversary in 2007 of the abolition of the slave trade to persuade the Royal Parks, after some lobbying, to erect a stone tablet to Sancho on the remaining wall of the house.[46] Similarly, in 2000, Westminster Council erected a local council (green) plaque on the site of 73 Riding House Street, where Equiano formerly lived. These memorials belatedly register the black presence in British history but, unlike their abolitionist peers, they remain excluded from national sites of memory such as Westminster Abbey. That such memorials have even been considered is mostly down to the lobbying of groups such as the Equiano Society and the Black and Asian Studies Association, both formed in the 1990s to publicise the life and works of Africans and Asians in British history in an attempt to redefine the contemporary identity of multicultural Britain.[47]

Asians in Britain

Whilst there has been a recent focus on the presence of the African diaspora in Britain, the settled presence of Asians in the capital from the seventeenth century onwards should also be recognised. The Asian presence was mostly linked to the activities of the East India Company, the world's first transnational corporation, which operated out of the city of London for over 250 years. There are some visual traces of the company's influence around the city. East India Dock now exists in name only but East India Dock Road and Commercial Road, both purpose built to bring East India goods into the company's warehouses at Cutler's Wharf in the city, still survive. There is a plaque on the site of the company's former warehouses, now called Cutler's Gardens, at the back of the Swiss Re building in the city, a coat of arms painted on the roof of the former East India Company Chapel, St Matthias Church in Poplar, and a mural by Spiridione Roma, 'The East offering its riches to Britannia', commissioned for the East India Company and located in the entrance of the Foreign and Commonwealth Office. (Unfortunately, this mural is only open to viewing by the public on the annual Open House weekend.)

There are, however, statues linked to the activities of the East India Company in the symbolic centre of London. In Trafalgar Square, the statue of Sir Henry Havelock by the sculptor William Behnes and another of General Sir Charles Napier by George Cannon Adams remind the public of their service in the name of empire in Burma, Afghanistan and India. Outside the Foreign Office is a statue of Robert Clive, first Baron Clive of Plassey. His victory over the Nawab of Bengal at Plassey in 1757 reversed the trend of bullion flowing eastwards and ushered in the period of the 'unrequited trade' between Britain and the Asian sub-continent.[48] Sculpted by John Tweed, it stands as another example of the period of 'self-confident hero worship' before the First World War.[49]

The Gurkha regiments, formed by the East India Company in 1815, have been recently commemorated in 1997 by a seven-foot bronze statue by sculptor Philip Jackson. Its location off Whitehall, the site reserved for military memorials, serves to remind people of the colonial troops who loyally served the empire for nearly 200 years. Despite this loyal service, in 2006, some of these same Gurkhas could be found marching past the monument, asking for the same pension received by other British soldiers.[50] There is a further reference to the service of Asian servicemen and women at Memorial Gates military memorial in Hyde Park unveiled in 2002, which commends the whole continent for its service in both World Wars.[51] But loyalty to the empire has not been the only theme of the few memorials relating to the Indian subcontinent. Outside Finsbury Town Hall in Islington is a plaque to Dadabhai Naoroji, Britain's first Asian Member of Parliament in 1892 and a staunch opponent of British rule. As well, the Gandhi statue, sculpted by Fredda Brilliant, unveiled in the 'Peace' space of Tavistock Square in Bloomsbury in 1966, also reminds us of the subcontinent's resistance to British rule. And while Trafalgar Square may be a symbol of empire, is has also been the site of many protests against British rule in India.[52]

A Victorian heroine

Loyalty in the service of Britain or empire, however, is no guarantee of a memorial. There is currently no memorial to Mary Seacole

(1805–81), the Jamaican nurse who set up a hospital on the Crimean peninsula during the Crimean War. She was recently voted the 'greatest black Briton' in a poll.[53] Public recognition of Seacole was granted to her in her lifetime but she was subsequently forgotten. Recovery work by a new generation of scholars and activists has re-established her place in the public memory of the Crimean War. A blue plaque erected by the Greater London Council in 1986 in George Street where Mary lived was removed in a dispute and only replaced in 2005 by a Westminster Council green plaque. A campaign is currently running to have a blue plaque erected to her in Soho Square and a memorial statue fund was launched in 2003.[54] A portrait of Seacole by Albert Charles Challen, painted in 1869 and accidentally discovered in 2005, has been lent indefinitely to the National Portrait Gallery by its owner, Helen Rappaport.[55]

Monument mania revisited

A public visual memory of Britain's expansionist and imperial past occupies a constant presence across the land, in both spatial and temporal terms.[56] It is possible, however, to read the landscape of London's sites of memory both as glorification of imperial values and as moments of resistance to these same values. London can be viewed as an embodiment of the profits of the slave trade or the site where slavery was undermined. What is clear is that many see physical markers as important in this battle for memory in London's 'contested public spaces'.[57] Memorial 2007, for example, believes a memorial will cut across the collective amnesia on the subject of the slave trade.[58] The organisers – individuals linked to the Black and Asian Studies Association who are sponsored by the Museum in Docklands – are attempting to raise £1.25 million to erect a permanent memorial, amongst the plethora of memorials, in the Rose Garden of Hyde Park to 'honour and acknowledge the millions of enslaved Africans and their descendents'.[59] They hope that the publicity surrounding the 200th anniversary of the abolition of the slave trade will raise awareness of the fact that there is no monument in London's public space directly connected to the transatlantic slave trade.

Given the selective nature of history and public memory, it is hardly surprising that some people feel disenfranchised from this process of history-making and excluded from its national symbols of identity. Katharine Hodgkin and Susannah Radstone have written:

> [T]he establishment of memorial sites, places where the past is not only preserved as fetish but also transmitted as signification, is inevitably a focus for struggle over meaning: whose monument is permitted and what meanings may it convey? And since these sites are also publicly established or at least sanctioned, they are inescapably implicated in the construction of narratives – or perhaps maps – of national identity.[60]

Similarly, in his analysis of how black Britons feel about heritage and identity, Stuart Hall has suggested that 'National heritage is a powerful source of meaning; those who can't see themselves reflected in the mirror are therefore excluded.'[61] London can only claim to be a truly representative home to its multicultural inhabitants if it sanctions in its public spaces a 'monument mania' of a broader kind.

Notes

1   Graffiti in the male public toilets of the Tate Britain, 2007.
2   Greater London Authority, 'Parliament Square to get Statue of Nelson Mandela', *The Londoner*, June 2007, p. 5; A statue to Nelson Mandela was duly sited in Parliament Square on 29 August 2007. At the ceremony, Mandela joked: 'we hoped that one day a statue of a black person would be erected here'.
3   R. Moore, 'Stop this Monument Mania', *Evening Standard*, 27 September 2005.
4   F. Driver and D. Gilbert, 'Imperial Cities: Overlapping Territories, Intertwined Histories', in F. Driver and D. Gilbert (eds) *Imperial Cities: Landscape, Display and Identity* (Manchester and New York: Manchester University Press, 1999), pp. 1–3.
5   P. Nora, 'Between Memory and History: Les Lieux de Mémoire', in G. Fabre and R. O'Meally (eds) *History and Memory in African American Culture* (Oxford: Oxford University Press, 1994), pp. 284–300.
6   S. J. Morgan, 'My Father's Photographs: The Visual as Public History', in H. Kean, P. Martin and S. J. Morgan (eds) *Seeing History: Public History in Britain Now* (London: Francis Boutle, 2000), pp. 22–3.
7   Driver and Gilbert, *Imperial Cities*, p. 3.
8   J. Siblon, 'A Mistaken Case of Identity', *History Workshop Journal*, 52 (2001) 253–60.
9   P. K. Gilbert (ed.) *Imagined Londons* (Albany: State University of New York Press, 2002), p. 2.
10 R. Samuel, *Theatres of Memory: Past and Present in Contemporary Culture*, vol 1 (London: Verso, 1994), p. 4.
11 *ibid*, p. 7.
12 Kean *et al*, *Seeing History*, p. 15.

13 This definition is inadequate as 'black' is open to wide interpretation and 'Asian' denotes someone from a vast geographical area. However, I am using it only to avoid the problematic usage of the definition 'black' only. When I was young, I was called 'black', now I am called 'Asian' although, strictly speaking, I am neither.

14 See N. Myers, *Reconstructing the Black Past: Blacks in Britain 1780–1830* (London: Frank Cass, 1996), pp. 7–8.

15 P. Gilroy, *The Black Atlantic: Modernity and Double Consciousness* (London: Verso, 1993), p. 15.

16 A. Tyrrell and J. Walvin, 'Whose History Is It? Memorialising Britain's Involvement in Slavery', in P. A. Pickering and A. Tyrrell with M. T. Davis, N. Mansfield and J. Walvin, *Contested Sites: Commemoration, Memorial and Popular Politics in Nineteenth-century Britain* (Aldershot: Ashgate, 2004), p. 162.

17 R. Mace, *Trafalgar Square: Emblem of Empire*, 2nd edn (London: Lawrence and Wishart Ltd, 2005), p. 12.

18 Mace, *Trafalgar Square*, pp. 103–4.

19 Gilroy, *The Black Atlantic*, p. 13.

20 C. Spence, 'Seeing Some Black in the Union Jack', *History Today*, 52: 10 (2002) 30–7.

21 J. Marsh, 'The Black Presence in British Art 1800–1900', in J. Marsh (ed.) *Black Victorians: Black People in British Art 1800–1900* (Aldershot: Lund Humphries, 2005), p. 18.

22 G. Courtauld, *The Pocket Book of Patriotism* (London: Halstead Books Ltd, 2004).

23 Mace, *Trafalgar Square*, p. 11.

24 J. R. Oldfield, *'Chords of Freedom': Commemoration, Ritual and British Transatlantic Slavery* (Manchester: Manchester University Press, 2007), p. 56.

25 S. Hall, quoted in T. Hunt, 'Whose History Is It Anyway?', *History Today*, (October 2006) 28–30.

26 Y. Alibhai-Brown, *Who Do We Think We Are? Imagining the New Britain* (London: Penguin Books, 2001), pp. 184–5.

27 R. Drayton, 'The Wealth of the West was Built on Africa's Exploitation', *The Guardian*, 20 August 2005.

28 http://www.nationalarchives.gov.uk/pathways/blackhistory/about.htm

29 *Public Advertiser*, 17 November 1769 as quoted in P. Ward-Jackson, *Public Sculpture of The City Of London, Volume VII, Public Sculpture of Britain series* (Liverpool: Liverpool University Press, 2003), p. 163.

30 D. Knight, *Gentlemen of Fortune: The Men who Made their Fortunes in Britain's Slave Colonies* (London: Frederick Muller Limited, 1978), p. 52; M. Dresser, 'Set in Stone? Statues and Slavery in London', *History Workshop Journal*, 64 (2007) 174.

31 Samuel, *Theatres of Memory*, p x; M Dresser, 'Set in Stone? Statues and Slavery in London', *History Workshop Journal*, 64 (2007) 175–86.

32 M. Wood, *Blind Memory: Visual Representations of Slavery in England and America 1780–1865* (Manchester: Manchester University Press, 2000), p. 7.

33 T. Hunt, 'Easy on the Euphoria', *The Guardian*, 25 March 2006.

34 Wood, *Blind Memory*, p. 8.

35 Oldfield, *'Chords of Freedom'*, p. 59.

36 *ibid*, p. 59.
37 *ibid*, p. 57.
38 http://www.westminster-abbey.org/library/burial.
39 S. Walker, 'Black Cultural Museums in Britain: What Questions do they Answer?', in E. Hooper-Greenhill, *Cultural Diversity: Developing Museum Audiences in Britain* (London: Leicester University Press, 1997), p. 36.
40 Tyrrell and Walvin, 'Whose history is it?', p. 156.
41 *ibid*, p. 158.
42 See P. Edwards and D. Dabydeen (eds) *Black Writers in Britain 1760–1890: An Anthology* (Edinburgh: Edinburgh University Press, 1991).
43 I. Sancho, *Letters Of The Late Ignatius Sancho, An African*, first published 1782 (London: Penguin Books Reprint, 1998); O. Equiano, *The Interesting Narrative and Other Writings*, first published 1772 (London: Penguin Books Reprint, 1995); O. Cugoano, *Thoughts and Sentiments on the Evil and Wicked Traffic of the Slavery and Commerce of the Human Species, etc.'*, first published London, 1787 (New York: Penguin Classics, 1999).
44 M. Sherwood, *After Abolition: Britain and the Slave Trade since 1807* (London: I. B. Tauris & Co. Ltd, 2007), p. 10.
45 The National Portrait Gallery held a small exhibition on Sancho in 1997 called *Ignatius Sancho: An African Man of Letters* and Birmingham Museum and Art Gallery held a major exhibition on Equiano between September 2007 and January 2008 called *The Equiano Exhibition*.
46 http://www.friendsofgreenwichpark.org.uk.
47 http://www.blackandasianstudies.org.uk; http://www.brycchancarey.com/equiano.
48 N. Robins, *Loot: In Search of the East India Company*, http://www.open-democracy.net/, accessed 22 January 2003; N. Robins, *The Corporation that Changed the World: How the East India Company Shaped the Modern Multinational* (Ann Arbor MI: Pluto Press, 2006).
49 The statue was erected in 1912 and moved to its current location, the former India Office, in 1916. J. Blackwood, *London's Immortals: The Complete Outdoor Commemorative Statues* (London: Savoy Press, 1989), p. 14.
50 'Gurkhas March on No.10', *Metro*, 15 December 2006.
51 http://www.mgtrust.org/.
52 J. Schneer, 'Anti Imperial London: The Pan-African Conference of 1900', in Driver and Gilbert, *Imperial Cities*, pp. 254–67.
53 http://www.100greatblackbritons.com.
54 http://www.maryseacole.com.
55 C. Higgins, 'Historic Portrait of Crimean War Nurse Unveiled', *Guardian*, 11 January 2005; http://www.npg.org.uk/live/prelseacole.asp.
56 D. Massey, 'Places and Their Pasts', *History Workshop Journal*, 39 (1995) 186.
57 D. Walkowitz and L. M. Knauer (eds) *Memory and the Impact of Political Transformation in Public Space* (Durham: Duke University Press, 2004), p. 2.
58 A. Rice, *Radical Narratives of the Black Atlantic* (London and New York: Continuum, 2003), p. 213.
59 http://www.Memorial2007.org.uk.
60 K. Hodgkin and S. Radstone, *Contested Pasts: the Politics of Memory* (London: Routledge, 2003), p. 14.
61 Hall, 'Whose History Is It Anyway?', 28–30.

9
Museum Theatre: Children's Reading of 'First Person Interpretation' in Museums

Vasiliki Tzibazi

> a commitment to the idea of public history is a commitment to a concern with audience and an awareness of the relationship between audience, historical practice and institutional context.[1]

Introduction

Museums are one of the many sites in which people engage with history. Institutionally, they are as diverse as are their audiences, and they employ a range of historical practices. One of these is museum theatre, which has been used increasingly to present history to children to allow them to understand not just content but a subject's concepts, methods and structures. This constructivist model has arisen in the context of a questioning of the traditional historical canon. Museum theatre, however, has not been without its critics.

Robert Hewison, in his polemical work *The Heritage Industry*, described the nostalgic turn to heritage as a 'distortion of the past' and a 'stifling of the culture of the present'.[2] His concerns focused on the use of heritage as a consumable product that offered an unreal view of the past and reinforced a selective national identity. He posed questions about the kind of past that the tourist industry and agencies such the English Heritage and the National Trust decided to preserve and promote in the name of education. He viewed such preservations of the past as 'simulacra', which, with the use of actors in costume and guided tours, invited the pupils to take a step back into the past without exploring the complexity of the historical processes.[3] Similar views on the use of living history in museums and heritage sites were expressed by others.[4] Notable amongst these voices was Peter Fowler, who pointed out that although living history programmes can be based on historical research, the feelings that these programmes evoke 'cannot be "historical"'.[5] According to this view it would be misguided to think that the programmes could allow the participants to feel what it was like to be a Tudor or a Roman and hence to experience how life was in the past: 'such created pasts may be convincing ... but they can never be realistic, genuine recreations of what once was, for the simple reason that *we* are different'.[6]

Those, like Hewison, who privilege traditional historical practices, argue that these alone can produce 'authentic' history. Heritage, in this view, is mere entertainment, and 'living history' in museums only trivialises the past. Others have put forward contrary views. Roy Rosenzweig and David Thelen's major American study *The Presence of the Past* and its Australian counterpart, *Australians and the Past* by Paul Ashton and Paula Hamilton, have reinforced claims that history operates in a variety of ways in the culture.[7] Raphael Samuel viewed the various forms of 'living history' as democratic scholarship that transformed museums from 'being temples for the worship of the past' to widely accessible places that promoted engagement with history.[8] For Samuel, 'history is not the prerogative of the historian ... it is rather a social form of knowledge'.[9] It was within this conceptual framework that Samuel 'saw "living history"' as one vital part of the 'ensemble of activities and practices in which ... a dialectic of past-present relations is rehearsed.'[10] In this process participants do not simply consume pre-packaged views of the past. As in any reading, they exercise historical reflection and thinking. Such an approach would entail a pedagogy that would – through the narratives' framing devices such as a contrast between present and past – facilitate the construction of historical understanding.[11]

Such an approach is also vital to sustainable museum practices. As James Gardner of the Smithsonian Institution's National Museum of American History has observed, the 'public needs to understand how museums have shifted from [a] preoccupation with the authenticity of artefacts to issues of significance and meaning'.[12] This entails 'sharing what we do as historians and curators', making history about people, not just ideas, events or things and embracing diversity.[13]

What is 'museum theatre'?

Museums that have a prominent focus on education and communication have adopted a variety of live interpretation methods including a range of theatrical styles as a means of finding new ways to respond to their visitor's needs for meaningful experiences.[14] Re-enactments, first/third person interpretation events and role-play are among the most common theatrical forms of interpretation in museums, galleries and heritage sites, and are commonly defined as forms of 'museum theatre'. However, 'museum theatre' should be understood as a term that encompasses various forms of theatre in museums rather than as a concept defined in fixed terms. The term was formally introduced with the establishment of the International Museum Theatre Alliance (IMTAL) in 1990 and was used instead of terms such as 'interpretive theatre', 'living history' and 'theatre in museums' which up until that time had all been used in the relevant literature. Currently, the term is mainly used by IMTAL members when referring to interpretation where performers assume the role of characters to communicate ideas, facts and concepts via fictional activity.[15] First person interpretation programmes were one of the first forms that were classified as museum theatre, while in a few cases the two terms are used interchangeably. In particular, in first person interpretation programmes the interpreters, by adopting the role of a historically documented or a fictional character, act as if they live in a different historical time and either acknowledge that the visitors are in the present or act as though the visitors have moved to the characters' time. Key elements of the form are its partially improvisational and interactive nature as the actors, without breaking out of role, might encourage the visitors' participation.[16]

This chapter illustrates how the participants – and in particular school children – make sense of the first person interpretation programmes' content and format. The term content denotes the event's interpretive points integrated into the fictional context. The term format refers to the practices and the theatrical components employed for the construction of the event. The programmes are not considered autonomous entities in themselves but are products of agendas and relationships between the parties involved such as the museums' agenda and the schools' curriculum and agenda. Thus, the views, expectations and intentions of all participants in the construction of the event are taken into account to provide an insight into how the meaning emerges and consequently how the event is used as an interpretive medium of the past.

Every year 40,000 pupils in school groups visit the Museum of London, of which 60 per cent are at Key Stage Two.[17] The museum has an established tradition of providing live interpretation programmes since 1995–96 that aim to 'personalise' the galleries and to give visitors the feeling that they can relate to another person from a different historical period.[18] Two theatrical events at the Museum of London were selected for study as 'typical' first person interpretation events and also for their potential to provide a wider perspective on the use of theatre as a learning and interpretive tool in museum and heritage settings. Differences and commonalities between the two events were identified in order to highlight the children's interpretation of the event and the parameters that shape first person interpretation. Each case study is understood as a 'bounded system'[19] and is viewed in relation to two (Key Stage Two) school classes' participation.[20] The selection of the schools and the year groups (year four and five, 9–10 years of age) depended on issues of accessibility and practicality.

Description of the events

In Event A, the year four class met a female character called Martia Marina. The character is a Roman maidservant around 30 years of age who lives in AD 300. When she was about eight, her mother, who could not afford to keep her, sold her into slavery thinking that she might save her life by doing so. In her mid twenties, her master Rufus Martius Comitalis freed her. However, she chose to keep working for Rufus and his family. She is in love with a Roman soldier (who is a character in Event B). A maidservant in a nearby house, jealous of Martia Martina's good fortune, has put a curse on her by writing her name backwards on a piece of lead.

In Event B, the year five class meets Marcus Alpius Peregrinus. Marcus is a 41-year-old Roman army veteran who served for 25 years in the army. He is a citizen and was posted to many different places during his time in the army. When the class meets him it is AD 300, a year after he retired. He now lives at the home of his friend Rufus Marius Comitalis, whom he met when serving in London. Marcus intends to marry Martia Martina who works as a servant in Rufus' house.

The characters, although fictional, are drawn to be as historically accurate as possible through research conducted by the actor and the museum's curator. The intention is to develop characters that will project a well-defined personality, such that each character will be a 'real person having real feelings' with whom the children can identify. Allowing the personality to be expressed in the actor's performance, combined with interactive and humorous elements is intended to create memorable learning experiences. Both programmes, being educational, develop themes that to a certain extent are related to the setting and the relevant Qualification and Curriculum Authority schemes of the Key Stage Two national curriculum.

Before exploring the parameters that shape the children's reading of the first person interpretation events, I will describe briefly the development of 'museum theatre' and the debates around it to set the context for this research.

Tracing 'museum theatre'

The conceptual roots of using theatre in museums can be traced back to 1891 when the first experiment with living history took place at the Skansen Open Air Museum in Sweden. In order to engender a sense of cultural identity without being 'a dead museum', actors and artists were dressed up to represent customs and aspects of a traditional lifestyle.[21] This first use of people-based historical interpretation influenced the development of several exhibitions in North America at the end of the nineteenth century,[22] and the practice was used a few decades later by various open-air museums.[23] It is estimated that by the early 1980s more than 800 sites in the USA employed first-person interpretation.[24]

The initial use of the medium took the form of costumed interpreters who acted as people living in the past in a 'they were, they did' style of presentation and was mainly associated with representations of everyday life in the past.[25] As indoor use of museum theatre gradually expanded, it was criticised for portraying an idealised past that reinforced cultural identity and stereotypes.[26] In response to this criticism, institutions such as the National Museum of American History[27] and the Canadian Museum of Civilization developed scripted dialogues to address controversial issues such as the subjects of slavery and historically remote cultural attitudes, values and preconceptions. These initiatives provided the impetus for the development of various styles of museum theatre as a means for exploring the past and the subjective interpretation of history. At the beginning of the 1990s, 'museum theatre', scripted or within an interactive format – while remaining contested – focused on the intercourse with the visitor rather than on 'giving life' to static exhibits.[28]

The development of the medium in North America did not leave the British Isles unaffected. During the 1970s particular emphasis was placed on the use of the country's heritage as an educational resource for organised school groups.[29] National Trust sites demonstrated a real interest with the establishment of the Young National Trust theatre in

1976. During the 1980s the theatre toured various sites to perform pieces of theatre-in-education for primary school children the related to the sites' history.[30] With the English Heritage sites' interest in hosting re-enactment events, various societies and groups were also performing all over the country.[31] It was this enthusiasm for its educational functions that was associated with what was known in 1980s as the 'Heritage Industry debate' which centred around Wright's and Hewison's work.

By the end of the 1980s the first residential[32] and non residential 'museum theatre' companies were established in the UK.[33] These were orientated to the use of more interactive techniques and, in particular, first person interpretation. Their founders, who had a background in the theatre-in-education and drama-in-education movements and/or were trained in North American museums, employed and trained actors and educators who over the years developed projects in a wider range of museums.

However, the development of the medium cannot be traced in a linear path. For many years its use as an interpretive means was perceived as controversial by many museum professionals, whereas the diversity of professional backgrounds of 'museum theatre' practitioners posed difficulties in finding a common ground for discussion of its nature.[34] This scepticism and diversity was particularly reflected in the first conference organised in Liverpool in 1991 to examine issues surrounding 'museum theatre'. From the museum professionals' side, questions were posed about the actors' appropriateness as interpreters, the entertaining nature of the medium and its potential to trivialise history and distort the past.[35] Disputes amongst practitioners partially subsided towards the end of 1990s with the emergence of the 'museum theatre' professional and the establishment of associations[36] that advocated the medium's potential to reach a wide range of visitors and add depth to the museum experience.[37] However, tension regarding its validity as an educational medium was never resolved. Evaluation was perceived as the main path via which professionals could provide evidence about its efficiency as an interpretive tool.[38]

Methodology and aims

The research methodology was located under an interpretivist paradigm: it viewed the participants in the event as intentional actors that interpret their own and others' actions.[39] In particular, a number of issues were taken into account during the conduct of the research such as gaining the children's informed consent and issues of confidentiality and power.[40] This approach was consistent with the classification of children as 'research participants' who 'should be informed, involved and consulted about all activities that affect their lives'. In a similar way, we understood 'meaning-making' from a constructivist point of view: that is, as an active and constantly evolving construction that depends on one's previous expectations, understandings and experiences. The following discussion explores children's 'meaning-making' of the theatrical events in association with their own learning agenda. As with any other participants in the 'living history' or 'museum theatre' events, children bring their own preconceptions of history, their own understandings and expectations. The extent to which the children's activities before and after their visit to the museum shape their understanding will be investigated, as will the ways in which they understand and view the events' format and content. This will illuminate the main parameters that shape the theatrical event and its use as a learning/interpretive tool. Also, considering that 'meaning-making' is not a static process, I attempt to identify the understandings reached by the children, as shaped by time. Thus, the children's learning agenda and interpretation of the 'museum theatre' experience is examined at three stages: before, during and after participation in the event.

Thus, for the research's exploratory inquiry, qualitative data generation techniques were employed such as participatory observation in the museum and the classroom setting, children's drawings, group interviews before and after the classes' participation in the event and individual interviews four months later. Overall, 15 children participated in the research. The children's interpretations emerged via grounded theory analysis. Grounded theory was approached as an act of understanding the meaning of lived experience and not as a mechanical process bound to certain rules. Consistent with the constructivist paradigm, the findings showed that multiple interpretations amongst the children were constructed, especially in regard to the content (interpretive points) of the event.

Within this theoretical framework, which views the cognitive and social aspects of learning as operating in congruence with each other, the analytic process took into account both the individual and the collective experience. The children's individual perspective was gained through their comments expressed during group interviews, from classroom and museum-based observations and in individual drawings and interviews conducted after the event. On a collective level, the group interviews held before and after the event facilitated the social construction of meaning. In combination with the children's observed interaction during the 'museum theatre', the group interviews offered an insight into the 'taken-as-shared' aspects of the children's experience and their interpretation of it.

Children's reading of the first person interpretation events

The classes as interpretive communities bring their own agendas, expectations and pre-understandings to the 'museum theatre' events. These preconceptions were investigated to the extent possible via prolonged participatory observations and group interviews. It was found that they were mainly shaped via the classes' prior museum visits, classroom-based learning, preparatory activities for participation in the event and children's prior 'museum theatre' experiences, if any.

A range of themes emerged from the children after the events. The examination of the main themes for both events suggests several parameters that shape the use of the medium as an interpretative tool in museums.[41] Two of these parameters are discussed below and demonstrate the extent to which the interplay between the children's own agenda and the medium's theatrical and pedagogical form can affect children's reading of the events and understanding of the past.

Accepting the big lie: 'what about these lights ... they are not Roman'

The children's agenda, as expected, reflected the classroom discussions about the history topic. In the case of the year five class it was orientated towards the Roman Army and military life, while the year four class' agenda included themes not only from the Roman conquest but also from everyday life. However, a common pattern that emerged in both groups that affected the children's reading of the events' fictional context was the perception of Romans as 'fighters' and 'invaders'. Although moral undertones were expressed – Group two: 'I hate them because they invaded Britain', 'they were nasty', 'they were killing people' – it was the children's understanding of the Roman army as 'the most well-organised one' that shaped mainly the boys' admiration for it: Group two: 'I like them because they did things different to us and they knew how to fight.' (Also, see Figure 9.1.) These preconceptions about the Romans, not challenged within the context of the children's classroom-based learning, affected their belief in the events' fictional context and reading of the characters as fictional personas.

Figure 9.1 Child's drawing before the museum visit, Year 5: 'I done the drawing because when I read about the Romans and when they went to war I thought about how they battled and that's what I imagined.'

Within the realm of the educational drama, the establishment of the 'make-believe' in the fictional context is considered a prerequisite for the participants' engagement in the dramatic process.[42] How this element was deployed requires further discussion, in particular when the children were not prepared for the events' format and hence were not aware of the fictional lenses through which they could view the event.

Given that in a 'museum theatre' event the visitors sample the characters' behaviour and personality solely through their interaction with them, this study suggests that it is important for this interaction to take place without breaking the event's fictional context. The first contact with the actors and the building of trust between the actor/ interpreter and the audience is essential for the children's meaningful participation in the event. In the form of 'interactive theatre' that focuses on the creative participation of the audience, the experience 'can be fulfilled only through the willing collaboration of the audience'.[43] When, for example, at the beginning of Event B an explicit contract was drawn by the actor regarding the children's participation in the event, with references made to schooling modes of communication, the actor's 'out-of-role' response to the group provoked interpretations contrary to his intentions that he be seen as a 'real' Roman. ('He looked like a Roman with the clothes he wore but he did not act supreme'; 'he was practically telling us that he was not a Roman although he sounded like if he would make himself seem that he was like a real Roman'.) The actor's interaction within a didactic mode stripped the event of its theatrical quality and undermined the children's genuine participation in it. They did not value the event for its educational content, while during the event, instead of posing questions that could expand upon their understanding of the period, they focused on challenging the actor's plausibility as a Roman character.

It was evident in both events that the actors' plausibility as fictional characters was important in challenging the children's preconceptions and facilitating the reading of the events through the fictional frame. The characters that both actors selected to take over were 'composite' characters resembling real people in Roman times rather than roles of known historical personas. It is noted by Beth Goodacre and Gavin Baldwin that this type of character might be particularly demanding for actors as it involves empathetic immersion in a character whose social and physical features are located in an unfamiliar context.[44] To facilitate the establishment of the make-believe, the actors might need to move beyond mere role-play to create an identity that has a temporal existence and is clearly signalled through a theatrical mode. Indeed, the children read the characters for their naturalistic plausibility and theatricality, as expressed by changes in the rhythm and pace of narration, in the actor's body language and their proximity to the audience. For example, during event A, the actor used the 'space visualisation' technique, which involves looking over the heads of the visitors when describing a memory.[45] The children understood the moment for its theatricality and suggested that it contributed to the acceptance of the event's 'big lie': 'I thought she was talking to a prince or something like that, talking to the soldier ... I can see her, I can see the household'; 'she is not a real person but you felt like she was really like a real person'.

It was this reading of the characters' theatricality and, by extension, the events' theatrical elements, which was associated with the reading of the narratives' interpretive content. For example, the interpretive theme of heating was communicated to the children within a theatrical mode that challenged the boundaries of the real. The actor invited the children to put out their hands to feel if there was heat coming from the floor. The actor, unexpectedly and in loud voice, addressed the slave underneath that was supposed to be taking care of the furnace. For the

class the moment was unexpected, as indicated in their immediate reaction – they pulled their hands back and remained silent – and also in
the comments elicited in the follow up group interviews. ('When he
shouted my heart was beating fast, I did not expect that'; 'I really liked
the bit when he shouted at the floor: "wake up". You know the slaves
were living downstairs and they had to make fire so he can get warm'.)
The moment was memorable in the long term and in the case of some
children it motivated them to search for more information on the
subject. (See Figures 9.2 and 9.3.)

From present to past: an interaction between the real and fictional

In first person interpretation programmes, interaction between visitors
and actors usually takes place from the present to the past. The actors
might develop a number of techniques to address the issue of time in
their interaction with the visitors. For example, roles might be allo-
cated to the visitors that also situate them in the past, visitors might
pass through time travel machines or statements might be made by the
actors hinting that the event takes place in a different time.

The approach which was followed in the case study events is known
as the 'my time/your time approach', where the actors, although
coming from the past, acknowledge the visitor's time period and make
comparisons.[46] Via a series of questions the actors encouraged the children to describe the interpretive themes through their own time frame
and pointed out, through anachronisms, the differences and similarities between the present and the past. If the children's own frame of
reference and prior understandings about the subject matter could be
defined as 'real', it could be suggested that it was the process of oscil-
lating between the 'real' and the 'fictional' context that played a
significant role in the construction of meaning. The 'fictional context'
might be interpreted here using John O'Toole's model on the elements
of the dramatic form: 'the fictional context is finite and selective...
[but] with established parameters [for] the human subjects, their relationships and the environment which would exist if the context were
in fact real'.[47]

Perhaps what differentiates the fictional context of 'museum theatre'
events from other theatrical forms is its operation within a layer of
'authenticity'. This is usually illustrated in the 'museum theatre' professionals' intention to integrate interpretive themes in the events,
which need to be well researched and linked to the gallery's setting

Figures 9.2 and 9.3   Drawings conducted in the individual interviews four months after the event, Year 5 child: 'This man wearing sandals, he was just like Caesure because he was a rich man. He had slaves underneath turning this big wheel so heat would come on. Every time it was cold when he was standing on floor would shout them to turn the wheel harder. It would be like that and the long stick would come out here.'

and museum collections. It is also expressed in the quality that the school children attribute to the experiences, objects and displays they encounter within the museum setting.[48] Indeed, in the interviews conducted before the events, the value of 'authenticity' was tacitly expressed in the children's expectations that the 'museum theatre' experience will be an opportunity for learning. Museums are viewed as legitimate sources to gain knowledge about the past and, in particular, to view objects related to the period under study: 'a museum is a part of history that you learn about the Romans'; 'mostly our visit will be about objects and artefacts because there are lots of history things in a history museum'.

In this respect, the children were willing to read the interpretive themes that were provided in the characters' narratives as 'facts' about life in Roman times. The findings suggest that the communication of these themes, through the contrast between the children's and the character's timeframe, appears to facilitate the recollection of the interpretive themes within a period of five months after the event. When the children were asked to reflect on the event, they communicated the interpretive themes by recalling the responses they provided to the actor.[49] The children's participation in the event via their frame of reference seems to be in tune with radical constructivism's perspective on the process of learning. This postulates that any process of interpretation originates in the interpreter's encouragement to participants to interact in the event through their own context of familiarity.[50] By bringing the past and present together through the interaction between the real and the fictional they build a bridge between what they already know and the new interpretive themes: 'we told her that in our time we have radiators and she was telling us about what they use ... the heat comes through ... and it goes all the way up the walls and if you have another house it goes up as well through the ceiling. But the Celts never had that. They lived in houses made out of wood. But Romans got stone'.

The extent to which the construction of meaning affected the children's preconceptions about the Romans was elucidated through this research. Given that the majority of the children arrived at the museum viewing the whole experience as an opportunity for learning, it could be assumed that such a perception affected the children's tendency to read the specific details given about the characters' lives on a more abstract level. However, for these readings they brought instinctive human, emotional and affective understandings, as well as prior understandings or knowledge, which shaped the way they made sense of the past. It has been argued by theorists whose work has focused on aesthetic learning that, within this construction of meaning, feelings are inseparable from cognition.[51] As argued by Chris Husbands and Anna Pendry, in history teaching, tasks or strategies that enable pupils to unpack the 'emotional and affective complexity of learning about the past' are of equal importance to cognitive tasks.[52]

The 'first person interpretation' events at the museum entail, as any form of drama, a process of creating imaginary worlds wherein the parameters of 'what can be seen as legitimate knowledge' can be expanded to facilitate the exploration of issues of human concern and intellectual enquiry.[53] It provides a site for constructing meaning that, according to what Augusto Boal defines as 'the metaxis phenomenon', operates between the actual world and that of the fiction.[54] The children contrast these double worlds and move from the known to the possible. The visual aspect of the experience, combined with the interaction with a person pretending to 'come from the past', added a more humanised dimension to the children's perception of the setting. They viewed it as a place where real people would have lived. For example, one child commented in his drawing: 'I think it's important because poor people had to live there so I feel sorry for them'; 'I thought there were not such things as love in Roman times'. Such interpretations might suggest that the children view the past and read the setting within a humanistic context.

These 'museum theatre' events offer important opportunities for the exploration of children's preconceptions and understandings. But are the museums willing to negotiate the events' format and encourage interaction that is not set on a predetermined structure and script? If Wolfgang Iser's position is taken into account – that effective text is one that 'forces the reader into a new critical awareness of his or her customary codes and expectations' – then questions can be posed about the case study events' potential to challenge all children's preconceptions and to enable them to act as self-reflectors in the construction of meaning.[55]

Conclusion

The children's interpretations of the first person interpretation events underline the subjectivity of the theatrical experience and suggest that the potential of the medium lies in its performative quality and also in its interactive nature with the audience. When the theatrical framework possesses certain pedagogic qualities it can enhance the long-term recollection of objects, facilitate the understanding of social history and promote the children's perception of the past as real and human. The interplay between the event's format/ content and the experience's fictional/real context is evident in the children's interpretation of their 'museum theatre' experience. The participants view history in the context of their perception of time and place. What they experience, together with their personal engagement with the everyday past in the museum, affects their understanding of history. History needs to become part of the present, to be recreated and challenged. Museum theatre is a medium congruent with the curricular requirements for the subject of History with the potential to enhance the children's learning 'from the past' and also to highlight history's relevance to the present.[56]

In the field of museum interpretation a shift is taking place 'from the object centeredness to an emphasis on the promotion of experience'.[57] Subjectivity has a vital role to play in the transition of museums from being institutions that promote constructed representations of reality to being places where the fabrication of experiences is celebrated. Perhaps the effective use of 'museum theatre' that embraces and explores participants' meaning-making could be the answer to the criticism that museums as keepers of the past offer neat packages of the past for contemporary consumption. For museums there is much to gain from a dialogue with their visitors and the development of a common quest for what defines museums' identity and interpretive practices.

Notes

1 A. Curthoys and P. Hamilton, 'What Makes History Public?', *Public History Review*, 1 (1993) 13.

2 R. Hewison, *The Heritage Industry: Britain in a Climate of Decline* (London: Methuen, 1987), p. 10.

3 *ibid*, p. 135.

4 References to publicised material that provoked debates at the time can be found in A. Jackson, 'Inter-acting with the Past: The Uses of Participatory Theatre at Museums and Heritage Sites', *Research in Drama Education*, 5: 2 (2000) 199–215.

5 P. J. Fowler, *The Past in Contemporary Society: Then, Now* (London and New York: Routledge, 1992), p. 114.

6 *ibid*, p. 115.

7 R. Rosenzweig and D. Thelen, *The Presence of the Past: Popular Uses of History in American Life* (New York: Columbia University Press, 1998); P. Ashton and P. Hamilton (eds) *Australians and the Past*, special issue of *Australian Cultural History*, 22 (2003).

8 R. Samuel, *Theatres of Memory: Past and Present in Contemporary Culture* (London: Verso, 1994), p. 177.

9   *ibid*, p. 8.
10 *ibid*.
11 *ibid*, pp. 271, 284. However, the extent to which Samuels' views on the dynamic nature of 'living history' and Hewison's reservations about the medium's educational quality were reflected in the development of the medium is yet to be determined.
12 J. B. Gardner, 'Contested Terrain: History, Museums, and the Public', *The Public Historian*, 26 (2004) 15.
13 *ibid*, pp. 16–17.
14 Live interpretation is a broad term used to denote activities that provide 'active, face-to-face contact between the interpreter and the visitor'. See P. Risk, 'People-based Interpretation', in R. Harrison (ed.) *Manual of Heritage Management* (Oxford and Boston: Butterworth-Heinemann Ltd and the Association of Independent Museums, 1994), pp. 320–30. When the activities have a theatrical character focusing on historical and cultural interpretation then they can be identified with the term living history. The historian Jay Anderson interprets living history as simulation of life in the past and describes three main uses of the medium/approach: (a) for interpretive purposes (b) as a research tool and (c) for personal entertainment by nostalgic enthusiasts. See J. Anderson, *Time Machines: The World of Living History* (Nashville, Tennessee: The American Association for State and Local History, 1984). It is within the context of the first and the last approach that the term is utilised within the museum world to describe historically authentic activities that take place in an appropriate context and often in heritage sites and open-air museums. (For an example of the use of the term in published papers see D. Camp, 'Does He Smell Right?: Living History at Culzean Castle', in *GEM News*, 54 (1994) 7–8 and G. E. Burcaw 'Can History be too Lively?' *Museums Journal*, 80: 1 (1980) 5–7. Within the key definitions provided by organisations such as IMTAL and American Alliance for Theatre and Education (AATE), living history appears as a form of 'museum-theatre' while in earlier papers it is used as a synonym for re-enactments to denote the recreation of a variety of activities ranging from domestic life to military services. See A. Robertshaw, 'Acts of Imagination', *Museums Journal*, 90: 3 (1990) 30–1; A. Robertshaw, 'From Houses into Homes: One Approach to Live Interpretation', in *Social History in Museums: Journal of the Social History Curators Group*, 19 (1992) 14–20 and J. Malcolm-Davies, 'Living Interpretation in Museums', in *Heritage Interpretation*, 43 (1989) 12–14. For key definitions see IMTAL, http://www.imtal.org/keyDefs.php last accessed on 10/12/2004 ; American Alliance for Theatre and Education (AATE), Museum Theatre, http://www.aate.com/museumtheatre.html, last accessed on 13 March 2007.
15 The term appears initially in North American bibliography: C. Hughes, 'Theatre and Controversy in Museums', *Journal of Museum Education*, 23: 3 (1998) 13–15; S. Roth, *Past into Present: Effective Techniques for First-person Historical Interpretation* (North Carolina: The University of North Carolina Press, 1998) and later in the European IMTAL website created in 2003.
16 This broad definition emerges from various sources such as the IMTAL website; the AATE website; Risk, 'People-based Interpretation', pp. 320–30; S. Beck 'Use of Improvisation in Museums Theatre', in L. Maloney and

C. Hughes (eds) *Case Studies in Museum, Zoo and Aquarium Theatre* (Washington, DC: American Association of Museums, 1999), pp. 21–7 and Roth, *Past into Present*, pp. 50–3.

17 School Policy Document, Museum of London, Internal Document, 2003.

18 V. Tzibazi, 'Researching the Children's Meaning Making of First Person Interpretation Programmes', *Journal of Education in Museums,* 25 (2004) 28–32.

19 The term 'case study' is used here as 'a choice of what is to be studied' rather than as a form of inquiry itself with further methodological implications. See R. Stake, 'Case Studies', in N. K. Denzin and Y. S. Lincoln (eds) *Handbook of Qualitative Research*, 2nd edn (Thousand Oaks, CA: Sage Publications, 2000), p. 435.

20 J. Platt, 'What can Case Studies Do?', in R. G. Burgess (ed.) *Studies in Qualitative Methodology*, vol. 1 *Conducting Qualitative Research* (Greenwich, Connecticut: JAI Press, 1988), pp. 1–23.

21 J. Anderson, *Time Machines*, p. 19; E. Andren, *Skansen: Buildings and Animals. A Short Guide for Visitors* (Stockholm: Nordiska Museet, 1947), pp. 4–5; N. E. Baehrendtz *et al*, 'Skansen – A stock taking at 90', *Museum XXXIV*, 82: 3 (1982) 177.

22 Examples of exhibitions are given in B. Goodacre and G. Baldwin, *Living the Past*: Reconstruction, Recreation, Re-enactment and Education at Museums and Historical Sites (London: Middlesex University Press, 2002), p. 47.

23 Since the 1940s the Colonial Williamsburg in Virginia has been using costumed guides and craft demonstrators on a systematic basis to simulate life in the past. See A. Greenspan, *Creating Colonial Williamsburg* (Washington, DC and London: Smithsonian Institution Press, 2002). This example inspired other North American open-air museums, such as the Plimoth Plantation, the Old Sturbridge Village, the Farmer's Museum and the Mystic Seaport to incorporate living history programmes into their range of offerings. See Anderson, *Time Machines*, p. 33; A. Robertshaw '"A Dry Shell of the Past": Living History and the Interpretation of Historic Houses', *Interpretation*, 2: 3 (1997) 17–20.

24 A. Robertshaw, 'Acts of Imagination', in *Museums Journal*, 90: 3 (1990) 30.

25 Risk, 'People-based Interpretation', p. 325.

26 S. Alsford and D. Parry, 'Interpretive Theatre: A Role in Museums?', *Museum Management and Curatorship*, 10 (1991) 8–23; Greenspan, *Creating Colonial Williamsburg*.

27 At the beginning of 1980s the National Museum of American History developed a scripted dialogue entitled 'Buyin' Freedom' between two actors raising issues of slavery. It was one of the first programmes that brought live interpretation indoors centered around a dialogue. See M. E. Munley, 'Evaluation Study Report of Buyin' Freedom: An Experimental Live Interpretation Program', in *Perspectives on Museum Theatre* (Washington, DC: American Association of Museums, 1993), p. 70.

28 J. Cannizzo and D. Parry, 'Museum Theatre in the 1990s: Trail-blazer or Camp-follower?', in S. M. Pearce (ed.) *Museums and the Appropriation of Culture* (London: The Athlone Press, 1994) pp. 43–64; Alsford and Parry, 'Interpretive Theatre'.

29 Dressing up, play acting and participating in hands-on activities can be traced back to the late 1960s mainly in historic houses. See M. Harrison,

Changing Museums: Their Use and Misuse (London: Longmans, 1967); M. Harrison, *Learning out of School: A Teacher's Guide to the Educational Use of Museums* (London: Ward Lock Educational, 1970). Although this kind of interpretation cannot be easily classified as theatre, it could still be considered as the precursor of future developments in the field. In 1975 organisations such as The Association for Heritage Interpretation and the Heritage Trust were founded to encourage high standards of educational provision including also more dramatic approaches. See M. Dyer, 'The Heritage Education Trust: A Personal View of an Evolving Role', in Dyer (ed.) *Heritage Education Handbook* (Kettering: Heritage Education trust, 1986), pp. 25–188. However, widespread interest in heritage education was better established in the 1980s during which time a variety of school services was developed across museums and heritage sites in the UK including demonstrations, direct teaching, hands-on sessions and the use of drama. See E. Hooper-Greenhill (ed.) *The Educational Role of the Museum* (London and New York: Routledge, 1994), p. 243.

30 S. Woodhead and A. Tinniswood, 'Making Things with your Heart', in Woodhead and Tinniswood (eds) *'No Longer Dead to Me': Working with Schoolchildren in the Performing and Creative Arts* (London: The National Trust, 1996) pp. 4–7; S. Mayo, '"I Didn't Know I Liked History so Much": Reflections on Three Years with the Young National Trust Theatre', in *GEM News*, 52 (1993) 7–8.

31 Such as the White Company and the History Re-enactment workshop which perform for a wide range of visitors. See J. Malcolm-Davies, 'Living Interpretation in Museums', in *Heritage Interpretation,* 43 (1989) 12–14; A. Robertshaw (1999) personal communication.

32 Residential companies are companies which, although formed independently, were resident in and contracted by a specific museum.

33 The first professional companies created in the UK were the MOMI Actors' Company, performing at the Museum of Moving Image since its opening in 1988; the Spectrum Company, resident in the Science Museum in London since 1987; and the Past Pleasures Company, founded in 1987. These shaped the future development of 'museum theatre' in the country. See C. Ford, 'The "theatre-in-museum" Movement in the British Isles', (PhD dissertation: The University of Leeds, 1998); interviews with the companies' directors: A. Ashmore (1999), G. Thomas (2000) and the Past Pleasures Company's website:http://www.pastpleasures.co.uk. Last accessed on 6 January 2007.

34 J. Price, 'Theatre of the Absurd', in *Museums Journal,* (March 1992) 200–21.

35 See Ford, 'The "theatre-in-museum" Movement'; J. Malcolm-Davies, 'Living Interpretation in Museums', 12–14.

36 For example, the International Museum Theatre Association, established in 1990, and the American Alliance for Theatre and Education – set up by the Museum Theatre Network in 2003 – both advocate for the use and dissemination of the medium.

37 This shared understanding was especially supported by the directors' of various institutions at the 1998 American Association of Museums Conference ("Directors Support Museum Theatre", IMTAL session).

38 See D. Jones, 'Museum Theatre and Evaluation: An Overview of What we Know'; L. Silber, 'Bringing Theatre into the Mainstream'; and L. Roberson 'Do We Speak the Same Language? Theatre in Science and History Museums',

all in *Insights, IMTAL Online Journal* (Museum of Science, 1999) at http://www.mos.org/learn_more/imtal-insights8.html accessed on 11 December 2000.

39 T. A. Schwandt, 'Constructivist, Interpretivist Approaches to Human Inquiry', in N. K. Denzin and Y. S. Lincoln (eds) *The Landscape of Qualitative Research: Theories and Issues* (Thousand Oaks, CA: Sage Publications, 1998), p. 225; J. Smith, *The Nature of Social and Educational Inquiry: Empiricism Versus Interpretation* (New Jersey: Ablex Publishing Corporation, 1989), p. 124.

40 C. Robinson and M. Kellett, 'Power', in S. Fraser *et al* (eds) *Doing Research with Children and Young People* (Thousand Oaks, CA: Sage Publications in association with the Open University, 2004), p. 86.

41 For an extensive discussion of the themes that emerged in this study see V. Tzibazi, 'Researching Primary School Children's "museum theatre" Experiences' (PhD dissertation: Leicester University, 2006).

42 Amongst the drama theorists and practitioners who advocate the value of suspending the participants' disbelief in the drama process are Dorothy Heathcote, Jonothan Neelands, John O'Toole and Cecily O'Neil. See B. J. Wagner, *Dorothy Heathcote: Drama as a Learning Medium* (London: Hutchinson, 1999); L. Johnson and C. O'Neil (eds) *Dorothy Heathcote: Collected Writings on Education and Drama* (London: Hutchinson Education, 1984); J. Neelands, *Learning through Imagined Experience: Teaching English in the National Curriculum* (London: Hodder & Stoughton, 1992); J. O'Toole, *The Process of Drama: Negotiating Art and Meaning* (London and New York: Routledge, 1992); C. O'Neil, *Drama Worlds: A Framework for Process Drama* (Portsmouth: Heinemann, 1995).

43 J. Wirth, *Interactive Acting* (Oregon: Fall Creek Press, 1994), p. 87.

44 Goodacre and Baldwin, *Living the Past*, p. 123.

45 Roth, *Past into Present*, p. 98.

46 *ibid*, p. 16.

47 O'Toole, *The Process of Drama*, p. 14.

48 A. Jackson and H. Rees Leahy, '"Seeing it for Real....?": Authenticity, Theatre and Learning in Museums', *Research in Drama Education*, 10: 3 (2005) 319.

49 However, it should be mentioned that in the interviews conducted four months after the event, the children's recollection of the character's actual narrative was fragmentary due to the time passed. The children's recollection of the themes was subjective depending on the children's prior and after the event agendas.

50 E. von Glasersfeld, 'On the Concept of Interpretation', *Poetics*, 12 (1983) 207–18.

51 D. Best, *The Rationality of Feeling: Understanding the Arts in Education* (London: The Falmer Press, 1992); W. R. Witkin, *The Intelligence of Feeling* (London: Heinemann Educational Books, 1974); M. Henry, 'Drama's Ways of Learning', *Research in Drama Education*, 5: 1 (2000) 45–62.

52 C. Husbands and A. Pendry, 'Thinking and Feeling: Pupils' Preconceptions about the Past and Historical Understanding', in J. Arthur and R. Phillips (eds) *Issues in History Teaching* (London and New York: Routledge, 2000), p. 132.

53 J. Carroll, 'Terra Incognita: Mapping Drama Talk', *NADIE Journal*, 12: 2 (1988) 21.

54 A. Boal, *The Rainbow of Desire: The Boal Method of Theatre and Therapy* (London and New York: Routledge, 1995).

55 T. Eagleton, *Literary Theory: An Introduction*, 2nd edn (Oxford: Blackwell Publishers, 1996), p. 68.
56 The revised curriculum orders for England (DfEE and QCA) address the aim to enhance children's historical understanding as knowledge about the past. However, they have been criticised for failing to make explicit how the pupils will make connections between the present and the past. See D. Henson, 'Archaeology in Schools', in D. Henson *et al* (eds) *Education and the Historic Environment* (London and New York: Routledge, 2004), pp. 26–7.
57 H. S. Hein, *The Museum in Transition: A Philosophical Perspective* (Washington, DC: Smithsonian Institution Press, 2000), p. ix.

Section 3   Material Culture, Memory and Public Histories

In different ways the contributors to this section challenge the conventional idea that historical researchers go to the archive to read and analyse material to ascertain how the past 'really was'.[1] Carolyn Steedman, however, in her collection *Dust*, privileges the role of the researcher in creating meaning from the ephemera of an archive. As she suggests, 'we have to be less concerned with History as *stuff* ... than as *process*'.[2]

And that process does not stop with the presentation of history either. In his chapter, Jon Newman, himself a professional archivist, reveals how, even when the curators of an exhibition explicitly acknowledge the constructed nature of an exhibition, they cannot control the way in which others will view such artefacts. On display were the images from a professional photographer's studio, carefully arranged to evoke the composition of the former studio. For the local visitors to the exhibition this archival montage was not merely a public display but material that evoked memories and associations with their own pasts and necessitated a direct intervention into the format of the display. Engagement with the material, then, had a starting point in the public arena, returned to personal pasts and memories only then to be re-formulated into a collective memory of a local community.

Outside of the public archive, other contributors here explore the role of personal archives and collections as part of an historiographical process. For collectors, as Walter Benjamin noted, 'the world is present, and indeed ordered, in each of his objects'. Artefacts have the merit of allowing the past to be represented in our space and our time. We do not displace our being back into their time but 'they step into our life'.[3] The personal archives discussed here include the collections of a nineteenth-century Scottish shepherd and autodidact emigrant to New Zealand, a male primary school teacher working in London in the decades after the Second World War and those of men who fought in different twentieth-century wars. Saved artefacts include a teapot, a theological treatise, campaign medals from the First World War and a collection of children's poetry.

Arguably these are personal materials, the type of ephemera used for writing family history, and the people whose lives they summon up are known to the researcher personally or through family stories. Such work might be dismissed by some as mere family or personal history.[4] Indeed as Ruth Finnegan, the chair of the team responsible for an innovative course on family and community history run by the Open University, has noted, that course was regularly described by traditional academics as 'amateur', 'antiquarian' and not 'proper' history.[5] But as Graeme Davison has observed, there are 'radical possibilities' in apparently personal history. He particularly notes the 'significant role it now performs in the political and spiritual life of those whose ancestral claims were most rudely denied by patriarchal history, the Aborigines'.[6] Moreover he emphasises the changing *forms* of family history writing which significantly 'begin in the here and now, with the writer, and describe a journey backwards in time, and often through space, towards an uncertain destination.'[7] Histories that start with everyday materials and experiences are also contextualised by, and inform, the broader picture, as Alessandro Portelli has recently reminded us.[8] Thus in their use of artefacts from personal collections Mary Stewart, Martin Bashforth, Hilda Kean and Brenda Kirsch are also re-figuring ways of approaching narratives of international migration, national memory and transgenerational stories of paternal absence.

All contributions in this section begin in the here and now and with the writer explicitly present in their chapter, as an ancestor, a subject or a participant in the making of history. Toby Butler, for example, shares with us the ways in which his personal knowledge and experience of living on a boat on the Thames enabled him to create different ways of exploring the memories and pasts of others living on its banks. His consciousness of his present physical locality as much as his intellectual concerns were significant in his approach.

Contributors have not ignored personal experiences and memories. Rather they have interrogated the personal – family accounts of a London mob's attacks on a German great grandmother's shop while her son fought for the British on the Western front; the failure of a marriage; lack of success at primary school – to re-think the past. The 'people' in this section may be those talking to the researcher on a journey along the Thames, but they are also those listening to the recordings made previously by the researcher while making their *own* journeys along the same river. They are the relatives who share their own researches and materials with the author who is also engaged in writing the family history. They are the visitors to an exhibition who make their own contributions to the proceedings. They are the children who sat the 11+ exam decades ago. But the 'people' also include the writers of these chapters. The pasts and presents discussed here may be personal but they are also public histories.

Notes

1 For further discussion on the conventional view of history, see Ranke's approach in R. J. Evans, *In Defence of History* (London: Granta Books 1997), p. 17 and W. Benjamin, 'Theses on the Philosophy of History', in *Illuminations* (London: Cape, 1970), p. 247.
2 C. Steedman, *Dust* (Manchester: Manchester University Press, 2001), p. 67. See also J. Sassoon, 'Phantoms of Remembrance: Libraries and Archives as "The Collective Memory"', *Public History Review*, 10 (2003) 55.
3 W. Benjamin, *The Arcades Project* (London: Belknap Press 1999), pp. 206–7.
4 See for example, E. Hobsbawm, History from Below, *On History* (London: Abacus, 1998), pp 266–8. For a supportive position, see R. Samuel, 'Introduction: Exciting to be English', in R. Samuel (ed.) *Patriotism: The Making and Unmaking of British Identity* (London: Routledge, 1988), p. xlv; R. Samuel, 'Local History and Oral History', *History Workshop Journal*, 1 (1976) 191–208; H. Kean, *London Stories: Personal Lives, Public Histories* (London: Rivers Oram Press, 2004).
5 R. Finnegan, 'The Open University Course on Family and Community History', *Genealogists' Magazine*, 25: 2 (1995) 49. Thanks to Phil Coward for drawing our attention to this article. M. Drake, 'Inside-Out or Outside-In? The Case of Family and Local History', in R. Finnegan (ed.) *Participating in the Knowledge Society: Researchers Beyond the University Walls* (Basingstoke: Palgrave Macmillan, 2005), pp. 118–19.
6 G. Davison, *The Use and Abuse of Australian History* (Sydney: Allen & Unwin, 2000), p. 98. See also B. Attwood, '"Learning about the Truth": The Stolen Generations Narrative', in B. Attwood and F. Magowan (eds) *Telling Stories: Indigenous History and Memory in Australia and New Zealand* (Sydney: Allen and Unwin, 2001).
7 Davison, *The Use and Abuse*, p. 101.
8 A. Portelli, 'So much depends on a red bus, or, innocent victims of the liberating gun,' *Oral History*, 34: 2 (2006) 30.

10
A Nation's Moment and a Teacher's Mark Book: Interconnecting Personal and Public Histories

Hilda Kean and Brenda Kirsch

Introduction[1]

A teacher's mark book, an 'official' school photograph of a class of East London children about to leave primary school, another photo of the teaching staff and a collection of writing by these same children: such materials are not the stuff to excite the conventional historian. They appear to be mere traces of personal pasts and so commonplace as to be scarcely the subject of grand narratives. However, such small things can also be those that surprise and become keys to larger issues.[2]

Figure 10.1   Infant and junior teachers, 1956

By examining these seemingly ordinary artefacts we hope to raise questions about the relationship between personal and public histories. David Vanderstel, the executive director of the American National Council on Public History, has recently defined public history in terms that counterpose 'professionals' and the 'public'. Writing in *Oral History* he described public history as 'the means of making what historians do understandable and relevant for a larger public. It is taking historical scholarship and adapting it to historic sites, exhibitions, documentaries, public policy and issues of the day'.[3]

But if we draw on other understandings of the term, which emphasise the value of people both in terms of making history and in using their own experience to understand the past, we can begin to see the possibilities for cutting across the divide between a passive 'public' and an active historian.[4] Both personal and local practice are key factors in the construction of the past. Within his definitions of history Raphael Samuel privileged the role of memory, and championed a 'different order of evidence and a different kind of inquiry'.[5] This inclusion of personal and collective memory within history has inevitably opened up new dimensions to the study of history. Katharine Hodgkin and Susannah Radstone, for example, situate their work on memory and history as a development of Samuel's approach while arguing that work on social and cultural memory 'has come to be known as "public history"'.[6]

Certainly, the way in which personal possessions can, and do, provide tangible links between the past and the present has been fruitfully explored, particularly by Roy Rosenzweig and David Thelen in the US, and by Paul Ashton and Paula Hamilton in Australia.[7] In their respective studies they have analysed the way people make sense of their lives in the present through their understanding of personal and national pasts. If history is seen as an activity rather than a profession, 'the numbers of its practitioners might be legion.'[8] This idea might be a useful starting point in constructing different sorts of histories about a past experience shared by nearly all living adults in, at least, the western world – namely the experience of schooling.

Most scholarship looking at education has focused on ideas of teacher professionalism and organisation rather than how the teacher might accrue personal value through student outcomes – that is, the teacher's relationship to the work produced by their students.[9] Further, while education has been included in grand-theme volumes by historians such as Ross McKibbin or Pat Thane[10] the detailed unpacking of the history of educational experience has become the specific remit of those working in education departments of universities rather than public historians. In turn this has led to a privileging of the empirical subject matter of schooling and a relegation of the nature of the process of history-making. Indeed, in the British mainstream *History of Education Journal* only very recently do we find articles dealing with the historiographical questions of the role of memory, or oral history, questions that have been widely embraced by both public and cultural historians. Defining themselves as separate from mainstream historiography by virtue of their subject matter, educational historians have therefore seen the role of material culture in histories of schooling as highly original. As Martin Lawn and Ian Grosvenor have recently realised, material culture 'has tended to stay with museum specialists and not historians of education. The pencil, cheap paper, colour printing and intelligence tests are the tools of schooling, which allow the grand narratives to function'.[11] That is, they are artefacts that are valuable as historical materials for larger narratives.

Objects, collecting and archives

For our study we looked at material traces of schooling in a working-class primary school in Hackney, east London from the late 1950s to the early 1960s. These things – the photographs, the mark book and poetry – did not belong to us but had been kept by the class teacher Mr E alongside similar material from different years when he had taught the 'top class', preparing them for the 11+ exam. As the photo suggests, the intake was overwhelmingly white, the largest 'ethnic minority' being Jewish children.[12] The artefacts had been kept in Mr E's home and were subsequently retained by his widow who had been a school secretary for most of her married life. She too had placed some value on them and had not discarded them on her husband's death.

Conventionally, when undertaking research using the past, historians visit archives since, as Carolyn Steedman has suggested, here is a 'place where a whole world, a social order, may be imagined by the recurrence of a name in a register through a scrap of paper, or some other little piece of flotsam'.[13] However, we had not been searching for a past in the archives; this material had been presented as a personal gift to one of the authors. The material was not part of the performance that archival institutions play in shaping the way we see the past.[14] The inert and 'everyday' nature of the mark book, if not the apparent occasion of the photo, interested us as a way of challenging

Figure 10.2   Class photograph of children about to leave junior school, 1960

an idea of history as simply event-driven, consisting of dramatic inter-ruptions to normality.[15] It also, as we shall explore later, provided a potentially unsettling meeting of our past and current selves.

Usually teachers' marks books are not collected in public archives. In the London Metropolitan Archives (LMA), which holds the records of the former London County Council (LCC) and the later Inner London Education Authority (ILEA) – between them, locally respons-ible for this particular school and for schooling in London generally between 1889 and 1990 – one might find official logbooks, compiled by head teachers, and individual registers of pupil enrolment from some inner London schools. But narratives of individual children are rare unless the 'extraordinary' has occurred, for example a child's acci-dent.[16] The standard of work of different classes of children may be discussed in official documents but the individual marks of individual children are outside this discourse. Personal stories are irrelevant.

Ostensibly Mr E's mark books and collections of children's writing were the artefacts of a personal collector. As Russell Belk has explored in his important study, a 'benefit' of collecting is the 'enlarging [of] the collector's sense of self'.[17] Belk suggests that the collector usually requires dedication to 'the hunt' for a particular object.[18] But Mr E needed to make no extra effort to acquire the artefacts; they were items created at least in part by himself during his professional work and he had always owned them. These were not items of conventional status, such as furniture, cars, or jewellery.[19] Rather these were everyday items of a working life that may have been collected as a form of practical memory. According to Sue Waterman, 'we collect at those places where we, for whatever reason, are connected to the world'.[20] The mark book is a multi-layered conduit of personal stories, public events, a passage of time connecting personal knowledge and experience to broader social contexts. This artefact was as much about the teacher as his charges.

These documents had a personal value for him – but also for us, two of his former pupils. They may indeed have contributed to the collector's sense of a past and acted as a way of remembering a particular time in his life.[21] However, if Mr E chose to remember his pupils through this device it was in a form mediated by him, with his methods of categorising and valuing children through the marks they obtained in his class. It is an indicator of his own role in ensuring the desired outcome: the pupils' passing of the 11+ exam and obtaining a coveted place at a grammar school. The apparent professionalism of the teacher – the neat handwriting, the careful lists – is also a personal act of self-approbation.

The moment of the 11+

These artefacts might be read as items of everyday interest divorced from event-driven dramatic interruptions to the quotidian.[22] But they are simultaneously part of a broader national past in which the 11+ was a key moment: personal artefacts may be valuable in creating a different form of history at a particular cultural moment in the life of the nation.[23]

In the 1950s and 1960s, places in free grammar schools, as created by the 1944 *Education Act*, were an object of desire by middle- and working-class parents alike. Their children competed for a restricted supply of places, which, like the examination itself, were regionally determined. Thus the 'likelihood of a working class boy receiving a selective education in the middle fifties and sixties was very little different from that of his parents' generation thirty years earlier'.[24] From the early 1950s the testing system for admission into grammar schools – the 11+ – had been criticised as inefficient and unfair, since it implied fixed notions of intelligence, which could be accurately measured by testing.[25]

Publishers, producing books for parents to coach their children with, realised the anxiety caused to parents by the process. As one primer explained: 'The 11+ – does it worry you? It needn't … You, the parent, can do much to prepare your child for the difficult tests in this all-important exam'. The anxious parent was encouraged to give the child 'your personal help and guidance in the most difficult and important test of his young life'.[26] Children were schooled in passing exams that might include examples such as: the following two mixed up words mean the same thing – spell them correctly: EREPC and RWLAC (or) HWRLI and PINS; complete the following comparison: Bread is to baker as bark is to (shin, shed, tree, house, pig); or general knowledge:'Of which countries are these national emblems (sic) – swastika? daffodil?'[27]

The specific mark book we now possess contains children's marks for regular tests taken both before and after the important 11 + exam taken in the spring. It includes the marks for weekly tests in 'mental', 'free expression', 'mechanical', 'verbal reasoning', 'spellings, 'arithmetic tests' and 'problems'. (An example of a 'problem' is: 'A lady gets four pints of milk every weekday and five pints on a Sunday. How much milk [in gallons, etc] does she get in the month of March if the first of March is a Saturday?')[28] It also records who was deemed sufficiently worthy to obtain a prize for overall attainment, progress, scripture, needlework or 'character'. At the start of the year the teacher had noted the children's reading ages, though, significantly, not their chronological ages; near the end of the year he noted the schools to which they were accepted (implicitly indicating whether or not the children had passed the 11+). Of the 38 registered at the start of the year, 21 obtained a grammar school place.[29]

Both in the form of the knowledge required to pass the exam and in the way in which it was recorded, the mark book is of a particular cultural moment in the life of the nation. Girls' names are listed separately from boys; no attention is paid to a child's age or particular learning problems. Its taxonomy of gender and learning is itself an indication of its time.

The collected and illustrated poems – produced as part of 'free expression' – are clearly circumscribed by a particular cultural moment of the time, and of course, the teacher's own frameworks. Topics penned by these Hackney children include: 'A countryside walk', in which the author finds a 'bubbling spring'; 'spring', describing daisies covering all country lanes (sic); and 'Christmas', a topic covered by Christian and Jewish children alike. The poems might also give glimpses of the children as an aspirational group who knew that they were destined to sit the 11+ and who, being in the top form, carried the burden of their parents' hopes. This might be seen in the pastiches of Lewis Carroll's poem *Jabberwocky* or in poems based on the music heard on the radio programmes for schools such as 'Ralph Vaughan Williams the piano did play/His works were particularly English some people say', or the affectation of poems about the 'Prima Ballerina' or 'The Nutcracker Suite'.

The epistemological constructs were not personal, even if the documents were the personal possessions of the teacher. They suggest the relationship between his personal and public life. And for us they also have meaning. The mark book, however, rather than the poetry collection or

Figure 10.3 Example of poetry for the grammar school in the teacher's collection

photos, related most closely to our memories. We had both remembered that we were at the bottom of the class. Indeed ranking was reinforced physically, with children being obliged to move seats or rows into different fixed desks as a result of the regular tests. We were inevitably placed in the bottom row where the teacher might see us; we weren't, we knew, the favoured ones. We were also not selected for the privileged positions of class prefect, dinner, stock, library or stairs monitors. Neither of us even acquired the status of 'reserve dinner monitor' which the mark book records. We did not win academic prizes, though it seems Brenda won recognition for her 'character'. And the failure to see the blackboard, due to our short-sightedness, probably accounted for our low marks in arithmetic and 'mechanical'. 'Free expression', at which we did well, did not require the ability to read distances.

For Brenda, one of about 12 Jewish children in the class, the mark book evoked again a memory of exclusion (if not, in retrospect, possible discrimination) by this particular teacher. She has vivid recollections that no Jewish pupils were called on to be monitors, and of a shared, secret glee amongst the Jewish children when Mr E picked on Christina C to be a monitor. Despite her forename they knew that her dad was Jewish: did he? In fact, the mark book showed that some Jewish children did do well but these achievements were more likely to be based on 'objective' criteria than the teacher's personal opinion.

Some public historians have used personal memory to interpret change over time.[30] The existence of the mark book with its recording of the name of every child in the year, triggered for us a memory of the other children but also, in different ways, memories of potential marginalisation. If individual memories are constructed within culture, so too are cultural memories constituted by individual memories.[31] One discourse running through the school year was that of inclusion and exclusion – the former epitomised by acceptance into the grammar school place, the latter by relegation to a secondary modern or 'comprehensive' school.[32] The mark book helped us recall and refigure memories but it also led to different readings and understandings beyond that of personal experience.

In our cases, born in August and July, we were nearly a year younger than the vast majority of the class. Our reading ages – presumably at the September of that final year of primary school when we were just over 10 years old – were recorded as 12 years and three and four months respectively. Only 11 children out of the 38 had lower reading ages. But our poor showing as summer-born children was not, it appears, simply a personal failure. The difficulties of so-called 'summer children' were raised at the time by those campaigning against the 11+ and streaming in primary school. The selection exam was becoming highly competitive and, simultaneously, its unreliability was becoming increasingly apparent.[33] One effect of the exam was the streamlining of juniors and even infants in schools, with the top stream being pressed forward with the examination in view.[34] A national survey in 1964 concluded that, as a result of constant grading and classification, children who were born from May to August[35] were most likely to be disproportionately represented in the C stream. Autumn-born children may have had up to 50 per cent more schooling than the summer children when it came to grade them for streamed A, B or C classes.[36] Despite – or because of – our schooling, we did in fact both pass the 11+ exam and proceeded to grammar school and from there on to higher education at 18 years of age.

The personal and the public

What is personal and what is 'public' in a narrative is often uncertain and blurred.[37] Here the teacher's mark book had the effect of invoking and validating our negative memories but also of situating our personal memory as explicitly social. Our memories of primary school had not been positive, nor had we been mis-remembering them due to particular psychological traits; the mark book confirmed our perception of a time of comparative failure. In the term in which we successfully sat the exam, we were ranked twenty-first and twenty-fifth in the class. But it also enabled us to situate the personal experience within a broader moment.

Yet our memories were more than just personal. Here was a distinctive record of particular moments in the cultural life of the nation, affecting children, teachers and parents alike. While these artefacts are about specific people – the teacher and two of his pupils – they are also about the fusing of subject and object as so often occurs in the use of memory in history. Conventionally, written records are anonymous or impersonal, whereas oral sources, the summoning up and articulation of memory, involve a remembering and a telling. According to Alessandro Portelli, the 'tale and the memory may include materials shared with others, but the rememberer and the teller are always individual persons who take on the task of remembering and the responsibility of telling.'[38] Here the rememberers, the tellers and the modern recorders are synonymous and the written document is personal to us in evoking our own memories.

People of particular generations can often still remember, sometimes with much emotion, their feelings around the exam and its outcome.[39] Reference to the deleterious effects of the categorisation that occurred and the development of comprehensive schools designed to cater (in theory) for children of all abilities became a key motif in the national political debate from the 1950s into the 1970s.[40] The memory of this personal event has elided into a collective memory of the nation's past and an internalisation of the experience. As Jeremy Black has discussed, the public use of history is frequently a matter of collective memory and its usages.[41]

If the authors' educational past can be configured as part of a particular post-war moment, so too can the teacher's own educational past. Mr E was not a conventionally trained teacher, having been one of the 27,000 new teachers trained under the aegis of the 'Emergency Training Scheme for Teachers' at the end of the war.

Although the majority of new teachers in the 1950s were women,[42] many men had been recruited under the scheme.[43] Faced with a lack of recruitment during the war itself and the loss of approximately 20,000 teachers who left schools for some form of war service,[44] the state had to recruit some 40,000 new teachers as quickly as possible after the war. A two-year funded course with extra grants for dependants was established[45] for mature people from the armed forces and other national services who possessed 'a sufficient background of general education, and culture to enable them to become worthy members of the teaching profession'.[46] Possession of a school certificate, while desirable, was not essential and the course was designed to relate to previous knowledge and experience.[47] Mr E came from a working-class, clerical, East London background and had served with the RAF in the war. As a Sunday school teacher in the local Congregational church, he had had experience of working with children. But without the war – and his active service – it is unlikely that Mr E could have become a teacher.[48]

Thus the mark book might be less a repository of children's success than a symbol of the teacher's own 'success' in even being in the classroom in this role. Male staff in the school – as the photo of the teachers' group indicates – were in the minority. But for many years Mr E had shared the prestigious teaching of the top fourth-year class with another (male) teacher. Perhaps the very keeping of the document implies an uncertainty about his status, a validation through others' successes. The mark book is simultaneously a personal and official document serving as an artefact for the creation of public histories in the culturally important decades ushered in after the 1944 Education Act and the 1948 training scheme. As Ken Jones suggests, the 'very fact that new institutions had emerged, charged with the welfare of the mass of the population, and staffed by professional groups committed at least to some extent to ideas of the public good, meant that the ground had been prepared for a slow shift of cultural power, in which the meanings and values treasured by conservatives were placed under siege.'[49]

Personal stories and archival silences

Our starting point was personal, deriving from material we saw to be 'about' us; it did not lead, however, to nostalgia. We did not, and do not, wish to remember those times, or ourselves at that age. We had remembered the class photo the teacher had retained but perhaps significantly, neither of us had kept a copy. After accessing the Friends Reunited website and discussing the merits of pursuing this line of inquiry, we realised we did not want to meet our classroom peers from those days. In their exploration of the role of the Friends Reunited website Paul Long and David Parker have situated the website as bestriding the official and unofficial consensual view of schooldays as being 'the best days of your life.'[50] They note the appeal of the site at its zenith, located, as described by the then co-owner Steve Pankhurst, in 'the huge wave of nostalgia sweeping the UK'. They rightly situate the contributions and messages to the website as a shifting archive of memory, and explore who it is that speaks and how.[51] Refusing the task of creating particular notions of a unified and continuously coherent self, this was a past we did not wish to bring into the present.

While the 11+ had been an important moment in the nation's psyche, its normative character has, ironically, resulted in an absence of material from the archive. Many of the tests were commissioned from the National Foundation for Educational Research (NFER) or Moray House, now part of Edinburgh University. However, despite its past work in this field the NFER possessed nothing from that period, and Moray House, which had regularly set papers for local educational authorities, could not find material relating to this period in inner London and held scant examples of papers.[52] Even the London Metropolitan Archives, which holds the archive of the former LCC (and ILEA), did not have 'ordinary' examples of 11+ papers – and unfortunately not the exams we had sat.

The typical had proved insufficiently valuable to be collected. Although the LCC had been one of the local authorities that had promoted comprehensive education in the 1960s,[53] it had not seen fit to keep documentation of a discredited past which both its elected members and officials had sought to change.[54] What had been the commonplace was not held in a public archive; the ordinary, the everyday, the examples of life inside the authority's schools, was absent. The 11 + exam had been an important moment but, in the absence of official material in the public archive, memory and personal artefacts might need suffice.

The only examples of 11+ papers in the LCC archive were those from 1958. The papers include two 'comprehension' passages on animals. In one narrative of a hopping bird and 'Daisy the pony' children had to pick out examples of nouns and verbs. In another passage, describing the habits of Brock the badger, the qualities of the badger are lauded and a local touch is added: 'a few families even live within the County of London at Ken Wood'. There were also papers on arithmetic and topics for a 20 minute composition: 'Your adventures when you lost your way home on a foggy evening'; 'How to grow a flower from seed'; 'A visit to a famous building'; or a story beginning – 'There was a scratching at the door and in the dim light I could see that it was slowly opening ...'.

The files contained complaints from one or two head teachers about the contents of these papers. For example, 'Brock' could have been misunderstood as a proper name for this particular badger rather than another name for badgers in general. But the files also had letters of complaint concerning grammatical corrections for 11+ papers for other years, although the actual papers had not been filed.

Despite our disappointment that the 'personal moment' of the 11+ exam we sat was not part of a 'public' archive, the archives revealed another meeting of different personal and public moments. The head teacher of our primary school had sat on the LCC junior leaving exam sub-committee between 1957 and 1960. In 1958 the sub-committee had suggested greater use of the record of a child's progress, especially during the final year, alongside a series of tests to replace the 11+. It recommended that before the results of any such tests be finalised,

Figure 10.4 The authors – and artefacts – at an infants' open day

head teachers should submit lists of boys and girls 'setting out in order of merit' with recommendations for transfer to appropriate secondary schools.[55] Our personal success, our 'progression' to the local grammar school, might well have been different if this proposal had been implemented in our time.

Conclusion

The 'discovery' of the mark book, the children's poetry and class photo led to a different reading of family photographs which had been taken at open days in the primary school. Ostensibly these were personal records in a family album taken by a father of his only child. But they also included other children in the background, images of pedagogical practice around the room, a particular cultural context that an electronic scanner could now reveal. In comparing a modern 'largely bare' classroom with his own secondary English classroom as a student, Ken Jones has argued that we need to 'rely... on [our own] collective memory to fill in for the systematic history which has yet to be written'.[56] But material in personal archives, family albums and handed down images might well substitute for the absences in the official record.[57] These photos in their content and process – produced by a father entering the school for open days with his camera – are of a particular time. They might also be used now as part of a shared past to write different histories of that time.

Writing about 'The return of history' several years before a framework for a national curriculum for history was introduced into British higher education,[58] Raphael Samuel presciently noted that the 'subject would be cut off from its lifeblood if it were to contract to a uniform grid'. Instead he advocated an approach to history that not only addressed the record of the past but the hidden forces 'shaping contemporary understandings of it, the imaginative complexes in and through which it is perceived.'[59] The same article concluded by suggesting that history could be a means of undoing and questioning a sense of self, offering 'more disturbing accounts of who we are and where we come from than simple identifications would suggest'.[60] His statement has analogies with Luisa Passerini's conclusion that: 'If I had not heard the life stories of the generation of '68 I would not have been able to write about myself; these stories have nourished mine, giving it the strength to get to its feet and speak.'[61]

The absence of material culture of the 11+ in the public domain is an important issue for historians concerned with the relationship between personal pasts and public history. Here a teacher's horded personal material helps to fill the absences in public archives and to evoke personal memories. In such ways new histories and understandings might be created and developed which allow for the involvement of many agents in the creation of histories. The public moment is made personal, and the personal is made public.

Notes

1   Thanks to Ken Jones and participants at the 'People and their Pasts' conference for their comments on earlier drafts.
2   J. Parr, *These Goods are Canadian-made: An Historian Thinks about Things* (Ottawa: University of Ottawa Press, 1999), p. 30
3   D. Vanderstel, 'Vox Pop', *Oral History*, 33: 1 (2005) 32.
4   H. Kean, 'Public History and Raphael Samuel: A Forgotten Radical Pedagogy?', *Public History Review*, 11 (2004) 51–62.
5   R. Samuel, *Theatres of Memory: Past and Present in Contemporary Culture* (London: Verso, 2004), p. 8.
6   K. Hodgkin and S. Radstone, *Contested Pasts: The Politics of Memory* (London: Routledge, 2003), p. 3.
7   R. Rosenzweig and D. Thelen, *The Presence of the Past: Popular Uses of History in American Life* (New York: Columbia University Press, 1998); P. Ashton and P. Hamilton, 'At Home with the Past: Background and Initial Findings from the National Survey', *Australian Cultural History*, 22 (2003) 5–30.
8   Samuel, *Theatres*, p. 17.
9   M. Lawn and G. Grace (eds) *Teachers: The Culture and Politics of Work* (London: Falmer Press, 1987); R. V. Seifert, *Teacher Militancy: A History of Teacher Strikes 1896–1987* (London: Falmer Press, 1987); A. Tropp, *The School Teachers* (London: Heinmann, 1957). Exceptions include J. Miller, *School for Women* (London: Virago, 1996) and C. Steedman, *The Tidy House: Little Girls Writing* (London: Virago, 1982).
10 R. McKibbin, *Classes and Cultures in England 1918–1951* (Oxford: Oxford University Press, 1998), pp. 206–71; P. Thane, *Foundations of the Welfare State*, 2nd edn (London: Longman, 1996), pp. 213–17.
11 M. Lawn and I. Grosvenor (eds) *Materialities of Schooling: Design, Technology, Objects, Routines* (Oxford: Symposium, 2005), p. 7.
12 The school still exists but appears to have no records of this part of its history.
13 C. Steedman, *Dust* (Manchester: Manchester University Press, 2001), p. 81.
14 J. Sassoon, 'Phantoms of remembrance: libraries and archives as the "collective memory"', *Public History Review*, 10 (2003) 41.
15 J. Moran, 'History, Memory and the Everyday', *Rethinking History*, 8: 1 (2004) 57.
16 H. Kean, *Deeds not Words: The Lives of Suffragette Teachers* (London: Pluto Press, 1990), p. 8.
17 R. W. Belk, *Collecting in a Consumer Society* (London: Routledge, 1995), p. 89.
18 *ibid*, p. 92.

19 S. Pearce , 'The Construction of Heritage', *International Journal of Heritage Studies*, 4: 2 (1999).
20 S. Waterman, 'Collecting the Nineteenth Century', *Representations*, 90 (2005) 121.
21 Belk, *Collecting*, pp. 91, 67.
22 Moran, 'History, Memory and the Everyday', p. 57.
23 H. Kean, *London Stories: personal lives and public histories* (London: Rivers Oram Press, 2004), pp. 128–31.
24 A. H. Halsey, A. Heath and J. M. Ridge, *Origins and Destinations: Family, Class and Education in Modern Britain* (Oxford: Oxford University Press, 1980), p. 202, as cited in K. Jones, *Education in Britain 1944 to the Present* (Cambridge: Polity Press, 2003), p. 46.
25 Jones, *Education in Britain*, p. 47.
26 *Grammar School Entrance tests: 11 plus Aid Book* (London: Mellifont Press, n.d.).
27 J. M. Charlton, *Test Papers in Intelligence* (London: Macmillan, 1961); N. C. Hayward and F. T. Walton, *Graded General Knowledge and Intelligence Tests, Book One, General Knowledge Juniors* (London: University Tutorial Press, 1956).
28 *Grammar School Entrance Tests*.
29 Twenty-one of 27 children listed had presumably passed the 11+ since they are recorded as obtaining places at grammar schools. (There were 38 in September). It is not recorded whether the places were taken up.
30 P. Thompson, 'Believe it or Not: Rethinking the Historical Interpretation of Memory', in J. Jeffrey and G. Edwall (eds) *Memory and History: Essays on Recalling and Interpreting Experience* (Lanham, MD: University Press of America, 1994), p. 11.
31 Hodgkin and Radstone, *Contested Pasts*, p. 5.
32 Given the large number of grammar schools in Inner London at this time the few comprehensive schools rarely attracted large numbers of pupils who had passed the 11+.
33 B. Simon (ed.) *New Trends in English Education: A Symposium* (London: MacGibbon and Kee, 1957), p. 12.
34 *ibid*, p. 12.
35 *ibid*, p. 13.
36 B. Jackson, *Streaming: An Education System in Miniature* (London: Routledge & Kegan Paul, 1965), pp. 23–6.
37 A. Portelli, 'Oral History as Genre'; M. Chamberlain and P. Thompson, *Narrative and Genre* (London: Routledge, 1998), p. 26.
38 A. Portelli, *The Order Has Been Carried Out: History, Memory, and Meaning of a Nazi Massacre in Rome* (Basingstoke: Palgrave Macmillan, 2003), p. 14.
39 This happened, for example, when we presented a version of this chapter at the People and their Pasts conference.
40 D. Thom, 'Politics and the People: Brian Simon and the Campaign Against Intelligence Tests in British Schools', *History of Education*, 33: 5 (2004) 515–30.
41 J. Black, *Using History* (London: Hodder Arnold, 2005), p. 9.
42 R. Lowe, *Education in the Post War Years: A Social History* (London: Routledge, 1988), p. 104.

43   *Challenge and Response: An Account of the Emergency Scheme for the Training of Teachers*, Ministry of Education pamphlet no 17, (London: HMSO, 1950).

44   P. Gosden, *Education in the Second World War: A Study in Policy and Administration* (London: Methuen, 1976), p. 124.

45   *Emergency Recruitment and Training of Teachers,* Circular 1652, interim report, (London: Board of Education, 15 May 1944).

46   L. Martin, *Into the Breach: The Emergency Training Scheme for Teachers* (London: Turnstile Press, 1949), pp. 2–3.

47   *Challenge and Response,* p. 23; *Emergency Recruitment,* p. 3 para 6.

48   *Challenge and Response,* p. 116.

49   Jones, *Education in Britain,* p. 14.

50   P. Long and D. Parker, '"Friends" Reunited? Official and Unofficial School Histories', unpublished paper, 'Unofficial and Official histories', Third Public History Conference, Ruskin College, Oxford, May 2002.

51   *ibid.*

52   Email correspondence with NFER and Moray House. The University of London's Institute of Education has no examples of the papers for London and few from elsewhere.

53   The ILEA, established in 1964, was Labour controlled until 1967. It decided to increase the number of comprehensives to 113 by 1970, which would have had the effect of including nearly all secondary schools. See I. G. K. Fenwick, *The Comprehensive School 1944–1970* (London: Methuen, 1976), pp. 139–41. Thanks to Ken Jones for this reference.

54   Opposition to such changes helped the Conservatives win the 1967 Greater London Council elections. Withdrawing Labour's plan to increase the number of comprehensives, they produced their own, which would increase the number of comprehensives to 78 by 1975; leaving 10 per cent of the school population still in grammar schools. Fenwick, *The Comprehensive School, ibid.*

55   Junior Leaving Examination Sub-committee of the Central Consultative Committee of Headmasters and Headmistresses (CCCHH), 8 October 1958, LCC (London Metropolitan Archives). The proposal was approved by the CCCHH but opposed by the London Head Teachers' Association 8 February 1959. William Houghton, the chief education officer, proposed the end of the 11+ in May 1963.

56   C. Jewitt and K. Jones, 'Managing Time and Space in the New English Classroom', in Lawn and Grosvenor, *Materialities of Schooling,* p. 202. Thanks to Ken Jones for clarifying his position.

57   See Kean, *London Stories.*

58   http://www.qaa.ac.uk/academicinfrastructure/benchmark/honours/history.asp, accessed 27 January 2007. See also A. Munslow, 'Getting on with History', *Rethinking History,* 9: 4 (2005) 497–501.

59   R. Samuel, 'The Return of History', originally published 14 June 1990 in *London Review of Books,* reproduced posthumously in R. Samuel, *Island Stories: Unravelling Britain* (London: Verso, 1998), p. 222.

60   *ibid,* p. 223.

61   L. Passerini, *Autobiography of a Generation: Italy 1968* (London: University Press of New England, 1996), p. 124.

11
Absent Fathers, Present Histories

Martin Bashforth

Introduction

There is a lack of serious and sustained debate about the value of family history, both in its own right and in its potential relationships to other genres and disciplines including public history.[1] In this chapter I will draw attention to several of these relationships, while concentrating specifically on the relationship between family history and the archive.[2]

Family historians do not so much make a cult of the archive as act as its slaves.[3] They pursue names in lists produced during the course of state, business and institutional activities: what may usefully be called 'the public archive' and consisting primarily of documentation. Their core activity bears a close resemblance to 'family reconstitution' techniques, shading into 'community reconstitution' techniques.[4] Standards may vary between one researcher and another but good practices are promulgated within the organised family history community, particularly in the UK by the Institute of Heraldic and Genealogical Studies (IHGS) and the Federation of Family History Societies (FFHS). The proliferation of family history societies, magazines devoted to the subject and family history fairs in the UK are an indication of how seriously the community of family historians see themselves. They are probably the single biggest constituency of practising historical researchers within the wider public history community.[5]

Family historians researching the most recent three or four generations perhaps pay greater attention to materials found in domestic collections of ephemera, objects, documents and photographs directly connected with the people being researched: that is, 'the private archive'.[6] One of the peculiar characteristics of the private archive, which differentiates it from the public archive, is the frequent inclusion of almost any item of material culture as well as documentation.[7]

Compared with other genres, family history research can be intensely personal. One can be simultaneously the gatherer of materials from private and public domains (the archivist or curator) and the one who interprets the materials and presents this interpretation to the world (the historian) while physically and emotionally being an object of the research. This is particularly true when studying the more recent past.

These concerns were brought to mind when I had been researching my grandfather, killed in the First World War in 1918. He left almost nothing tangible in the form of a private archive and there are only limited records in the public domain. During this same period I was attempting to create a private archive for my late father from a miscellaneous set of papers, photographs and objects, a particular selection of which he had hidden away from the rest of the family. I was setting out to identify the items, list them and box them formally. These experiences confronted me with a dangerous thought concerning my self-conscious position in relation to what might constitute my own private archive.

Such concerns are personal but have resonance at a professional level. I work as a para-professional archivist, have been trained conventionally as an academic historian and in my spare time research a variety of micro-histories, each with a strong family history basis.[8] However, in the case of my grandfather, father and myself, I am directly involved as part of a continuum of stories and memories covering four generations. What follows is a discussion of some of the issues brought to light so far, at the core of which is how the personal archives of 'ordinary' people may survive and the forces involved, using my own family history as a case in point.[9]

Absent fathers

In my paternal lineage the absence of fathers has been a constant thread over several generations. My grandfather, Thomas Bashforth, was born illegitimate in Workington, Cumberland, now Cumbria, in October 1888. His mother, Ellen Bashforth, later married a former soldier called John McGlasson, who thus became stepfather to Thomas. There were five further children who survived infancy. The family moved around the north of England following opportunities for work until they settled in Darlington, County Durham. Here Thomas married Florence Wood in 1912. They had three children before Thomas was killed in action in France in March 1918, leaving the children without a father and no direct memory of him.[10] The body was not identified after the war and Thomas Bashforth has no known grave, being listed as one of the 'missing' on the Pozières Memorial northeast of Amiens, France.[11] The lack of a grave marker adds a dimension of absoluteness to the sense of absence.

The youngest of Thomas' children was my father, Raymond Bashforth, born 5 November 1917. His mother married John Neary in 1922 and they had four more children who survived infancy. Thus Ray, with his brother and sister, was brought up by a stepfather as part of a family of mixed parentage. John Neary, his stepfather, had also been born illegitimate and brought up by a stepfather.

The next generation was disrupted in a slightly different way. As a youth Ray Bashforth joined the Territorial Army.[12] Along with his friends he was called-up in September 1939 at the outbreak of the Second World War. His close friend Joe Hinnigan was killed in a tragic accident within the first week, leaving a pregnant wife and two infant girls. Ray kept in touch with the widow during the war and in 1943 they married. They had one child, myself, born in 1945. Ray became a stepfather before he was a father and strenuously avoided favouring me in any way over my half sisters and brother. He had a stepfather of his own to act as role model as well as a personal empathy with the bereaved family, the son in particular.

Clearly this past is a problem for me as a 'historian'. I grew up sensing an emotional distance between myself and my father, a perception of paternal 'absence' that may be imagined or the outcome of other factors in my upbringing. This perception is not a fixed entity. It was brought to my attention in the course of counselling therapy as a means of both understanding Ray's behaviours and my own. During the development of this chapter the dimensions of that perception have changed, influenced by questions raised at its original presentation and in response to subsequent research and successive revisions of this text.[13]

In the course of time, my first marriage failed and (as I see it) I became 'absent' to my daughter, as I moved away both geographically and emotionally, absorbed by new priorities. We have worked hard in recent years to build a new relationship, but this also adds depth to the question of what I might choose to leave as a personal archive and the questions that my daughter in her turn might wish to have answered.

This is the basic story around which the subsequent discussion about personal archives will weave. It is a common enough experience for families over the past century or more, which makes it relevant beyond my own family history. It illustrates how the search for information about the past is not simply a pragmatic hunt through the archives – public and private – nor simply an exercise of the intellect, but a struggle with the emotions. In this kind of family history truths become various, elusive and contested, in our own minds and within our own personal networks.

This chapter will not be primarily concerned with issues and theories about absent fathers or with issues concerning masculine identity. It is about absence and the archive, absence and family history and contingent emotional questions.[14]

Archivists and boxes

Conventionally the records of a particular individual will be organised by an archivist into an arrangement dependent on the size and complexity of the contents. This creates the illusion of a discrete entity that confines the objects and documents through which an individual's story may be approached. A semblance of order is brought to such a collection by a process of sorting, arranging and listing the contents to form a catalogue.[15] The artificial creation of the professional archivist bears only a loose resemblance to what happens in everyday life, particularly with regard to the formation of private archives.

For most ordinary individuals those items that might make up a private archive seldom receive professional treatment in a public repository. This is the situation with regard to my grandfather and father and in the anticipated course of events will be no different for myself. Individual people sort, sift and reject the detritus of their own lives on a daily basis and may do something more or less systematic for departed relatives. The creation of a personal archive itself has a history. I can best illustrate this with reference to my own family. Imagine, then, three boxes.

Box 1: Thomas Bashforth 1888–1918

The imaginary archive box for my grandfather would need to be very small. His personal archive comprises three photographs, three campaign medals from the First World War, a bronze plaque and a certificate sent to his widow recording his ultimate sacrifice. While he had a personal connection to the photographs, the other objects were presented to the family only after his death. In one sense these may have acted as a substitute for the missing body of Thomas Bashforth. It is perhaps fitting that the medals and plaque now form part of a public display at the Durham Light Infantry Museum where several private histories have become public history and are presented in the context of values that are public rather than personal and private. In the museum they appear in the Medal Room and details are accessible on the museum's website under the heading 'Local Heroes'.[16] Gathering the stories associated with these objects under such a simplistic caption evades a more complex dimension of historical meanings.

The photographs all show him as a soldier – as a new recruit in 1914 in his first uniform, in a family group as a corporal in 1915 before he went to France and finally in an odd arrangement superimposed onto a photograph of the adoptive McGlasson family. This is 14956 Thomas Bashforth, 16th and 11th (Service) Battalions, Durham Light Infantry, defined for all time as a soldier of the First World War. The items in this small box and the items in the museum fall into an uneasy space where personal and public interpretations are in contest. For me they possess an emotional resonance as a connection to a missing grandfather. But any attempt to understand them has to negotiate almost a century of meanings overlaid by public myth about the First World War. My personal response has been to go to the public archive to try to reconstruct my own version of my grandfather's story. I have visited the locations in northern France with which this story is associated. In the process I have experienced the emotions that both the archive and the locations evoke, symbolised when I adopted a surrogate grave as my grandfather's last resting place.[17]

Such a small collection is unremarkable for a working-class man of his time. What may be more remarkable – apart from the uniformity already noted – is how these things were hidden. My Gran sent the medals to the DLI Museum and, although I had visited her regularly for years, she had never shown them to me or mentioned Thomas Bashforth at all. Although I knew as a child that my grandfather had been killed in this long ago war it was never discussed or elaborated upon. Not until my mid-fifties did my father produce the postcard of my grandfather in uniform during a casual conversation about the family tree. He said I could keep it, as this was not his 'real father', as this title was best reserved for John Neary who had brought him up.[18]

Imagine how this small personal archive came into being. At the time of his death Thomas Bashforth had other identities: as a father, a husband, a plasterer, a brother and a friend. But these were caused to disappear. His widow kept, was allowed to keep or perhaps thought it politic to keep only the few photographs – later passed to her children – and the medals and plaque. If she spoke about him to the children,

Figure 11.1   Private 14956 Thomas Bashforth, Durham Light Infantry. Undated, probably October 1914. Postcard given to the author by Ray Bashforth in 1997 (Author's collection)

Figure 11.2 Corporal Thomas Bashforth on pre-embarkation leave, summer 1915, with wife Florence and children, Edith (standing) and Thomas junior (Author's collection: permission Thomas Bashforth)

none of them have remembered anything she said and none of them remembered the man himself. Perhaps with a new husband and family it was best to honour only this small fragment of the man.

Joanna Bourke has commented on the emotional strategies adopted by the widows and families of the missing from the First World War and those encouraged by the State.[19] She described how people responded to the creation of local war memorials, were moved by events surrounding the Unknown Warrior or more privately turned to spiritualism as a means of keeping contact with the missing. However, she did not consider the thousands of 'private burials' that took place when widows chose to set aside their private grief in an act of denial. I have no memory of parents or grandparents ever wearing Remembrance Poppies, although I do remember gruff dismissals of the official State ceremonies. Private disdain for the public mainstream of remembrance has been marginalised as an issue but may be more common than usually recognised. Examination of more cases such as that of my forebears may reveal a more widespread form of refusal. Individual stories have the ability to stand outside of the mainstream, but it is precisely this exceptionality that is so often denied by the institutions of public history, a denial that might be usefully subverted by the millions of stories available in the family history community.

Box 2: Ray Bashforth 1917–2001

Imagine now a second box, which holds the personal archive of Thomas' son and my father, Ray Bashforth. I can describe it in detail, having been its 'archivist'. Its contents are more numerous and more diverse, since Ray lived longer than his father did and died only a few years ago. There are three significant aspects that deserve special attention.

Firstly, there are documents and objects that fairly typically reflect a working-class man of his generation. There are medals, photographs and certificates from his service in the Second World War. More unusual is a large foolscap notebook containing his course notes from the school of the Army Catering Corps. There are small objects, such as his blood donor badge and silver medals he won in boxing championships in the army. These items were always readily accessible in the home, stored in a cupboard by my mother and ceremoniously produced from time to time. Susan Pearce has commented on how women tend to be the custodians and interpreters of the collective domestic heritage and this is certainly true in the case of my mother.[20]

The second group of materials comprises memorabilia, mainly photographs, collected by other members of the family. My mother has the wedding photographs and she, my sisters and I each have our own sets of photographs in which Dad and we feature, often from holidays or family visits.

The third group seems to represent that part of my father that was truly absent. Wherever my father lived the centre of his domestic life was the shed in the yard or at the bottom of the garden. In this shed my father practised what Joanna Bourke has characterised as 'masculine housework'.[21] Occasionally my brother and I were inculcated into some of the minor mysteries of the trade, enlisted to chop firewood, clean everyone's shoes and dig potatoes. By and large, however, we were kept at bay from my father's sacrosanct space. My mother was guardian of the 'family heritage' and kept it in her space in the living room, while my father had his own space in which he demonstrated to an extreme the 'male tendency to distance self and its material from the family'.[22]

Figure 11.3   The tool chest in which Ray Bashforth hid his private collection of mementoes. The box was at the back of the second drawer down
(Photograph: the author, August 2005)

Moving from one shed to another over 60 years was a set of drawers in which Ray kept his tools and other equipment. This piece of furniture holds the same fascination for me today as it did when, as a small boy, I pulled out drawers to touch the mystery that was, and remains, my father.[23] He did not teach me any of his manual skills, so the various tools acquired the character of totems and I remain fascinated to this day with the skilled artisans that populate my ancestral lines. I no doubt unconsciously still associate manual labour with masculinity, much as Joanna Bourke has described.[24]

After my father's death a tin was found hidden away at the back of a drawer in this chest. Contents included photographs of him from the 1930s, before he was married, mostly showing him as a Territorial soldier in uniform or at annual camp. My mother at 94 recognised none of the faces of the other young men in the photographs. There were also mementoes from the Second World War, notably a patch of red cloth as worn by prisoners of war in the Italian prison camps, his army dog tags and a Royal Signals cap badge.[25] There was his army pay book and form CRO 24 from the Ministry of Works registering him in his trade under Defence Regulations 56 AB. Items such as these are easy to identify and can be related to other things kept elsewhere and to various public records.

Some items, however, are a complete mystery. A small book on *The Art of Lettering and Layout,* dated 1931, and inscribed with the name S/179687 RASC Holman Heaps, may relate to his apprenticeship as a painter and decorator. The name is unfamiliar to anyone in the family and, as my father did very little in the way of sign writing, it seems an odd item for a keepsake, especially squeezed into a tin box. A cheap set of charms, comprising a cross, heart and anchor, may have been a 'good luck' charm my father carried during the war. But my mother does not recognise it and its original significance is lost. Thus I would dispute Susan Pearce's contention that because such things represent 'an intensively individual past – no one is interested in other people's souvenirs'.[26] If that individual is connected to us through family or friendship, such objects exercise a fascination founded in that relationship and we enter into a search for meaning.[27]

Susannah Radstone and Katharine Hodgkin have commented on how memory is reliant on 'props' and that the subjective identity of private objects of this nature may not easily become public, as 'neither the prop nor the memory need have the same resonance for an outsider'.[28] I would suggest that for such items the only way they can have meaning is if they relate to a story about the individual in question.

Figure 11.4   Ray Bashforth at Royal Signals Territorial Army summer camp, circa 1935, with Ray Bashforth middle front row among unknown friends. Photograph from Ray's 'hidden archive'. Was it also a hidden identity?
(Author's collection)

In my father's secret collection there is a membership card for the aero-modelling club of which he was once secretary. It shows him paid up until 22 February 1947. My brother and sisters told me that my mother stopped him going 60 years ago because she disapproved of his habit of going for a drink after club meetings. Thus, apart from its significance in itself, the small piece of card may be also a clue to the other items in this secret collection. Perhaps the box represented for him a complex of regrets and private memories – a former identity made absent in time and space. What particular significance they had for him can only be a matter for speculation. It is not even clear if he ever took them out of the tin and looked at them. They may represent an emotional casualty in what Joanna Bourke has described as a struggle for power in the domestic space between husband and wife in the early decades of the twentieth century, thus linking the personal story to the public.[29] Less dramatically, they may represent a mixture of 'selected and consciously chosen documentation from the past' along with 'the mad fragmentations that no one intended to preserve and that just ended up there'.[30] It is also possible that 'the real story' is that as interpreter I am trying to confirm some sense of myself in relation to my father, driven by my unconscious needs, rather than by something about my father as such.[31]

As an archive, this is more complex than that of my grand-father. The illusion of a discrete individual entity created by the neat, acid-free, archive box is challenged by the number of items that have a public origin or that represent connections with other individuals and networks. Because I have a personal connection with the subject of this collection the items are not silent and inert; they speak to me through my own memories of the man, challenging my attempt to use my archival training as a means of containing what they represent.

The secret collection questions what I thought I knew about my father. Behind the identity of the man I struggled to know there was apparently yet another identity, more truly absent and now only accessible through conjecture. Ray's secret collection contrasts the experience recounted by Sally Morgan in relation to the album of photographs her father put together in a deliberate desire not to be forgotten. She was able to characterise this action as a form of writing history in images: 'he was giving me his own narrative of his own life'.[32] By contrast Ray has hidden away an alternative narrative, the structure and meaning of which I can only reconstitute by imagination and inference.

Box 3: Martin Bashforth 1945–present

As yet there is no archive box that might contain the personal archive that would represent my life. There are suitable materials for several such boxes, while decisions made in the past have already influenced what could potentially be there. Having now been alerted to the fundamental issue of how personal archives might come into existence, I find myself in a unique position. Just as my father had control over his secret box, so I have potential control over everything that might form my own personal archive.

My response to this situation was to seek an alternative viewpoint, so I asked my daughter what she would want such an archive to tell her about me. She provided a list of questions about home life in childhood, education, jobs, family relationships and key moments of transition in my life story. There were questions about emotional experiences, about sensations of the world around me, about hopes and dreams and how they turned out and about public events in which I had a part.

Her final paragraph reads: 'As the daughter of an absent father, my requirements are more biographical than historical, I would like to understand what life has been like for you so that I can draw comparisons between our relative experiences and answer the question: Who is this man?'

Both my question and her answer have to be seen in the context of our relationship and where it stands at this point in time. My approach to her was both a device within our process of rediscovery and a means to access an alternative viewpoint from my own. It was not emotionally neutral and involved a leap of faith on both our parts.[33] As curator of my archive I want to be ethically dispassionate about what stays and what goes. As interpreter and historian my 'training' suggests the need to be objective in my judgements. As the person directly involved, being examined and weighed up by the next generation while simultaneously wishing to control my autobiography, the effect is to induce paralysis.

In relation to my personal archive my daughter's questions missed out whole aspects of my life that I consider extremely important to me. Greater knowledge of the contents might generate further questions. However, much of the 'evidence' relating to questions she asked has long since been destroyed. The traces that remain may provide less than satisfactory answers. Many of the questions demand answers from the two most elusive aspects of our human existence: what goes on inside our heads and hearts and what transpires in the realm of social interactions at the minute level. These were never documented.

While the questions my daughter asked are precisely the kind asked by biographers trying to reconstruct something of the essential humanity of their subject, they expose the limits of any archive in being able to perform this function. They illustrate just how strongly other kinds of 'evidence' are required by those wanting to write history from the bottom up, whether working in the academy, the museum, the archive or as freelance family historians.

The archive, memory and family history

Jacques Derrida has commented that the trouble with the archive is 'the trouble of secrets, of plots, of clandestineness, of half-private, half-public conjurations, always at the unstable limit between public and private, between the family, the society and the State, between the family and an intimacy even more private than the family, between oneself and oneself'.[34] In a related vein, Annette Kuhn has commented: 'People who live in families make every effort to keep certain things concealed from the rest of the world, and at times from each other as well. Things will be lied about, or simply never mentioned. Sometimes family secrets are so deeply buried that they elude the conscious awareness even of those most closely involved'.[35] Kuhn, exploring the power of 'memory work' in constructing a personal history, stressed the social pressures tending towards concealment, even in those histories that contained unpleasant discoveries. By contrast, Derrida explored the associated psychological processes leading to the deletion of memory.

My exploration of personal archives in the context of my own family history has demonstrated in microcosm some of their observations and concerns. These are not unknown to professional archivists. Colin Gale has raised the issue of how archivists handle public records that reveal uncomfortable aspects of history, such as the forcible removal of Aboriginal children in Australia, while acknowledging the need to retain items that personally repulsed him in a private archive he was called upon to accession.[36] Judith Everton has drawn the attention of fellow archivists to new developments in health provision whereby individuals are encouraged to research their immediate family roots. Often, she has written, 'individuals suffering from an unresolved loss of some kind will frequently have met lies, some of which may well have been meant to shelter them from information perceived to be unpalatable, but as a result of which they are likely to feel a diminished trust in adults and a reluctance to accept information offered to them'.[37]

The same pressures apply to the researcher or family member dealing with items of domestic heritage in terms of retention, disclosure and interpretation. The more uncongenial the item and the memory associated with it, the more acute may be the desire to suppress or discard. The wider history of family dislocation and dysfunction associated with the phenomenon of the 'absent father', however that absence might have occurred, is not something affecting isolated individuals. It forms part of the social history of the twentieth century and has profound contemporary resonance.[38]

I remember a saying from my working-class upbringing that you should not 'wash your dirty linen in public'; that is, you should not reveal family secrets to others outside the immediate circle. Even at its simplest level this represents a challenge to family historians if they are to progress from the practice of accumulating ancestors and distant cousins to the point where they can share their stories and, as my daughter has suggested, 'draw comparisons between our relative experiences' and move closer to an understanding of who we really are.

Such an approach to family history has yet to be seriously attempted. Earlier academic interest in family history tended to see it as the raw material for a study of communities and local history.[39] Raphael Samuel over 30 years ago suggested that oral history might transform family history, making possible 'a much more phenomenological account'.[40] More recently John Charlton has suggested that a combination of a linear family history with associated records linking to broader sets of community and institutional archives might help illuminate periods of social transition.[41] The use of oral history by Anna Davin in her evocation of London childhood is a brilliant example of how illuminating this kind of personal evidence can be.[42] Paul Thompson has commented on the potential of oral history to enhance family history by adding information about 'the ordinary family's contacts with neighbours and kin, or its internal relationships'.[43]

In the public history sector in recent years, local community projects, museums and archives in the UK have begun to develop the concept of the 'Community Archive', gathering materials from volunteer contributors in the locality to begin to illustrate how local people view their own community's past.[44] Roy Bradshaw has begun an ambitious project to link early nineteenth-century records to interactive mapping to create an unrivalled resource through which to study the development of Derby from the individual to the community.[45] Add to these examples the methodologies deriving from the inter-disciplinary use of psychology developed by those engaged in 'memory work',[46] the potential of family history to illuminate at least the twentieth century appears limited only by the sheer immensity of the task involved in working with so much data and so many contributors.

Conclusion

Early in the development of family history as a mass occupation, Stan Newens drew attention to the role of family historians – especially those organised into Family History Societies – in ensuring the continued opening up of archives and records offices to the general public.[47] The phenomenon has been acknowledged by archivists in the UK and elsewhere.[48] Newens commented that the vast majority of such researchers, if not actually working class themselves, were researching predominantly working-class and lower middle-class forebears.

I would go further than his tentative conclusions of 25 years ago and suggest that family historians collectively represent the most significant opportunity to thoroughly democratise the practice of history. The idea of thousands of families conducting three or four generation family history studies, using the products of family history research and being *organised among themselves* represents a revolution waiting to happen, notwithstanding the methodological issues regarding meaning and interpretation that this paper has exposed.[49] An in-depth study of linear successions of 'absent fathers' might have value in its own right as a contribution to historical socio-psychology, while in the process demonstrating the untapped potential of the millions of family histories that already exist in the private domain.

Notes

1 I am defining public history as a multi-disciplinary field of related forms of study and presentation of historical material, rather than a genre as such. There is no single universal definition but the one provided by the New York University to define its Graduate Program touches on most of the points around which agreement might cluster, without specifically mentioning family history. See http://www.history.fas.nyu.edu/object/history. gradprog.archivespublichistory.html, accessed 30 January 2007.
2 In the course of this chapter I will refer to 'the archive' as the general body of documentation available for researchers. More specific definitions will emerge during the discussion.
3 The concept of the 'cult of the archive' derives from Ludmilla Jordanova, *History in Practice* (London: Arnold, 2000), p. 186ff in which she states that 'the archive implies a kind of intimacy with particular aspects of the past

that are more personal, individual, private and hence worth looking at precisely because they concern "real life"' (p. 187). The relevance of her emphasis on the personal indicates the particular resonance archives may have for the family history researcher.

4 The method of 'family reconstitution' was pioneered in France by Louis Henry, and in the UK by E. A. Wrigley and the Cambridge Population Studies Group in their studies of historical demography. 'Community reconstitution' is of the same progeny and was pioneered in the UK by Alan MacFarlane.

5 Further reference to the significance of the family history community will appear throughout this chapter.

6 I will use the terms 'private archive' and 'personal archive' interchangeably throughout, to refer to the assemblage of materials relating to the personal life of a particular individual.

7 Hilda Kean brings this out very strongly in her discussion of the formation of the personal archives of her mother and father, in *London Stories: Personal lives, Public Histories* (London: Rivers Oram Press, 2004), p. 157ff. Non-documentary objects are seen to have enormous meaning in relation to the character and activities of their former owners.

8 These are primarily in connection with social networks and migration in eighteenth-century southwest Yorkshire, the story of the Barnsley Cord-wainers Society from 1747 and the human stories behind the history of the 11th Battalion Durham Light Infantry in the First World War. Through these projects I am trying to develop a methodology for handling this type of data in a way that enables historical analysis beyond simple genealogy.

9 I have used the catch-all term 'ordinary' to cover all those non-élite, non-celebrity people, usually defined as working-class or middle-class, though in my personal view they frequently are and often were extraordinary both as individuals and in the groups to which they variously belonged.

10 The eldest child, Ethel, was two years old when Thomas left for France and would have seen little or nothing of him before he was killed. The eldest son born in 1915 is still alive but has no memory of his father. My own father was only two months old when Thomas had his last home leave in January 1918.

11 The Pozières Memorial commemorates those Allied soldiers who lost their lives on the Somme battlefields during 1918.

12 The Territorial Army was established originally in 1912 to provide the UK with a reserve defence army. Members attended weekly training sessions and an annual summer camp. The branch in Darlington was attached to the Royal Corps of Signals.

13 The original paper was delivered at the First International Conference on Public History at Ruskin College, Oxford, UK in September 2005 and was followed by correspondence between myself and other participants.

14 At the conference where the original paper was presented the issue of the absent father dominated questions and discussion. It has great relevance to the study of family history and resonated emotionally and intellectually with the delegates. There simply is neither the time nor the scope to handle these questions satisfactorily here.

15 Archivists work to a set of standards overseen by professional bodies such as the International Council on Archives and in the UK by the Museums,

Libraries and Archives Council and the Society of Archivists. There are professionally monitored training courses and professional, para-professional
and voluntary workers in the field generally adhere to the same standards.

16 The Durham Light Infantry Museum website can be found at http://www.
durham.gov.uk/dli and the relevant section is found under Medal Collection.
Accessed 27 March 2007.
http://www.durham.gov.uk/dli/usp.nsf/pws/dli+-+dli+home+page

17 The grave is to an Unknown Soldier of the Durham Light Infantry at Bou-
choir, south east of Amiens, barely a kilometre from the spot where Thomas
Bashforth was killed and forming part of a group of four including one of
his named comrades and two other unknown soldiers.

18 In a significant parallel, my half brother would vehemently claim Ray Bashforth as his 'real father' and declare that the one buried in Darlington's
West Cemetery meant nothing to him. Both in his case and that of my
father I remember the tone of voice, perhaps not angry or bitter, but decisive and abrupt and clearly intended to cut the conversation dead.

19 J. Bourke, *Dismembering the Male: Men's Bodies, Britain and the Great War*
(London: Reaktion Books, 1999), pp. 228–52.

20 S. M. Pearce, 'The Construction of Heritage: The Domestic Context and its
Implications', *International Journal of Heritage Studies*, 4: 2 (1998) 101.

21 J. Bourke, *Working-Class Cultures in Britain 1890–1960: Gender, Class and
Ethnicity* (London and New York: Routledge, 1994), pp. 81–9.

22 Pearce, 'The Construction of Heritage', 93. While Pearce's study of domestic
heritage opened up an important way of understanding the processes of
material culture survival in the modern era it was slightly flawed in its
methodology and thus failed to bring out the gender issues sufficiently
strongly. In defining feelings about spaces, interviewees in the survey were
asked in which room they felt most 'at home'. For men this is a loaded
phrase, distinguished in particular from 'work' and other spheres of personal identity such as my father's shed. In this latter space he was certainly
happy, free and himself, but he would not have described it as the room in
which he most felt 'at home'.

23 The chest of drawers did not originally belong to my father. It was made in
1912 by my maternal great grandfather, a cabinet-maker by trade, for my
maternal grandfather as a wedding present. It therefore possesses multiple
significances for me.

24 Bourke, *Working-Class Cultures*, pp. 94–5

25 Ray was captured at Mersa Matruh in Libya in June 1942, held prisoner at
PG 78 Sulmona in the Abruzzo region of Italy, east of Rome, and escaped in
September 1943 following the signing of the Armistice between the Allied
Forces and the Italian Government. He arrived back in England in January
1944, having been helped by an Italian family.

26 S. M. Pearce, 'Collecting Reconsidered', in S. M. Pearce (ed.) *Interpreting
Objects and Collections* (London and New York: Routledge, 1994), p. 196.

27 Christopher Tilley, discussing archaeological objects, has suggested that no
object has an 'ultimate or unitary meaning that can be held to exhaust it'
and that we enter into a dialectical relationship with the object and create
our own meanings, very much in the present. See C. Tilley, 'Interpreting
material culture', in Pearce, *Interpreting Objects*, p. 72.

28 S. Radstone and K. Hodgkin (eds) *Regimes of Memory* (London and New York: Routledge, 2003), pp. 55–60.

29 Bourke, *Working-Class Cultures*, pp. 67–71.

30 C. Steedman, *Dust* (Manchester: Manchester University Press, 2001), p. 68.

31 Carolyn Steedman suggests that the archive reader is searching for something other than what is found: *ibid*, p. 77.

32 S. J. Morgan, 'My Father's Photographs: The Visual as Public History', H. Kean, P. Martin and S. J. Morgan (eds) *Seeing History: Public History in Britain Now* (London: Francis Boutle, 2000), p. 34.

33 It took considerable courage on my daughter's part to respond in the way she did, knowing that her response would become public. To say I am grateful is an understatement of how I feel about what she gave me.

34 J. Derrida, *Archive Fever: A Freudian Impression* (Chicago and London: University of Chicago Press, 1998), p. 90.

35 A. Kuhn, *Family Secrets: Acts of Memory and Imagination* (London and New York: Verso, 1995), pp. 1–2.

36 C. Gale, 'Record-keeping as an Ethical Imperative', *Journal of the Society of Archivists*, 27: 1 (2006) 17–27.

37 J. Everton, 'The Role of Archives in the Perception of Self', *Journal of the Society of Archivists*, 27: 2 (2006) 227–46.

38 To illustrate this, try typing the phrase 'absent father' into an internet search engine and see what proportion of the results relate to issues of contemporary public policy and single parenthood. This is not an exact science, but illustrates the point.

39 The Open University in the UK ran a series of linked courses leading students from analysis of their own family trees through to the study of community. Some of these students went on to form the Family and Community Historical Research Society, a rare example of collaborative work in illuminating aspects of social history but one which has long gone past any connection with family history research as such.

40 R. Samuel, 'Local History and Oral History', *History Workshop Journal*, 1: 1 (1976) 203.

41 J. Charlton, 'Family History from the Left', *London Socialist Historians Group Newsletter* 6 (1999) 2.

42 A. Davin, *Growing Up Poor: Home, School and Street in London 1870–1914* (London: Rivers Oram Press, 1996).

43 P. Thompson, 'The Voice of the Past: Oral History', in R. Perks and A. Thomson (eds) *The Oral History Reader*, 1st edn (London and New York: Routledge, 1998), p. 25.

44 Examples of these projects in the UK are numerous and have in many cases been supported not only by local authorities using regeneration funding, but by technical assistance from the National Archives and the website initiative Commanet.

45 'Digital Derby', a project in progress described by Roy Bradshaw of the University of Nottingham at a seminar on the uses of Geographical Information Science in historical research, University of York, 28 February 2007.

46 See, for example, Kuhn, *Family Secrets*; Radstone and Hodgkin, *Regimes of Memory*; K. Hodgkin and S. Radstone (eds) *Contested Pasts: The Politics of*

Memory (London and New York: Routledge, 2003); S. Radstone (ed.) *Memory and Methodology* (Oxford and New York: Berg, 2000).

47 S. Newens, 'Family History Societies', *History Workshop Journal*, 11 (Spring 1981) 154–9.

48 See, for example, R. Boyns, 'Archivists and Family Historians: Local Authority Record Repositories and the Family History User Group', *Journal of the Society of Archivists*, 20: 1 (1999) 61–74; E. G. Franz, 'What Makes an Archives successful?: The "House of History" Concept', *Journal of the Society of Archivists*, 16: 1 (1995) 71–6.

49 The emphasis is mine, as I think that museums, archives and academic institutions have a vital informative and critical role, but should allow the family history community itself to generate the research, the debates and the analysis. I believe the skills to do this are rapidly emerging in the constituency of family historians and they need only to become conscious of their collective power.

12
'Memoryscape': Integrating Oral History, Memory and Landscape on the River Thames

Toby Butler

Introduction

The story of how I found myself in a rowing boat, intensely following a piece of rubbish floating in the river Thames for 15 miles, is going to take some telling. It begins at the Museum of London where I worked as an advisor on a sound art installation, *Linked*, by the artist Graeme Miller.[1] This was a trail that ran alongside the M11 link road in Hackney, the site of the biggest anti-road protest Britain had ever seen. The trail was made up of oral testimony from people who had lost their homes in the process of the motorway construction, broadcast from lampposts in the streets alongside the new road. At certain points on the walk you listened to tracks at specific locations using audio equipment borrowed from local libraries, a little like the museum audio guides that most people are familiar with, but used in the outside landscape.

I wanted to develop the idea of the audio walk conceptually, as an active and immersive way to understand and map the cultural landscape, and more practically as a different way of presenting oral history. I created two audio walks of my own, playable on CD and mp3 players, along two sections of the Thames Path that runs alongside the river Thames in London. Adopting a term used by Miller, I later dubbed the walks that used oral history recordings 'memoryscapes' – landscape interpreted and imagined using the memories of others.[2] I wanted to experiment with presenting memories coherently in a spatial context, using some techniques borrowed from artistic, geographical, oral history and public history practice, and in the process encourage people to encounter parts of the river – and its culture – that they may not have considered exploring before.

In *Theatres of Memory*, Raphael Samuel looked beyond the discipline of academic history, museum studies and the heritage industry to argue that public history could encompass a broader range of practices.[3] In recalling Samuel's teaching pedagogy, Stuart Hall described his approach to the past:

> [Samuel] profoundly respected the depth and richness of lived experience which ... [gave his students] a historical sense of themselves and made them into the social historians of their own lives and cultures and the active custodians of their own popular memories.[4]

Samuel's concept of public history as work that can be both embracing and situated, has been consolidated and extended since his death. In Britain, two aspects of public history have been influential. First, its inclusive nature seems to have found a natural home in oral history, to the extent that there are dedicated public history pages in the Oral History Society's journal.[5] The second influence might be loosely termed historical reflexivity. Samuel was concerned that people drew on their own experiences and identities to make historical meaning in the world. This has continued at Ruskin College, Oxford, under the direction of Hilda Kean who jointly developed a public history programme with him and established an MA course in public history in 1996.[6] However, in the current higher education environment, this more democratic form of history-making may have a hard road to hoe.

While Samuel's brand of public history has many intellectual and political attractions, it is not the only path that might be followed. Jill Liddington and Simon Ditchfield have argued that history debate has been frozen about Samuel's idea of heritage and public history since his death.[7] They are right to warn against the stultifying effect of memorialisation and more debate can only help public history evolve intellectually. But I hope the public historians of the future can retain something of the spirit of Samuel's later work and keep the public history concept as elastic, open, interdisciplinary and inclusive as possible.

In this spirit, I will draw on disciplines outside of history to explain how I attempted to design an intrinsically open and outward-looking methodology to encounter an unknown, and unexpected, set of people to interview. If, as Samuel argued, history is at its heart an activity as opposed to a profession or an intellectual debate, then the 'doing', the process of research is significant.[8] I will consider how oral history recordings were used to curate an oral history walking trail and examine the process of weaving my own personal journey into the recording. The final element in this chapter will contain another public – the hundreds of people who actually experienced my memoryscape. A recording is lifeless until experienced; it is only when each listener walks through the landscape and brings their own unique set of memories, sensations and understandings to bear that what Samuel called the 'dialectic of past-present relations' can be performed.[9] Only after considering those responses can the whole creative process be truly understood.

As well as giving an artistic and experimental take on how a work of public history might be created, I also hope to provide some inspiration to those who are interested in using new media as a means of engagement. If we extend the term public history to encompass public space, there are now whole new avenues open for historians to offer interpretations of the outside world. The increasingly popular mobile platforms (GPS-enabled mobile phones, mp3 players, in-car navigation systems) can offer exciting opportunities to create multimedia oral, local and cultural histories. Such histories can now be easily and cheaply self-published online for downloading, thus potentially reaching a very wide public audience.[10]

Place, mobility and memory

Place and mobility has become a major concern for geographers and increasingly historians interested in narrating place. Older ideas that topography, geology and economic history 'made' a place have been questioned by writers like Doreen Massey who has argued that places have to be seen as very complex and shifting combinations of local, national and international networks. She argues that a really radical history of a place would not try to 'seal a place up into one neat and tidy "envelope of space-time"' but recognise that what comes together in a place is a conjunction of many histories and places.[11] From the 1970s the phenomenological ideas of Yi-Fu Tuan and Edward Relph have also been influential.[12] Tuan argued that humans get to know the world through place, so that topophilia, the 'affective bond between people and place' was a fundamentally important part of human experience.[13] Relph suggested that one of the fundamental aspects of being human was to live in a world that is filled with significant places, because place determines our experience.[14] Place, home and 'roots' are deep-seated human needs and they shape our cultural identity. This way of thinking, something that anthropologist Liisa Malkki has described as a fundamentally sedentary metaphysics, underpins much cultural thought and territorialises identity into commonplace assumptions about property, region and nation.[15] This philosophy of place is not without its difficulties. For example, Tim Cresswell's work on mobility and the tramp in America has explored the idea that such conceptions can lead to dualistic thoughts about people that are mobile, or displaced such as tramps, travellers or refugees as pathologically dangerous.[16]

A more positive and playful sense of mobility was famously celebrated by the Situationists, who were interested in the material and psychological patterns of the city street and their effects on the individual – a psychogeography.[17] Significance came from the 'dérive', literally a 'drift', an apparently aimless wandering that nonetheless revealed the psychic undercurrents of the city.[18] In his latest book *On the Move,* Cresswell explores some more positive valuations of mobility that have developed in social and cultural theory – a kind of 'nomadic metaphysics'.[19] For example Michel de Certeau argued that walking in the city is a performance, an acting out of place – he explains it in terms of direct comparison to language; walking, like language, are both creative acts where you can improvise, make connections, take short cuts, take thousands of decisions in the present.[20] Spoken memory can also be seen in these terms. The ability of spoken memory to make connections with other times, symbols and places make the act of memory a nomadic, mobile process – like our consciousness, it is always a work in progress.[21] It can therefore present a multifaceted, nuanced way of seeing the world. It is also fiercely independent, sometimes affirming dominant collective memory, but as Alessandro Portelli has shown, often opposing it.[22]

As well, the process of interviewing has a connective mobility of its own. Sometimes an oral history project can be the connecting network between people who scarcely know each other but share common ground. The interviewer has considerable connective agency in his or her power to take questions and problems from one interview to another – perhaps to someone directly responsible for a situation. This technique is most commonly used in news journalism, where it is normal practice to record the opinion of one person and then immediately relate the opinion to another for a response, to balance the story.[23] It can be extended to many sources to give great scope; in *Working,* for example, Studs Terkel investigated American attitudes to work by compiling interviews with people who may not be directly connected, but can offer different perspectives on a common theme. For example, in a chapter entitled 'cradle to grave', he records a baby nurse, schoolteachers, occupational therapist, retirement home nurse and an undertaker.[24]

The technique has more commonly been applied to places in the form of community-based oral histories of a village, locality or workplace. In some cases the community or group doesn't actually have to exist as an entity in the first place. In Islington, for example, an oral history trail is being constructed with people who live and work along the old main north road out of London, the A1, which runs through the borough. The project aims to tell 'the history and heritage of the A1 as told by the people who live and work along it', partly as a community building exercise.[25] Similarly Edward Platt used a routeway in *Leadville: A Biography of the A40*.[26] He knocked on the doors of residents in Western Avenue, another major road leading out of London, recording the words of anyone who was willing to discuss the road and their lives next to it. Like *Linked* mentioned already, Platt used the road as an organising principle to connect people. This more mobile, fractured perception of urban space does not necessarily coincide with historical, planning, government or place-name perceptions of place. The technique uses paths, routes, networks and trajectories to give a more complex idea of place, talking to a series of people who might not ordinarily meet, or consider themselves part of a group or a community.

There are parallels and strengths to be drawn from both the nomadic and the sedentary schools of thought, which are by no means mutually exclusive. The way that artists and oral historians have attempted to break free from rigid place-based conceptions of what makes up a community might be seen as 'mobile' practices. Yet in this work there is also a strong element of the sedentary or the topophilic. In terms of oral history, exploring alternative networks or paths through a community can reveal more complex connections between people, place and their identity, but place, home and roots still have a fundamentally important role.

Constructing a river-based oral history trail

I had lived in a houseboat on Ash Island, in the middle of the river Thames on the western borders of London, for ten years. I was acutely aware that the river in London was a mobile entity in itself that sustained a variety of river-based cultures. Yet many Londoners seemed to see it in sedentary terms as a border, an administrative and cultural dividing line between north and south. Henri Lefebvre has argued that our conceptions of 'abstract space' tend to be fragmented and broken, particularly when places are artificially sub-divided for purposes of administration and control.[27] The Thames in London is diced up in exactly this kind of way. Conservation areas and borough boundaries marked on maps are frequently plotted in the middle of the river.[28] The river and its tributaries are even governed by three different organisations in different parts of London.[29]

Living in the middle of the river made these divisions seem nonsensical. In my exploration of river culture I wanted the Thames to be appreciated as an entity, not merely a border or a backdrop for riverside development. I applied the Situationist idea of the drift to my own surroundings and found a way to incorporate the river as a powerful connecting force that ran through the centre of a city. I floated an object made out of driftwood and other things I found trapped by the

Figure 12.1   The float used for the drifting experiment was made from rubbish found floating in the river. It made a good image for the drifting CD (*Credit*: Simon Russell, Boing Graphics)

current of the river behind my boat. I planned to follow the float down the Thames from my houseboat at Hampton Court eastwards through London. I would follow in a rowing boat, noting, photographing and videoing its course. Where it touched the bank – or something else floating or moving in the river – I would record it as a point of inspiration for finding an interviewee. The concept had potential for human encounter, but involved the force of the river itself as something that introduces and brings together disparate places and people, as opposed to dividing them. This method also had the advantage of forcing me to look at places – and therefore people – that I would have never ordinarily considered. As I have discussed elsewhere, this inter-disciplinary methodology incorporated elements of hydrology, cultural geography, oral history, sound art and public history.[30]

Drifting: the dérive

Set adrift on a current of a river I began to feel a great sense of freedom and adventure. Huck Finn escaped his rule-bound home by travelling on a raft on the Mississippi: 'other places do seem so cramped up and smothery, but a raft don't. You feel mighty free and easy and comfortable on a raft'.[31] For a few weeks I could do the same; the theories and methodologies and references and precedents of my academic life were left behind. Out here on the current, it seemed like there were no constraints or rules – I genuinely had no idea where the float was going to take me next; it felt like my mind had to be kept truly open because anything might happen.

I followed the float for 15 miles in a process that took several weeks, until the strong tidal currents of the river made the experiment impossible to continue.[32] The landscape of the banks of the Thames in central London contains some of the most imposing architecture in Britain, as successive political and economic powerhouses were built along the prestigious waterfront (palaces, bridges, parliaments and corporate headquarters).[33] Many of these buildings have such a strong historical, visual and political gravitational force that they are all but impossible to ignore. Yet the float managed to do so. On long, straight stretches the float would move fast, disregarding palaces, industries and entire localities. The flow gave a strange, unpredictable structure to my river-combing, providing me with a fresh set of memory places, which, like the neighbourhood tours, parish mappings, public art and gardening projects going on elsewhere, challenges dominant cultural practices associated with places of national significance.[34]

The drifting experiment also forced me to consider talking to people outside my social circle at unexpected locations. Several times the drifter took me directly to people's feet; bungalow owners, boat builders, a lock keeper. At times this became something akin to Jill Fenton's description of attending a Surrealist walk in Paris in which Jean-Pierre Le Goff traced an image of a clock onto a street map and led people to each number in turn. Fenton described a series of encounters that seemed to defy pure chance; small details seemed to acquire new meaning as if it was part of some strange pattern.[35] This is the experience of making the landscape fresh by narrating your own adventure. Like memory-making, significances and patterns emerge in the experience, and again in the retelling. In my experiment I became the lead actor in a strange play. Pieces of floating detritus were props, storylines and even characters, re-entering the stage at unexpected moments.

Another way of understanding this process would be as a process of curating. The artist and public historian (or as he terms his practice, nu-curator) Tim Brennan has experimented with both incorporating and escaping physical sets of triggers situated in the landscape.[36] His guided walks include inscriptions, sculptures, statues and memorials, but he introduces new readings and experiences by introducing quota-

Figure 12.2   The author (right) interviewing Steve Bolam, Molesey Lock Keeper and node of river culture
(*Credit*: Steve Whiting, loopimages.com)

tions that might or might not be related to the triggers or even each other. In this way he encourages the walker to be reflexive and make their own meaning from the different elements.[37] The construction of the drifting trail might be seen in similar terms. I had used the current of the river to set up a series of collisions, connecting a series of unrelated sites in a reflexive way. The interviewing process might also be seen in these taxonomical terms, although for me it was a much more personal and organic experience. Questions from one interview were taken to another; my own life and memories were bound up in the story when the float hit places that had great personal significance,

Figure 12.3 The houseboat wedding that was aurally recreated by editing together interviews with the wedding guests
(*Credit*: Author's photograph)

such as the place where I got married; friends and relations as well as strangers were included in this narrative.

The narration became an important feature in the recordings and strengthened the experience as a more coherent, situated process. I encouraged the listener to engage physically with the drifting process by trying to move at the same speed as the river for a while; to get a physical sense of what such a journey might feel like:

> As an experiment, try walking for a little while at the same speed as the river. Look out for a leaf or something floating on the surface to gauge the speed. This will give you a good idea of how long my experiment took.[38]

This situated approach also gave the narration additional authenticity as I tried to establish that my role was not that of the educated outsider, but an insider. I tried to acknowledge the fact that I was curating my own experience, my own locality – my own life. I made parts of the journey autobiographical, in this example by including details of my home at Ash Island:

> Up ahead on your right you will soon see some houseboats moored on the other side of the river. This is Ash Island. I lived on a houseboat here for nearly 10 years. It's a very strange sensation to live and sleep inches away from the moving water for such a long time. I often wondered about the river further down stream, running through the heart of London. What was it like to drive a paddle steamer or live in a riverside bungalow or work in London's docks? Was there anything that connected us, apart from the ever-flowing river?[39]

Overall I wanted to convey that the recordings were situated and particular to my journey, but also to present the listener with a chance to make other connections. By combining the recordings with their own memories and the physical experience of walking through the riverscape, the listener can build up a very active impression of the river and its cultural significance. This is a very dynamic process; sometimes the listener's presence, or their life experience, will synchronise with what they are listening to and it will become very meaningful; other times there might be some dissonance; maybe the landscape has changed or something happened to disrupt the experience; the memory might not have much function in the listener's present (although it might another time, or with someone else). The result should be a unique set of reflective experiences.

I was concerned that listening to the interviews with headphones would remove the listener's consciousness from their surroundings. I wanted to draw attention to the listener's environment, so the sound track was layered with binaural recordings of the riverbank – that is, recordings made with a stereo two-part microphone that is placed in each ear of the recorder, which picks up sound in the same way as the human head. The result is a startling 'surround sound' – if footsteps are recorded behind you, it will sound as if someone is behind you when you listen. These recordings gave the walk a temporal dimension. If the walker's experience matches the recording at any point on the walk, the recorded sound will tend to blend in and go unnoticed. But if the sound doesn't match, it creates a little prick of consciousness – like a boat passing, or the sound of a wave lapping on the shore. The walker looks in vein and realises that the thing creating the sound must have been there at some other time. They are reminded of their present surroundings, and like any river journey, it cannot be travelled in the same way twice.

The result was a carefully constructed three-mile walk containing a total of an hour of memories from 14 different people. The whole design of the walk was meant to slow people down, to take more notice of the cultural landscape and therefore make place more meaningful. Breaks from the soundtrack between listening locations allowed people to reflect, process and have their own adventure. The overall effect has been described by one reviewer as being a little like a Zen koan:[40]

> [*Drifting* is] a fluid pattern of multiple agendas, effecting and being effected by the Thames and its social, political, historical and economic sectors. Each location and narrator is accompanied by the river's own music, its aural ebbs and flows, the creaking of wooden boat joints, the wash, a tugboat toot, bodying the world of a major urban riverway.[41]

The public view

I placed my sound walks into the public domain, making sure that they were available for free download from the memoryscape website, in local bookshops, museums, libraries and tourist information centres, and publicised the walks in the local press and on local radio.[42] In

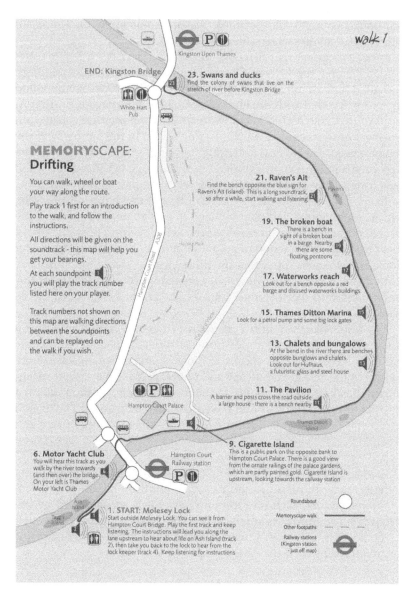

Figure 12.4 The drifting route map, showing walkers where to play each oral history track
(*Credit*: Author's design)

19 months at least 14,000 people experienced the memoryscapes in one way or another. Audience evaluation, using questionnaires and interviews with nearly 150 adults, revealed an overwhelmingly positive reaction from those who experienced the walk. The evaluation process also revealed some interesting benefits to the memoryscape concept. Several people remarked that they felt empathy towards the people that they listened to despite the fact that they were from a different age, class or culture. This 'normalisation' effect seemed to come from a combination of factors including the listening environment, the style of speaking and the fact that the listener could not see the interviewee. Listeners seemed to respond particularly well to the variety of voices used which gave the experience authenticity and emotional impact – they enjoyed hearing from 'real' people as opposed to a mono-vocal guide. Listening in the riverscape gave people visual 'hooks' to understand the context of the memories they were hearing, and the reality of the present environment seemed to temper feelings of past nostalgia.

The *drifting* walk also seemed to engender a feeling of identity with the landscape. Respondents reported that using a variety of senses, the imagination, and references in the landscape, as well as physically participating and getting an 'insiders' take on the riverscape, all helped to make the experience more meaningful and therefore memorable. Creating these connections, or links to place seems to have led to a feeling of closeness, or rootedness for some people. One newcomer to West London wrote, 'Now I know a sense of a beginning attachment'. Another walker described the process as 'deepening my attachment to the river. Like roots shooting off into the soil.'

Several people talked about the experience adding a new reality, or a new dimension of reality to the existing landscape. Furthermore, listeners who visit the same landscape again can use those links to remember something of the stories that they heard: 'Memoryscape has made me consider the part the river has played in so many people's lives. I think about this whenever I visit the river since listening to the recording *drifting*.' Perhaps this aspect of the experience could be of interest to those wishing to encourage feelings of belonging and identity in a particular community or location if memorable links can be made between individuals and the cultural topography of a place – past and present.

Bruce Chatwin's celebrated book *The Songlines* explores the Australian Aboriginal tradition of walking and singing mythic and actual topographies into being.[43] Iain Chambers has pondered on whether mobile media players could offer us a similar experience of our landscape:

> Perhaps it still continues to echo inside the miniaturised headphones of modern nomads as the barely remembered traces of a once sacred journey intent on celebrating its presence in a mark, voice, sign, symbol, signature, to be left along the track.[44]

Listening to memories in the outside world can actually give us a semblance of this feeling. The acts of voicing and listening to stories and to everyday sounds seem to entwine quite easily with the rhythm of walking; the effect for some can be very powerful, a drifting sense of place that is both rooted and shifting, sedentary and mobile. After more than a century of recording the human voice, the stories and myths that have been passed down through generations don't have to be merely 'barely remembered': presenting oral history in public places can really make the landscape sing.

Conclusion

My aim was to explore the potential of the audio medium to locate oral history in the landscape, make it reverberate publicly and in doing so elaborate a more nuanced, complex and open sense of place. Charles Hardy, excited by the historical possibilities of authoring spoken words and sound, wrote that:

> Perhaps multi-channel aural histories represent an important tool for the authoring of 'post modern' histories by providing a means of sharing authority, privileging multiple rather than univocal perspectives, and opening space – using simultaneity and dimension in the presentation of history that is not possible in the printed word, bound as it is by linear unfolding.[45]

In some regards 'drifting' might be thought of as a linear experience, a journey with a beginning and an end. But in all other respects it echoes Hardy's vision.

I have created just this kind of history; it is something that incorporates multiple perspectives, including my own, in its selection and presentation of oral history; it does use simultaneity, both in the listening to those histories in the context of the present landscape and in the temporal and multi-channel sound design. I also hope it opens up and 'thickens' space by placing sounds and memories back in the outside world. It is simultaneously a situated, personal cultural exploration, a presentation of oral history and an intrinsically active and 'open' experience in which there is an opportunity for the listener to make sense of the different memories in their own way and make their own connections. The process of reintroducing memories back into their geographical habitat is not without its representational, political and ethical difficulties.[46] But if 'drifting' has realised anything of the potential of the medium, the experience should be dramatically different to reading a set of edited transcripts in a book, and I hope it might offer real potential for public historians wishing to create multiple and cross-cultural understandings of place.

Notes

1 G. Miller, *Linked: A Landmark in Sound, an Invisible Artwork, a Walk* (Sound installation, London: 2003). See www.linkedm11.info/

2 T. Butler and G. Miller, 'Linked: A Landmark in Sound, a Public Walk of Art', *Cultural Geographies*, 12: 1 (2005) 77–88, reprinted in R. Perks and A. Thomson (eds) *The Oral History Reader* 2nd edn (London: Routledge, 2006).

3 R. Samuel, *Theatres of Memory: Past and Present in Contemporary Culture* (London: Verso, 1994), p. 8.

4 S. Hall, 'Raphael Samuel, 1934–96', *New Left Review*, 221 (January/February 1997) 124–5.

5 J. Liddington and G. Smith, 'Crossing Cultures: Oral History and Public History', *Oral History*, 33: 1 (2005) 42.

6 H. Kean, 'Public History and Raphael Samuel: A Forgotten Radical Pedagogy?', *Public History Review*, 11 (2004), 51–62.

7 J. Liddington and S. Ditchfield, 'Public History: A Critical Bibliography', *Oral History*, 33: 1 (2005) 42.

8 Samuel, *Theatres of Memory*, p. 17.

9 *ibid*, p. 8.

10 T. Butler, 'Memoryscape Audio Walks' (2005). See www.memoryscape.org.uk.

11 D. Massey, 'Places and Their Pasts', *History Workshop Journal*, 39 (1995) 191.

12 T. Cresswell, *Place: A Short Introduction* (Oxford: Blackwell Publishing, 2004).

13 Y. F. Tuan, *Topophilia: A Study of Environmental Perception, Attitudes, and Values* (Englewood Cliffs, NJ: Prentice-Hall, 1974), p. 4.

14 E. C. Relph, *Place and Placelessness* (London: Pion Limited, 1976), p. 43.

15 L. Malkki, 'National Geographic: The Rooting of Peoples and the Territorialisation of National Identity Among Scholars and Refugees', *Cultural Anthropology*, 7: 1 (1992) 24–44.

16 T. Cresswell, *The Tramp in America* (London: Reaktion Books, 2001) pp. 14–19; T. Cresswell, *On the Move: Mobility in the Modern Western World* (London and New York: Routledge, 2006), pp. 39–42.

17 S. Ford, *The Situationist International: A Users Guide* (London: Black Dog Publishing, 2005), p. 33.

18   *ibid*, p. 34.
19   Cresswell, *On the Move*, pp. 47–55.
20   M. de Certeau, *The Practice of Everyday Life* (Berkeley: University of California Press, 1984), p. 97.
21   P. Thompson, 'Believe It or Not: Rethinking the Historical Interpretation of Memory', J. Jeffrey and G. Edwall (eds) *Memory and History: Essays on Recalling and Interpreting Experience* (Lanham: University Press of America, 1994), p. 11.
22   A. Portelli, 'The Peculiarities of Oral History', *History Workshop Journal*, 12 (1981) 96–107.
23   D. Randall, *The Universal Journalist* (London: Pluto Press, 1996), p. 72.
24   S. Terkel, *Working, People Talk about What They Do All Day and How They Feel About What They Do* (New York: Pantheon Books, 1974).
25   T. Timothy, 'Report on the Sept 9th Forum Event: A1 Audio Tour: Brief Description', *Arts for Islington Forum Monthly Bulletin*, (3 October 2005) 19.
26   E. Platt, *Leadville: A Biography of the A40* (London: Picador, 2001).
27   H. Lefebvre, *The Production of Space* (Oxford: Blackwell Publishers, 1991).
28   Physically the Thames cuts through the heart of London, yet it is on the very edge of the territory of the City of London and 16 of the 32 London boroughs that share the riverside. Commentators have noted that the river has, until recently, been perceived in policy terms as on the edge, rather than at the centre of coherent planning. C. Sumner, 'Historic waterscapes', I. Munt and R. Jaijee (eds) *River Calling: The Need for Urban Water Space Strategies* (London: London Rivers Association, 2002), p. 65.
29   British Waterways administers London's canals and some docks and tributaries; the Environment Agency administers the 'non-tidal' Thames; and the Port of London Authority administers the tidal Thames (downstream from Teddington Lock).
30   T. Butler, 'A Walk of Art: The Potential of the Sound Walk as Practice in Cultural Geography', *Social and Cultural Geography*, 7: 6 (2006) 889–908.
31   M. Twain, *The Adventures of Huckleberry Finn* (New York: Bantam Books, 1981) p. 113.
32   As the river can be dangerous to navigate at night, I retrieved the float at the end of each day and started again from where I had finished the day before.
33   Hampton Court Palace, the Houses of Parliament, the Tower of London, the Greater London Authority building and the Millennium Dome are perhaps the most famous examples.
34   K. Till, 'Places of Memory', in J. Agnew, K. Mitchell and G. Ó Tuathail (eds) *A Companion to Political Geography* (Oxford and Cambridge: Blackwell Publishing, 2003), pp. 294–6.
35   J. Fenton, 'Space, Chance, Time: Walking Backwards Through the Hours on the Left and Right banks of Paris', *Cultural Geographies*, 12: 4 (2005) 412–28; D. Pinder, 'Arts of Urban Exploration', *Cultural Geographies*, 12: 4 (2005) 397.
36   T. Brennan, 'Manoeuvre' (2003) http://mysite.wanadoo-members.co.uk/manoeuvre/page1.html accessed 17 November 2006.
37   T. Brennan, 'Mercator Manoeuvre', *Cultural Geographies*, 12: 4 (2005) 514–20.

38 T. Butler, *Drifting*, track 3 (Audio walk, London: Memoryscape Audio Walks, 2005).
39 *ibid*, track 2.
40 A Zen Buddhist story, parable or statement that helps lead to awakening or spiritual insight.
41 J. Friedman, 'Media Review: Drifting, from Memoryscape Audio Walks. Produced by Toby Butler', *Oral History Review*, 33: 1 (2006) 109.
42 See T. Butler, www.memoryscape.org.uk for further information, and to download audio and maps of the walk. An online version is also available here for those who are unable to walk the trails.
43 B. Chatwin, *The Songlines* (London: Vintage Classics, 1987).
44 I. Chambers, 'The Aural Walk', in C. Cox and D. Warner (eds) *Audio Culture: Readings in Modern Music* (New York: Continuum, 2004), p. 101.
45 C. Hardy III, 'Authoring in Sound: Aural History, Radio and the Digital Revolution', in Perks and Thompson, *The Oral History Reader* p. 398.
46 T. Butler and R. Wilson, 'Interview with Toby Butler', ReadySteadyBook (2007) http://www.readysteadybook.com/Article.aspx?page=tobybutler accessed 20 February 2007.

13
Expanding the Archive: The Role of Family History in Exploring Connections Within a Settler's World

Mary Stewart

Introduction

My exploration of the life and thoughts of my great, great grandfather, William McCaw (1818–1902), blended what are often regarded as separate pursuits: family history and academic history.[1] In 1880 McCaw, a shepherd, writer and amateur theologian, moved from Scotland to New Zealand with his large family. Generations of my extended family have preserved the memory of McCaw, treasuring his letters and newspaper articles and passing down photographs, objects and stories relating to the McCaw family. I mined my family archive in order to build up a holistic picture of my ancestor and his views upon the world, through which I accessed and explored wider historical theories. I undertook this research on McCaw for a postgraduate degree at the University of Otago, but until I attended the 2005 public history conference at Ruskin College and began to write this chapter I had not looked into public history. The new works I read made me reflect more closely on the history I had written. Where did my research sit – and did this matter?

My use of my family's stories, photographs and documents to construct a history fitted with family history and genealogy – an area that is booming both in England and New Zealand.[2] My consideration of how and why my family has remembered our ancestor sat within the remit of public history, which has long explored how non-academics and non-professional historians view and construct a sense of the past. Yet, unlike many public historians in New Zealand, I studied within a university with funds from a university scholarship, rather than work for a government agency, museum or independent organisation. The primary aim of my thesis was to use a microhistory of my great, great grandfather to engage with debates within the historical academy about migration to New Zealand in the nineteenth century. My role as both academic enquirer and a member of the family at the centre of the research meant that I took care to produce a piece of writing that would be accessible to my extended family and also stand up to academic scrutiny.

It became increasingly clear that I could not pick out which parts of my work were family history, which were public history and which academic history: I had engaged with elements of all three. Indeed, over the last ten years, both in New Zealand and worldwide, there has been significant debate about the boundaries of these disciplines – particularly as regards the meaning of public history.[3] Bronwyn Dalley has argued that to focus on crystallising the boundaries between public and academic history can be unhelpful, as it can distract from exploring the ways in which history is created and consumed within New Zealand.[4] In this chapter, rather than spending time categorising the components of my research, I argue that valuing family archives, reflecting upon how they have been constructed and relating the experience of individuals and families to wider historical theories can bring fruitful results to anyone who wishes to explore our pasts. Positioning my research in this way I hope that my work can, in some small part, tap into what David Thelen described as a participatory historical culture 'in which using the past could be treated as a shared human experience and opportunity for understanding, rather than a ground for suspicion and division.'[5]

I start with an exploration of how my family has remembered William McCaw and contend that this set of family sources constitutes an archive of material that rivals any institution's, in diversity if not in volume. I then explore the construction of this family archive because any insight McCaw's story could offer to wider histories was mediated through the prism of my family's sense of their past. The variety of sources within my family archive is one of its greatest strengths, which stands in contrast to the views of many historians who have attached relative values to the types of material family archives contain – be it published or unpublished text, object or image. Finally, I show how I have used McCaw as case study to engage with wider historical ideas: exploring the space between this personal narrator and the many historical accounts and theories about migration to New Zealand in the late nineteenth century.

Remembering William McCaw

My study of William McCaw drew on an eclectic group of sources from my family history that are not an academic's usual means of analysing our pasts. However, the family stories, letters and photographs used regularly by genealogists and, increasingly, by historians to capture information about our pasts are as interesting and challenging resources as any other. American academic G. Thomas Tanselle's exploration of the term archive is useful: it is 'important to recognise that individuals, over the course of their lifetimes, amass archives no different in kind from those preserved by firms, institutions, and organisations.'[6] All the McCaw relatives who have helped with my study have shared knowledge and material from their personal archives, which has in turn strengthened my own.

I introduce you to my great, great grandfather, William McCaw, here pictured with his wife Isabella. Since I was a small child I have been aware of my rather stern ancestors because my parents, aunts and grandparents all had copies of this iconic photograph. As I met family

Figure 13.1   Painted photograph of William and Isabella McCaw, original photograph 1896
(Jessie Stewart Private collection)

members in England and New Zealand in the course of my research, this photograph stared out at me from many a wall, bookshelf or mantelpiece. Despite our very different lives numerous McCaw descendants had kept alive the memory of this rather serious old man, through the simple act of displaying the photograph in their homes. Who was this individual that generations of the family had chosen, above any other, to remember?

Born in Dumfriesshire, Scotland, in 1818, William McCaw was employed as a shepherd on an isolated farm where he lived with Isabella and their ten children who had survived infancy.[7] When McCaw was made redundant in 1880, aged 61, the adult members of the family started to consider what course of action to take, as William faced unemployment that would also cause the family to lose their home.[8] After several months of deliberation, the family decided to move together to New Zealand. McCaw explained in a speech at the village school the night before the family departed that although he was 'not an emigration enthusiast', the family had decided to move because the children would have better employment opportunities and he thought that in the colonies he could use his small savings to better effect.[9] In September 1880 the McCaws arrived in New Zealand, settling in Glenore, South Otago on the east coast of the South Island. Whilst McCaw continued to farm at Glenore until 1899, his children married and moved away, the daughters settling in South Otago and the sons further afield. In 1899 the family were reunited once more because the second eldest child Marion, who had stayed in Scotland with her husband, sailed to New Zealand to join the celebrations for William and Isabella's Golden Wedding. This trip was timely because in 1902, just three years later, McCaw died.

This tale, in itself, is similar to those of thousands of other migrants from Scotland in the nineteenth century. The difference is that my family has actively remembered and celebrated McCaw's existence, constructing an archive of material about our common ancestor. Recent researchers into the construction, politics and use of archives in colonial history contend that the act of creating an archive deserves as much scrutiny as its contents. Most of this research has focused on the archives of British colonial states in South Asia, exploring how the documents kept by colonial administrations have shaped the history one can reconstruct. Voices of the non-literate, women and others who came into little contact with the colonial state are not represented in these archival collections, further stressing the importance of other archival sources – such as family history.[10] This research is useful because it leads us to question not only the provenance of the books, letters or photographs contained in an archive, but recognise that the existence of an archive is, in its own right, worthy of scrutiny.

My family's remembrance of William McCaw has been enabled, primarily, by his own prodigious output of writing. Although he completed only two winters of formal schooling, McCaw read widely and published several theological works, based on his devout Reformed Presbyterian faith. Following the tradition of the radical Covenanters in the sixteenth century, the Reformed Presbyterian Church – following Calvinist principles – stressed the need for each believer to read the Gospel. The most successful of McCaw's books was his 1855 essay *Truth Frae 'Mang the Heather* in which he used logical argument and scriptural evidence to argue that the Bible was true.[11]

After this success, McCaw became a regular correspondent to his local newspaper, the *Dumfries and Galloway Standard*, engaging in debates about topics as diverse as theology, the electoral franchise and the identity of the inventor of the bicycle.[12] He continued to contribute to the *Standard* after he migrated, writing each month, without fail, a round-up of news and thoughts entitled 'Notes from New

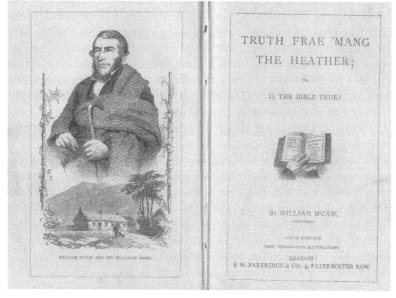

Figure 13.2 Frontispiece of *Truth Frae 'Mang the Heather*, 6th edition c1884 (Jessie Stewart Private Collection)

Zealand'. He also found time to write, albeit less frequently, to the local press and Presbyterian church magazines in Otago, as well as maintaining regular correspondence with his daughter in Scotland, his siblings in America and Australia, and his children who gradually scattered across New Zealand.[13]

Despite McCaw's volumes of writing, were it not for the intervention of one of his children I doubt that I would have known enough about my ancestor to consider studying him further. In 1947 the McCaws' youngest son, William Armstrong McCaw, (known as Uncle Willie) compiled, published and distributed a collection of McCaw's writing to the family worldwide.[14] This pamphlet, *The Memoir and Remains of William McCaw*, was republished by the McCaw Family Reunion Committee in 1981, alongside a family tree, as part of the celebrations of the centenary of the McCaws' arrival in New Zealand.[15] My grandmother, Jessie Stewart, kept a vast collection of letters, newspapers and photographs of the McCaws, often given to her for safekeeping by others in the extended family.[16] As well as collating his father's work for publication, Uncle Willie was a keen photographer whose skills provided generations of McCaws with images of family occasions including the iconic picture of his parents. By displaying this photograph in their homes the descendants of William McCaw have kept him as part of their present lives and identities, whether or not they have ever read his letters, articles or books. The family's use of this image illustrates Anne Else's description of the power of photography 'to make available to ordinary people long-lasting and portable depictions of absent people and places closely connected to them.'[17] Other remaining McCaw artefacts have been carefully treasured by the extended family, such as the engraved watch given to William and the electroplated teapot presented to Isabella when they left for New Zealand.[18]

In addition to books, photographs and objects, we McCaws have a place to visit to remember our ancestors. Cormilligan, the isolated cottage in north Dumfriesshire inhabited by McCaws from 1780 to 1880, still stands. McCaws have made the pilgrimage back to Cormilligan since the First World War, when some of the McCaw men in the military used their leave to travel to Scotland.[19] For at least the last 40 years, the Wilson family, who farm the land adjacent to Cormilligan, have received a steady stream of McCaws. Dilapidated, inaccessible by road and uninhabited since the 1930s, the McCaw clan have reclaimed Cormilligan as our own. On one wall, above the main fireplace, is an array of signatures of McCaw descendants, etched into the crumbling plaster. I took this photo of Cormilligan on a cold winter's day in 2003,

Figure 13.3   Teapot presented to Isabella McCaw as the family left Tynron. The inscription reads, 'presented to Mrs McCaw by her friends on leaving Cormilligan for New Zealand, May 28th 1880.' Teapot in the keeping of the Allison family. (Photograph: Mary Stewart)

when visiting with my siblings. We added our signatures below our grandmother's, next to those of our father and two of his sisters. It is not only the McCaw clan who have found Cormilligan a deeply affecting place. Dumfriesshire poet Rab Wilson discovered it whilst retracing the footsteps of the Victorian schoolmaster James Shaw. Intrigued by the signatures on the wall Wilson made contact with several McCaws in New Zealand and was sent the *Memoir and Remains*. Inspired by the story of the family's migration Wilson wrote 'Cormilligan', a haunting sonnet in Scots verse.[20]

Why he has been remembered is a difficult question to answer because each family member may have had different and multiple motivations. I suspect that the desire to maintain some of the closeness of the original family was fulfilled by the act of celebrating the famous family patriarch. Reunions, the publication of the *Memoir and Remains*

Figure 13.4 Cormilligan, Dumfriesshire, Scotland, January 2003
(Photograph: Mary Stewart)

and the Family Tree all tied the disparate members of the extended family together and commemorated the journey from old home to new. Yet without McCaw's literacy and the publication of his words, I am certain that knowledge of my ancestor would have struggled to survive into the twenty-first century. McCaw's books, letters and the iconic photograph have acted as a scaffold upon which the family have hung the stories, photographs and memories, tying his descendants together through their knowledge, and pride, in him.

I used this diverse collection of sources with the knowledge that there will be much else that McCaw does not mention in his writing, and events and instances that the family has not remembered, whether consciously or unconsciously. In the case of the McCaws, the dark corners and hints of unhappiness in our family's history have not been passed down through the generations – in text or in word – or have not reached my ears, leaving William McCaw as the family's stable and talismanic figure. However, these rememberings and omissions are no more or less apparent for McCaw than for the biography of any person, organisation or even nation. As Tanselle helpfully concludes: 'To regard the truthfulness of archives as an issue for discussion is therefore pointless unless we understand that the question being asked is how we find truth anywhere.'[21] Both the material I have used from my family's and other archives, and the archives themselves, should not be free from critical evaluation. In fact, it is this evaluation that is integral to any history we write and read.

The challenge: making family history relevant to a wider audience

My family's remembrance of this ancestor echoes the results of major quantitative and qualitative surveys of the meaning of the 'past' in America and Australia, where most respondents explored history through family stories, memories and objects.[22] Analysing the results of their American survey, Roy Rosenzweig and David Thelen describe that: 'the interviews were filled with intimate talk about the past. Families and their stories dominated the numbers as well as the words.'[23] Not only did the wider family's sense of history bring this man to my attention, their bookshelves, photograph albums and memories provided me with many of the sources to study him. My challenge, as family member and historian, was to fashion a history from these sources that would not only serve my family as an account of our ancestor, but also explore wider historical theories. As Rosenzweig describes, some family histories can be so parochial that they do not engage or reflect upon any stories of those outside that particular small group. Conversely, the American survey itself was born from the frustration felt by a group of academics that conventional history teaching and academia had become increasingly disconnected from wider 'popular' audiences, losing touch with how Americans engaged with the past.[24] In his article considering the function of oral history, Alessandro Portelli offers a useful framework to help bridge this gap:

> Oral history, in essence, is an attempt to reconnect the local, native point of view from below and the global, scientific point of view from above: to contextualize the local, and to enable the global to recognize it. Oral history, then, brings history from above and history from below into the same text – as it were, to the negotiating table – creating an equal dialogue between the historians' awareness of the broad spatial and temporal patterns, and the local narrator's closely focused personal narrative.[25]

My study was not an oral history, but it did use a local narrator as a means to explore wider historical ideas, just as in *London Stories* Hilda Kean argues that her materials were, 'in some senses, about my family but are also part of broader cultural and social histories'.[26] My study in no way purported to describe the experience of a typical migrant, but instead to see how this one man felt and functioned as he moved hemisphere. Of course, I am not alone in valuing family history as a route into exploring our pasts. In the New Zealand context, *whakapapa*, genealogy in traditional Maori oral history, is a vital resource for any historian exploring Maori history.[27] Family stories have definitely been valued in *Te Ara*, the online encyclopedia of New Zealand, which features the stories and photographs of many migrants to New Zealand, most of whom have not contributed to any type of formal history before.[28] Traditionally, while few New Zealand historians have been actively dismissive of family historians studying settlers' heritage, they have rarely engaged with these groups except where the family history is of a notable New Zealander.[29] Research on settlers such as McCaw, famous only within his family circle, therefore offers fresh personal perspectives on life in colonial New Zealand.

Valuing the diversity of material in family archives

I was able to explore the space between the personal and the global that Portelli describes only because I valued all the resources in my family archive, building up a detailed and rounded portrait of my ancestor. This gave me a new route into other archives as I sought all that pertained to this one individual and also into secondary literature as I then researched all the themes that he raised. I was not searching the archives for the stories of migrants from one country or category, nor was I using one type of source, although all are common and valid approaches to colonial history. Information gleaned from my family archive directed me to a variety of material – including published works, such as McCaw's newspaper articles and his pamphlet *The Gospel and Total Abstinence* held in the British Library.[30] In a similar vein, Hilda Kean used family stories and ephemera to instigate and inform further archival and genealogical research to uncover her family's, and London's, pasts.[31] Piecing together an analysis of McCaw, his ideas and identity, from such a patchwork of sources was an occasionally frustrating experience. But I came to appreciate that the diversity of source material was one of my study's greatest assets.

The photograph of workers eating lunch at McCaw's Glenore farm revealed a facet of his life that was not apparent from the written sources alone. Moving to New Zealand, a modern reader might immediately think that McCaw's most frequent encounters with other ethnic

Figure 13.5   Lunch or tea break for the farmworkers at McCaw's Glenore farm, 1890s
(Republished with the permission of the Tokomairiro Historical Society, Milton)

groups would be with Maori, but there were few Maori in the local vicinity.[32] Instead, McCaw lived in an area with a sizeable Chinese community, who had flocked to the goldfields around Glenore.[33] McCaw discussed the treatment of Chinese in only four of his 200 'Notes from New Zealand', focusing instead on the land, lives and politics of the settler population. Although McCaw explains in one of these four articles that he 'met with Chinese daily,' the infrequency of his articles on the topic and the brevity of these few discussions, makes the Chinese community appear a peripheral part of his Otago life.[34] It is only when I discovered this photograph in the Milton Museum, in South Otago, amongst papers donated after my grandmother's death, that I began to appreciate that McCaw 'met with Chinese daily', not in the street, but because at least one Chinese man worked on his farm. Who this man was and the length and nature of his employment remains a mystery, but nonetheless, he is sitting and eating with the rest of group. This photograph, by adding a visual dimension, uncovered more about McCaw and his relationship with Chinese, so often feared and discriminated against, than the words in the newspaper could ever have shown.[35]

In contrast to many studies of migration in this period I have valued published works alongside unpublished family letters. In his long correspondence with the *Dumfries and Galloway Standard* McCaw's articles followed regular patterns describing the changing seasons, the weather and annual events such as Church Synods. The famous Otago historian A. H. McLintock discounted the 'Notes from New Zealand' as a source for his 1949 *History of Otago*, presumably because his London researcher deemed the articles 'a repetition of what has been said, so I am not bothering with them.'[36] Historians of emigrant correspondence have long taken seriously personal letters in family archives, but have also tended 'not to bother' with published correspondence. American historian Charlotte Erickson's groundbreaking work stresses the personal letter as the most valuable source to give insight into the colonial experience of the migrant, an argument followed by historians of Irish migration to Australasia, Angela McCarthy and David Fitzpatrick.[37] These scholars have discounted published letters as a means of delving into the emotional world of the migrant, because they have viewed them as marketing tools to sell migration to the masses and, in Fitzpatrick's case, as text where 'editorial excisions' cannot be identified.[38]

Tanselle's exploration of the term archive is, once again, useful. He asserts that the historian must recognise that an archive of unpublished material is also shaped by human decisions: which documents are kept, where they are stored and how they are catalogued. If the historian recognises that an archive is not a collection of documents untouched by human hand, Tanselle continues, then 'is there any reason to believe that unpublished manuscripts contain more accurate information than published books?'[39] These three historians assess the effect published letters may have had in stimulating migration, but they do not address the colonial author's motivations for writing, nor the emotional effect upon those at 'home' reading them – which I explore later in this chapter. As shown in these two examples, to view a family archive as whole, exploring what has been remembered and by whom, allows the enquirer to uncover a more textured sense of our pasts than if one type of source is pulled out and viewed in isolation.

Uncovering the local and global connections of William McCaw

I used the portrait of McCaw I had built up from my family archive to explore areas of history that are often treated as separate fields of historical enquiry: how McCaw's faith affected his relationship to the communities in which he lived, his ideas on agricultural management and the ownership of land and his theological reasoning and interpretation of biblical text. In all these areas I used McCaw as a case study to test out how historians had depicted our pasts, not to prove any theory right or wrong, but simply to see how McCaw's story could reflect upon them. In this chapter, I shall explore this process in relation to McCaw's sense of local, national and international belonging. Peter Gibbons reflects a growing mood in the New Zealand historical community in his call for a reconsideration of the nation-state as the focus of New Zealand history, which has traditionally been focused on tracing the country's path to nationhood.[40] Gibbons suggests instead two possible approaches to counter this trend. First, a 'macro' approach, which identifies the 'linkages of local centres to the world system archipelago,' and second, the use of 'microhistories' that create 'interesting and instructive vignettes of individual experiences.'[41] My study of McCaw blends these two approaches, using the microhistory of one man's experience to reflect upon a settler's life in colonial Otago and his links with the wider world.

McCaw, like any individual, did not have one simple sense of belonging: he connected to various family members via letters, to the natural world via his memories of the landscape, to other Presbyterians through his faith and to a local community via the *Dumfries and Galloway Standard*. I have found Tony Ballantyne's model of a web of connections a useful framework to help make sense of McCaw's many layers of belonging as he accessed, and created, networks of information exchange and emotional ties. Ballantyne uses the analogy of a web to characterise the relationships between the metropole, the periphery and between colonies within the British Empire. He asserts that 'we need to reconstruct the networks that structured the empire and trace the transmission of ideas, ideologies and identities across space and time. The web captures the integrative nature of this cultural traffic.'[42] I have used the web analogy on a personal scale, tracing and analysing McCaw's web of connections.

Certainly, McCaw recognised that he had ties to two nations – Scotland and New Zealand – but these sentiments of national belonging were referred to infrequently, running against the grain of much recent work on Scottish migration.[43] As Patrick O'Farrell warns, a focus purely on the ethnic identity of migrants has the danger of assuming its intrinsic value for each migrant, without contextualising what ethnic belonging meant for them.[44] Ethnicity was a fluid idea, moulded by the migration experience, as Alison Clarke's study of nineteenth-century

Otago clearly illustrates.[45] Scottishness was important to McCaw, but it was only one of the many strands within his web of connections and identities.[46] Similarly, although McCaw recognised, and at times celebrated the British Empire, his thoughts on the imperial endeavour were not straightforward. He often expressed disappointment at the flouting of the Empire's purpose, which, in his eyes, was to spread the word and principles of Christianity.[47] Far more central to McCaw's world were his links closer to home: his family and his local communities, both in Scotland and New Zealand.

The written word was central to McCaw's web of connections. Well before migration to New Zealand, letters served an important function in facilitating relationships within the McCaw family, as the children working away from home kept up with the family through the exchange of letters. Later, letters helped to bridge the wider geographical gaps both between Scotland and New Zealand and between McCaw and his siblings in America and Australia, sharing news of the family, common friends and acquaintances. In 1899, William wrote to his unknown grandchildren in Scotland, fulfilling his role as patriarch of the family by guiding them in their Biblical study and belief in God.[48] By reinforcing the knowledge of known faces and personalities, the letters sent between members of the McCaw family acted as a bond tying the distant parts of the family together.

McCaw's published letters gave great insight into his sense of belonging, which I could tease out because I viewed them in the context of all the other sources in the family archive. Fitzpatrick argues that the personal letter was a 'cultural institution, transcending the particular information that it conveyed,' but in McCaw's case, this concept can be extended to include his published correspondence.[49] Regardless of the verity of the images of colonial life they portrayed, the 'Notes from New Zealand' served a vitally important purpose for McCaw in adjusting to his new home. McCaw delighted in receiving the mail from home, in 1894 describing the receipt of the *Standard* as 'a refreshing shower upon dry land,' which he and the family 'drank in with pleasure'.[50] It was not only the reception of the newspaper upon which McCaw relied. He so enjoyed writing back that he sent his column even when he felt there was little news to tell. He wrote in January 1898:

An Irishman was going to write the history of snakes in his native country, and it was contained in three words – "There is none." The

> New Zealand news at present are about as scarce as the Irish snakes, so I might as well say there is none and have done with it.[51]

Despite this opening McCaw wrote an article of average length. As these passages reveal, McCaw wrote the 'Notes from New Zealand' not only to convey news, but to maintain a link with his community at home. In this sense what he wrote was inconsequential – it was the process of writing itself that was important. Thus, it was not just family letters that helped mitigate McCaw's homesickness. Writing to and receiving the newspaper also had a 'consolatory function' for McCaw, something that David Cressy also discovered in his study of seventeenth-century migrants to America.[52]

According to Ballantyne, the people and institutions within the web of empire each formed a node, or connection point, linking to other such nodes throughout the web. The *Standard* acted as a vital node in McCaw's web, as its global circulation allowed him, and many other migrants, to feel part of the community at 'home.' Indeed, McCaw was not the only 'Foreign and Colonial Correspondent' because news was sporadically sent into the *Standard* from several American states as well as Hawaii, Canada, all the Australian colonies and from others in New Zealand.[53] In 1900 a young soldier in India wrote to the *Standard*, and included a poem for the attention of McCaw, demonstrating that a newspaper in Scotland could link readers that were continents apart.[54] Facilitated by the global reach of the postal system, the readership of the *Standard* spanned the globe, forcing Ballantyne's web analogy to stretch outside the bounds of the British Empire.

Through the exchange of the *Standard*, those in Scotland could glimpse into the local colonial world and McCaw could keep abreast of events in Dumfriesshire. The 'Notes from New Zealand' concentrated on local news, the vast majority focusing on the environment, people and church activities of South Otago. McCaw regularly explained that he was only familiar with his local area: 'I cannot go all over New Zealand, and restrict my note to the part I best know. The plain of Tokomairiro'.[55] In his family memoir *Vanished Kingdoms* Patrick O'Farrell explores the link to the local, noting that for his forebears to meet an Irishman was 'a matter of very mild interest,' but to meet someone from their local area in Ireland was 'noteworthy'.[56] McCaw fits this description, as his articles included news of other Dumfriesians in New Zealand, regardless of whether he had known them before his migration.[57] Of course, the need to find people and news in common with his readers in Dumfriesshire may well have influenced McCaw's decision to include these pieces of news. These two local communities linked by the global circulation of the printed and written word dovetails with Rollo Arnold's detailed studies of New Zealand settler communities, where he concluded that settlers viewed their world not in terms of national boundaries, but instead connected the 'village and the globe.'[58]

Ballantyne's model of a web, with its spider-like imagery, also signals that the connecting threads within McCaw's web were liable to be broken, changed or spun anew. Throughout his colonial life McCaw created new links to local newspapers, his New Zealand based family and the Otago natural world. As his life in the colonies progressed, McCaw's strong personal links with his Scottish familial and local worlds became more fragile. Generations of family, in Scotland, America and Australia, were unknown to the aging McCaw, and friends, acquaintances and political foes in Dumfriesshire began to die.[59] Throughout his life, no matter how much the individual strands within McCaw's webs of belonging were weakened by distance or death, he derived an overwhelming sense of global community not from a sense of national identity, the British Empire, nor his fellow readers, but from his Presbyterian faith. One can appreciate the role of faith in his life, though it is so often written out of histories of the nineteenth century.[60] The night before he left Scotland, he said these words to his gathered friends and family:

> Cormilligan is not Heaven. Scotland is not perfection. The kind hearts here are not the only kind hearts on earth. I have had much enjoyment in the land of my nativity, but it is not necessarily at an end even though we take our departure even to the end of the earth. There is an all-wise, all-powerful and Gracious Ruler presiding over all things, and will bring all things to a glorious issue for everyone of us if only we make His precepts the men of our counsel. [61]

Alison Clarke's assessment that the thought of reunion in heaven helped many migrants to dull the pain of separation on earth fits neatly with the McCaws' experience.[62] James McCaw, who had moved to America in the 1870s, wrote to his brother:

> But here the blessed assurance of a bright hereafter comes in with its cheery hope of a glorious reunion where there will be no pain and

none of those who are faithful unto death will be absent. May we all be included.[63]

For the McCaws, God's arms embraced the entire globe.

Conclusion

My study of McCaw placed this one migrant within the context of the nineteenth century's vast movements of people, goods and ideas, using family history to mediate the space between the personal and global perspectives in history that Portelli describes. This has only been possible because I used my family archive as a route into McCaw's story, drawing on material both published and previously hidden from the wider historical record. Although I used my family history in an academic endeavour, far more of the McCaw clan, in both New Zealand and Britain, have read the results than fellow historians. My work, touching upon aspects of history that are often placed in the separate domains of family history, public history and academic history, illustrates how explorations of the past often relate to and reflect upon all three. I am certain that further strengthening of this interaction can inform and enrich all types of history we produce, helping to achieve a more textured explanation of our pasts.

Notes

1 My thanks to Kiran Chauhan, Hilda Kean and Rob Perks for their constructive comments on this chapter.
2 A. Else, 'History Lessons: The Public History You Get When You're Not Getting Any Public History,' in B. Dalley and J. Phillips (eds) *Going Public: The Changing Face of New Zealand History* (Auckland: Auckland University, 2001), pp. 125–7.
3 J. Liddington, 'What is Public History? Publics and their Pasts, Meanings and Practices,' *Oral History Journal*, 30: 1 (2002) 83–93.
4 B. Dalley, 'Finding the Common Ground: New Zealand's Public History,' in Dalley and Phillips, *Going Public*, pp. 16–29.
5 D. Thelen, 'Afterthoughts', in R. Rosenzweig and D. Thelen (eds) *The Presence of the Past: Popular Uses of History in American Life* (New York: Columbia University Press, 1998), p. 190.
6 G. T. Tanselle, 'The World As Archive,' *Common Knowledge*, 8: 2 (2002). http://muse.jhu.edu/journals/common_knowledge/v008/8.2tanselle.html accessed on 2 February 2004.
7 W. McCaw, 'A Brief Biography Read on the 50th Anniversary of his Marriage: 5th January 1849–January 1899', in W. Armstrong McCaw (ed.) *Memoir and Remains of William McCaw: Cormilligan, Tynron, Dumfriesshire, Scotland and*

Glenore, Otago, New Zealand 1st edn (Invercargill: Family Publication, c1947), pp. 6–8.

8   McCaw Family Reunion Committee, *Memoir and Remains of William McCaw*, 2nd edn (Milton: McCaw Family Reunion Committee, 1982), p. 51.

9   *Dumfries and Galloway Standard* (hereafter *DGS*), 2 June 1880, p. 7.

10   For example, A. Burton, *Dwelling in the Archive: Women Writing House, Home, and History in Late Colonial India* (Oxford: Oxford University Press, 2003).

11   See the sixth edition: W. McCaw, *Truth Frae 'Mang the Heather, or Is the Bible True?* 6th edn (London: S. W. Partridge and Co, c1884).

12   For examples see the six-part 'Prophetic Numbers' series, *DGS* February–March 1865; 'Money or Morals,' in scrapbook of newspaper clippings published by *DGS* August 1869: both in Box NZ487 Jessie Stewart (née Lockhart), Archives of the Presbyterian Church of Aotearoa New Zealand, Knox College, Dunedin (hereafter APCANZ); *DGS*, 1 April 1869, p. 6.

13   See McCaw, *Memoirs and Remains*, p. 38. Letters from William's siblings in America are found in Box NZ487, APCANZ.

14   McCaw, *Memoir and Remains*, 1st edn.

15   *Memoirs of William McCaw*, 2nd edn; D. Currie (ed.) *McCaw Family Tree 1656–1982* (Milton: McCaw Family Reunion Committee, 1982).

16   Box NZ487, APCANZ; Tokomairiro Historical Society at the Milton Museum and Information Centre, South Otago; Jessie Stewart Private Collection held by Janet Anderson, Central Otago.

17   Else, 'History Lessons', p. 128.

18   The watch was treasured by the late Keith McCaw of Mosgiel and the teapot by the late Stewart McCaw Allison of Milton.

19   Selection of photographs taken by Alexander McCaw (son of William Armstrong McCaw) in Scotland c1918, Jessie Stewart Private Collection.

20   R. Wilson, 'Cormilligan,' *Lallans*, 62 (2003) 12–33.

21   Tanselle, 'The World As Archive.'

22   P. Ashton and P. Hamilton, 'At Home with the Past: Background and Initial Findings from the National Survey', special issue of *Australian Cultural History*, 22 (2003) 27.

23   Rosenzweig and Thelen, *The Presence of the Past*, p. 9.

24   Rosenzweig 'Afterthoughts,' p. 186 and Rosenzweig and Thelen, 'Introduction', in *The Presence of the Past*.

25   A. Portelli, 'So Much Depends on a Red Bus, or, Innocent Victims of the Liberating Gun', *Oral History*, 34: 2 (2006) 30.

26   H. Kean, *London Stories: Personal lives, Public Histories* (London: Rivers Oram Press, 2004), p. 10.

27   Else, 'History Lessons,' pp. 125–8.

28   www.teara.govt.nz/ *Te Ara* features letters by William McCaw and his children Jean Kydd and William Armstrong McCaw.

29   For example, C. Fitzgerald (ed.) *Letters from the Bay of Islands: The Story of Marianne Williams* (Auckland: Penguin, 2004). This volume has been deservedly popular with historians and the general public.

30   W. McCaw, *The Gospel and Total Abstinence: The Gospel Indispensable and Pre-eminent as a Means of Social Reformation, but Total Abstinence from All Intoxicating Drinks a Christian Duty* (London: Partridge & Co, 1857), British

Library, London. Note: McCaw's name is standardised as MacCaw in the British Library integrated catalogue.

31 Kean, *London Stories*, pp. 10–15.

32 A. Anderson, *The Welcome of Strangers: An Ethnohistory of Southern Maori A.D. 1650–1850* (Dunedin: University of Otago Press/Dunedin City Council, 1998), figure 10.1, p. 168.

33 See J. Ng, *Windows on a Chinese Past*, 4 vols (Dunedin: Otago Heritage Books, 1993–1999).

34 *DGS*, 11 July 1888, p. 7. The other articles are *DGS*, 5 October 1881, p. 3; 11 July 1888, p. 7; 16 August 1899, p. 7.

35 B. Moloughney and J. Stenhouse, 'Drug-besotten, Sin-begotten Fiends of Filth: New Zealanders and the Oriental Other, 1850–1920,' *New Zealand Journal of History*, 33: 1 (1999) 43–64.

36 Mrs F. G. Soper to A. H. McLintock, 23 October 1946, Box 129, Otago Settlers Museum, Dunedin.

37 C. Erickson, *Leaving England: Essays on British Emigration in the Nineteenth Century* (Ithaca, NY: Cornell University Press, 1994).

38 A. McCarthy, 'A Good Idea of Colonial Life: Personal Letters and Irish Migration to New Zealand,' *New Zealand Journal of History*, 35: 1 (2001) 1–21; D. Fitzpatrick, *Oceans of Consolation: Personal Accounts of Irish Migration to Australia* (Cork: Cork University Press, 1994), pp. 26–7.

39 Tanselle, 'The World As Archive'. See also E. D. Swain, 'Oral History in the Archives: Its Documentary Role in the Twenty-first Century', in R. B. Perks and A. Thomson (eds) *The Oral History Reader*, 2nd edn (London: Routledge, 2006).

40 P. Gibbons, 'The Far Side of the Search for Identity: Reconsidering New Zealand History,' *New Zealand Journal of History*, 37: 1 (2003) 39.

41 *ibid*, pp. 41, 45. Gibbons argues that the best method of uncovering these micro and macro viewpoints is to focus on networks of the acquisition, distribution and consumption of goods. I feel that this approach is limiting.

42 T. Ballantyne, 'Race and the Webs of Empire: Aryanism from India to the Pacific', *Journal of Colonialism and Colonial History*, 2: 3 (2001). http://muse.jhu.edu/journals/journal_of_colonialism_and_colonial_history/v002/2.3ballantyne.html accessed 2 October 2002.

43 See for example C. Cumming, 'Scottish National Identity in an Australian Colony', *The Scottish Historical Review*, 72: 203 (1993), 22–38.

44 P. O'Farrell, 'Varieties of New Zealand Irishness: A Meditation', in L. Fraser (ed.) *A Distant Shore, Irish Migration and New Zealand Settlement* (Dunedin: University of Otago Press, 2000), p. 25.

45 A. Clarke, 'Feasts and Fasts: Holidays, Religion and Ethnicity in Nineteenth Century Otago' (PhD dissertation, University of Otago, 2003).

46 Tom Brooking's recent survey of the history of Scottish migration to Otago does seem to accept this point. T. Brooking, 'Weaving the Tartan into the Flax: Networks, Identities, and Scottish Migration to Nineteenth-Century Otago, New Zealand', in A. McCarthy (ed.) *A Global Clan: Scottish Migrant Networks and Identities Since the Eighteenth Century* (London: I. B. Tauris, 2006) pp. 185–6.

47 McCaw built a cairn on his farm to celebrate Victoria's Diamond Jubilee *DGS*, 14 August 1897, p. 3. His last published article argued against the Boer War *DGS*, 23 April 1902, p. 6.

48 McCaw, *Memoir and Remains*, pp. 9–10.
49 Fitzpatrick, *Oceans of Consolation*, p. 472. This is a point that Charlotte Erickson has recently conceded: Erickson, *Leaving England*, p. 17.
50 *DGS*, 24 Feb 1894, p. 3.
51 *DGS*, 9 March 1898, p. 7. See also 29 March 1890, p. 3; 24 April 1889, p. 3.
52 D. Cressy, *Coming Over: Migration and Communication between England and New England in the Seventeenth Century* (Cambridge and New York: Cambridge University Press, 1987), pp. 232–4, 246.
53 For a list of foreign correspondents to the *Standard* see M. Stewart, 'Notes from New Zealand: A Window into a Settler Mind', MA thesis (Otago: University of Otago, 2004), p. 124. Rev MacKenzie of Nelson, New Zealand, occasionally wrote to the *Standard*. For example, see *DGS*, 1 June 1898, p. 3; 24 August 1898, p. 7.
54 *DGS*, 21 February 1900, p. 6.
55 *DGS*, 31 August 1887, pp. 6–7.
56 P. O'Farrell, *Vanished Kingdoms: Irish in Australia and New Zealand: a Personal Excursion* (Kensington, Australia: New South Wales University Press, 1990), p. 50.
57 For examples see Stewart, *Notes from New Zealand*, pp. 98–101.
58 R. Arnold, *New Zealand's Burning: The Settlers' World in the mid 1880s* (Wellington: Victoria University Press, 1994), pp. 118–20.
59 See Stewart, 'Notes from New Zealand,' pp. 112–18.
60 J. Stenhouse, 'God's Own Silence: Secular Nationalism, Christianity and the Writing of New Zealand History', *New Zealand Journal of History*, 38: 1 (2004), 52–71. See also M. Stewart, 'Calvinism, Migration and Settler Culture: The Case of William McCaw', in J. Stenhouse (ed.) *Christianity Modernity and Culture: New Perspectives on New Zealand History* (Adelaide, Australia: ATF Press, 2005) pp. 32–56.
61 *DGS*, 2 June 1880, p. 7.
62 A. Clarke, 'Heavenly Visions: Otago Colonists' Concepts of the Afterlife', unpublished paper (University of Otago History Seminar, 2004) p. 11.
63 James McCaw, New York to William McCaw, South Otago, 20 November 1898, Box NZ487, APCANZ.

14
Harry Jacobs: The Studio Photographer and the Visual Archive

Jon Newman

> Modern memory is, above all archival. It relies entirely on the materiality of the trace, the immediacy of the recording, the visibility of the image.[1]

Introduction

This is an account of how a local authority archive acquired the print collection of a studio photographer and some of the implications arising from the decision to exhibit it. Lambeth Archives obtained the Harry Jacobs archive of several thousand portrait photographs in 1999 upon his retirement. The collection was distinctive and significant because Jacobs had become a photographer in Brixton in the late 1950s just as the major migration of people from the Caribbean to urban Britain in general and to South London in particular was getting under way. Jacobs was from a Jewish family out of East London but he became the de facto studio photographer for this nascent black community just as Brixton, in the borough of Lambeth, was becoming a major centre for, particularly, Jamaican settlement. Many of the passengers on the *Empire Windrush*, the first boat to bring post-war migrants from the Caribbean to England in 1948, had settled in this area of South London and these Caribbean and West African communities continued to grow throughout the rest of the twentieth century. Today Brixton rivals Harlem in New York in the popular imagination as an iconic black urban centre; it has become shorthand for 'Black London' or arguably 'Black Britain'. The Jacobs' photographic archive provides an unselfconscious record of the growth and aspirations of this black community from the late 1950s until 1999.

The acquisition and display of the Jacobs' archive involved Lambeth Archives and myself, as the Archive Manager at Lambeth Archives, in an exploration of a number of issues that cross over between archive practice and public history. The collection was an important means for engaging new audiences with their recent history and, through the exhibition, it provided the community that Jacobs had served with an opportunity to interrogate and re-appraise these self-images. However, the very actions of archival preservation and public display also raised some ethical issues about the public ownership and display of personal or family material and the institutional transformation that such materials undergo in that transition from private collection to public archive or 'heritage asset'. Finally, because of the nature of the collection and the fact that Jacobs' customers had been largely from the local black community the process also involved dealing with issues around perceived cultural appropriation.

There is a growing expectation that archives, museums and other heritage institutions should hold, and proactively seek, content that is 'relevant' to current, new and future audiences. This expectation is in part shaped by central government agendas that inform policy and funding issues but is also driven by bottom-up demands and expectations of communities and individuals as to the perceived shortcomings of public collections. For example, the 2004 report of the Archives Task Force, *Listening to the Past, Speaking to the Future*, identifies 'access to all' as one of its key aims in order to 'increase community participation in UK archive activities with particular focus on engaging hard-to-reach communities'. Naturally there is an ongoing debate as to both the meaning of this relevance and the nature of those audiences.[2]

There is an obvious and important intersection here with the domain of public history. Archives, libraries and museums, operating as they do outside of the traditional academic setting, are increasingly required to position themselves as conduits for more informal, communal, participative and owned practices, which includes forms of public historical practice. They are well positioned to provide neutral and accessible spaces for such engagement with local groups. At the same time there is an expectation that such activities can no longer simply be delivered by heritage professionals but that they require the endorsement and involvement of the people who are the subject of the historical activity, as well as the audience. This becomes particularly, but not exclusively, significant when predominantly white museum or archive institutions are dealing with content that relates to other ethnic groups. In London the Mayor's Commission on African and Asian Heritage identified 'Empowering community-based heritage' as one of its five key areas and noted that it 'is therefore important that

African, Asian and other diverse communities have opportunities to navigate their own ways into heritage, ensuring that the ownership of their cultural identity is maintained.'[3] The Jacobs' archive, with its obvious crossovers with family life and history, local community identity, and racial and cultural identity, clearly linked with these public historical issues in a way that other research collections would not have.

Family photographs

The Jacobs' archive might technically be described as a business archive of a studio photographer. However, it must also be read as a collection of disparate family photographs. Essentially it comprises second copies of privately commissioned work that had been kept by the photographer. For the purposes of this chapter I use the term family photographs to mean those accumulations of formal and informal images of family, friends, domestic events and objects that are assembled over time and have a particular and cumulative meaning and resonance for a defined audience. These were once held in photograph albums or carried in wallets but now tend to be stored on computer hard drives and displayed as screen savers on monitors or mobile phones. What the Jacobs' archive lacks is that particular and cumulative meaning associated with family collections. However, as I will suggest, it does have other and larger values as a collection.

One of the defining features of such family photographs is their ethereality; the rapid falling away of meaning they undergo across time. This historical process undoubtedly affects all types of records, but I am arguing that there is a particular and critical distinction to be made between such private images and other categories of public records including photographic ones. The significance and the narratives attached to such private collections of photographs are either lost or harden and simplify as they are transmitted down generations, particularly where they depend on oral and remembered rather than written narratives to sustain them. To take a personal example from my family, a great aunt assembled a collection of her photographs and snapshots of family members, taken between 1917 and the 1950s, which she assembled as a single framed collage. It was a significant and symbolic arrangement: the cruciform design of pansies, for remembrance, suggests a symbolic structure and a highly personal meaning. The original significances of many of the images and their narratives and associations died with her. My mother still knows many of the

Figure 14.1 Great-aunt Jo's photo-collage. Family photographs risk losing their original meaning when they enter a public archive
(Photograph, nd, author's collection)

people's names and has her own contexts for some of them. For me, two generations on, these images are haemorrhaging meaning. If I show them to my own children I can only recount the grimly poignant story of my great grandparents (top, left and right), Catholic emigrants to London from Bavaria and of their son (centre) who was killed in the British army at Ypres while a mob threw bricks through his parents' bakers shop window in Marylebone because of the German name over the door. A single family story has been distilled from the multiple images and meanings of the collage and that story has to serve as an exemplar within the grand narrative of war because all former personal and more nuanced contexts are lost.

If we agree that there is an inherent vulnerability to such collections within families, then what are the implications for such images when they cross over from the private family domain to the public, institutional one of a museum or archive? If I were to offer my family items to a public collection what meaning might they have to future researchers or visitors? Archives and museums are increasingly being offered and in some cases actively collecting such personal ephemera be it a family photo album, studio photographers' archives or collections of copy photographs assembled by family historians.[4]

The personal family album is becoming a legitimate field for public access and research in a way that Walter Benjamin never anticipated for his own when, writing in 'A Small History of Photography', he wryly recalls: 'Uncle Alex and Aunt Riekchen, little Trudi when she was still a baby, Papa in his first term at University... and finally, to make our shame complete, we ourselves: as a parlour Tyrolean, yodelling, waving our hat against a painted snowscape'.[5]

Benjamin goes on to recall the shared experience of visiting such studios at the turn of the nineteenth century, 'the period of those studios, with their draperies and palm trees, their tapestries and easels, which occupied so ambiguous a place between execution and representation, between torture chamber and throne room'.[6] The experience was a universally memorable one, although it is not always clear whether it is the actual event or the subsequent and enduring image produced from it that is being recollected. Harry Jacobs, whose own studio was to become such a shared and remembered place for people in Brixton, recalled his own first visit to a studio in the 1920s:

> My mother took us to a small photographer in Whitechapel by the name of Jerome, round the corner from where we lived in Stepney. I think I was about six; I had my elder brother with me, my other

brother, my sister and my mother. I can't remember the reason the photo was taken, but it must have been important because I was wearing my school cap and a lightweight belted overcoat, short trousers and socks and polished black shoes. My mother was wearing her best cloche hat. This photographer produced postcard size prints, three for sixpence halfpenny. We couldn't afford a frame in those days, but it went on the mantelpiece in the holy of holies, what was known as the 'front room', that was only used for weddings, funerals and bar mitzvahs.[7]

Such portraits at their creation and through a subsequent shared and known descent among family members can contain the most intense personal and cultural meaning, but upon their entry into the public domain of the archive or museum that all changes. That these simulacra of personal identity, focused on the face and drawing the viewer to the eyes and the mouth, should end up carrying so little residual meaning (frequently not even a name) is a disturbing paradox. Archivists and curators, attempting to catalogue and assign retrospective meanings to these items are left with the footnotes – dates inferred from costume, motives for the studio visit ascribed from internal evidences – a soldier going to war? A couple getting married? A young man starting work in a new suit? Sometimes there is an elliptic note written on the back, or an inked cross on the front that once distinguished a certain child from an otherwise indistinguishable sea of faces in a classroom photograph. Confronted by such loss of meaning the cataloguer is reduced to inventories, dimensions and details; the photograph, once an image freighted with personal meaning, has become an object. Catalogue texts and exhibition captions reflect this uncertain reification: 'Anonymous albumen portrait print, *carte de visite* card mount, 10 cm × 6 cm, subject not known, some colour retouching to cheeks and neck tie'; 'Pair of ambrotypes, possibly taken prior to the marriage of George and Elizabeth Cooke before 1857, oval gilt frame, 8 cm × 6 cm, photographer(s) unknown'.

This recalls the dichotomy that Roland Barthes struggles with in *Camera Lucida*. That work starts by developing a considered, theoretical analysis of the meaning of the photographic image. Halfway through this process the death of Barthes' mother usurps theory and reconfigures the work into an achingly personal response to photography and to this loss: one that condenses around a particular rediscovered childhood image of his mother. He discusses and describes this 'Winter Garden' image at length but tellingly – and unlike the many other published photographs that intersperse his text – he does not reveal the actual image to the reader:

> I cannot reproduce the Winter Garden Photograph. It exists only for me. For you it would be nothing but an indifferent picture, one of the thousand manifestations of the 'ordinary'; it cannot in any way constitute the visible object of a science; it cannot establish an objectivity, in the positive sense of the term; at most it would interest your *studium*: period, clothes, photogeny; but in it, for you, no wound.[8]

Harry Jacobs

This issue of the significance of individual photos or family collections becomes considerably more problematic when one is confronted with the archive of a photographic business. Lambeth Archives acquired the Jacobs archive in 1999 after I was alerted to Harry's imminent retirement. I negotiated the purchase of whatever remained in the shop, but at this stage was uncertain just what that might constitute. In the subsequent exhibition catalogue I describe what awaited us when I went with a colleague to collect the archive:

> What remained was the 'human wallpaper' that enveloped most of both floors of the shop. Harry had meticulously constructed this over several decades; the principle was that whenever he took a photograph that he liked, he stapled a second copy of it to the wall where it served as a combination of wallpaper, free advertising and exhibition piece. This remarkable mosaic of several thousand images, butted up end to end with no gaps or chinks, completely covered two walls of the downstairs office, continued up the stairs and had encroached all over the back wall of the upstairs studio, opposite the famous landscape scene – the background to so many of the actual photographs. Secured by rusty staples, Harry's former clients stared from the walls: an extraordinary confusion of proud faces and special moments; in their work uniforms and party frocks, displaying their latest hairstyles and babies, sporting new suits and swim suits, offering wedding toasts and eating funeral meats. They stretched back across Harry's career, from the earliest black and white prints taken in the late 1950s on their now yellowing card mounts to more recent, though equally fading, colour work from the 70s and 80s.[9]

Jacobs has generally been seen as a 'black studio photographer' or, more accurately, a photographer who worked almost exclusively with a black

Figure 14.2   Harry Jacobs in his studio
(Self-portrait photograph, c1968 © Lambeth Archives)

clientele. Although he did plenty of other work and was available for all customers, it is not an unreasonable perception. As he noted: 'I suppose I became a bit of an institution for the black community in Brixton. First of all I was the only photographer they could go to; later on there was Campbell's studio on Vining Street; I knew him, and his brother who ran the travel agency round the corner.' Jacobs used to claim, only half-jokingly, that like 'Boots *the* Chemist', he was 'Harry Jacobs *the*

Photographer'. It is a view confirmed by former customers: 'It was a popular place at the time; a lot of West Indians used him, you know, and the rumour goes round among the Caribbean community. In those days, it was early days for us and he was kind enough, mild enough … We must have used him several times; once we sponsored a christening of a child, another time we took our daughter there, another time on our own, always dressed up for the occasion.'[10]

This adoption by the black community was tested during the Brixton Riots when many neighbouring premises were either looted or fired. The special status afforded the shop during the events of April 1981[11] seems to confirm that Jacobs was not exaggerating:

> I think being Jewish helped. The racism back then was awful; but it was directed almost as much at me as it was at black people. They used to say: 'You're one of us; you're ostracised too'. So when the riots were on in Brixton in 1981, and the crowds came along Stockwell Road and into Landor Road, breaking windows (this is what one of the women opposite the shop told me) when the crowd came into Landor Road, there was a group of them in front of my shop, shouting: 'Don't smash his windows; that's Harry Jacobs'; he's one of us'.[12]

Into the archive

Lambeth Archives removed over 5,000 images from Jacobs' studio: some 3,000 mounted prints that had been stapled to the walls of the shop, studio and stairs; and a further 2,000 loose prints. They were all privately commissioned studio portraits, for weddings, funerals, new jobs, award ceremonies and new babies, among other things. They presented a number of problems aside from the practical ones of their physical condition and long-term preservation needs.

The copyright in this disparate collection was problematic. Lambeth Archives owned the photographic prints but myriad, anonymous individuals who had commissioned the photos held the intellectual rights to the images. This presented both a legal and an ethical issue; Lambeth Archives held this collection that we knew was of great local interest and had research value as a record of the black community in Brixton. But it was a collection assembled from multiple privately commissioned images that had only originally been intended for a closed audience of family and friends. If such images were exhibited, one of the effects would be that, 'the original context of the private commission, printed at an intimate scale for a specific audience is lost upon entry [of the images] into these public spaces. They become anonymous through their multiplicity and iconic through the process of selection and framing. They are represented as artistic and cultural images for general consumption, beyond the personal confines of the family album or the front room mantelpiece and its ornaments.'[13]

Another difficulty about holding such a collection was to do with community expectations. There is a quite understandable wariness among some newer communities towards attempts by museums and archives to collect, interpret and represent their cultural heritage. Archive provision in the UK is still substantially delivered by local authority archives. There are of course subject specialised and community archives emerging and approaches like 'Archives 4 All' and the National Council on Archives' Community Archives Development Group are encouraging a new diversity of approach towards issues of community heritage.[14] Nevertheless, the local authority archive with a collecting policy that covers a geographical area – borough, district or county – has traditionally collected not just its own authority's 'official' records, but has also provided a place of deposit for the records of any local business, organisation or individual that cared to place them there.

That such archives have always been more effective at collecting the records of established or 'establishment' organisations should not surprise us. By definition and in the eyes of more recent or marginalised communities local authority record offices are part of the local 'establishment'. At the same time such communities naturally tend to retain their own cultural property. If one considers the historical response of Catholic, Jewish and Huguenot communities – which was to create closed archives of their own (initially religious) organisations' records – this can be seen not only as a response to their own marginal or illegal status within larger society. It can also be viewed as a way of retaining control over their communities' cultural property and identity; and still serves as a model for marginal groups today, be they black, Muslim or white working class communities.[15] This problem is starting to be addressed through work around the concept of community archives, for example. And the archive establishment is starting to acknowledge the existence of communities for whom the traditional archival 'offer' for a collection (physical removal of collections to a record office that can be geographically, intellectually and culturally remote, and the 'professional' management of storage and access arrangements) is unacceptable. This may perhaps be a product of such communities' desire to control their own cultural property. Certainly such property has greater significance to them as an important and also vulnerable part of their personal and group identity.[16]

This is not to suggest that there was an alternative place for the Jacobs' archive to go, or that the local black community was not pleased that it had been preserved in this way. It was rather that, as Lambeth Archives, we understood that there needed to be an empathetic approach to holding and accessing the collection and particularly in the way that it was displayed, if indeed we chose to exhibit it. We also looked at ways of, if not challenging, then at least acknowledging the concern that public history is not simply professional historians, archivists or curators providing accessible exhibitions for 'the public'.

Lambeth Archives chose to do this in partnership with Black Cultural Archives (BCA) and to use their gallery in central Brixton for the exhibition. BCA is an established heritage organisation that defines itself as a custodian of black British history, both locally and nationally.[17] We recognised that an exhibition on this subject curated solely by Lambeth Archives would have less credibility and attract less support and interest than a joint venture. BCA's support and imprimatur helped validate the project. One particular concern was the copyright in the individual images and the fact that rights to all the photos were held by thousands of unknown individuals whom we were unable to contact to obtain permission. We dealt with this by issuing a joint statement with BCA acknowledging the absence of copyright and the difficulties of tracing individual owners. It said: 'We hope that we have also done this [the exhibition] in a way that is both respectful and celebratory in its selection, description and treatment of the photographs and that [it] will be supported by the local community.'[18]

Twin Lens Reflex

In the end the *Twin Lens Reflex* exhibition was a pairing of Jacobs' work with that of a Nigerian photographer, Bandele 'Tex' Ajetunmobi, who had lived in Stepney, East London, from 1948 until 1994. This was another rescued archive saved, literally, from the skip by his niece, Victoria Loughran, after Tex's death and held by her. The dynamic of the exhibition came from the contrasting ways in which these two contemporaries had recorded black Londoners – one as a professional studio photographer, the other as an informal amateur. The exhibition ran for eight weeks over Christmas 2004–05 at BCA's gallery and had over 1,500 visitors. It was well attended and extremely popular. Most visitors were local black people who knew or knew of Jacobs and his work.

At the time of the exhibition, Harry Jacobs was still living locally although he was now elderly and frail. I had discussed the exhibition with him and interviewed him for the exhibition catalogue. He found the notion that his studio work was to be displayed in a gallery gratifying but also puzzling. He maintained a defiantly pragmatic and business-like approach. While he could recognise the value his collection had to the community he was suspicious of any attempt to elevate his studio photography as art. 'There was no artistry to it', he commented, 'everyone wanted absolute mirror images of what they looked like; I couldn't do anything fancy with lighting and shadow or they would complain; I produced what they wanted ... I didn't do any of the printing, never, not even the black and white stuff; I just pointed the camera and "click".'[19]

To try to quantify the success of the exhibition and to understand its meaning for the community it represented I offer some analysis of comments from the BCA's visitors' book. Putting aside general approving remarks, the comments fell substantially into two categories. The first were those visitors who came with memories of the studio and the photographs: 'Great to relive memories of that wonderful shop window of Harry's photos in Landor Road which I often gazed at in passing by'; 'We've all been in those studios'; 'Looked for myself, it brought back good feelings'; 'Great seeing these images second time around'; 'Great to see Harry Jacobs' photos rescued'; 'My mum saw a lot of people she knew'; 'I couldn't find myself'; 'Wonderful pictures, I recognised people from the late 80s'; 'Great to see Harry's work again well displayed and cared for'.[20]

For these visitors the exhibition seemed to include and extend their own sense of family, locality and community. Many of them knew Harry personally and his studio was a familiar landmark; visiting it and using it had been a shared and known experience. Although the photographs were privately commissioned, the comments remind us again of their previous communal existence on the walls of Harry's shop, long before they entered the public archive. Indeed, many of these comments suggest that they had always been recognised as a quasi-public collection; indeed, there was almost an expectation that, somehow, these images would continue to be so.

They also remind us that Jacobs' work had always occupied an extended, communal domain. These images of family celebration and success (nurses in uniform, degree ceremonies, new babies) had previously been sent 'home' to the Caribbean and West Africa, back a generation to adorn the mantelpieces of aunts, grandparents and siblings as

Figure 14.3 Marcia finds her uncle. A visitor to the *Twin Lens Reflex* exhibition finds a previously unknown photograph of her relative
(Photograph Nilu York, 2004 © Lambeth Archives)

a record of the achievements of the post-war Diaspora. Jacobs recalled that: 'They used to send these pictures home to their families. I used to get phoned up in the middle of the night at home from Jamaica or Nigeria, what with the time difference; people used to get the number off of the photographers mount card and think it was their relative's new address, "Can I speak to Donald?", "Where is my daughter living; tell her she hasn't replied to the letter I wrote". I had to say, "Look, I don't know, I'm just the photographer."'[21]

The second category of visitor comment moves beyond these personal reflections. Rather it locates the significance of the collection in a public notion of history – and specifically of a local black history. These disparate and private images, when brought together, serve as a 'legacy', 'record', 'history' and 'heritage' (these terms recur throughout the visitors book) of the local black community: 'Very important and necessary for our community, I am very proud'; 'Good to know where we come from, an invaluable legacy'; 'Being here makes me feel proud and beautiful'; 'Good to be able to go back to our roots'; 'Well done Harry for holding on to our history'; 'Thanks for spending time with our British, English, West Indian, African history'; 'Great to see a display of someone's work in our community who did well for the good of our peoples'.[22]

Does the subsuming of the personal and the communal in these responses to an exhibition of private photographs resolve the initial dilemma? The nervously anticipated conflict between private and public did not emerge. There appeared to be an accommodation between those who took pleasure in finding themselves, their family and their friends publicly displayed and those who found in the exhibition some overarching record of shared community endeavour. Specifically no one was offended or embarrassed by the exhibition.

This engagement and ownership was most tellingly illustrated by the way that visitors responded to 'the wall of images'. When we first planned the exhibition there had been much discussion about how to display Jacobs's photographs. To frame individual portraits would have inevitably turned them into iconic, gallery objects, resulting in a further distancing process from their domestic and personal origins. Another possible approach was that adopted in the *We are the People* exhibition at the National Portrait Gallery, where Tom Phillips thematically grouped his collection of postcard photographs of 'the previously unknown and unsung'– Man and Child, Women in Uniform, Soldiers, and so on.[23]

Our solution was to replicate the way we had first found the images in Jacobs' shop and studio by reconstructing a wall of photographs at one end of the gallery. This accommodated about 250 photographs, secured behind a 12′ × 8′ Perspex screen and using the same rusty staple holes that had originally held them to the walls of the Landor Road studio. This was a pleasing solution in several ways: it respected the archival provenance of the collection by replicating its original display format; and it possessed an ethical dimension, which the other options of individual framing or thematic grouping did not seem to have. We did not have a photographic record of the layout of the original studio walls so there was no possibility of scrupulously replicating them image for image. Instead, a deliberately randomised recreation was a way of dealing with an editorial process of selection (250 images out of 5,000), which respected the group anonymity and the individual identities of both the exhibited portraits and those excluded from the display.

Many visitors clearly recognised this attempt to recreate the feel of the studio. Indeed for one visitor the simulacrum was so successful that he assumed it was a studio and he could have a photograph taken there. What were even more pleasing, if unanticipated, were people's responses

Figure 14.4 The self-captioning exhibition. 'Post-it' notes left by visitors to the *Twin Lens Reflex* exhibition identifying individual portraits (Photograph Gabrielle Bourn, 2005 © Lambeth Archives)

to the deliberate, uncaptioned anonymity of this wall of faces. This was left undone so that visitors could identify the portraits of people that they knew. The process started when guests at the private view asked for 'post-it' notes and started attaching descriptions of people over the photographs. Although we had not expected this, the response seemed blindingly appropriate and the 'post-it' notes were left up and pads of blank notes and pens were made available. Over eight weeks the contributions grew and by the end of the show there were over 40 brief CVs 'Stafford Baker, resident of Brixton frontline'; 'Martin Ade Olubayo, died Nigeria Jan. 1990, daughter Justine McKay-Bayo'; 'Members of the Small Axe Posse – D, Juicy & Michael'; 'Paul Williams, top barber in Brixton, Jan Austin his client was a trainee barrister'; 'Aunty Sonia Caballero, she is doing very well'.[24]

Conclusion

The act of 'saving' the collection – of preserving and removing it from the studio walls, of boxing, numbering, stamping, cleaning, encapsu-

Figure 14.5   'Members of the Small Axe Posse; D, Juicy & Michael'. Caption to anonymous portrait photograph provided by an exhibition visitor in 2005 (Photograph Harry Jacobs, 1982 © Unknown)

lating in inert polyester sheets, of selectively digitising, using for exhibition, publicising and writing about – in short all the activities that a public archive engages in with their collections has had the effect of creating or imposing new and official meanings on the collection. As Pierre Nora suggests, the archival process has transformed what was previously personal, intuitive and temporary into the 'material trace'.[25]

This transformative process encourages the creation of new uses and significances for the archive. Local people still come to trawl through the collection, looking for old family members or friends or even to track down pictures of themselves as children. That direct connection with the collection's original function is unusual: a contemporary genealogy, exclusively available to Jacobs' South London clientele. But increasingly other users are coming to take the collection in different directions. Some researchers investigate the history of hairstyles, African fabrics or fashion designs, theatre set designers look for props, historians of black freemasonry use the collection and educational publishers search for material for the teaching of 'citizenship'. One should not be surprised at the discovery of new or unanticipated research values in archive collections.

To invoke the mantra of current heritage-speak, the Jacobs' archive is now 'accessible'.[26] Yet at the same time it is exposed to new risks and dangers. Its physical integrity might now be assured but it is vulnerable to that loss of autonomy, significance and integrity that its previous quirky status as unofficial community gallery had given it. Arguably such a loss is something that all collections undergo to varying degrees when they cross the threshold of the archive. What happened with the spontaneous captioning at the *Twin Lens Reflex* exhibition was a temporary re-appropriation of meaning by the local community that 'owned' the collection. The guerrilla captions posted on the images were a refusal to allow these photographs to turn into the merely emblematic or representational of whatever – 'black youth', '1970s fashion', 'Windrush migrant', 'Caribbean nurse'. Instead of the cryogenic after-existence of the archive, they were briefly reacquiring the shared life and meaning that they had once held for the individuals who commissioned and owned them and for the extended families and community who understood their significances.

Notes

1   P. Nora, 'From Lieux de Mémoire to Realms of Memory', preface to P. Nora and L. D. Kritzman (eds) *Realms of Memory: Rethinking the French Past, vol 1* (New York: Columbia University Press, 1996).

2   Archives Task Force report, *Listening to the Past, Speaking to the Future* (London: MLA, 2004). See also the National Council on Archives Road to Relevance Conference, 2003 and MLA London *Revisiting Collections* research, 2005–7 http://www.mlalondon.org,uk.

3   The Mayor's Commission on African and Asian Heritage, *Delivering Shared Heritage* (London: Greater London Authority, 2005), p. 41.

4   See for example the use of the Paddy Fahey collection held by London Borough of Brent Archives in F. Whooley, *Irish Londoners* (Gloucestershire: Sutton Publishing, 1997). On the use of two Malian studio photographers' work see M. Lamunière, *You Look Beautiful Like That: The Portrait Photographs of Seydou Keïta and Malick Sidibé* (New Haven and London: Yale University Press, 2001).

5   W. Benjamin, 'A Small History of Photography', in Benjamin, *One Way Street* (London: NLB, 1979), p. 246.

6 *ibid.*
7 Transcript of interview with Harry Jacobs, July 2004, Lambeth Archives Department.
8 R. Barthes, *Camera Lucida: Reflections on Photography* (London: Jonathan Cape, 1982).
9 J. Newman, *Twin Lens Reflex, The Portrait Photographs of Harry Jacobs and Bandele 'Tex' Ajetunmobi* (London: Lambeth Archives, 2004), p. 2.
10 Transcript of interview with Boniface Amos, July 2004, Lambeth Archives Department, cited in *Twin Lens Reflex.*
11 The Brixton riots between young people from the black community and the police took place over three days in April 1981. Over 150 buildings were damaged and 30 were burned. During that summer similar rioting took place in other black communities of Handsworth, Toxteth, Moss Side and Southall.
12 Transcript of interview with Harry Jacobs, July 2004, Lambeth Archives Department, cited in *Twin Lens Reflex.*
13 *ibid*, p. 15.
14 Archives 4 All, http://www.nationalarchives.gov.uk/partnerprojects/a2a/ National Council on Archives' Community Archives website, http://www.communityarchives.org.uk/
15 See for example the collecting policies of secular Jewish archives in the UK such as the Wiener Library, http://www.wienerlibrary.co.uk/collections.aspx or the University of Southampton Libraries special collections http://www.archives.lib.soton.ac.uk/holdings.shtml.
16 See, for example, *Final Report of the Community Access to Archives Project* (London: The National Archives, 2004). See also the National Council on Archives' Community Archives website http://www.communityarchives.org.uk/.
17 Black Cultural Archives (BCA) was established as an educational charity in Brixton 1981. Its main objectives are to collect, document, preserve and disseminate the history and culture of black people of African and Caribbean ancestry living in Britain. BCA's aim is to develop a centre of excellence for black history and heritage in Brixton with national and international reach. www.bcaheritage.org.uk.
18 *Twin Lens Reflex*, p. 16.
19 Transcript of interview with Harry Jacobs, July 2004, Lambeth Archives Department, cited in *Twin Lens Reflex.*
20 Black Cultural Archives, visitors' book, selected entries, 22 November 2004–28 January 2005.
21 Transcript of interview with Harry Jacobs, July 2004, Lambeth Archives Department, cited in *Twin Lens Reflex.*
22 Black Cultural Archives, visitors' book, selected entries, 22 November 2004–28 January 2005.
23 *We are the People*, National Portrait Gallery exhibition, March–June 2004. http://www.npg.org.uk/live/wearepeople.asp.
24 Harry Jacobs' archive, Lambeth Archives Department, IV/233, viewer descriptions added to collection.
25 P. Nora, 'From Lieux de Mémoire to Realms of Memory', preface to Nora and Kritzman, *Realms of Memory.*

26 'An archival heritage unlocked and made open to all citizens in a way that engages them and empowers them to use archives for personal, community, social and economic benefit.' Vision Statement of the Archives Task Force report, *Listening to the Past, Speaking to the Future.*

Select Bibliography

Abrams, J. F. 'Lost Frames of Reference: Sightings of History and Memory in Pennsylvania's Documentary Landscape', in Hufford, M. (ed.) *Conserving Culture: A New Discourse on Heritage* (Urbana and Chicago: University of Illinois Press, 1994), pp. 24–38.

Ackroyd, P. *London: The Biography* (London: Chatto and Windus, 2000).

Alibhai-Brown, Y. *Who Do We Think We Are? Imagining the New Britain* (London: Penguin Books, 2001).

Alsford, S. and Parry, D. 'Interpretive theatre: A Role in Museums', *Museum Management and Curatorship*, 10 (1991), pp. 8–23.

Anderson, A. *The Welcome of Strangers: An Ethnohistory of Southern Maori A.D. 1650–1850* (Dunedin: University of Otago Press/Dunedin City Council, 1998).

Anderson, J. *Time Machines: The World of Living History* (Nashville, TN: The American Association for State and Local History, 1995).

Anderson, M. 'In Search of Women's Public History: Heritage and Gender', *Public History Review*, 2 (1993), pp. 1–17.

Andren, E. *Skansen: Buildings and Animals. A Short Guide for Visitors* (Stockholm: Nordiska Museet, 1947).

Appadurai, A. (ed.) *The Social Lives of Things: Commodities in Cultural Perspective* (Cambridge: Cambridge University Press, 1986).

Archibald, R. 'Narrative for a New Century', *Museum News*, November–December (1998).

Archives Task Force, *Listening to the Past, Speaking to the Future* (London, MLA, 2004).

Arnold, R. *New Zealand's Burning: The Settlers' World in the mid 1880s* (Wellington: Victoria University Press, 1994).

Arts NSW, *NSW Premier's History Awards 2006* (Sydney: Arts NSW, 2006).

Arthur, J. and Phillips, R. (eds) *Issues in History Teaching* (London and New York: Routledge, 2000).

Ashley, S. 'State Authority and the Public Sphere: Ideas on the Changing Role of the Museum as a Canadian Social Institution', *Museum and Society*, 3: 1 (2005), pp. 5–17.

Ashton, P. 'The Past in the Present: Public History in the City of Sydney', in Murray T. (ed.) *Exploring the Modern City: Recent Approaches to Urban History and Archaeology* (Sydney: Historic Houses Trust of NSW, 2003), pp. 1–23.

Ashton, P. and Hamilton, P. 'On not Belonging: Memorial and Memory in Sydney', *Public History Review*, 9 (2001), pp. 23–36.

Ashton, P. and Hamilton, P. 'At Home with the Past: Background and Initial Findings from the National Survey', *Australians and the Past*, special issue of *Australian Cultural History*, 22 (2003), pp. 5–30.

Ashton, P. and Hamilton, P. 'Facing Facts?: History Wars in Australian High Schools', *Journal of Australian Studies*, 91 (2007), pp. 45–59.

Ashton, P. and Hamilton, P. *History at the Crossroads* (Sydney: Halstead Press, 2008, forthcoming).

Ashton, P. and Keating, C. 'Commissioned History', in Davison, G., Hirst, J. and Macintyre, S. (eds) *Oxford Companion to Australian History* (Melbourne: Oxford University Press, 1998), pp. 139–41.

Atkinson, A. 'Heritage, Self, and Place', in Hamilton, P. and Ashton, P. (eds) *Australians and the Past*, special issue of *Australian Cultural History*, 22 (2003), pp. 161–71.

Attwood, B. (ed.) *In the Age of Mabo: History, Aborigines and Australia* (Sydney: Allen and Unwin, 1996).

Baehrendtz, N. E. *et al* 'Skansen – A Stock Taking at 90', *Museum XXXIV*, 82: 3 (1982), pp. 173–8.

Ballantyne, T. 'Race and the Webs of Empire: Aryanism from India to the Pacific', *Journal of Colonialism and Colonial History*, 2: 3 (2001).

Barley, N. *Native Land* (London: Penguin Books, 1989).

Barth, F. (ed.) *Ethnic Groups and Boundaries: the Social Organisation of Culture Difference* (London: George Allen & Unwin, 1969).

Barthes, R. *Mythologies* (Paris: Seuil, 1970).

Barthes, R. *Camera Lucida: Reflections on Photography* (London: Jonathan Cape, 1982).

Bassett, M. *The Mother of All Departments: The History of the Department of Internal Affairs* (Auckland: Auckland University Press, 1997).

Beck, S. 'Use of Improvisation in Museums Theatre', in Maloney, L. and Hughes, C. (eds) *Case Studies in Museum, Zoo and Aquarium Theatre* (Washington, DC: American Association of Museums, Professional Practice series, 1999), pp. 21–7.

Becker, C. L. *Everyman His Own Historian: Essays in History and Politics* (New York: Crofts & Co., 1935).

Belgrave, M. 'Something Borrowed, Something New: History and the Waitangi Tribunal', in Phillips, J. and Dalley, B. (eds) *Going Public: The Changing Face of New Zealand History* (Auckland: Auckland University Press, 2001), pp. 92–109.

Belgrave, M. *Historical Frictions: Maori Claims and Reinvented Histories* (Auckland: Auckland University Press, 2005).

Belk, R. W. *Collecting in a Consumer Society* (London: Routledge, 1995).

Benjamin, W. *Illuminations*, H. Arendt (ed.) (London: Cape, 1970).

Benjamin, W. 'Small History of Photography' in Benjamin, *One Way Street* (London: NLB, 1979).

Benjamin, W. *The Arcades Project*, trans. Eiland, H. and McLaughlin, K. (London: Belknap Press, 1999).

Benson, S., Brier, S. and Rosenzweig, R. (eds) *Presenting the Past: Essays in History and the Public* (Philadelphia: Temple University Press, 1986).

Bergmann, K. *et al* (eds) *Handbuch der Geschichtsdidaktik*, 1st edn (Düsseldorf: Schwann, 1979: five subsequent editions).

Best, D. *The Rationality of Feeling: Understanding the Arts in Education* (London: The Falmer Press, 1992).

Black, J. *Using History* (London: Hodder Arnold, 2005).

Blackwood, J. *London's Immortals: The Complete Outdoor Commemorative Statues* (London: Savoy Press, 1989).

Blatti, J. (ed.) *Past Meets Present: Essays about Historic Interpretation and Public Audiences* (Washington, DC: Smithsonian Institution Press, 1987).

Blomfield, G. 'Hidden History: Conflict and Community History', in Community History Program (CHP), *History and Communities: A Preliminary Survey* (Kensington: CHP University of New South Wales, 1990), pp. 59–70.

Boal, A. *The Rainbow of Desire: The Boal Method of Theatre and Therapy* (New York: Routledge, 1995).

Bodnar, J. *Remaking America: Public Memory, Commemoration, and Patriotism in the Twentieth Century* (Princeton, NJ: Princeton University Press, 1992).

Bookspan, S. 'Something Ventured, Many Things Gained: Reflections on Being a Historian-Entrepreneur', *The Public Historian*, 28: 1 (2006), pp. 67–74.

Bourke, J. *Working-Class Cultures in Britain 1890–1960: Gender, Class and Ethnicity* (London and New York: Routledge, 1994).

Bourke, J. *Dismembering the Male: Men's Bodies, Britain and the Great War* (London: Reaktion Books, 1999).

Boyns, R. 'Archivists and Family Historians: Local Authority Record Repositories and the Family History User Group', *Journal of the Society of Archivists*, 20: 1 (1999).

Breitbart, M. M. and Stanton, C. 'Touring Templates: Cultural Workers and Regeneration in Small New England Cities', in. Smith, M. K. (ed.) *Tourism, Culture and Regeneration* (Wallingford, UK: CABI, 2006), pp. 111–22.

Brennan, T. 'History, Family, History', in Kean, H., Martin, P. and Morgan, S. J. (eds) *Seeing History: Public History in Britain Now* (London: Francis Boutle, 2000), pp. 37–50.

Brennan, T. 'Manoeuvre' http://mysite.wanadoo-members.co.uk/manoeuvre/page1.html, 2003

Brennan, T. 'Mercator manoeuvre', *Cultural Geographies*, 12: 4 (2005), pp. 514–20.

Brooking, T. 'Weaving the Tartan into the Flax: Networks, Identities, and Scottish Migration to Nineteenth-Century Otago, New Zealand', in McCarthy, A. (ed.) *A Global Clan: Scottish Migrant Networks and Identities Since the Eighteenth Century* (London: I. B. Tauris, 2006), pp. 183–202.

Burcaw, G. E. 'Can History be too Lively?', *Museums Journal*, 80: 1 (1980), pp. 5–7.

Burton, A. *Dwelling in the Archive: Women Writing House, Home, and History in Late Colonial India* (Oxford: Oxford University Press, 2003).

Butler, T. *Drifting* (Audio walk, London: Memoryscape Audio Walks, 2005).

Butler, T. 'Memoryscape Audio Walks', www.memoryscape.org.uk, 2005.

Butler, T. 'A Walk of Art: The Potential of the Sound Walk as Practice in Cultural Geography', *Social and Cultural Geography*, 7: 6 (2006), pp. 889–908.

Butler, T. and Miller, G. 'Linked: A Landmark in Sound, a Public Walk of Art', *Cultural Geographies*, 12: 1 (2005), pp. 77–88.

Butler, T. and Wilson, R. 'Interview with Toby Butler', ReadySteadyBook http://www.readysteadybook.com/Article.aspx?page=tobybutler, 2007.

Byrnes, G. *The Waitangi Tribunal and New Zealand History* (Melbourne: Oxford University Press, 2004).

Camp, D. 'Does He Smell Right?: Living History at Culzean Castle', *GEM News*, 54 (1994), pp. 7–8.

Cannizzo, J. and Parry, D. 'Museum Theatre in the 1990s: Trail-blazer or Camp-follower?', in Pearce, M. S. (ed.) *Museums and the Appropriation of Culture* (London: The Athlone Press, 1994), pp. 43–64.

Carment, D. *A Past Displayed: Public History, Public Memory and Cultural Resource Management in Australia's Northern Territory* (Darwin: Northern Territory University Press, 2001).

Carr, D. 'The Need For the Museum', *Museum News,* March/April (1999), pp. 11–21.

Carrier, P. *Holocaust Monuments and National Memory Cultures in France and Germany since 1989* (Oxford: Berghahn Books, 2006).

Carroll J. 'Terra Incognita: Mapping Drama Talk', *NADIE Journal* 12: 2 (1988), pp. 13–21.

Carter, D. 'Working with the Past, Working on the Future', in Nile, R. and Peterson M. (eds) *Becoming Australia: The Woodford Forum* (St Lucia: University of Queensland Press, 1999), pp. 9–18.

Casey, D. 'Culture Wars: Museums, Politics and Controversy', *New Museum Developments and the Culture Wars,* special issue of *Open Museum Journal,* 6 (2003), pp. 8–10.

Certeau, M. de, *The Practice of Everyday Life,* trans. Rendall, S. (Berkeley: University of California Press, 1984).

Chambers, I. 'The Aural Walk', in Cox, C. and Warner, D. (eds) *Audio Culture: Readings in Modern Music* (New York: Continuum, 2004), pp. 98–101.

Champion, J. 'Seeing the Past: Simon Schama's "A History of Britain" and Public History', *History Workshop Journal,* 56 (2003), pp. 153–80.

Charlton, J. 'Family History from the Left', *London Socialist Historians Group Newsletter,* 6 (1999), p. 2.

Chatwin, B. *The Songlines* (London: Vintage Classics, 1987).

Clendinnen, I. 'The History Question: Who Owns the Past?', *Quarterly Essay,* 23 (2006), pp. 1–128.

Clifford, J. *Routes: Travel and Translation in the Late Twentieth Century* (Cambridge: Harvard University Press, 1997).

Cohen, A. P. (ed.) *Symbolising Boundaries: Identity and Diversity in British Cultures* (Manchester: Manchester University Press, 1986).

Cohen, D. J. 'The Future of Preserving the Past', *CRM: The Journal of Heritage Stewardship,* 2: 2 (2005).

Commonwealth of Australia, *Review of the National Museum of Australia, its Exhibitions and Public Programs. A Report to the Council of the National Museum of Australia* (Canberra: Commonwealth of Australia, 2003).

Community Access to Archives Project, *Final Report* (London: The National Archives, 2004).

Conard, R. *Benjamin Shambaugh and the Intellectual Foundations of Public History* (Iowa City: University of Iowa Press, 2002).

Courtauld, G. *The Pocket Book of Patriotism* (London: Halstead Books, 2004).

Cresswell, T. *The Tramp in America* (London: Reaktion Books, 2001).

Cresswell, T. *Place: A Short Introduction* (Oxford: Blackwell Publishing, 2004).

Cresswell, T. *On the Move: Mobility in the Modern Western World* (London and New York: Routledge, 2006).

Cressy, D. *Coming Over: Migration and Communication between England and New England in Seventeenth Century* (Cambridge and New York: Cambridge University Press, 1987).

Cugoano, O. *Thoughts and Sentiments on the Evil and Wicked Traffic of the Slavery and Commerce of the Human Species, etc.* first published London, 1787 (New York: Penguin Classics, 1999).

Cumming, C. 'Scottish National Identity in an Australian Colony', *The Scottish Historical Review,* 72: 203 (1993), 22–38.

Curthoys, A. and Hamilton, P. 'What Makes History Public?', *Public History Review*, 1 (1992), pp. 8–13.

Dalley, B. 'Finding the Common Ground: New Zealand's Public History', in Dalley, B. and Phillips, J. (eds) *Going Public: The Changing Face of New Zealand History* (Auckland: Auckland University Press, 2001), pp. 16–29.

Dalley, B. and Labrum, B. (eds) *Fragments: New Zealand Social and Cultural History* (Auckland: Auckland University Press, 2000).

Dalley, B. and McLean, G. (eds) *Frontier of Dreams: The Story of New Zealand* (Auckland: Hodder Moa Beckett, 2005).

Dalley, B. and Phillips, J. (eds) *Going Public: The Changing Face of New Zealand History* (Auckland: Auckland University Press, 2001).

Davin, A. *Growing Up Poor: Home, School and Street in London 1870–1914* (London: Rivers Oram Press, 1996).

Davison, G. 'Public History', in Davison, G., Hirst, J. and Macintyre, S. (eds), *The Oxford Companion to Australian History* (Melbourne: Oxford University Press, 1998), pp. 532–3.

Davison, G. *The Use and Abuse of Australian History* (Sydney: Allen & Unwin, 2000).

Davison, G. 'A Historian in the Museum: The Ethics of Public History', in Macintyre, S. (ed.) *The Historian's Conscience: Australia Historians on the Ethics of History* (Melbourne: Melbourne University Press, 2004), pp. 49–63.

Davison, G. and McConville, C. (eds) *A Heritage Handbook* (Sydney: Allen and Unwin, 1991).

Dean, D. and Rider, P. E. 'Museums, Nation and Political History in the Australian National Museum and the Canadian Museum of Civilization', *Museum and Society*, 3: 1 (2005), pp. 35–50.

Denning, G. 'Some Beaches are Never Closed: Foundation and Future Reflections on the History Institute, Victoria', *Rostrum*, 19 (2001), pp. 23–9.

Derrida, J. E. *Archive Fever: A Freudian Impression,* trans. Prenowitz (Chicago and London: University of Chicago Press, 1998).

Dicks, B. *Culture on Display: The Production of Contemporary Visitability* (UK: Open University Press, 2004).

Ditchfield, S. 'It Pays to Help the Public Meet the Ancestors', *The Times Higher Education*, 20 April 2001.

Darien-Smith, K. and Hamilton, P. (eds) *Memory and History in Twentieth-Century Australia* (Melbourne: Oxford University Press, 1994).

Drake, M. 'Inside-Out or Outside-In?: The Case of Family and Local History', in Finnegan, R. (ed.) *Participating in the Knowledge Society: Researchers Beyond the University Walls* (Basingstoke: Palgrave Macmillan, 2005), pp. 110–23.

Dresser, M. 'Set in Stone? Statues and Slavery in London', *History Workshop Journal*, 64 (2007), 175–86.

Driver, F. and Gilbert, D. (eds) *Imperial Cities: Landscape, Display and Identity* (Manchester and New York: Manchester University Press, 1999).

Durbin, G. (ed.) *Developing Museum Exhibitions for Lifelong Learning* (London: Stationery Office Books, 1996).

Dyer, M. 'The Heritage Education Trust: A Personal View of an Evolving Role', in Dyer (ed.) *Heritage Education Handbook* (Kettering: Heritage Education Trust, 1986).

Eagleton, T. *Literary Theory: An Introduction* 2nd edn (Oxford: Blackwell Publishers, 1996).

Edwards, B. 'Avebury and Not-so-ancient-places: The Making of the English Heritage Landscape', in Kean, H., Martin, P. and Morgan, S. J. (eds) *Seeing History: Public History in Britain Now* (London: Francis Boutle, 2000).

Edwards, P. and Dabydeen, D. (eds) *Black Writers in Britain 1760–1890: An Anthology* (Edinburgh: Edinburgh University Press, 1991).

Else, A. 'History Lessons: The Public History You Get When You're Not Getting Any Public History', in Dalley, B. and Phillips, J. (eds) *Going Public: The Changing Face of New Zealand History* (Auckland: Auckland University Press, 2001), pp. 123–40.

English, J. R. 'The Tradition of Public History in Canada', *The Public Historian*, 5: 1 (1983), pp. 46–59.

Equiano, O. *The Interesting Narrative and Other Writings*, first published 1772 (London: Penguin Books reprint, 1995).

Erickson, C. *Leaving England: Essays on British Emigration in the Nineteenth Century* (Ithaca, NY: Cornell University Press, 1994).

Evans, R. J. *In Defence of History* (London: Granta Books, 1997).

Everton, J. 'The Role of Archives in the Perception of Self', *Journal of the Society of Archivists*, 27: 2 (2006), pp. 227–46.

Fabre, G. and O'Meally, R. (eds) *History and Memory in African American Culture* (Oxford: Oxford University Press, 1994).

Faulkner, W. *Requiem for a Nun* (Harmondsworth: Penguin, 1960).

Fenton, J. 'Space, Chance, Time: Walking Backwards Through the Hours on the Left and Right Banks of Paris', *Cultural Geographies*, 12: 4 (2005), pp. 412–28.

Finnegan, R. 'The Open University Course on Family and Community History', *Genealogists' Magazine*, 25: 2 (1995), pp. 49–54.

Fitzgerald, C. (ed.) *Letters from the Bay of Islands: The Story of Marianne Williams* (Auckland: Penguin, 2004).

Fitzpatrick, D. *Oceans of Consolation: Personal Accounts of Irish Migration to Australia* (Cork: Cork University Press, 1994).

Foard, G. 'Field Offensive', *British Archaeology*, 79 (2004), accessed at www. britarch.ac.uk.

Foner, E. *Who Owns History?: Rethinking the Past in a Changing World* (New York: Hill and Wang, 2002).

Ford, S. *The Situationist International: A Users Guide* (London: Black Dog Publishing, 2005).

Fowler, P. J. *The Past in Contemporary Society: Then, Now* (London and New York: Routledge, 1992).

Franz, E. G. 'What Makes an Archives Successful? The "House of History" Concept', *Journal of the Society of Archivists*, 16: 1 (1995), pp. 71–6.

Friedman, J. 'Media Review: *Drifting* from Memoryscape Audio Walks. Produced by Toby Butler', *Oral History Review*, 33: 1 (2006), pp. 107–9.

Frisch, M. (ed.) *A Shared Authority: Essays on the Craft and Meaning of Oral and Public History* (Albany: State University of New York Press, 1990).

Fussell, P. *The Great War and Modern Memory* (Oxford: Oxford University Press, 1975).

Gale, C. 'Record-keeping as an Ethical Imperative', *Journal of the Society of Archivists*, 27: 1 (2006), pp. 17–27.

Gapps, S. 'Out of Time, Out of Place: Re-enacting the Past of a Foreign Country', *Public History Review*, 9 (2001), pp. 61–9.

Gapps, S. 'Authenticity Matters: Historical Re-enactment and Australian Attitudes to the Past', in Hamilton, P. and Ashton, P. (eds) *Australians and the Past*, special issue of *Australian Cultural History*, 22 (2003), pp. 105–16.

Gardner, J. B. 'Contested Terrain: History, Museums, and the Public', *The Public Historian*, 26: 4 (2004), pp. 11–21.

Gardner, J. B. and LaPaglia, P. S. (eds) *Public History: Essays from the Field* (Malabar, Florida: Krieger Publishing Company, 1999).

Gibbons, P. 'The Far Side of the Search for Identity: Reconsidering New Zealand History', *New Zealand Journal of History* 37: 1 (2003), pp. 38–47.

Gilbert, P.K. (ed.) *Imagined Londons* (Albany: State University of New York Press, 2002).

Gilroy, P. *The Black Atlantic: Modernity and Double Consciousness* (London: Verso, 1993).

Glaser, L. *Hopewell Furnace National Historic Site: Administrative History* (Philadelphia and Boston: National Park Service, Northeast Regional Office, 2005).

Glasersfeld, E. von 'On the Concept of Interpretation', *Poetics*, 12 (1983), pp. 207–18.

Glassberg, D. *Sense of History: The Place of the Past in American Life* (Amherst, MA: The University of Massachusetts Press, 2001).

Goodacre, B. and Baldwin, G. *Living the Past: Reconstruction, Recreation, Re-enactment and Education at Museums and Historical Sites* (London: Middlesex University Press, 2002).

Goodall, H. 'Museum Reviews: The Historical Museums of Ottawa; Canadian Museum of Civilization', *The Public Historian*, 24: 1 (2002), pp. 55–64.

Gorman-Murray, A. 'Gay and Lesbian Public History in Australia', *Public History Review*, 11 (2004), pp. 8–38.

Gosden, P. *Education in the Second World War: A Study in Policy and Adminis-tration* (London: Methuen, 1976).

Gough, P. 'Sites in the Imagination: The Beaumont Hamel Newfoundland Memorial on the Somme', *Cultural Geographies*, 11: 3 (2004), pp. 235–58.

Gough, P. 'Corporations and Commemoration: First World War remembrance, Lloyds TSB and the National Memorial Arboretum', *International Journal of Heritage Studies*, 10: 5 (2004) 435–55.

Gough, P. and Morgan, S. J. 'Manipulating the Metonymic: The Politics of Civil Identity and the Bristol Cenotaph, 1919–1932', *Journal of Historical Geographies*, 30 (2004), pp. 665–84.

Greenspan, A. *Creating Colonial Williamsburg* (Washington, DC and London: Smithsonian Institution Press, 2002).

Grele, R. J. 'Clio on the Road to Damascus: A National Survey of History as Activity and Experience', *The Public Historian*, 22: 1 (2000), pp. 31–4.

Griffith, G. 'The Historical View from the Royal Australian Historical society', in The Local History Co-ordination Project (LHCP), *Locating Australia's Past* (Kensington, NSW: LHCP, 1988), pp. 1–6.

Hackney, S. 'The American Identity', *The Public Historian*, 19: 1 (1997).

Hall, S. 'Raphael Samuel, 1934–96', *New Left Review*, 221 (January/February 1997), pp. 119–27.

Hamilton, P. '"Stranger than Fiction": the *Daily Mirror* "Historical Feature"', in Rickard, J. and Spearritt, P. (eds) *Packaging the Past? Public Histories*, special issue of *Australian Historical Studies*, 24: 96 (1991), pp. 198–207.

Hamilton, P. 'Memory studies and cultural history', in Teo, H. and White, R. (eds) *Cultural History in Australia* (Sydney: University of NSW Press, 2003), pp. 81–97.

Hamilton, P. and Ashton, P. (eds) *Australians and the Past*, special issue of *Australian Cultural History*, 22 (2003).

Handler, R. 'Is 'Identity' a Useful Cross-Cultural Concept?', in Gillis, J. R. (ed.) *Commemorations: The Politics of National Identity* (Princeton: Princeton University Press, 1994).

Handler, R. and Gable. E. *The New History in an Old Museum: Creating the Past at Colonial Williamsburg* (Durham and London: Duke University Press, 1997).

Hansen, G. 'White Hot History: the Review of the National Museum of Australia', *Public History Review*, 11 (2003), pp. 39–50.

Hardy III, C. 'Authoring in Sound: Aural History, Radio and the Digital Revolution', in Perks, R. and Thomson, A. (eds) *The Oral History Reader* 2nd edn (London: Routledge, 2006), pp. 393–405.

Hardy III, C. 'A People's History of Philadelphia: Reflections on Community Oral History Projects and the Uses of the Past', *The Oral History Review*, 33: 1 (2006), pp. 1–32.

Harootunian, H. *History's Disquiet: Modernity, Cultural Practice and the Question of Everyday Life* (New York: Columbia University Press, 2000).

Harries, M. and Harries, S. *The War Artists: British Official War Art of the Twentieth Century* (London: Michael Joseph, in association with the Imperial War Museum and the Tate Gallery, 1983).

Harrison M. *Learning out of School: A Teacher's Guide to the Educational Use of Museums* (London: Ward Lock Educational 1970).

Hayden, D. *The Power of Place: Urban Landscapes as Public History* (Cambridge, Massachusetts: MIT Press, 1995).

Hayward, J. and Wheen, N. (eds) *The Waitangi Tribunal: Te Roopu Whakamana i te Tiriti o Waitangi* (Wellington: Bridget Williams Books, 2005).

Hein, H. S. *The Museum in Transition: A Philosophical Perspective* (Washington, DC: Smithsonian Institution Press, 2000).

Henry, M. 'Drama's Ways of Learning', *Research in Drama Education,* 5: 1 (2000), pp. 45–62.

Henson, D. 'Archaeology in Schools', in Henson, D., Stone, P. and Corbishley, M. (eds) *Education and the Historic Environment* (London: Routledge, 2004).

Henson, D., Stone, P. and Corbishley, M. (eds) *Education and the Historic Environment* (London and New York: Routledge, 2004).

Hewison, R. *The Heritage Industry: Britain in a Climate of Decline* (London: Methuen, 1987).

Hilliard, C. 'James Cowan and the Frontiers of New Zealand History', *New Zealand Journal of History*, 31: 2 (1997), pp. 219–33.

Hilliard, C. 'Stories of Becoming: the Centennial Surveys and the Colonization of New Zealand', *New Zealand Journal of History*, 33: 1 (1999), pp. 3–19.

Hilliard, C. 'Textual Museums: Collection and Writing in History and Ethnology, 1900–1950', in Dalley, B. and Labrum, B. (eds) *Fragments: New Zealand Social and Cultural History* (Auckland: Auckland University Press, 2000), pp. 118–39.

Hobsbawm, E. and Ranger, T. *The Invention of Tradition* (Cambridge: Cambridge University Press, 1983).

Hodgkin, K. and Radstone, S. *Contested Pasts: The Politics of Memory* (London: Routledge, 2003).

Hooper-Greenhill, E. (ed.) *The Educational Role of the Museum* (London and New York: Routledge, 1994).

Hooper-Greenhill, E. (ed.) *Cultural Diversity: Developing Museum Audiences in Britain* (London: Leicester University Press, 1997).

Hoskins, J. *Biographical Objects: How Things Tell the Stories of People's Lives* (London: Routledge, 1998).

Hufford, M. (ed.) *Conserving Culture: A New Discourse on Heritage* (Urbana and Chicago: University of Illinois Press, 1994).

Hughes, C. 'Theatre and Controversy in Museums', *Journal of Museum Education*, 23: 3 (1998), pp. 13–15.

Hughes, R. *The Fatal Shore: A History of the Transportation of Convicts to Australia, 1787–1868* (London: Collins, 1987).

Hughes-Warrington, M. *History Goes to the Movies: Studying History on Film* (Abingdon: Routledge, 2007).

Hunt, T. 'Whose History Is It Anyway?', *History Today* (October 2006), pp. 28–30.

Husbands, C. and Pendry, A. 'Thinking and Feeling: Pupils' Preconceptions about the Past and Historical Understanding', in Arthur, J. and Phillips, R. (eds) *Issues in History Teaching* (London and New York: Routledge, 2000), pp. 125–34

Jackson, A. *Anthropology at Home* (London: Routledge, 1986).

Jackson A. 'Inter-acting with the Past: The Use of Participatory Theatre at Heritage Sites', *Research in Drama Education*, 5: 2 (2000), pp. 199–215.

Jackson, B. *Streaming: An Education System in Miniature* (London: Routledge & Kegan Paul, 1965).

Jensen, B. E. *Historie – livsverden og fag* (Copenhagen: Gyldendal, 2003).

Jewitt, C. and Jones, K. 'Managing Time and Space in the New English Classroom', in Lawn, M. and Grosvenor, I. (eds) *Materialities of Schooling: Design, Technology, Objects, Routines* (Oxford: Symposium, 2005), pp. 201–14.

Johnson, L. and O'Neil, C. (eds) *Dorothy Heathcote: Collected Writings on Education and Drama* (London: Hutchinson Education, 1984).

Jones, D. 'Museum Theatre and Evaluation: An Overview of What we Know', in *Insights, IMTAL online journal* http://www.mos.org/learn_more/imtal-insights8.html, 1999.

Jones, K. *Education in Britain 1944 to the Present* (Cambridge: Polity Press, 2003).

Jordanova, L. *History in Practice* (London: Arnold Publishers, 2000).

Kalela, J. 'Politics of History and History Politics: Some Conceptual Suggestions as to Political Aspects of History', *Ajankohta*, Finland (2004).

Kaplan, F. (ed.) *Museums and the Making of 'Ourselves': The Role of Objects in National Identity* (London: Leicester University Press, 1994).

Karp, I. and Lavine, S. D. (eds) *Exhibiting Cultures: The Poetics and Politics of Museum Display* (London: Smithsonian Institution Press, 1991).

Kean, H. *Deeds not Words: The Lives of Suffragette Teachers* (London: Pluto Press, 1990).

Kean, H. 'Public History and Raphael Samuel: A Forgotten Radical Pedagogy?', *Public History Review*, 11 (2004), pp. 51–62.

Kean, H. *London Stories: Personal lives, Public Histories* (London: Rivers Oram Press, 2004).

Kean, H. 'Personal and Public Histories: Issues in the Presentation of the Past', in Graham, B. and Howard, P. (eds) *The Ashgate Research Companion to Heritage and Identity* (Aldershot: Ashgate, 2008).

Kean, H., Martin, P. and Morgan, S. J. (eds) *Seeing History: Public History in Britain Now* (London: Francis Boutle, 2000).

Kelley, R. 'Public History: Its Origins, Nature and Prospects', *The Public Historian*, 1: 1 (1978).

Kingston, B. 'The Use and Function of Local History', in The Local History Co-ordination Project, *Locating Australia's Past* (Kensington: University of New South Wales Press, 1988), pp. 3–8.

Kirshenblatt-Gimblett, B. *Destination Culture: Tourism, Museums, and Heritage* (Berkeley: University of California Press, 1998).

Kirshenblatt-Gimblett, B. 'World Heritage and Cultural Economics', in Karp, I. *et al* (eds) *Museum Frictions: Public Cultures/Global Transformations* (Durham, North Carolina: Duke University Press, 2006), pp. 160–202.

Knight, D. *Gentlemen of Fortune: The Men who made their Fortunes in Britain's Slave Colonies* (London: Frederick Muller Limited, 1978).

Kuehl, J. 'History on Film: T.V. History', *History Workshop Journal*, 1 (1976), pp. 127–35.

Kuhn, A. *Family Secrets: Acts of Memory and Imagination* (London and New York: Verso 1995).

Kurin, R. 'Cultural Conservation through Representation: Festival of India Folklife Exhibitions at the Smithsonian Institution', in Karp, I. and Lavine, S. D. (eds) *Exhibiting Cultures: The Poetics and Politics of Museum Display* (London: Smithsonian Institution Press, 1991).

Kyriakopoulos, B. 'Can there be an Official History?', *BBC History Magazine*, 8: 3 (2007), p. 90.

Ladd, B. *The Ghosts of Berlin: Confronting German History in the Urban Landscape* (Chicago: University of Chicago Press, 1997).

Lamunière, M. *You Look Beautiful Like That: The Portrait Photographs of Seydou Keïta and Malick Sidibé* (New Haven and London: Yale University Press, 2001).

Lawn, M. and Grosvenor, I. (eds) *Materialities of Schooling: Design, Technology, Objects, Routines* (Oxford: Symposium, 2005).

Lefebvre, H. *The Production of Space*, trans. Nicholson-Smith, D. (Oxford: Blackwell, 1991).

Leon, W. and Rosenzweig, R. (eds) *History Museums in the United States: A Critical Assessment* (Urbana: University of Illinois Press, 1989).

Levinson, S. *Written in Stone: Public Monuments in Changing Societies* (Durham, NC: Duke University Press 1998).

Liddington, J. 'What is Public History? Publics and their Pasts, Meanings and Practices', *Oral History*, 30: 1 (2002), pp. 83–93.

Liddington, J. 'Public history in Britain', *NCPH Public History News*, 23: 3 (2003), pp. 1–2.

Liddington, J. and Ditchfield, S. 'Public History: A Critical Bibliography', *Oral History*, 33: 1 (2005), 40–5.

Liddington, J. and Smith, G. 'Crossing Cultures: Oral History and Public History', *Oral History*, 33: 1 (2005), pp. 28–31.

Lowe, R. *Education in the Post War Years: A Social History* (London: Routledge, 1988).

Lowenthal, D. *The Past is a Foreign Country* (Cambridge: Cambridge University Press, 1985).

Lowenthal, D. *Possessed by the Past: The Heritage Crusade and the Spoils of History* (London: Viking, 1996).

Lubar, S. and Kendrick, K. M. *Legacies: Collecting America's History at the Smithsonian* (Washington, DC: Smithsonian Institution Press, 2001).

Luke, T. W. *Museum Politics: Power Plays at the Exhibition* (Minneapolis: Minnesota University Press, 2002).

MacCannell, D. *The Tourist: A New Theory of the Leisure Class* (Berkeley: University of California Press, 1976).

Macdonald, S. 'On "Old Things": The Fetishization of Past Everyday Life', in Rapport, N., *British Subjects: An Anthropology of Britain* (Oxford: Berg, 2002).

Macdonald, S. 'Undesirable heritage: Fascist Material Culture and Historical Consciousness in Nuremberg', *International Journal of Heritage Studies*, 12: 1 (2006), pp. 9–28.

Mace, R. *Trafalgar Square: Emblem of Empire* 2nd edn (London: Lawrence and Wishart Ltd, 2005).

Macintrye, S. (ed.) *The Historian's Conscience: Australia Historians on the Ethics of History* (Melbourne: Melbourne University Press, 2004).

Macintyre, S. and Clark, A. *The History Wars* (Melbourne: Melbourne University Press, 2003).

Malkki, L. 'National Geographic: The Rooting of Peoples and the Territorialisation of National Identity Among Scholars and Refugees', *Cultural Anthropology*, 7: 1 (1992), pp. 24–44.

Malcolm-Davies, J. 'Living Interpretation in Museums', *Heritage Interpretation*, 43 (1989), pp. 12–14.

Malcolm-Davies, J. 'Keeping it alive', *Museums Journal*, 90: 3 (1990), pp. 25–9.

Maloney, L. and Hughes, C. (eds) *Case Studies in Museum, Zoo and Aquarium Theatre* (Washington, DC: American Association of Museums, 1999).

Marsh, J. (ed.) *Black Victorians: Black People in British Art 1800–1900* (Aldershot: Lund Humphries, 2005), pp. 12–22.

Martin, L. *Into the Breach: The Emergency Training Scheme for Teachers* (London: Turnstile Press, 1949).

Massey, D. 'A Global Sense of Place', *Marxism Today* (June, 1991), pp. 24–9.

Massey, D. 'Places and their Pasts', *History Workshop Journal*, 39 (1995), pp. 182–92.

Massey, D. *For Space* (London: Sage, 2005).

Mauss, M. *The Gift: The Form and Reason for Exchange in Archaic Societies* (London: Routledge, 1967).

Mayo, S. '"I Didn't Know I Liked History so Much": Reflections on Three Years with the Young National Trust Theatre', *GEM News*, 52 (1993), pp. 7–8.

Mayor's Commission on African and Asian Heritage, *Delivering Shared Heritage* (London: Greater London Authority, 2005).

Miller, D. 'Artefacts and the Meaning of Things', in Ingold, T. (ed.) *Companion Encyclopedia of Anthropology: Humanity, Culture and Social Life* (London: Routledge, 1994).

McCarthy, A. 'A Good Idea of Colonial Life: Personal Letters and Irish Migration to New Zealand', *New Zealand Journal of History*, 35: 1 (2001), pp. 1–21.

McClean, S. '"Progress the Iconoclast": Campaigns, Ideologies and Dilemmas of Historic Building Preservation in New South Wales, 1900–1939', *Public History Review*, 7 (1998), pp. 25–42.

McIntyre, D. J. and Werner, K. (eds) *National Museums Negotiating Histories: Conference Proceedings* (Canberra: National Museums of Australia, 2001).

McGibbon, I. '"Something of Them is Here Recorded": Official History in New Zealand', in Grey, J. (ed.) *The Last Word? Essays on Official History in the United States and the British Commonwealth* (Westport, CT: Praeger Publishers, 2003) and www.nzetc.org.

McKibbin, R. *Classes and Cultures in England 1918–1951* (Oxford: Oxford University Press, 1998).

McKinnon, M. (ed.) *Bateman New Zealand Historical Atlas* (Auckland: David Bateman Ltd/Department of Internal Affairs, 1997).

Merriman, N. 'Diversity and Dissonance in Public Archaeology', in Merriman (ed.) *Public Archaeology* (London: Routledge, 2004).

Merriman, N. (ed.) *Public Archaeology* (London: Routledge, 2004).

Moloughney, B. and Stenhouse, J. 'Drug-besotten, Sin-begotten Fiends of Filth: New Zealanders and the Oriental Other, 1850–1920', *New Zealand Journal of History*, 33: 1 (1999), pp. 43–64.

Moran, J. 'History, Memory and the Everyday', *Rethinking History*, 8: 1 (2004), pp. 51–68.

Morris-Suzuki, T. *The Past Within Us: Media, Memory, History* (London: Verso, 2005).

Morgan, S. J. 'My Father's Photographs: The Visual as Public History', in Kean, H., Martin, P. and Morgan, S. J. *Seeing History: Public History in Britain Now* (London: Francis Boutle, 2000), pp. 19–35.

Munley, M. E. 'Evaluation Study Report of Buyin' Freedom: An Experimental Live Interpretation Program', *Perspectives on Museum Theatre* (Washington, DC: American Association of Museums, 1993), pp. 69–94.

Museum of Sydney, *Sites: Nailing the Debate: Archaeology and Interpretation in Museums* (Sydney: Historic Houses Trust of New South Wales, 1996).

Museums in Australia 1975: Report of the Committee of Inquiry on Museums and National Collections (Canberra: Australian Government Publishing Service, 1975).

Myers, N. *Reconstructing the Black Past: Blacks in Britain 1780–1830* (London: Frank Cass, 1996).

Neelands, J. *Learning through Imagined Experience: Teaching English in the National Curriculum* (London: Hodder & Stoughton, 1992).

Nelson, K. and Fivush, R. 'The Emergence of Autobiographical Memory: A Social Cultural Developmental Theory', *Psychological Review*, 111: 2 (2004), pp. 86–511.

Newell, A. S. '"Home is What You Can Take Away with You": K. J. Ross Toole and the Making of a Public Historian', *The Public Historian*, 23: 3 (2001), pp. 63–71.

Newens, S. 'Family History Societies', *History Workshop Journal*, 11 (Spring 1981), pp. 154–9.

Newman, J. 'Twin Lens Reflex, the Portrait Photographs of Harry Jacobs and Bandele "Tex" Ajetunmobi' (London: Lambeth Archives, 2004).

Ng, J. *Windows on a Chinese Past*, 4 vols (Dunedin: Otago Heritage Books, 1993–1999).

Nile, R. and Peterson, M. (eds) *Becoming Australia: The Woodford Forum* (St Lucia: University of Queensland Press, 1999).

Nora, P. 'Between Memory and History: Les Lieux de Memoire', in Fabre, G. and O'Meally, R. (eds) *History and Memory in African American Culture* (Oxford: Oxford University Press, 1994), pp. 284–300.

Nora, P. (ed.) *Les Lieux de mémoire*, 7 vols (Paris: Edition Gallimard, 1984–1992).

Nora, P. (ed.) *Realms of Memory: Rethinking the French Past*, vol. 1 – *Conflicts and Divisions*, trans. Goldhammer, A. (New York: Columbia University Press, 1996).

O'Farrell, P. 'Varieties of New Zealand Irishness: A Meditation', in Fraser, L. (ed.) *A Distant Shore: Irish Migration and New Zealand Settlement* (Dunedin: University of Otago Press, 2000).

Oldfield, J. R. *'Chords of Freedom': Commemoration, Ritual and British Transatlantic Slavery* (Manchester: Manchester University Press, 2007).

Oliver, W. H. (ed.) *The Dictionary of New Zealand Biography*, vol. 1 (1769–1869) (Wellington: Allen and Unwin/Department of Internal Affairs, 1990).

O'Neil, C. *Drama World: A Framework for Process Drama* (Portsmouth: Heinemann, 1995).

O'Toole, J. *The Process of Drama: Negotiating Art and Meaning* (London and New York: Routledge, 1992).

Palmer, C. 'An Ethnography of Englishness: Experiencing Identity Through Tourism', *Annals of Tourism Research*, 32 (2005), pp. 7–27.

Parr, J. *These Goods are Canadian-made: An Historian Thinks about Things* (Ottawa: University of Ottawa Press, 1999).

Passerini, L. *Autobiography of a Generation: Italy 1968* (London: University Press of New England, 1996).

Pearce, S. M. (ed.) *Interpreting Objects and Collections* (London and New York: Routledge, 1994).

Pearce, S. M. *Museums and the Appropriation of Culture* (London: The Athlone Press, 1994).

Pearce, S. M. 'The Construction of Heritage: The Domestic Context and its Implications', *International Journal of Heritage Studies*, 4 : 2 (1998), pp. 86–102.

Pearson, M. and Sullivan, S. *Looking After Heritage Places: The Basics of Heritage Planning for Manager, Landowners and Administrators* (Melbourne: Melbourne University Press, 1995).

Perks, R. 'A People's History of Industrial Philadelphia: Reflections on Community Oral History Projects and the Uses of the Past', *Oral History Review*, 33: 1 (2006).

Perks, R. and Thomson, A. (eds) *The Oral History Reader* 1st edn (London and New York: Routledge, 1997).

Philips, J. 'Our History, Our Selves: The Historian and National Identity', *New Zealand Journal of History*, 30: 2 (1996), pp. 107–23.

Pickering, P. A. and Tyrrell, A. with Davis, M. T., Mansfield, N. and Walvin, J. (eds) *Contested Sites: Commemoration, Memorial and Popular Politics in Nineteenth Century Britain* (Aldershot: Ashgate, 2004).

Pinder, D. 'Arts of Urban Exploration', *Cultural Geographies*, 12: 4 (2005), pp. 383–411.

Platt, E. *Leadville: A Biography of the A40* (London: Picador, 2001).

Platt, J. 'What Can Case Studies Do?', in Burgess R. G. (ed.) *Studies in Qualitative Methodology*, vol. 1 *Conducting Qualitative Research* (Greenwich, Connecticut: JAI Press, 1988), pp. 1–23.

Portelli, A. 'The Peculiarities of Oral History', *History Workshop Journal*, 12 (1981), pp. 96–107.

Portelli, A. *The Battle of Valle Giulia: Oral History and the Art of Dialogue* (Madison: University of Wisconsin Press, 1997).

Portelli, A. 'Oral history as Genre', in Chamberlain, M. and Thompson, P. *Narrative and Genre* (London: Routledge, 1998) pp. 23–45.

Portelli, A. *The Order Has Been Carried Out: History, Memory, and Meaning of a Nazi Massacre in Rome* (New York: Palgrave Macmillan, 2003).

Portelli, A. 'So Much Depends on a Red Bus, or, Innocent Victims of the Liberating Gun', *Oral History*, 34: 2 (2006), pp. 29–43.

Price, J. 'Theatre of the Absurd', *Museums Journal* (March 1992), pp. 200–21.

Purbrick, L. 'The Architecture of Containment', in Wylie, D. (ed.) *The Maze* (London: Granta, 2004), pp. 91–110.

Radstone, S. (ed.) *Memory and Methodology* (Oxford and New York: Berg, 2000).

Radstone, S. and Hodgkin, K. (eds) *Regimes of Memory* (London: Routledge, 2003).

Rainey, R. M. 'The Memory of War: Reflections on Battlefield Preservation', in Austin, R. L. (ed.) *Yearbook of Landscape Architecture* (New York: Van Nostrand Reinhold, 1983).

Randall, D. *The Universal Journalist* (London: Pluto Press, 1996).

Read, P. '"Before Rockets and Aeroplanes": Family History', in Hamilton, P. and Ashton, P. (eds) *Australians and the Past*, special issue of *Australian Cultural History*, 22 (2003), pp. 131–41.

Relph, E. C. *Place and Placelessness* (London: Pion Limited, 1976).

Renwick, W. (ed.) *Creating a National Spirit: Celebrating New Zealand's Centennial* (Wellington: Victoria University Press, 2005).

'Review of the National Museum of Australia, its Exhibitions and Public Programs: A Report to the Council of the National Museum of Australia (Canberra: Commonwealth of Australia, 2003), NMA website www.nma.gov.au.

Rice, A. *Radical Narratives of the Black Atlantic* (London and New York: Continuum, 2003).

Rickard, J. and Spearritt, P. (eds) *Packaging the Past? Public Histories*, special issue of *Australian Historical Studies*, 24: 96 (1991).

Ricoeur, P. *Time and Narrative*, vol. 1, trans. McLaughlin, K. and Pellauer, D. (Chicago: University of Chicago Press, 1984).

Risk, P. 'People-based Interpretation', in Harrison, R. (ed.) *Manual of Heritage Management* (Oxford and Boston: Butterworth-Heinemann Ltd and the Association of Independent Museums, 1994), pp. 320–30.

Roberson, L. 'Do We Speak the Same Language? Theatre in Science and History Museums', *Insights, IMTAL online journal*, http://www.mos.org/learn_more/imtal-insights8.html, 1999.

Robertshaw, A. 'Acts of Imagination', *Museums Journal* 90: 3 (1990), pp. 30–1.

Robertshaw, A. 'From Houses into Homes: One approach to Live Interpretation', *Social History in Museums, Journal of the Social History curators group*, 19 (1992), pp. 14–20.

Robertshaw, A. '"A Dry Shell of the Past": Living History and the Interpretation of Historic Houses', *Interpretation*, 2: 3 (1997), pp. 17–20.

Robins, N. *The Corporation that Changed the World: How the East India Company shaped the Modern Multinational* (Ann Arbor MI: Pluto Press, 2006).

Robinson, C. and Kellett, M. 'Power', in Fraser, S. *et al* (eds) *Doing Research with Children and Young People* (Thousand Oaks, CA: Sage Publications, 2004), pp. 81–96.

Rosenzweig, R. 'Not A Simple Task: Professional Historians Meet Popular History-makers', *The Public Historian*, 22: 1 (2000), pp. 35–8.

Rosenzweig, R. 'Everyone a Historian' http://chnm.gmu.edu/survey/afterroy.html#32.

Rosenzweig, R. and Thelen, D. *The Presence of the Past: Popular Uses of History in American Life* (New York: Columbia University Press, 1998).

Roth, S. *Past into Present: Effective Techniques for First-person Historical Interpretation* (North Carolina: The University of North Carolina Press, 1998).

Ryan, A., 'Developing a Strategy to "Save" History', *Australian Historical Association Bulletin*, 87 (1998), pp. 39–49.

Samuel, R. 'Local History and Oral History', *History Workshop Journal*, 1: 1 (1976), pp. 191–208.

Samuel, R. 'History Workshop Methods', *History Workshop*, 9 (1980), pp. 162–76.

Samuel, R. *Theatres of Memory: Past and Present in Contemporary Culture*, vol. 1 (London: Verso, 1994).

Samuel, R. *Theatres of Memory. vol 2: Island Stories: Unravelling Britain* (London: Verso, 1998).

Samuel, R., Bloomfield, B. and Boanas, G. (eds) *The Enemy Within: Pit villages and the Miners' Strike of 1984–5* (London: Routledge and Kegan Paul, 1986).

Samuel, R. and Thompson, P. (eds) *The Myths We Live By* (London: Routledge, 1990).

Sancho, I. *Letters Of The Late Ignatius Sancho, An African,* first published 1782 (London: Penguin Books reprint, 1998).

Sassoon, J. 'Phantoms of Remembrance: Libraries and Archives as "The Collective Memory"', *Public History Review*, 10 (2003), pp. 40–60.

Schama, S. *Landscape and Memory* (London: HarperCollins Publishers, 1995).

Schadla-Hall, T. 'The Comforts of Unreason: The Importance and Relevance of Alternative Archaeology', in Merriman, N. (ed.) *Public Archaeology* (London: Routledge, 2004).

Schlereth, T. J. *Cultural History and Material Culture: Everyday Life, Landscapes, Museums* (Charlottesville: University Press of Virginia, 1992).

Schörken, R. *Geschichte in der Alltagswelt. Wie uns Geschichte begegnet und was wir mit ihr machen* (Stuttgart: Klett-Cotta, 1981).

Schörken, R. (ed.) *Der Gegenwartsbezug der Geschichte* (Stuttgart: Klett, 1981).

Schneer, J. 'Anti Imperial London: The Pan-African Conference of 1900', in Driver, F. and Gilbert, D. (eds) *Imperial Cities: Landscape, Display and Identity* (Manchester and New York: Manchester University Press, 1999).

Schwandt, T. A. 'Constructivist, Interpretivist Approaches to Human Inquiry', in Denzin, N. K. and Lincoln, Y. S. (eds) *The Landscape of Qualitative Research: Theories and Issues* (Thousand Oaks, CA: Sage Publications, 1998).

Sebald, W. G. *On the Natural History of Destruction* (London: Penguin, 2003).

Sherwood, M. *After Abolition: Britain and the Slave Trade Since 1807* (London: I. B. Tauris & Co. Ltd, 2007).

Siblon, J. 'A Mistaken Case of Identity', *History Workshop Journal*, 52 (2001), pp. 253–60.

Silber, L. 'Bringing Theatre into the Mainstream', *Insights, IMTAL online journal*, http://www.mos.org/learn_more/imtal-insights8.html, 1999.

Simon, B. (ed.) *New Trends in English Education: A Symposium* (London: MacGibbon and Kee, 1957).

Simpson, M. *Making Representations: Museums in the Post-Colonial Era* (London and New York: Routledge, 1996).

Smith, J. *The Nature of Social and Educational Inquiry: Empiricism Versus Interpretation* (New Jersey: Ablex Publishing Corporation, 1989).

Smith, L. *Uses of Heritage* (London: Routledge, 2006).

Spence, C. 'Seeing Some Black in the Union Jack', *History Today*, 52: 10 (2002), pp. 30–7.

Spurway, J. 'The Growth of Family History in Australia', *The Push: Journal of Early Australian Social History*, 27 (1989), pp. 7–12.

Stake, R. 'Case Studies', in Denzin, N. K. and Lincoln, Y. S. (eds) *Handbook of Qualitative Research*, 2nd edn (Thousand Oaks, CA: Sage Publications, 2000), pp. 435–54.

Stanley, P. 'Happy Birthday HRS: A Decade of the Australian War Memorial's Historical Research Section', *Public History Review*, 2 (1993), pp. 54–65.

Stanton, C. 'Serving Up Culture: Heritage and its Discontents at an Industrial History Site', *International Journal of Heritage Studies*, 11: 5 (2005), pp. 415–31.

Stanton, C. *The Lowell Experiment: Public History in a Postindustrial City* (Amherst and Boston: University of Massachusetts Press, 2006).

Stearns, P. N. *et al* (eds) *Knowing, Teaching, and Learning History: National and International Perspectives* (New York: New York University Press, 2000).

Steedman, C. *Dust* (Manchester: Manchester University Press, 2001).

Stenhouse, J. 'God's Own Silence: Secular Nationalism, Christianity and the Writing of New Zealand History', *New Zealand Journal of History*, 38: 1 (2004), pp. 52–71.

Stenhouse, J. (ed.) *Christianity, Modernity and Culture: New Perspectives on New Zealand History* (Adelaide, Australia: ATF Press, 2005), pp. 132–56.

Stewart, M. 'Calvinism, Migration and Settler Culture: The Case of William McCaw', in Stenhouse, J. (ed.) *Christianity Modernity and Culture: New Perspectives on New Zealand History* (Adelaide, Australia: ATF Press, 2005).

Stowe, N. J. 'Public History Curriculum: Illustrating Reflective Practice', *The Public Historian*, 28: 1 (2006), pp. 39–66.

Sumner, C. 'Historic Waterscapes', in Munt, I. and Jaijee, R. (eds) *River Calling: The Need for Urban Water Space Strategies* (London: London Rivers Association, 2002).

Swain, E. D. 'Oral History in the Archives: Its Documentary Role in the Twenty-first Century', in Perks, R. B. and Thomson, A. (eds) *The Oral History Reader* 2nd edn (London: Routledge, 2006).

Szekeres, V. 'A Place for All of Us', *Public History Review*, 4 (1995), pp. 59–64.

Tanselle, G. T. 'The World As Archive', *Common Knowledge*, 8: 2 (2002) http://muse.jhu.edu/journals/common_knowledge/v008/8.2tanselle.html.

Tennant, M. 'History and Social Policy: Perspectives from the Past', in Dalley, B. and Tennant, M. (eds) *Past Judgement: Social Policy in New Zealand History* (Dunedin: University of Otago Press, 2004), pp. 19–21.

Terkel, S. *Working; People Talk about What They Do all Day and How They Feel about What They Do* (New York: Pantheon Books, 1974).

Teutonico, J. M. and Fidler, J. (eds) *Monuments and the Millennium* (London: James and James, 2001).

Thane, P. *Foundations of the Welfare State* 2nd edn (London: Longman, 1996).

Thelen, D. 'History Making in America', *The Historian*, 53 (1991), pp. 631–48.

Thelen, D. 'But Is It History?', *The Public Historian*, 22: 1 (2000), pp. 39–44.

Thelen, D. 'A Participatory Historical Culture', http://chnm.gmu.edu/survey/afterdave.html.

Thom, D. 'Politics and the People: Brian Simon and the Campaign against Intelligence Tests in British Schools', *History of Education*, 33: 5 (2004), pp. 515–30.

Thompson, P. 'Believe It or Not: Rethinking the Historical Interpretation of Memory', in Jeffrey, J. and Edwall, G. (eds) *Memory and History: Essays on Recalling and Interpreting Experience* (Lanham: University Press of America, 1994).

Till, T. 'Places of Memory', in Agnew, J., Mitchell, K. and Ó'Tuathail, G. (eds) *A Companion to Political Geography* (Oxford and Cambridge: Blackwell Publishing, 2003), pp. 289–301.

Timothy, T. 'Report on the Sept 9th Forum Event: A1 Audio Tour: Brief Description', *Arts for Islington Forum Monthly Bulletin* (3 October 2005).

Trapeznik, A. (ed.) *Common Ground? Heritage and Public Places in New Zealand* (Dunedin: University of Otago Press, 2000).

Trask, D. F. and Pomeroy III, R. W. (eds) *The Craft of Public History: An Annotated Select Bibliography* (Connecticut: Greenwood Press for NCPH, 1983).

Tuan, Y. F. *Topophilia: A Study of Environmental Perception, Attitudes, and Values* (Englewood Cliffs: Prentice-Hall, 1974).

Twain, M. *The Adventures of Huckleberry Finn*, first published 1884 (New York: Bantam Books, 1981).

Twain, M. *The Wayward Tourist: Mark Twain's Adventures in Australia* (Melbourne: Melbourne University Press, 2006), p. 65; extracts from Mark Twain, *Following the Equator*, first published 1897.

Tyler, W. *Survey 2000: A Report of the Survey of Member Societies of the Federation of Australian Historical Societies* (Canberra: Federation of Australian Historical Associations, 2000).

Tyrrell, A. and Walvin, J. 'Whose History Is It? Memorialising Britain's Involvement in Slavery', in Pickering, P. A. and Tyrrell, A. with Davis, M. T., Mansfield, N. and Walvin, J. (eds) *Contested Sites: Commemoration, Memorial and Popular Politics in Nineteenth-century Britain* (Aldershot: Ashgate, 2004).

Tyrrell, I. *Historians in Public: The Practice of American History, 1890–1970* (Chicago: University of Chicago Press, 2005).

Tzibazi V. 'Researching the Children's Meaning Making of First Person Interpretation Programmes', *Journal of Education in Museums*, 25 (2004), pp. 28–32.

Vanderstel, D. 'The National Council on Public History', *Public History Review*, 10 (2003).

Vanderstel, D. 'Vox Pop', *Oral History*, 33: 1 (2005), p. 32.

Wagner, B. J. *Dorothy Heathcote: Drama as a Learning Medium* (London: Hutchinson, 1999).

Walker, S. 'Black Cultural Museums in Britain: What Questions do they Answer?', in Hooper-Greenhill, E. (ed.) *Cultural Diversity: Developing Museum Audiences in Britain* (London: Leicester University Press, 1997).

Walkowitz, D. 'Series in Public History: "Around the Globe"', *Radical History Review*, 75: 79 (1999).

Walkowitz, D. and Knauer, L. M. (eds) *Memory and the Impact of Political Transformation in Public Space* (Durham NC: Duke University Press, 2004).

Walkowitz, D. and Knauer, L. M. (eds) *Narrating the Nation: Memory, Race and Empire* (Durham NC: Duke University Press, 2007).

Wallace, M. *Mickey Mouse History and Other Essays on American Memory* (Philadelphia: Temple University Press, 1996).

Ward-Jackson, P. *Public Sculpture of The City Of London, Volume VII, Public Sculpture of Britain series* (Liverpool: Liverpool University Press, 2003).

Waterman, S. 'Collecting the Nineteenth Century', *Representations,* 90 (2005), pp. 98–128.

Weiner, A. *Inalienable Possessions: the Paradox of Keeping-While-Giving* (Berkeley: University of California Press, 1992).

Welzer, H. and Markowitsch, H. J. 'Towards a Bio-psycho-social Model of Autobiographical Memory', *Memory,* 13:1 (2005), pp. 63–78.

Whittick, A. *War Memorials* (London: Country Life, 1946).

Whooley, F. *Irish Londoners* (Gloucestershire: Sutton Publishing, 1997).

Wilson, R. 'Cormilligan', *Lallans,* 62 (2003), pp. 112–33.

Windschuttle, K. 'How Not to Run a Museum: People's History at the Postmodern Museum', *Quadrant,* 45: 9 (2001).

Wirth, J. *Interactive Acting* (Oregon: Fall Creek Press, 1994).

Witkin, W. R. *The Intelligence of Feeling* (London: Heinemann Educational Books, 1974).

Wolschke-Bulmahn, J. (ed.) *Places of Commemoration: Search for Identity and Landscape Design* (Washington, DC: Dumbarton Oaks, 2001).

Wood, M. *Blind Memory: Visual Representations of Slavery in England and America* (Manchester: Manchester University Press, 2000).

Woodhead, S. and Tinniswood, A. 'Making Things with your Heart', in Woodhead, S. and Tinniswood, A. (eds) *'No Longer Dead to Me' Working with Schoolchildren in the Performing and Creative Arts* (London: The National Trust, 1996), pp. 4–7.

Woodward, C. *In Ruins* (London: Vintage, 2002).

Wright, P. *On Living in an Old Country: The National Past in Contemporary Britain* (London: Verso, 1985).

Wright, P. 'Restoration tragedy', *The Guardian,* 13 September 2003.

Young, C. 'Recasting School History: For Better or For Worse?', *Public History Review,* 7 (1998), pp. 9–12.

Young, C. 'Historical Revivalism', *Australian Historical Association Bulletin,* 88 (1999), pp. 23–5.

Young, L. 'Federation Flagship', *Meanjin,* 60: 4 (2001), pp. 149–59.

Zerubavel, E. *Time Maps: Collective Memory and the Social Shape of the Past* (Chicago and London: The University of Chicago Press, 2003).

Zuckerman, M. 'The Presence of the Present: The End of History', *The Public Historian,* 22: 1 (2000), pp. 19–22.

Zukin, S. *Loft Living: Culture and Capital in Urban Change* (Baltimore and London: Johns Hopkins University Press, 1982).

Index